ANCIENT INDIAN TRADITION & MYTHOLOGY

TRANSLATED BY

A BOARD OF SCHOLARS

AND EDITED BY

Dr. G.P. BHATT

VOLUME 49

ANCIENT INDIAN TRADITION AND MYTHOLOGY SERIES

[PURĀṆAS IN TRANSLATION]

VOLUMES

ŚIVA 1-4
LIṄGA 5-6
BHĀGAVATA 7-11
GARUḌA 12-14
NĀRADA 15-19
KŪRMA 20-21
BRAHMĀṆḌA 22-26
AGNI 27-30
VARĀHA 31-32
BRAHMA 33-36
VĀYU 37-38
PADMA 39-48
SKANDA, PART I 49

VOLUMES UNDER PREPARATION

SKANDA, PARTS II—XIX
BHAVIṢYA
BRAHMAVAIVARTA
DEVĪBHĀGAVATA
KĀLIKĀ
MĀRKAṆḌEYA
MATSYA
VĀMANA
VIṢṆU
VIṢṆUDHARMOTTARA

THE SKANDA-PURĀṆA

PART I

TRANSLATED AND ANNOTATED BY

Dr. G.V. TAGARE

MOTILAL BANARSIDASS PUBLISHERS
PRIVATE LIMITED . DELHI

First Edition: Delhi, 1992

ISBN: 81-208-0966-1

Also available at:
MOTILAL BANARSIDASS
41 U.A., Bungalow Road, Jawahar Nagar, Delhi 110 007
120 Royapettah High Road, Mylapore, Madras 600 004
16 St. Mark's Road, Bangalore 560 001
Ashok Rajpath, Patna 800 004
Chowk, Varanasi 221 001

UNESCO COLLECTION OF REPRESENTATIVE WORKS— Indian Series
This book has been accepted in the Indian Translation Series of the UNESCO Collection of Representative Works, jointly sponsored by the United Nations Educational, Scientific and Cultural Organization (UNESCO) and the Government of India

PRINTED IN INDIA
BY JAINENDRA PRAKASH JAIN AT SHRI JAINENDRA PRESS, A-45 NARAINA INDUSTRIAL AREA, PHASE I, NEW DELHI 110 028 AND PUBLISHED BY NARENDRA PRAKASH JAIN FOR MOTILAL BANARSIDASS PUBLISHERS PVT. LTD., BUNGALOW ROAD, JAWAHAR NAGAR, DELHI 110 007

PUBLISHER'S NOTE

The purest gems lie hidden in the bottom of the ocean or in the depth of rocks. One has to dive into the ocean or delve into the rocks to find them out. Similarly, truth lies concealed in the language which with the passage of time has become obsolete. Man has to learn that language before he discovers that truth.

But he has neither the means nor the leisure to embark on that course. We have, therefore, planned to help him acquire knowledge by an easier course. We have started the series of Ancient Indian Tradition and Mythology in English Translation. Our goal is to universalize knowledge through the most popular international medium of expression. The publication of the Purāṇas in English Translation is a step towards that goal.

EDITORIAL

We have planned the publication of the *Skanda Purāṇa* in English translation in nineteen *Parts* (AITM Vols. 49-67), of which the present one is the first. The Purāṇa is divided into seven *Books*, i.e. major divisions, viz. *Māheśvarakhaṇḍa*, *Vaiṣṇavakhaṇḍa*, *Brāhmakhaṇḍa*, *Kāśīkhaṇḍa*, *Āvantyakhaṇḍa*, *Nāgarakhaṇḍa* and *Prabhāsakhaṇḍa*, out of which six are further divided into several *Sections* each, totalling twenty-five, the sixth *Book* being an exception. As planned, *Book I* will be published in three *Parts*, *Book II* in three, *Book III* in two, *Book IV* in two, *Book V* in three, *Book VI* in three and *Book VII* also in three *Parts*.

The present *Part I*, that is AITM Volume 49, comprises the whole of *Kedārakhaṇḍa* which is the first *Section* of *Book I*, i.e. *Māheśvarakhaṇḍa*, along with an *Introduction* and *Index*. This *Section* has thirty-five chapters which treat of the oft-repeated themes of the self-immolation of Satī in the sacrifice of Dakṣa, the churning of the ocean, the elimination of demon Vṛtra, the story of how Bali is outwitted by Vāmana, the burning of Kāmadeva by god Śiva and the celebration of latter's marriage with Pārvatī who wins him over by her severe penance, and the slaying of demon Tāraka by Kārttikeya or Skanda after whom the Purāṇa is named. In addition, the main objective of this Purāṇa being glorification of god Śiva and inculcation of devotion to him and his worship, it also includes many stories and legends about Śiva, the importance of the worship of *Liṅga* and of that of Gaṇeśa, the meritoriousness of wearing *Tripuṇḍra*, *Rudrākṣa*, *Vibhūti* etc. Though every now and then the Purāṇa harps upon the supremacy of god Śiva, Viṣṇu is not underrated but held on a par with Śiva and no opportunity is lost in trying to reduce the gulf between Śaivism and Vaiṣṇavism.

Here the title *Kedārakhaṇḍa* calls for a comment. Kedāra or Kedāranātha is a place of pilgrimage situated in the snowy Himalayas in District Garhwal of Uttara Pradesh, to the north of Haridwar, enshrining one of the twelve great *Liṅgas* of Mahādeva or Śiva. One would naturally expect that the Section bearing this name should contain a description and glorification of Kedāranātha at least and of surrounding geographical region and also of neighbouring holy places such as Badarīnātha, Jośīmaṭha, Haridvāra etc. But disappointingly enough, it contains nothing like that. Surprisingly, the name 'Kedāra' itself is conspicuous by its complete absence in the text of the Section. It appears thas the name is here as arbitrary as that of a person named Kailāsanātha or Banārasīdāsa, who might have never seen Kailāsa or Banārasa in his life. One wonders what could have been the intention of the author(s) in so naming the Section.

Lastly, a word about the ascetic Lomaśa whose name occurs as the narrator of the stories of this Section in response to the queries of a group of ascetics with Śaunaka as their leader in the Naimiṣa forest, modern Nimsar. There is one sage Lomaśa mentioned frequently in the *Mahābhārata,* who, according to Sörensen's *An Index to the Names in the Mahābhārata,* "accompanied the Pāṇḍavas and pointed out to them the different tīrthas and told their various legends" and was one "among the ṛshis who surrounded Bhīshma on his arrow-bed" etc., but his parentage and other antecedents are not clearly given. Our Lomaśa, on the other hand, has been spoken as not only a disciple of sage Vyāsa (SkP I.i.1.3) but is positively identified with Sūta (Ibid I.i.1.20; I.i.15.25 etc.), the well-known story-teller and disciple of Vyāsa and the son of Lomaharṣaṇa. Elsewhere in the Purāṇa (SkP I.ii.1.2. etc.) he is also alternatively called Ugraśravas, the one who is usually addressed as 'Sūta' but whom *Mahābhārata* (Ādiparva 1.1) calls "Lomaharṣaṇaputra Ugraśravāḥ sautiḥ" i.e. Ugraśravas, the son of Sūta. It may be borne in mind that 'Sūta' was not a proper name but a designation meaning a 'charioteer', 'son of a Kṣatriya by a woman of Brāhmaṇa caste', a 'story-teller' etc. and that Lomaharṣaṇa and Ugraśravas both were 'Sūta'. The conclusion we arrive at is that Lomaśa, according to the author(s) of the Purāṇa, was another name of Ugraśravas, the Sūta.

G.P. BHATT

CONTENTS

ABBREVIATIONS

Common and self-evident abbreviations such as Ch(s)—Chapter(s), p—page, pp—pages, v—verse, vv—verses, Ftn—Footnote, Hist. Ind. Philo.—History of Indian Philosophy are not included in this list.

ABORI	*Annals of the Bhandarkar Oriental Research Institute*, Poona
AGP	S.M. Ali's *The Geography of Purāṇas*, PPH, New Delhi, 1973
AIHT	*Ancient Indian Historical Tradition*, F.E. Pargiter, Motilal Banarsidass (MLBD), Delhi
AITM	*Ancient Indian Tradition and Mythology* Series, MLBD, Delhi
AP	*Agni Purāṇa*, Guru Mandal Edition (GM), Calcutta, 1957
Arch. S. Rep.	Archaeological Survey Report
AV	*Atharva Veda*, Svādhyāya Maṇḍal, Aundh
BdP	*Brahmāṇḍa Purāṇa*, MLBD, Delhi 1973
BG	*Bhagavadgītā*
BhP	*Bhāgavata Purāṇa*, Bhagavat Vidyapeeth, Ahmedabad
Br	*Brāhmaṇa* (preceded by name such as Śatapatha)
BsP	*Bhaviṣya Purāṇa*, Vishnu Shastri Bapat, Wai
BVP	*Brahma Vaivarta Purāṇa*, GM, 1955-57
CC	*Caturvarga Cintāmaṇi* by Hemādri
CVS	*Caraṇa Vyūha Sūtra* by Śaunaka, Com. by Mahīdāsa
DB	*Devī Bhāgavata*, GM, 1960-61
De or GDAMI	*The Geographical Dictionary of Ancient and Mediaeval India*, N.L. De, Oriental Reprint, Delhi, 1971
DhS	*Dharma Sūtra* (preceded by the author's name such as Gautama)

ERE	*Encyclopaedia of Religion and Ethics* by Hastings
GP	*Garuḍa Purāṇa,* ed. R.S. Bhattacharya, Chowkhamba, Varanasi, 1964
GS	*Gṛhya Sūtra* (preceded by the name of the author such as Āpastamba)
HD	*History of Dharma Śāstra*, P.V. Kane, G.O.S.
IA	*The Indian Antiquary*
IHQ	*The Indian Historical Quarterly*
JP	*Purāṇa* (Journal of the Kashiraj Trust), Varanasi
KA	*Kauṭilya Arthaśāstra*
KP	*Kūrma Purāṇa*, Veṅkaṭeśvara Press Edn., Bombay; also Kashiraj Trust Edn., Varanasi, 1971
LP	*Liṅga Purāṇa*, GM, 1960; also MLBD, Delhi, 1981
Manu	*Manusmṛti*
Mbh	*Mahābhārata*, Gītā Press, Gorakhpur, VS 2014
MkP	*Mārkaṇḍeya Purāṇa*
MN	*Mahābhārata Nāmānukramaṇī*, Gītā Press, Gorakhpur, VS 2016
MtP	*Matsya Purāṇa,* GM, 1954
MW	Monier Williams' *Sanskrit-English Dictionary*, MLBD, Delhi, 1976
NP	*Nāradīya* or *Nārada Purāṇa*, Veṅkaṭeśvara Press, Bombay
PCK	*Bhāratavarṣīya Prācīna Caritrakośa,* Siddheshwar Shastri, Poona, 1968
PdP	*Padma Purāṇa*, GM, 1957-59
PE	*Purāṇic Encyclopaedia*, V. Mani, English version, MLBD, Delhi, 1975
PR or PRHRC	*Puranic Records on Hindu Rites and Customs,* R.C. Hazra, Calcutta, 1948
ṚV	*Ṛg-Veda*, Svādhyāya Maṇḍal, Aundh
Śat Br	*Śatapatha Brāhmaṇa*
SC or SMC	*Smṛti Candrikā* by Devanna Bhaṭṭa

SEP	*Studies in Epics and Purāṇas*, A.D. Pusalkar, Bharatiya Vidya Bhavan (BVB), Bombay
SkP	*Skanda Purāṇa*
SP	*Śiva Purāṇa*
VāP	*Vāyu Purāṇa*
VR	*Vālmīki Rāmāyaṇa*
VdP	*Viṣṇudharmottara Purāṇa*
VmP	*Vāmana Purāṇa*
VP	*Viṣṇu Purāṇa*
VrP	*Varāha Purāṇa*

INTRODUCTION

All religions, be it Islam, Christianity or Hinduism, lay great emphasis on the sanctity of certain places and enjoin pilgrimage to them. Large rivers, mountains and forests have always been venerated as the abodes of gods.[1]

Ancient Sūtras and old Smṛtis like Manu and Yājñavalkya do not attach much importance to Tīrthas, but the later literature on this branch of Dharmaśāstra is very extensive. The *Mahābhārata* (Mbh) regards pilgrimage to Tīrthas more meritorious than sacrifices.[2]

Hence it was natural that Purāṇas and digests on Tīrthas vied with one another in glorifying their respective Tīrthas. The *Skanda Purāṇa* (SkP) is not one book but a library of such *Sthala-Purāṇas* or *Tīrtha-Māhātmyas*. Hence its importance for researchers in different disciplines.

The great oriental scholar, Dr. Jan Gonda, has succinctly emphasized the importance of these *Sthala Purāṇas* in his *Mediaeval Religious Literature in Sanskrit* as follows:[3]

> This genre of literature is not only very useful for deepening our knowledge of the cultural and religious history of India in general, but also most valuable for those who want to reconstruct the development of regional history and local cults or to gain a deeper insight into various religious institutions: for instance, the recommendation of pilgrimage to poor people

1. *sarvāḥ samudragāḥ puṇyāḥ,*
   sarve puṇyā nagottamāḥ|
   sarvam āyatanam puṇyam,
   sarve puṇyā vanāśrayāḥ||
   Devala, quoted in Parāśara-Mādhavīya
2. *tīrthābhigamanaṁ puṇyam|*
   yajñair api viśiṣyate|
   Mbh, *Vana* 82.13
3. J. Gonda, *Mediaeval Religious Literature in Sanskrit*, Weisbaden, 1977, pp. 276-82.

as a substitute for expensive sacrifice, into beliefs and practices e.g. 'those who bathe here go to heaven and those who die here are not born again', and in connection with the conviction in religious suicide and worship of the deceased and into the significance of holy places, local variants of myths and legends and so on. They give information on topography.

The SkP is thus a mine of social, cultural, political, historical, geographical, religious and philosophical information.

It need not however be supposed that the SkP or the Mbh underestimates the importance of moral purity. The SkP: *Kāśīkhaṇḍa* (IV.i.6.48-51) quotes Mbh, *Vana* 82.9-12 and exhorts the need of self-control, knowledge and penance for obtaining the full advantage of pilgrimage.[1]

The SkP is specially important as it covers practically the whole of India. Thus it describes the topography, cultural traditions etc. of the Himalayan region (in the *Kedārakhaṇḍa* and the *Badarikāśrama-māhātmya*), of Uttara Pradesh (in *Kāśīkhaṇḍa* and *Ayodhyā-māhātmya*), Orissa (in *Puruṣottama-kṣetra-māhātmya*), Malwa, Rajasthan and a part of Gujarat (in *Āvantya-khaṇḍa*), Western India along with Gujarat (in *Nāgara-* and *Prabhāsa-khaṇḍa*) and South India (in *Veṅkaṭācala-* and *Setu-māhātmya*). The SkP has thus covered the major part of India (except such states as Maharashtra and Punjab). The authors of each of these *Māhātmyas* knew their respective regions like the palm of their hand and describe the topography of the area, particular *Tīrtha*, its location, legendary history, its distance and directions from the main *Tīrtha*. Naturally these *Tīrtha-māhātmyas* came to be written at different times by different authors. Hence the criticism or evaluation of a particular *Khaṇḍa* should not be regarded as applicable to the whole of the SkP. Thus the ignorance about the beginning of the *Kali* Age or of the dates of

---

1. *yasya hastau ca pādau ca*
   manaścaiva susaṁyatam|
   vidyā tapaś ca kīrtiś ca
   sa tīrtha-phalam aśnute||
   SkP IV.i.6.48; Mbh, *Vana* 82.9.12
VāP 92.125, 127 endorses this.

Vikramāditya, Śaka, Pramati etc. in *Kaumārikākhaṇḍa*, should be attributed to the author of that particular *Khaṇḍa* and not to authors of other parts. Similarly the author of the *Kāśīkhaṇḍa* appears to be a gifted poet familiar with *Alaṅkāraśāstra*, but that does not mean that the whole of the SkP is of that poetic standard. The general literary standard of other authors, however, is certainly high.

THE TITLE

This Purāṇa is called *Skanda/Skānda*. According to the NP 104.2-4, Vyāsa named this Purāṇa *Skānda* and described it as consisting of a hundred thousand verses and "all the rites and rituals regarding Śiva have been revealed by Skanda (Ṣaṇmukha)."

The SkP in the concluding (44th) *Adhyāya* of the last (viz. *Prabhāsa*) *Khaṇḍa* informs us:

> This Skānda Purāṇa was formerly disclosed by Kumāra (Skanda).
> This Purāṇa contributing to longevity and pleasing to the people of four *Varṇas*, was certainly created by the great-souled Skanda (or Ṣaṇmukha).[1]

THE EXTENT

In the traditional list of Mahāpurāṇas, the SkP holds the thirteenth rank, but in its extent, in number of verses, it is the first.

The SkP is found in two versions or forms: (1) *Khaṇḍas* and (2) *Saṁhitās*. The *Saṁhitās* are six in number viz. (1) Sanatkumāra, (2) Sūta, (3) Śāṅkarī, (4) Vaiṣṇavī, (5) Brāhmī and (6) Saura. The total number of verses in these *Saṁhitās* is one hundred thousand.

---

1. *skāndam purāṇam etac ca kumāreṇa purodhṛtam/*
idam purāṇam āyuṣyam caturvarṇa-sukha-pradam/
nirmitam ṣaṇmukheneha niyatam sumahātmanā//
SkP VII. iv. 44.3-4

But the NP recognizes the *Khaṇḍa*-version. The SkP has the following seven *Khaṇḍas*:

(1) *Māheśvara*, (2) *Vaiṣṇava*, (3) *Brāhma*, (4) *Kāśī*, (5) *Avantī*, (6) *Nāgara* and (7) *Prabhāsa*. The NP 104.3 states that the SkP contains 81,000 verses, a figure confirmed by the SkP in the colophon of each *Adhyāya*. The MtP 53.41-42, the VāP 104 and the BhP 12.13 give 81,000 as the number of its verses. But the AP 272.17 states that the SkP has 84,000 verses, a view confirmed by the SkP[1] (!)

The Venkateshwar Press edition of the SkP which we translate, contains 94313 verses (*Purāṇa Journal* VII.2.339). The incidents mentioned in this Purāṇa took place in the *Tatpuruṣa Kalpa* (according to NP).

There are four editions of this *Khaṇḍa* type of SkP: (1) The Venkateshwar Press (VP), (2) Bangavasi (BV), (3) Naval Kishore Press, Lucknow and (4) The Gurumandala (GM), edition. But these editions vary in their contents. For example, the *Caturaśīti-liṅga-māhātmya* ('glorification of 84 Liṅgas') in Part I of the *Avantī-khaṇḍa* (VP and GM editions) is not found in the Lucknow edition. In part II of the *Avantī-khaṇḍa* (Lucknow Edition) some 110 chapters differ considerably from those in the VP edition. The GM includes the spurious *Satya-nārāyaṇa-māhātmya* in the *Revā-khaṇḍa* (pp. 1122-33) but it is not found in the VP edition.

TEXT-TRANSMISSION

The SkP VII.iv.44.1-2 states that the entire Purāṇa was narrated formerly by Skanda to Bhṛgu. Aṅgiras got it from Bhṛgu. Cyavana got it from Aṅgiras. Ṛcīka got it from Cyavana. It is thus traditionally handed down.[2] The Purāṇa is silent as to how it came up to Sūta through Vyāsa. The rest of that last chapter of the SkP is *Phalaśruti*.

---

1. *caturaśīti sāhasraṁ skāndam skanderitam mahat*|
2. *etat purāṇam akhilam purā skandena bhāṣitam*|
bhṛgave Brahma-putrāya tasmāllebhe tathā'ṅgirāḥ||
tataśca cyavanaḥ prāpa, ṛcīkaśca tato muniḥ|
evam paraṁparāprāptam sarveṣu bhuvaneṣvapi||
SkP VII.iv.44.1-2

The present text of the SkP is somewhat different from that of the 11th cent. A.D. Some of the verses then existing in the SkP and quoted as such by Lakṣmīdhara in the *Kalpataru* (A.D. 1110) are not found in the present day text of the SkP. For example, in the *Kalpataru* on Tīrtha (pp. 36-37) some 19 verses are quoted from the SkP, but they are untraced in the present text of the SkP, though they are found in LP 92.120-142. In the *Kalpataru* on p. 44 three verses are quoted from the SkP but are not found in our SkP text, though they are traced in the LP 92.97-99.

There is thus an urgent necessity of preparing a critical edition of the *Skanda Purāṇa*. I have, however, followed here the VP edition.

THE SKANDA AS A MAHĀPURĀṆA

The position of the SkP as a Mahāpurāṇa is not disputed by anyone. But the very nature of SkP being a library of *Kṣetra* and other *Māhātmyas*, is basically different from other Purāṇas, say the VP or the BhP. Hence we should not stretch the SkP on the Procrustean bed of *purāṇam pañcalakṣaṇam*. In fact (as observed by A.D. Pusalkar in *Studies in Epics and Purāṇas*, Bharatiya Vidya Bhavan, Bombay) the *pañca lakṣaṇas* are observed in their breach by a number of Purāṇas except the VP. The SkP not being one book, is not expected to follow the five *lakṣaṇas*. It is true that many books in the SkP share the Purāṇic ideas about *Sarga*, *Pratisarga*, *Manvantara*, but the *lakṣaṇas Vaṁśa* and *Vaṁśānucarita* are totally absent except a few unconnected semi-historical references in the *Kaumārikākhaṇḍa* and *Brāhmakhaṇḍa* (see *infra*, the section on "Semi-historical References in the Skanda Purāṇa").

SOCIAL CONDITION

As society in Purāṇic India is of utmost importance and interest, let us first see society as depicted in the SkP.

Like other Purāṇas, the SkP nostalgically remembers the ideal social condition in the *Kṛta* Age—a classless society, free provision of shelter, food, clothes and ornaments by trees, absence of the concept of Adharma etc. (SkP I.ii.40.176-183). The evolution of *Varṇas* like *Kṣatriyas* and the introduction of the performance of sacrifices appeared in *Tretā Yuga*.[1]

But, as P.V. Kane points out, *Varṇa* is not *Jāti* or caste. *Jāti* has the following characteristics:[2]

(1) Heredity: caste is assigned by birth

(2) Endogamy and Exogamy

(3) Certain restrictions as to food (what food is to be taken, from whom etc.)

(4) Occupation—A particular caste is to follow a particular occupation

(5) Gradation of castes on a social scale. *Jāti* thus lays special emphasis on birth or heredity, while *Varṇa* emphasizes duties.

But brāhmaṇa, kṣatriya, vaiśya and śūdra are *equally important* parts of the body of the Puruṣa (ṚV X.90.12). It thus represents the organic nature of the Hindu Society.

The SkP strongly asserts equality between man and man.

"Humanity being the common factor who is low and who is high?", asks SkP IV.ii.58.120. "If four sons are born from the same person from the same woman, how can they belong to four different *varṇas*?" (Ibid, 125). "The distinction between one *varṇa* and another does not hold water. Hence nobody should ever regard that there is difference between man and man (ibid. 126)." Like Śāṅkara Vedānta, the SkP also espoused elsewhere the stand of equality. Listing the created castes, god Brahmā asserts the equality of these castes to Nārāda: "All those subjects are born from parts of my body (VI.242.18) and hence are equal."

This equality is voiced in other Purāṇas as well, e.g. VāP I.i.6.71. All varṇas are born of the Person (of the Puruṣa). The respective duties of brāhmaṇas, kṣatriyas, vaiśyas and śūdras are based on old Smṛtis like Manu, Yājñavalkya. But even brāhmaṇas took to different vocations like agriculture, medical profession,

---

1. *varṇāśramapratiṣṭhā ca yajñas tretāsu cocyate*
SkP I.ii.40.194

2. HD, II.i, pp. 54-55.

begging at forbidden houses and became degraded (SkP III.ii. 39.287-289). It resulted in the creation of eleven castes among brāhmaṇas who neither dine dor marry *inter se.*[1]

GOTRAS OF BRĀHMAṆAS

The SkP III.ii.9.27-31 gives a list of 24 *gotras* of the brāhmaṇas who settled at Brahmāraṇya. They are as follows:

(1) Bhāradvāja, (2) Vatsa, (3) Kauśika, (4) Kuśa, (5) Śāṇḍilya, (6) Kāśyapa, (7) Gautama, (8) Chāndhana, (9) Jātukarṇya, (10) Vatsa (repetition), (11) Vasiṣṭha, (12) Dhāraṇa, (13) Ātreya, (14) Bhāṇḍila, (15) Laukika, (16) Kṛṣṇāyana, (17) Upamanyu, (18) Gārgya, (19) Mudgala, (20) Mauṣaka, (21) Puṇyāsana, (22) Pārāśara, (23) Kauṇḍinya, (24) Gānyāsana.

Vaiśyas who served their brāhmaṇa patrons adopted the same *gotra* as that of their patrons. Each *gotra* has a Devī associated with it.

Gotra is the latest ancestor or one of the latest ancestors of a person by whose name his family has been known for generations; while *pravara* is constituted by the sage or sages who lived in the remotest past, who were most illustrious and who are generally the ancestors of the *gotra* sages or in some cases the remotest ancestors alone. (HD Vol. II. Part i. p. 497)

By the way, it may be pointed out that the list of *gotras* and *pravaras* in the MtP is more comprehensive (vide Appendix II to V.S. Agrawal's *Matsya Purana—A study*).

CASTES AND SUB-CASTES

Due to a number of permutations and combinations of these *varṇas*, a number of *jātis* evolved and they followed different

---

1. *ekādaśa dvijās tataḥ||*
ekādaśa-samājñātir|
vikhyātā bhuvanatraye||
na teṣāṁ saha-saṁbandhaḥ|
na vivāhaśca jāyate ||
SkP III.ii.39.324-325

avocations (SkP V.iii.122.7). SkP I.ii.40.177-190 states that due to *moha* (delusion) and the development of sordid proclivities of man, a topsy-turvy social crisis based on difference of opinion (*matibheda*) arose.

The period of the SkP was an era of social crises. The followers of the Veda like brāhmaṇas, kṣatriyas were at sixes and sevens. Non-Vedic cults like Jainism and Buddhism mounted severe attacks on Brāhmaṇism. For example, the disputation between Jaina Prince Kumārapāla and brāhmaṇas on killing of animals in sacrifice (SkP III.ii.36.61-109) and the preaching of Viṣṇu in the form of a Buddhist monk Puṇyakīrti with Lakṣmī as a nun called Vijnānakaumudī (SkP IV.ii.58.82-126) may be noted. Her criticism of Varṇabheda is however valid.

INFLUX OF MLECCHAS

There was an influx of the Mleccha communities. The following Mleccha communities are mentioned:

From north-western India: Tuṣāras, Barbaras, Daradas (from Dardistan), Lumpas (or Lumpakas or Lamghans), Pahlavas (Persians?), Svagaṇas (from Sogdiana, i.e. the area around Bukhara and Samarkand), Śakas (Scythians), Yavanas (Ionians, Greeks).

The invasion by leaders of these people, e.g. Lohāsura, the iconoclast (SkP III.ii.23), indicates foreign invasions in a veiled manner.[1] The sense of nationalism was conspicuous by its absence as can be seen from the Buddhist co-operation with Arabs against the Hindu King Dahir in Sindha or Jayacanda, King of Kanauj's invitation to Shahbuddin Ghori against Pṛthvīrāja Cauhāna. Moreover, from mixed marriages were born *Pṛthag-varṇas* or *hīna-varṇas* 'lower castes' (V.iii.122.7) and they were regarded lower than śūdras. They were untouchables, *antyajas*, cāṇḍālas. These Jātis had to live outside the village. Naturally this inequitous system of caste was one of the important causes of the downfall of Hindus.

FORMS OF MARRIAGE

Family is the basis of social organization. Marriage, both in

1. Also see SkP VII.i.19.83 for reference to Mlecchas, Dasyus etc.

the patriarchal and matriarchal systems, is a *sine qua non* of family. From the times of the *Gṛhya Sūtras*, *Dharma Sūtras* and *Smṛtis*, forms of marriage are said to be eight, viz. *Brāhma, Prājāpatya, Ārṣa, Daiva, Gāndharva, Āsura, Rākṣasa* and *Paiśāca* (*Āśvalāyana Gr.* I.6, *Baudhāyana Dh. S.* I., *Manu* III.21). The SkP gives ten forms of marriage. Out of them the above mentioned eight forms of marriage are given in the SkP III.ii.6. 27-30, but in a different order, viz. *Brāhma*, *Daiva*, *Ārṣa*, *Prājāpatya*, *Āsura*, *Gāndharva* and *Paiśāca*. This order is also given in SkP IV.38. To this list SkP VI.241.36 adds *Prātibha* and *Ghātina*. Out of these the first four are the best forms. The rest are meant for *hīna-jātis* ('low castes').

The SkP III.ii.6. 27-30a give the essential features of these marriage-forms as follows:

(1) *Brāhma* : The bridegroom to be invited and the daughter well-decorated with ornaments to be offered.

(2) *Daiva* : The daughter duly ornamented to be offered to the priest who has performed one's sacrifice.

(3) *Ārṣa* : The daughter to be given after receiving a pair of cows or bulls from the bridegroom.

(4) *Prājāpatya* : The daughter to be offered with the blessing, "May both of you perform Dharma".

LOWER FORMS OF MARRIAGE

(5) *Āsura* : Purchase of a girl by paying money (IV. i.38.5)

(6) *Gāndharva* : Love-marriage by mutual friendship between a boy and a girl.

(7) *Rākṣasa* : Marriage by forcible abduction of a girl.

(8) *Paiśāca* : Marrying a girl by fraudulent means, the worst form.

The SkP III.ii.6.33 recommends endogamous marriage, though instances of exogamous marriages even of *Pratiloma* type are found. For example, king Durdharṣa married an apparently brahmin girl Candravadanā with the consent of her foster-father Kalpa (SkP V.ii.70. 8-20).

SAṀSKĀRA

Though the term *Saṁskāra* in the sense of 'refinement' does not occur in the ṚV and *Gṛhya Sūtras*, it occurs since the period of *Dharma Sūtras* (e.g. Gautama VII.8; Āpastamba I.1.1.9). Echoing *Smṛtis*, the SkP (VI.239.31) says, "By birth one is śūdra. He is called Twice-born (*Dvija*) through *Saṁskāras*." The ultimate aim is brāhmaṇahood, the attainment of which is very difficult (VII. i.207.56).[1] Brāhmaṇahood is attained by the performance of *Saṁskāras*. They turn a *śūdra-vipra* into a bonafide *vipra* (V.iii.20.50),[2] in the absence of which one is as good as a beast[3] (I.ii.29.147). The SkP classifies brāhmaṇas into eight categories in an ascending order:

Mātra, *Brāhmaṇa*, *Śrotriya*, *Anūcāna*, *Bhrūṇa*, *Ṛṣikalpa*, *Ṛṣi* and *Muni* (I.ii.5.110).

(1) One merely born in the family of a brāhmaṇa is *mātra*. He is devoid of rites.

(2) A person who practises the Vedas, is merciful and truthful is a *brāhmaṇa*.

(3) One who has studied at least one branch of the Veda along with the *Aṅgas* and performs six holy activities is a *śrotriya*.

(4) A brāhmaṇa conversant with Vedas and Vedāṅgas, teaching Vedas to a number of pupils is *anūcāna*.

(5) An *anūcāna*, a regular performer of *Yajñas* and study of Vedas and partaker of food after feeding others is a *bhrūṇa*.

---

1. *mānuṣyaṁ durlabham loke*
brāhmaṇyam adhikam tataḥ|
SkP VII.i.207.56

2. *brāhmaṇatvam tribhir lokaiḥ*
durlahham padmalocane|
SkP V.iii.20.50

3. *saṁskārarahitam janma yataśca paśuvat smṛtam*|
SkP I.ii.29.147

(6) A master of Vedic and of secular knowledge who always stays in a hermitage is a *ṛṣikalpa*.
(7) A person with sublimated sex-urge, competent to bless or curse is a *ṛṣi*.
(8) One, desisting from worldly activities, engaged in meditation and viewing gold and a lump of earth with equanimity is a *muni*.

This stage of *muni* is obtained by one who is born in a brāhmaṇa family and has undergone all Vedic *saṁskāras* (VI.147.46). All the *saṁskāras* beginning with *Niṣeka* or *Garbhādhāna* and ending with *Śmaśāna* are essential for all *Dvijas*, i.e. brāhmaṇas, kṣatriyas and vaiśyas. These *saṁskāras* are described in details in SkP IV.i.36.2 ff.

THE NUMBER OF SAṀSKĀRAS

The number of saṁskāras varies with different Smṛti authors from sixteen to forty-eight as in Gautama (VIII.14-24) followed by Śaṅkha, quoted in *Smṛticandrikā Subodhinī* on *Mitākṣarā* (a commentary on *Yājñavalkya Smṛti*) and SkP V. iii.20.50-59 and VI.115.26.

LIST OF SAṀSKĀRAS

(1) *Bījakṣepa* — Sowing the seeds
(2) *Garbhādhāna* — Conception
(3) *Puṁsavana* — Desire for a male child
(4) *Sīmanta* — Parting of hair
(5) *Jātakarma* — Rites after birth
(6) *Nāma* — Naming of the child
(7) *Niṣkrama* — Bringing the child out of the lying-in chamber
(8) *Anna-prāśana* — First feeding of the child with food
(9) *Cūḍā-karma* — The tonsure ceremony
(10) *Mauñjī-bandhana* — Investing with the sacred thread
(11) *Aiṣika* — Pertaining to Aiṣika, i.e. religious rites to be performed in the month of Āśvina (?)

(12) *Dārvika* — Oblation made with a ladle from *Darvī-homa* (MW 476b)
(13) *Saumika* — Pertaining to the *Soma* sacrifice(?)
(14) *Bhaumika* — Ceremony pertaining to the earth (MW 768)
(15) *Patnī-saṁyojana* — Marriage

16-41 are the various rites pertaining to:

(16) *Daiva-karma*
(17) *Mānuṣyam*
(18) *Pitṛkarma*
(19) *Daśama*
(20) *Aṣṭaka*
(21) *Bhūta*
(22) *Bhavya*
(23) *Iṣṭa*
(24) *Pārvaṇa* (*Śrāddha*)
(25) *Śrāvaṇī*
(26) *Agrāyaṇa*
(27) *Caitra*
(28) *Aśvayuji*
(29) *Darśa*
(30) *Paurṇimāsī*
(31) *Nirūḍha*
(32) *Paśu-savana*
(33) *Sautrāmaṇi*
(34) *Agniṣṭoma*
(35) *Atyagniṣṭoma*
(36) *Ṣoḍaśī*
(37) *Vājapeya*
(38) *Atirātra*
(39) *Āptoryāma*
(40) *Daśa Vājapeya*
(41) *Dayā* (Mercy to all) (See Gautama's list)
(42) *Kṣānti* (Forgiveness)
(43) *Anasūyā* (Absence of jealousy)
(44) *Śauca* (Purity)
(45) *Anāyāsa* (Non-exertion) (Not mentioned in the SkP but accepted from Gautama's list)
(46) *Maṅgalam* (Auspiciousness).
(47) *Akārpaṇya* (Absence of miserliness)
(48) *Aspṛhā* (Absence of covetousness or desirelessness

SkP follows Gautama and AP 32.1-12, 166.9-17.

SkP later states that forty-eight *saṁskāras* are prescribed by god Brahmā for excellent *Dvijas* (VI.115.26-27).

ABORIGINAL TRIBES

Apart from the followers of the Vedas, there was however a not-ignorable section of the society which was denied these *saṁskāras*. It included foreigners such as Tuṣāras, Barbaras, Daradas, Lumpas, Pahlavas, Svagaṇas, Śakas and Yavanas and Tribals of hill and forest areas like Pulindas, Ābhīras, Medakas and Niṣādas.

It is rather strange that we assimilated the foreigners in our society but did not show that humanitarian attitude to our Indian tribals.

STATUS OF WOMEN

The SkP declares that both men and women are evolved from the *Ardhanārīśvara* form of god Śiva (I.ii.22.38). Woman constitutes the household; hence she is called *Gṛhiṇī*. One is born as a son from her; hence she is called *Jāyā*. She protects the husband from the sinful world and hence she is called *Kalatra*. Devala says that *Vidyā* (learning) and wife are like luminaries. They should be attained with efforts (I.ii.15.7-10). Lest neglect should be done to the weaker sex, god Brahmā clearly exhorted in the *Śāstra* that bringing up a daughter is ten times more meritorious than bringing up a son (I.ii.23.44-47). Wife is necessary for the fruition of religious rites as for continuance of the family. Where women are delighted by being provided with good food, dress and ornaments, all goddesses happily stay there and all undertakings (of the householder) become successful (IV.i.40.59). The spiritual power of a chaste woman is eulogized. *Kāśikhaṇḍa* (i.4.60-69) has highly praised chaste women. Even the Sun is afraid of touching them with his rays. Even a glance from a chaste woman purifies the whole body.

Kāśīkhaṇḍa (i.4) prescribes a code of conduct for chaste women. A woman is not to desert her husband even if he be fallen or frigid. She is not to deck herself when her husband has gone away. The Purāṇa encourages Satī. But a very important point foolishly ignored by the Hindu society, for which criminal negligence they have been suffering a heavy social loss, is this Purāṇa's insistence on the natural purity of women:

"Women are pure in every part of their person." "Even if a woman is raped or has been in the custody of a robber, she should never be abandoned. This abandonment has no scriptural sanction." "Women become pure by their menstrual flow."[1]

Some scholars suspect Muslim influence on this Purāṇa due to the following two adjectives: (1) one who has covered her face with her garment (*vastra-nigūḍha-vadanā*) and (ii) one who has covered her face within her apparel (*vastrāntapihitānanā*) used in the case of Menā (Queen of Himālaya) and Pārvatī (an unmarried girl).

Most probably wearing of veils before strangers was an old custom in royal families; so no Muslim influence need be suspected here.

WIDOWS

The Purāṇa shows that the lot of widows was unenviable. *Kāśīkhaṇḍa* 1.4 prescribes inhuman restrictions on widows. A widow is to tonsure her head. She is to take one meal a day and perform *Vratas* involving fasting. She is not to use cosmetics, not to sleep on a bedstead. Her appearance is inauspicious. The prohibitions do have sanction of *Smṛtis* but that does not exonerate the charge that the treatment of widows was inhuman.

WOMEN'S EDUCATION

Since the *Upanayana* of girls went out of vogue and child marriages became common, common girls had little scope for learning. Girls in royal families could write (even love-letters) and were taught fine arts like dancing, singing and painting (III.iii. 1.45; III.iii.8.19-20). *Brahma-vādinīs* like Maitreyī, Kaṁsarī were very rare.

---

1. . . . स्त्रियो मेध्यास्तु सर्वत: ।। 46 ।।
बलात्कारोपभुक्ता वा चोरहस्तगताऽपि वा ।
न त्याज्या दयिता नारी नास्यास्त्यागो विधीयते ।। 47 ।।
संशुद्धी रजसा नार्या: ।। 48 ।।

SkP IV.i.40.46-48

DRESS AND ORNAMENTS

It was the fashion of the old to wear two clothes (*vastra-yugma*), the Dhoti and the upper garment. Women used clothes dyed in red and blue and of variegated colours (*citravastra*) (IV.i.28.81; IV.i.40.142). Clothes of cotton, silk, wool were used and the variety of clothes shows an advanced stage of society.

The SkP mentions the following ornaments: *Mukuṭa* (crown), *Nāsābharaṇa* (nose-ring III.i.50.54), probably a late borrowal, *Kuṇḍala* (ear-ring), *Hāra* (a pearl necklace), *Niṣka* or *Suvarṇa-niṣka* (necklace of gold coins?), bangles (of gold and silver), *Kaṭaka* (bracelet), *Aṅgulīyaka* (finger-ring), *Kāñcī* (girdle), *Nūpura* (anklets). If a woman wished long life to her husband, it was obligatory that she whose husband is living must use turmeric, saffron, vermillion, collyrium, betel (?) and other auspicious decorations like coiffure and ornaments for hands and ears (III.ii.7.28-29).

In general, it is a picture of a prosperous and happy society.

RELIGIONS IN THE SKANDA PURĀṆA

The text mentions three religions, viz. Brāhmaṇism, Jainism and Buddhism. There is found a veiled reference to Jagadguru Ādi Śaṅkara in I.ii.47.13-14 in the statement that Jagadguru 'Kūrma' re-established the Vedas (Vedic path), annihilated thousands of Buddhas and censured naked Jainas, and also an attempt to synthesize the five Brāhmaṇical sects, viz. those of Śiva, Viṣṇu, Śakti, Vināyaka and Sūrya. A positive recognition and accommodation of these sects is found throughout the Purāṇa. For example, *Kāśīkhaṇḍa,* though it is mainly devoted to Śiva and describes the 68 important Śaiva shrines along with their locations, supplies us with a list of 36 *Śaktipīṭhas* (in ii. 70), 56 Vināyaka temples along with their places and 12 Āditya shrines (of the Sun-god) (in i.46-50; ii.51).

The *Khaṇḍas* of the SkP though specifically meant for the glorification of Śiva, have sections on glorification of Viṣṇu. Though the Purāṇa is named after Skanda, yet he, as a god, is ignored in preference to Gaṇeśa or Śakti who are specially treated.

The major influence on the Purāṇa is that of *Advaita* philosophy of Śaṅkara. There is mention of one Rāmānuja (SkP, II.i.21) who is a devotee of Viṣṇu and preached *Pāñcarātra* doctrine. This may be a reference to Rāmānuja (b. 1017), the founder-exponent of *Viśiṣṭādvaita* philosophy. Attempt has been made to accommodate Vṛṣabha, the first *Tīrthaṅkara* of Jainas who preached *Pāramahaṁsya* (the highest order of *Saṁnyāsa*)[1] and Buddha, the founder of Buddhism as *Avatāras* of Viṣṇu but Viṣṇu's function as Buddha is to mislead the Asuras.[2]

The list of Viṣṇu's *Avatāras* (II.ix.18-26) is interesting. It is as follows:

(1) Divine Boar	(2) The Fish
(3) The Tortoise	(4) Man-lion
(5) Vāmana	(6) Kapila
(7) Datta	(8) Vṛṣabha
(9) Bhārgava Rāma	(10) Dāśarathi Rāma
(11) Kṛṣṇa	(12) Kṛṣṇa Dvaipāyana (Vyāsa)
(13) Buddha	(14) Kali

This accommodativeness did not cut much ice with Jainas. Kumārapāla who confiscated the Agrahāra of Brāhmaṇas (in *Dharmāraṇyakhaṇḍa* in the *Brāhmakhaṇḍa*) criticizes the Brāhmaṇas for performing animal sacrifices and asks them to give up that path. Jaina authors who use the stock argument against Brāhmaṇas forget (probably do not know) that animal sacrifices were formerly condemned by a Sāṅkhya, Māṭhara by name, whom *Nandīsūtra* of the Śvetāṁbara canon mentions along with another Sāṅkhya teacher Īśvarakṛṣṇa. Jainas often quote the following verse of Māṭhara:

"If by cutting trees for sacrificial posts and by killing animals one can go to heaven, what else is the way to hell?"[3]

---

1. SkP II.ix.18.26.
2. *chalena mohayiṣyāmi bhūtvā buddho' surān aham/*
SkP II.ix.18.41
3. *vṛkṣāṁś chitvā paśūn hatvā kṛtvā rudhira-kardamam/*
yadi vā gamyate svargaṁ, narakaṁ kena gamyate//

Viṣṇu's role is that of a crafty religious teacher. When Divodāsa could not be dislodged from Kāśī, Viṣṇu assumed the form of a Buddhist teacher Puṇyakīrti and Lakṣmī as Vijñānakaumudī. He preached that the world is beginningless and endless. Gods like Brahmā, Viṣṇu and Rudra are embodied beings like us. They too are afraid of death. All embodied beings being alike, have mercy on beings as mercy to living beings is the highest Dharma. There is heaven and hell on this earth alone, nowhere else. *Vijñāna* is the highest *Mokṣa*. Hence do not perform sacrifice involving *Hiṁsā* (IV.ii.58.82-110). Vijñānakaumudī mounted an attack on *Cāturvarṇya* (Ibid. 115-126).

The common man ignored such disputations and took to Yoga or *Bhakti*, a rosary of beads, muttering the name of Rāma etc., worship of Rādhā-Kṛṣṇa etc. (II.ix.26-29)

SEMI-HISTORICAL REFERENCES IN THE SKANDA PURĀṆA

If the *Pañca-lakṣaṇa* definition of Purāṇa be strictly applied to the SkP, it ceases to be a Purāṇa, as it has no description or enumeration of *Dynasties of Kings*, though there are references to many Purāṇic kings. It is, as stated above, a library of *Sthala-Purāṇas* with occasional references to a Purāṇic ruler or Purāṇa-type transformation of a historical king. Whatever references are found in the SkP are noted here region-wise.

Proceeding statewise, at first we come across Kanauj (Kānykubja). Leaving aside Purāṇic legendary rulers like Gādhi, Viśvāmitra, we meet Āma alias Nāgabhaṭa II of the Pratihāra dynasty in SkP III.ii.36. It is the pretext of a prediction about *Kali* Age made by Vyāsa to Dharma that we are told the historical legend about King Āma. Āma would be a powerful ruler devoted to the protection of his subjects (III.ii.36.34-36). From his wife Māmā, he would have a daughter Ratnagaṅgā who, under the influence of one Jaina teacher Indra-Sūri, would become Jaina and be married to a Jaina prince Kumbhīpāla (or Kumārapāla), the ruler of Dharmāraṇya. He would confiscate the Agrahāras of Brāhmaṇas. The Brāhmaṇas would go in appeal to King Āma, but the King, a convert to Jainism and surrounded by Jaina courtiers, would refuse to restore their lands etc., given by Lord Rāma till they produced the charter given by Rāma. The Brāhmaṇas would go to the South to Hanūmān, the Monkey-god. He would give them two of his hairs. On their return, they would appeal to King Āma again. In case he refused, they would drop down one hair of Hanūmān which would set ablaze the whole of Āma's palace and capital. Āma would surrender and agree to give back the Land etc. to Brāhmaṇas. The Brāhmaṇas then would drop the second hair of Hanūmān and everything that was burnt would be restored to him. People too would again re-embrace Vaiṣṇavism (III.ii.38.46-49).

This Purāṇic legend (except the submission of King Āma to Brāhmaṇas) finds support in the story of Bappabhaṭṭi in Rājaśekhara's *Prabandha Kośa*. Therein Āma was a Jaina king of Gwalior, son of Yaśovarmā (confused with Yaśodharmā). He defeated his rival Dharma, King of Gauḍa, when the stake was fixed on the result of the disputation between two court pandits, Bappabhaṭṭi for Āma and Vākpati for King Dharma of Gauḍa. Bappabhaṭṭi won but the kingdom of Gauḍa was given back to King Dharma.

But there is no reference to Hanūmān's hair and restoration of Dharmāraṇya to Brāhmaṇas.

The Legend about Brahmins from Dharmāraṇya going to the South and bringing Hanūmān's hair may possibly be associated with the crushing defeat inflicted on Nāgabhaṭa by Rāṣṭrakūṭa king Govinda III of South. Rāṣṭrakūṭa records (e.g. Pathari Pillar Inscription E.I. IX.255) state that he (Rāṣṭrakūṭa King Govind III) destroyed the valour of Nāgabhaṭa who in fear vanished "nobody knew whither" and after having "devasted his home" and overrun his dominions proceeded up to Himalayas" (*Imperial Kanauj*, pp. 26-27). This is possibly 'the destructive hair' of Hanūmān in the South. The epithets given to kings in the official genealogy recorded in royal charters show that four generations of Pratihāra kings beginning with Devarāja were devotees respectively of Viṣṇu, Śiva, Bhagavatī and Sūrya (*Imperial Kanauj*, p. 28). The story of conversion of Nāgabhaṭa to Jainism shows the influence of the Jaina tradition on this Purāṇa. Nāgabhaṭa (alias Nagāvaloka) ended his life by immersion into the waters of Gaṅgā in A.D. 833 (*Prabhāvaka-caritra*). This shows Nāgabhaṭa's religious temperament, testified by his performance of religious ceremonies enjoined by the Vedas (*Imperial Kanauj*, p. 28).

The credibility of this legend in the SkP becomes a suspect when Kumārapāla, a Śaiva Cālukya ruler of Gujarat (A.D. 1143-71) who embraced Jainism in A.D. 1164, is made the son-in-law of the Pratihāra King of the 8th century A.D.

BHOJA

Another important king noted by the SkP is Bhoja, king of Kanauj (A.D. 836-82). He was a person with large eyes, long mighty arms, learned, eloquent, sweet-speaking and endowed with all auspicious qualities (SkP VII.ii.6.21). One day his forest officer from Raivataka reported about a lady with the head of a deer. The king got her brought to his capital. Though duly washed and decorated, she could not speak. Due to the efficacy of a Tīrtha, she became a woman with a beautiful face and told the king that she was the king's wife during the last seven births. They married and lived happily (VII.ii.7.32).

Once sage Sārasvata glorified the pilgrimage to Vastrāpatha. The king wanted to abdicate his kingdom in favour of his son and go on pilgrimage to Vastrāpatha, but sage Sārasvata dissuaded the king from doing so as deities like Śiva and Viṣṇu could be worshipped even at home.[1]

Bhoja performed the pilgrimage with his family and without abdicating his throne; he died and went to the highest heaven.[2]

The quotation is given to show that Bhoja did not abdicate his kingdom at all. Hence Dr. H.C. Roychoudhuri's inference[3] that Bhoja abdicated his throne in favour of his son is not correct.

---

1. *gṛhe'pi devā hara-viṣṇumukhyā*
   jalāni darbhā nṛpate tilāśca|
   aneka-deśāntara-darśanārtham
   mano nivāryaṁ nṛpate tvayeti || SkP VII.ii.10.19

2. *tato yathokta-vidhinā sa bhojo nṛpa-sattamaḥ|*
   vastrāpatha-kṣetrayātrām parivārajanaiḥ saha|
   kṛtvā kṛtārthatām prāpto jagāmānte param padam|| SkP VII.ii.19.34

3. A Note on the *Vastrāpatha Māhātmya* of Skanda Purāṇa (IHQ, V, pp. 129-35).

KĀŚIRĀJA CANDRADEVA

SkP VI.106.6 refers to Aila Candradeva, king of Kāśī: *Ailasya candradevasya kāśirājasya sanmateḥ*. As Gahadwal kings of Kanauj were called Kāśirājas, Kāśirāja Candradeva is most probably a king of Kanauj.[1]

PALLAVAS OF TOṆḌAMAṆḌALA (KĀÑCĪPURAM AREA)

As the SkP deals with the entire traditional Cakravartī Kṣetra from the Setu to Kedāra,[2] historical references to the South Indian kings like Pallavas of Toṇḍamaṇḍalam, Colas and Pāṇḍyas of Madura are natural. Out of them Pallavas are described in details due to their connection with *Veṅkaṭācala Māhātmya*.

PALLAVAS OF TOṆḌAMAṆḌALA (Based on SkP II.i.9-11)

The origin of Pallavas is still obscure.[3] In the SkP II.i.9.53-54 we are told that King Toṇḍamāna was born of Sudhīra or Suvīra and Nandinī and belonged to the Lunar dynasty (*Soma Kula*).

He married Padmā, daughter of a Pāṇḍya king. He was a devotee of Viṣṇu. He established his capital at Nārāyaṇapura.

This account in the SkP that Toṇḍamāna was born of an age-old royal Kṣatriya family shows that he was not a foreigner—'*Pahlava*' as held by some scholars. The promotion from the epithet '*rāja*' in early part of the chapter (II.i.10.22) to '*rājarāja*' in its later part (II.i.10.96, 101) shows his increase in power and status. It was through the grace of Lord Śrīnivāsa of Śeṣācala that a Śūdra Raṅgadāsa of Pāṇḍyadeśa became a high-caste Kṣatriya King Toṇḍamāna. As per advice of sage Śuka, Toṇḍamāna bathed in Padmasaras and when he returned home, his father abdicated the throne for him—a traditional Kṣatriya

---

1. A.B.L. Awasthi, *Studies in Skanda Purana*, Vol. I, p. 196.
2. *pṛthvīm ā setu kedārāt*| SkP I.iii. (Uttarārdha) 22.8
3. Rao, B.V.K., *A History of the Early Dynasties of Andhradesh*, p. 135.

practice. Toṇḍamāna was indirectly invited by Śrīnivāsa as follows: "Śrīnivāsa in a boar form used to graze Śyāmāka grains of a Niṣāda (an aboriginal, possibly a Kuruva). When the Niṣāda chased him he disappeared down in the earth. When the Niṣāda tried to dig this place, he became unconscious. But to the Niṣāda's son, the divine Boar said to go to the king Toṇḍamāna and ask him to build a shrine for him as a Boar resting on a rock and wash the anthill (*Valmīka*) thereof with the milk of a black cow." The Niṣāda and his son conveyed that message to the king. The king conveyed this message to his ministers and queens. When he slept Lord Śrīnivāsa conducted Toṇḍamāna to his (Śrīnivāsa's) cave and the entire road to the cave was marked with sprouts (*pallavas*) scattered there. The next day the king found that the route to Śrīnivāsa's cave was strewn over with *pallavas*. Toṇḍamāna enclosed the Śrīnivāsa cave in his palace, built his capital (Nārāyaṇapura, mod. Tirupati) there, ruled as Kings' King (*Rājarāja*, *Nṛpendra*) over the earth. He was asked by Śrīnivāsa to respect two trees *Tintiṇī* (tamarind tree) and *Campaka* (a sweet-smelling flower plant) as they represented Viṣṇu and Lakṣmī respectively.

This is an attempt to explain why Toṇḍamāna dynasty came to be known as Pallavas (of Kāñcī). *Toṇḍai* is the name of a creeper (*Capparis Horrida*). *Toṇḍaiyar* is the Tamil rendering of *Pallava*. "The theory of the Toṇḍamaṇḍalam origin of the Pallavas of Kāñcī best explains the historical fact relating to the problem of their origin"[1], though historians doubt what the relation was, if any, between the Tiraiyar-Toṇḍaiyar and the Pallavas and what the interval was between the two lines of rulers at Kāñcī.[2]

The Purāṇa does not give the personal name of Toṇḍamāna. But if he be the founder of the Toṇḍamāna (or Toṇḍaiyar) dynasty, his personal name is probably Iḷandiraiyan. If this guess be correct, he was the younger contemporary of the famous Cola King Karikāla.

SkP (II.i.3-5) mentions another line of rulers of Toṇḍaimaṇḍala: Mitravarman→Viyad or Ākāśa→Vasudāna. Mitra-

1. *The Classical Age*, BVB, Bombay, p. 257.
2. Majumdar and Altekar, *Gupta-Vakataka Age*, pp. 303-04.

varmā of the Lunar Race (Somakula) ruled at Nārāyaṇapura. He married a Pāṇḍya princess (II.i.3.15-18). Their son Viyad or Ākāśa, a powerful sovereign, discovered a beautiful girl Padminī while ploughing. She was married to Lord Veṅkaṭeśa (Ibid, 3.21-30), Vasudāna, the son of Viyad or Ākāśa and Dharaṇī. SkP III.i.9.12-13 mentions the defeat of a powerful athlete Malla-Balī from the South by Aśokadatta, a protege of Pratāpamukuṭa of Kāśī. The identification of this athlete Malla-Bali with the Pallava King Narasiṁhavarman I is doubtful.

COLA

According to SkP (II.iv.26, 27) Cola is the name of a sovereign who ruled from Kāñcī[1] and the ancient country called Coladeśa is named after the ruler. During his reign there was no person destitute, miserable or wicked (*pāpabuddhi*). He was a pious Vaiṣṇava devotee of Anantaśayana (i.e. Viṣṇu reclining on the serpent Śeṣa). He performed so many sacrifices that both the banks of the river Tāmraparṇī were decorated with golden sacrificial posts. Though he observed sacred vows under the guidance of his preceptor Mudgala, the Lord was not pleased with him. So Cola placed his sister's son (*bhāgineya*) on the throne and immolated himself in fire. He is thus credited to have started the matriarchal system of inheritance.[2]

PĀṆḌYA RULERS

The SkP (III.i.48.2, Ibid, 50.42, VI.63.6) refers to Pāṇḍya kings of Madurai frequently. They were matrimonially related to Toṇḍamaṇḍala kings (e.g. Toṇḍamāna and Padmā II.i.9.55). The SkP mentions the following Pāṇḍya kings: Śaṅkara Pāṇḍya (SkP III.i.48.2), his son Suruci (Ibid, III.i.48.66), Puṇyanidhi (III.i 50.2-3), Padmavarṇa or Padma-miśra (III.iii.4.40-47), Vajrāṅgada (I. iii 22.6). Little is known about them dynastically or historically. In SkP (III.i.48) a few details are

1. The ancient capital of Cola was Uraiyur on the Kāverī in the 2nd cent. A.D. and Kāñcīpura in the 11th cent. A.D. (De, 51)—a point worth noting in determining the date of the text.

2. SkP II.iv.27.25-26.

given about Śaṅkara Pāṇḍya. He was a great king (*Rājaśekhara*, III.i.48.7), a pious follower of *Varṇāśramadharma*, a tolerant ruler worshipping Śiva, Viṣṇu and other gods. One day, while hunting, he killed an ascetic inadvertently. To atone for it, he placed his son Suruci on the throne and immolated himself in fire. Pāṇḍya King Vajrāṅga tried to circumambulate Aruṇācala on horseback and was punished for this insult to Śiva (ibid, ch. 22). But according to the advice of a Vidyādhara, Vajrāṅga became a devotee of Śiva, donated everything for the *Pūjā* of Śiva, performed penance at the hermitage of Gautama and attained *Mokṣa* (ibid, chs. 23-26).

The semi-historical references show that the spread of Brāhmaṇism had culturally united both the north and south India.

STRAY REFERENCES IN VARIOUS KHAṆḌAS

Māheśvara Khaṇḍa

Kaumārikā Khaṇḍa (KK): Kali Age began in 3101 B.C. The author of KK is unaware of it or perhaps believed differently and in a predictive way (in the future tense) makes the following statements:

(1) *The Nanda dynasty* "will come into being" in *Kali* 3310 (SkP, I.ii.40.251). This means that dynasty came to rule in A.D. 209 (*Kali* 3310—3101 B.C.—the beginning of the *Kali* Age). *The Age of Imperial Unity*, pp. 31-35 states that the Nanda dynasty began in 364 B.C.

(2) Vikramāditya: In *Kali* 3020, the kingdom of Vikramāditya "will come into being" (I.ii.40.252-54); so the Purāṇa states that Vikrama *Saṁvat* began in B.C. 81 (Kali 3020—3101 B.C.—beginning of Kali = B.C. 81). Actually the *Saṁvat* started in 57 B.C.

(3) In *Kali* 3100, the Śaka era 'will begin' (I.ii.40.254): It means the Śaka era began in 1 B.C. (*Kali* 3100—3101 B.C.—beginning of the *Kali* Age). Actually that era started in A.D. 78: In the notes I have given more such instances. We do not know if the Purāṇa writer had some other evidence about the beginning of the *Kali* Age.

(4) Śūdraka(?): A great heroic king, the Lord of warriors in 3290 after *Kali* (I.ii.40.250). *The Age of Imperial Unity* (BVB Vol. II, p. 264) regards him to be a legendary person.

(5) Buddha, King of Magadha: (Purāṇic date *Kali* 3600—3101 B.C.—beginning of the *Kali* = A.D. 499) Son of Hemasadana and Añjanī. Noble-hearted, subduer of Jyotir-bindu and other fierce enemies, enjoyed seven continents for 64 years (I.ii.40.255-60). He is identifiable with Buddhadatta of the Gupta dynasty who subdued Hūṇas and Tāmramukhas. He died in A.D. 498.

(6) Pramati (I.ii.40.259-62): This king was of Candramas *Gotra*. He "will destroy millions of Mlecchas and exterminate completely *Pāṣaṇḍas*. He will re-establish Vedic religion and restore stability in the *doab* of Gaṅgā and Yamunā." His date will be *Kali* 4400: *caturṣu ca sahasreṣu śateṣvapi caturṣu ca*/

(I.ii.40.259)

Kali 4400 works out to be A.D. 1299 (4400-3101 B.C.).

This is the period of Allauddin Khilji. History knows no such a powerful Hindu king in this era.

SkP VII.i.19.72-81 refers probably to this Pramati of Candramas *Gotra* who established Dharma in Madhyadeśa. One Pramati is mentioned in MtP 144.51-64 and V.S. Agrawal identifies him with Candragupta alias Vikramāditya (*Matsya Purāṇa—a Study*, pp. 228-31).

(7) Ādi Śaṅkara: In I.ii.47.13-14, we get stray references about Śaṅkara as follows: Jagadguru Kūrma re-established the Vedas (Vedic Path). He annihilated thousands of Buddhists and censured the naked Jainas.

(8) Does the epithet *Jñāna-sambandha-nātha* in I.iii.9.6 have a veiled reference to the Tamil saint Thiru Jñānasambandara?

(9) SkP II.i.21 mentions Rāmānuja and he is shown to have preached *Pāñcarātra* doctrines. Hence this may be an indirect reference to Rāmānuja, the teacher of *Viśiṣṭādvaita* school of Vedānta.

The above conjectures need substantiation.

POLITY IN THE SKANDA PURĀṆA

Though the SkP mainly consists of the glorification of sacred places (*Tīrtha Māhātmyas*) and does not deal specifically with Polity or *Rājadharma* as we find it in the *Śāntiparva* of the Mbh, the Purāṇa does refer to *Rājanīti* (II.ii.11-29), *Daṇḍanīti* (IV.i. 29.88) and also to *Rājadharma* (II.iv.32.2). But the Purāṇas do not appear to be interested in the theories about the nature of the state, varieties of state-government and such other matters as we find them in the works of Kauṭilya and Śukra or in the works of later European thinkers like Hobbes, Locke, Hegel and others. In fact the theory of nation-state is of a late origin.

From the description of *Kṛta Yuga*, we find that Purāṇa-authors believed in an idyllic state in ancient times when all people were good and law-abiding and needed no law-enforcing authority. That stateless state was blissful.[1] Even Locke and Rousseau believed in such a state of nature in pre-government days. But as Mārkaṇḍeya tells Yudhiṣṭhira[2]:

> Due to greed of men, *Mātsya Nyāya* ('Might is right') prevailed. So if there be no state-government, there would be chaos and the world will perish (V.iii.146.38). When *Dharma* (Law or Order) is lost there will be dominance of *Adharma* (Lawlessness) which will ultimately lead people to hell (V.iii.146.40).

Hence ancient sages established an order based on scriptures.[3] Mārkaṇḍeya gives a list of Law-givers (Smṛti-writers) such as Manu, Atri, Viṣṇu, Hārīta, Yājñavalkya, Uśanas and others.[4] Mārkaṇḍeya here hints at the theory of social contract. But more importantly, he gives the credit of "Setting in motion an organized state of Law" to the Creator (i.e. god Brahmā). The Mbh supports this theory and states that when people got tired of Lawlessness they approached the Creator (Brahmā) for a controller of affairs. God Brahmā then appointed Manu as their king. Manu in the *Manusmṛti* (VII.3-4) supports the Divine origin of Kingship. States Manu: "When anarchy prevailed and people fled out of

1. SkP I.ii.40.177-79; also *na vai rājyam ca rājāsīn na ca daṇḍo na dāṇḍikaḥ| dharmeṇa ca prajāḥ sarve rakṣanti ca parasparam||*
Mbh, *Śānti* 59.14

2. SkP V.iii.146.37ff.
3. SkP V.iii.146.41.
4. SkP I.ii.40.205-209; V.iii.171.2-3.
5. Mbh, *Śānti*, 67.18-21.

fear, the Lord created the King (Kingship) for the protection of all. The king was created out of the inherent particles (i.e. powers) of Indra, Vāyu, Yama, Sūrya, Agni, Varuṇa, Soma and Kubera." That is, the functions of the king are those of the *Dikpālas.* Elsewhere in the Mbh the name of the ruler appointed by the Creator is given as Virajas. This theory of the divine agency of the king is modified by *Baudhāyana Dharma Sūtra* which says that king was the servant of the subjects on the remuneration of one-sixth of the produce (of the land).[1]

The Mbh, *Śānti Parva* proposes the theory of social contract of kingship. It tells us that when Manu was hesitating to accept kingship, "The people themselves assured Manu that Law would be followed and the sin (of punishing) will go to law breakers and not to the king, their punisher. They further agreed to pay one-tenth of the grain produced as tax."[2]

It is worth noting that even though a divine agency is hinted, a Hindu king, either Vedic or Purāṇic, did not discharge the function of a priest as in ancient Egypt, Rome or Greece.

The social contract theory becomes more evident when we find that a plunderer-king like Purūravas or a tyrant like Vena was killed by the sages and their sons were installed as kings. In fact, Pṛthu took the royal oath that in thought, word and deed he would impartially administer justice and would never allow unlawful mixed marriage.[3]

If kingship was a social contract, was kingship elective or hereditary? The last line of people's assurance of obedience to Manu, viz. *pāhyasmān sarvato rājan devān iva śatakratuḥ*, raises the question whether the office of the king was elective or hereditary. We get such reference in the ṚV X.124.8 where people (*Viśas*) appear to elect a king. In the *Arthaśāstra* (II.4.2) hope is expressed that the king to be coronated be selected by the people (*tvām viśo vṛṇatām rājyāya*). But we find Vedic as well as Purāṇic kingship was hereditary and that too by

1. *ṣaḍbhāga-bhṛto rājā rakṣet prajām|*
Baudhāyana Dh. S. I.10.6.
2. Mbh, *Śānti* 67.23-28.
3. Pṛthu was called to take the oath before becoming a king.

primogeniture. As the Rāmāyaṇa put it, "Among the Ikṣvākus the eldest born becomes the king."[1]

KINGSHIP IN SkP

As far as our Purāṇa is concerned it states that god Brahmā appointed Ripuñjaya (alias Divodāsa) (and not Manu or Virajas) as the king (V.ii.74), thus endorsing the divine origin of kingship. But the author knew that kingship was a military need for protection and its pattern was patriarchal. For carrying out the onerous duties of kingship, the king must have the following twenty-six (which is a misprint for thirty-six) qualities and qualifications. This is, in fact, a quotation from Mbh, *Śānti*, Ch. 70.

I quote the Sanskrit Text of SkP VII.ii.17.84-94a:

षड्विंशगुणसंपन्नो राजा राज्यं करोति च ।
स राज्यफलमाप्नोति, श्रृणु तत्कथयाम्यहम् ॥ 84 ॥

चरेद् धर्मानकटुको, मुञ्चेत्स्नेहमनास्तिके ।
अनृशंसश्चरेदर्थं, चरेत् काममनुद्धत: ॥ 85 ॥

प्रियं ब्रूयाद्, अकृपण:, शूर: स्यादविकत्थन: ।
दाता चाऽऽयामवर्ज: स्यात् प्रगल्भ: स्यादनिष्ठुर: ॥ 86 ॥

संदधीत न चानार्यान्, विगृह्णीयान् न बन्धुभि: ।
नानाप्तैश्च चारयेच्चारान्, कुर्यात्कार्यमपीडयन् ॥ 87 ॥

अर्थान् ब्रूयान्न चापत्सु, गुणान् ब्रूयान्न चात्मन: ।
आदद्यान्न च साधुभ्यो, नासत्पुरुषमाश्रयेत् ॥ 88 ॥

नापरीक्ष्य नयेद्दण्डं न च मन्त्रं प्रकाशयेत् ।
विसृजेन्न च लुब्धेभ्यो, विश्वसेन्नापकारिषु ॥ 89 ॥

आप्तै: सुगुप्तदार: स्याद्रक्ष्यश्चान्यो घृणी नृप: ।
स्त्रियं सेवेत नात्यर्थं मृष्टं भुंजीत नाऽहितम् ॥ 90 ॥

---

1. *ikṣvākūṇām hi sarveṣām rājā bhavati pūrvajaḥ*|
VR. II.110.31

अस्तेय: [v. 1. अस्तव्य: in Mbh.]पूजयेन् मान्यान्
गुरुं सेवेदमायया।
अर्च्यो देवो न दम्भेन, श्रियमिच्छेदकुत्सिताम् ॥ 91 ॥

सेवेत प्रणयं कृत्वा [v. 1. हित्वा in Mbh.] दक्ष:
स्यादथ कालवित्।
सान्त्ववाक्यं सदा वाच्यमनुगृह्णन्न चाक्षिपेत् ॥ 92 ॥

प्रहरेन्न च विप्राय, हत्वा शत्रून्न शेषयेत्।
क्रोधं कुर्यान्न चाकस्मान्, मृदु: स्यान्नापकारिषु ॥ 93 ॥

एवं राज्ये चिरं स्थेयं यदि श्रेय इहेच्छसि ॥ 94a ॥

QUALITIES AND QUALIFICATIONS OF A KING

These *Guṇas* are enumerated by Nārada to Bali. A king has (i.e. should have) the following duties:

(1) Performance of duties without bitterness.
(2) Non-contact or no-friendship with an atheist.
(3) To acquire wealth without being harsh with the subjects.
(4) To enjoy pleasures without being arrogant or overindulgent.
(5) Gentleness or courtesy in speech.
(6) To be brave without boastfulness.
(7) Liberality with some restraint.
(8) To be valiant, bold without being ruthless.
(9) No association with the ignoble (*Anārya*).
(10) Not to get alienated from relatives.
(11) Not to employ spies of doubtful loyalty.
(12) To perform duties without causing trouble to anyone else.
(13) To be reserved about one's plans in emergency (i.e. time of distress).
(14) To praise another person's merits but not one's own.
(15) To collect wealth (taxes) but not from sages.
(16) Not to seek the support of the wicked.
(17) Never to inflict punishment without proper enquiry.

(18) To keep counsel confidential or secret.

(19) To donate but not to the greedy.

(20) Repose confidence except in those who have injured you.

(21) Proper protection of queens through faithful and trusted guards.

(22) To protect other good rulers (as allies).

(23) No over-indulgence in the company of women.

(24) To eat pure, wholesome food abstaining from harmful.

(25) To pay respects to the venerable.

(26) To worship gods sincerely without hypocrisy.

(27) To acquire wealth not polluted or earned by immoral or infamous means.

(28) To venerate Śrī (Royalty or State) with affection and attachment.

(29) To be alert and expert in performing one's duties at the proper time.

(30) To speak kind and conciliatory words.

(31) Not to insult anyone while doing favours.

(32) Not to punish a Brāhmaṇa.

(33) To destroy enemies completely.

[Mbh, *Śānti Parva* adds: (34) One should not attack an enemy without knowing his strength and position. A.B.L. Awasthi (*Studies in* SkP, p. 242) adds from the NKP Edition:]

(35) To show anger but not without cause.

(36) Not to be mild with the enemies.

A similar list of these *guṇas* is given in the Mbh, *Śānti*, ch. 70.

Only a person gifted with all these attributes should be appointed as the head of the state.

Kauṭilya and Kāmandaka classify these qualities or qualifications under the heads: *Adhigāmī Guṇas*, *Dhī-guṇas*, *Utsāha-guṇas* and *Ātmasaṁpad* i.e. personal *guṇas*.

FUNCTIONS OF A KING

As stated above, kingship is meant for the protection of the state and society (SkP III.ii.10.50). King is the leader of men and head of the State. The duties of a king may be briefly stated below:

(1) *Prajā-pālana* — Protection of subjects.

(2) *Prajā-rañjana* — Enhancement of public weal and pleasure.

(3) Observance of religious functions and practices.

(4) *Dharma-pālana* — Protection of Law.

(5) Protection of the prevailing social order (*Cāturvarṇya*).

(6) *Daṇḍa-dhara* or *Niyāmaka* — Dispensing justice and punishment.

(7) *Nṛpati-vṛtti* — King being the servant of his subjects, is to get one-sixth of the produce of the land, as his wages.

(8) *Paternal attitude* — Subjects are to be treated like one's children and looking after their welfare like a parent.

(9) *Divinity of King* — SkP believes in the divine origin of kingship and projects him as god Viṣṇu on the earth.

(10) *Safety of king* — Advises that a king should be protected carefully as the security and welfare of the state depends on him.

(11) *Yuvarāja* — A crown prince should have learning, humility, merits necessary for popular rulership, experience in statecraft.

(12) *Succession* — Kingship was hereditary by the law of primogeniture. In Cola land, kingship went to sister's son.

(13) *Sapta-ratna* (*Seven jewels*) — A *Samrāṭ* (emperor) is blessed with seven excellent 'jewels', viz. excellent elephant, horse, *kalpa-vṛkṣa* ('wish-yielding tree') etc.

(I.ii.9.19-21). But the list in MtP 142-63 includes: excellent discus, chariot, jewel (diamond), queen, treasure, a horse and an elephant.

(14) *Abhiṣeka* — Consecration ceremony marking the beginning of a king's rule. The public ministers, Brāhmaṇas and important citizens were consulted before the *Abhiṣeka* of a crown-prince.

A.B.L. Awasthi[1] gives the essentials distinctive of kingship:

1. *Chattra* — royal umbrella
2. *Camara* — chowries
3. *Koṣāgārāṇi* — treasury, storehouse
4. *Āyudhāgāra* — arsenal
5. *Mahiṣī* — queen
6. *Rājaputras* — princes
7. *Gajas* — elephants
8. *Aśvas* — cavalry, horses
9. *Vimānāni* — palatial buildings
10. *Vāhanāni* — vehicles
11. *Śibikā* — palanquin
12. *Ratha* — chariots

THE EVOLUTION OF THE CONCEPT OF MONARCHY IN EUROPE

It is interesting to compare the evolution of the concept of monarchy or kingship in the West.

According to Herodotus both monarchy and democracy are inherently defective as the monarch tends to be a tyrant and democracy degenerates into mob-rule. A government by the

1. *Studies in the Skanda Purāṇa*, Part I, p. 266.

best men is certainly preferable. Nothing can be better than the rule of one best man. Plato's idea of a philosopher-king is well-known. According to Aristotle the ends of the State are sovereignty of Law, freedom and equality of citizens, and perfecting of men in civilized life. For this monarchy is the best form of government, if a really wise and virtuous king can be found. It is thus an approximation to Plato's concept of philosopher-king.

The concept of divinity of king appears in the Hellenistic period. A true king is more than a military despot. He is divine because he brings harmony into his kingdom as God brings harmony into the world.

A king must be an *Animate Law*, that is a personalized form of the principles of Law and right that govern the whole universe. A king is thus distinctly different from the common man. King's authority has moral and religious sanction which his subjects recognize without a loss of their own moral freedom and dignity.

MONARCHY, HEREDITARY OR ELECTIVE?

Strangely enough, in mediaeval Europe, kings not only inherited and were elected but ruled "by the grace of God". Thus heredity, election and Divine grace combined in monarchy (Sabine 210). They believed "that secular rule was of divine origin, that the king was the vicar of God and that those who resisted him unlawfully were subjects of the Devil and the enemies of God"—that was the Christian duty of subjection to constituted authority. Even Thomas Hobbes in his political writings, sincerely believed that monarchy was the most stable and orderly form of government.

Later George Savile, First Marquis of Halifax, admits the advantage of absolute monarchy for unity and speed of execution but it destroys "the competent state of freedom" and hence recommends a "mixed monarchy"—a constitutional government divided between the monarch and the Parliament.

The philosophy of Hegel aimed at nothing less than a complete reconstruction of modern thought. In his *Philosophy of Right* he observes: Constitution is not manufactured. It is a work of centuries. The Monarch is a visible symbol of abstractions like national spirit, national Law and national state which is the real force in the background of Politics and History. To quote Hegel:

"In a well-organised monarchy, the objective aspect belongs to Law alone. The monarch's part is merely to set the law, the subjective 'I will'." (*Philosophy of Right*, Section 280)

As Purāṇic ideas belonged to circa 10th cent. A.D., we must confess that the Purāṇic concept of a monarch was not as advanced as that of Hegel and other modern European theorists.

Though ancient Indian thinkers have given such a great prominence to the king or the head of the state, he was regarded as a part of the state. They regarded body politic as consisting of seven limbs, viz. (1) the King, (2) Ministry, (3) Rāṣtra (Country), (4) *Durga* (Forts), (5) *Koṣa* (Treasury), (6) *Bala* (Army), (7) *Suhṛt* (Allies). AP[1] thinks that these seven *Aṅgas* are mutually helpful and they together constitute a *Rājya* (kingdom). The first *Aṅga* (kingship) is already discussed. The remaining *Aṅgas* are described briefly.

MINISTRY

Ancient Indian political thinkers regarded Ministry as the vital organ of the state. "Kingship is possible only with the help of ministers", states Kauṭilya.[2] As omniscience is impossible in a man and people are gifted with different aptitudes, the king should select them as ministers lest he should incur the destruction of the State—warns Śukra.[3] The SkP compares ministry-less state to a widow or a riverless (impure) country (SkP IV.ii.87.90-93).

1. *svāmyamātyaṁ ca rāṣṭraṁ ca durgaṁ koṣo balaṁ suhṛt |*
parasparopakāridaṁ saptāṅgaṁ rājyam ucyate || AP 239.1
The details of these are discussed in SkP VII.ii.17.162-63.

2. *sahāya-sādhyam rājatvam|*
Arthaśāstra, ch. 3.

3. *puruṣe puruṣe bhinnaṁ dṛśyate buddhi-vaibhavam|*
na hi tat sakalaṁ jñātum nareṇa kena śakyate|
ataḥ sahāyān vared rājā rājyābhivṛddhaye|
vinā prakṛtisammantrād rājya-nāśo bhaved dhruvam|
Śukranīti ch. II.

Designations:

The SkP uses three terms *Mantrī*, *Amātya* and *Saciva* to designate a minister and adjectives *mahā*, *mukhya*, *pradhāna* are added to them to express their dignified position. Out of these *Rājāmātya* and *Purohita* or *Purodhā* are regarded as the highest officers.[1] Between the two, the status of the royal priest was superior, practically equal to that of the king.[2]

Strength:

Though Manu advises seven or eight as the strength of the Ministry,[3] Kauṭilya quotes views recommending bigger ministries but Śukra (II.70) and *Nītivākyāmṛta* prefer smaller ministry. Our Purāṇa does not mention a fixed number though we have reference to the body of ministry (*Mantri-gaṇa*) in III.iii.13.13.

Caste-composition:

Though Smṛtis prefer Brahmins as ministers, Mbh, *Śānti* 87.5-8 recommends 4 Brāhmaṇas, 18 Kṣatriyas, 21 Vaiśyas and 3 Śūdras as members of the king's Privy Council. Majority of Vaiśyas and inclusion of Śūdras is surprising. But their qualifications are worth noting. Caste was no qualification for selection in the ministry. Śukra emphatically declares that only on occasion of dinner or marriage one should enquire about the caste and not when making appointment to ministry[4] (*Śukranīti* II.540). He further recommends that the military portfolio may be assigned to a Śūdra if he be capable or loyal.[5]

---

1. *rājopajīvināṁ śreṣṭhau rājāmātya-purohitau*|

SkP II.ii.8.48

2. *tayo rājasamaḥ pūjyaḥ purodhāḥ śāstra-sammataḥ*|

Ibid. II.ii.8.49

3. *sacivān sapta cāṣṭau vā kurvīta suparīkṣitān*|

Manu VII.54

4. *na jātyā na kulenaiva śreṣṭhatvaṁ pratipadyate*|
vivāhe bhojane nityam kula-jāti-vivecanam||

Sukra II.545

5. *svadharma-niratā nityaṁ svāmi-bhaktā ripu-dviṣaḥ*|
śūdrā vā kṣatriyā vaiśyā mlecchāḥ saṅkara-sambhavāḥ|
senādhipāḥ sainikāś ca kāryā rājñā jayārthinā|

Śukra II.139

SkP's glorification of Vāsudeva Kṛṣṇa as the ideal minister shows that the author entertained no caste bias for ministership except qualities and qualifications.

Qualities and Qualifications of Ministers:

The adjectives of ministers used in the above discussion show that knowledge of Vedas and *Śāstras*[1] and expertise in *Dharma Śāstra* were essential. Knowledge of *Mantra-śāstra* and *Mantra-rahasya* was an additional qualification. Experienced persons with welfare of the public at heart and loyalty were needed. Addicts to wine and women were unfit. Ministers must prove their worth by giving wise counsels to the king.[2]

Functions:

SkP refers to Council of Ministers. The king and ministers form one body, the king being the tree and ministers branches (VII.i.22.82). The deliberations in the Council of Ministers are to be kept secret (III.i.5.56; VI.100.2-10). They are to shoulder the responsibility of government in the absence of the king (VII.i.22.82). Vāsudeva Kṛṣṇa was held as the model of the best *Mantrī* (V.i.63.122).

KOṢA

Koṣa is essential for the maintenance of state civil and military services and for helping subjects during emergency. The rightfully acquired wealth (*Śuddhārtha*) in the Koṣa consists of tributes from conquered princes, taxes amounting to one-sixth of the produce of the land, fines etc. Stability of the state and happiness and prosperity of kings and subjects lie in sound financial position. Various kinds of wealth such as gold, jewels, coins and grains constitute the treasury. It should be stored in a number of rooms (V.iii.146.12-19). Due to weak financial

---

1. *amātyā veda-tattvajñāḥ sarvaśāstra-viśāradāḥ|*
SkP V.ii.80.37

2. *madirā-kāma-mattānāṁ mantritvaṁ vo na yujyate|*
hitam mantrayate rājñastena mantrī nigadyate||
SkP I.ii.32.4

position Puruyaśa, king of Pāñcālas, was ruined in a battle (II.vii.15.7-8). Śiva punished king Ajapāla for his attempt to defend his country by his spiritual power without collecting taxes (VI.95). Tax collection is a legitimate duty and power of the king but he should see that no harshness is used in tax collection. Kings used to tour their states to see that no coercion is resorted to by his officers (III.i.29.25 and II.vii.5.35-36).

FORTS (DURGA)

Forts were very important organ of the state as they afforded protection both to the king and the people. In the pre-gun-powder age a fort was compared to the strength of one thousand elephants and a hundred thousand excellent horses. Enemy cannot subdue a king well protected in a fort[1] (SkP IV.ii.76).

RĀṢṬAR

SkP like Kauṭilya gives the merits and demerits of a *deśa* or *rāṣṭra*. A good country should be free from enemies and protected by a powerful army (IV.i.24.3). A king should rule such a good country according to the precepts of *Rāja-dharma* (IV.i.24.19-22).

ARMY (BALA)

Army was the most important *Aṅga* of the state. It consisted of four limbs, viz. chariots, elephants, horses and infantry.[2] SkP mentions *bāhu-yuddha* (i.e. wrestling, boxing) in V.iii.48.58. It mentions military science (*Saṅgrāma Vidyā*), military experts (*Yuddha-viśārada*) and the science of archery. Navy formed an important constituent of the army. King Vasu led a naval expedition against Mlecchas of Kṣīradvīpa and defeated them

1. *durbalo' pi ākalayitum sahasā'rir na śakyate||*
kariṇām tu sahasreṇa, varāśvānāṁ na lakṣataḥ|
tat karma-siddhir nṛpater durgeṇaikena yad bhaved||
durgastho nābhibhūyeta vipakṣaḥ kenacit kvacit|
SkP IV. ii.76.20b-22a
2. There is a reference to six-limbed (*ṣaḍaṅga*) army in II.ii.12.16.

(V.iii.97.20-24). Camels also were probably used (III.iii.13.14). SkP describes an actual fight by a *caturaṅga dala* (VII.iv.36. 96-103). The chief of the army was called *Senāpati*. Kings used to participate in battles and were expected to be experts in *Śastra-vidyā* (II.i.16.22).

MITRA, SUHṚT (ALLIES)

There is no discussion of this topic in SkP, but Nārada explaining the beneficial effects of *Dāna* (religious gifts), remarks: "By Dāna even enemies turn into friends" (I.ii.2.83). Here *Dāna* is probably a euphemism for bribery.

UPĀYAS

Upāyas or political expendients, according to Bṛhaspati, are: (1) *Sāma* (2) *Dāma* or *Dāna*, (3) *Daṇḍa* and (4) *Bheda*. Their use brings stability to the state if the expediency of the time and place are taken into account.[1] The fundamental principles of foreign policy are: (1) *Sandhi*, (2) *Vigraha*, (3) *Yāma*, (4) *Āsana*, (5) *Saṁśraya* and (6) *Dvaidha*.[2] These are to be used for the destruction of enemy, for which employment of deceit, taking false oath etc. are recommended (VI.269.55-56). 'End justifies the means' seems to be the guiding principle (III.i.18.65). SkP encourages politicians to use *Mantra*, *Bala* and *Vīrya*, *Prajñā* and *Pauruṣa* (I.ii.21-258). *Sāhasa* is not enough. Kṛṣṇa was regarded as an expert in *Kūṭanīti* by Śukra (*Śukranīti* VI.1297).

RĀJYAŚRĪ

Sovereignty is the *sine qua non* of every state:

na rājyaṁ rājyamityāhū
rājya-śrī preyasī dhruvam/
saptāṅgam api tad rājyam
tayā hīnaṁ tṛṇāyate//

— SkP IV.i.34.98

---

1. *sāma dānaṁ ca bhedaśca caturthe daṇḍa eva ca/*
nītau kramāt prayojyāśca deśa-kāla-viśeṣataḥ//
SkP I.ii.16.39

2. SkP I.ii.16.40-41

No state is recognized as such without sovereignty. It is more desirable. Even if a state is endowed with seven constituents (*Saptāṅgam*), it is useless or insignificant like a blade of grass.

ADMINISTRATION

The king has theoretically absolute power over all executive, legislative and judiciary matters. But *Rājadharma* wielded control. The relation between Kṣatriya kings and Brāhmaṇas, the repositories of *Dharma*, was close like that of a tree and its roots (VII.i.22.80). Hence *Rājadharma* through Brāhmaṇas acted as a curb on kings. Kings were expected to take it as a sacred duty to treat subjects like their own children. Describing the rule of demon Jalandhara, SkP (II.iv.16.28) remarks: While he (Jalandhara) was ruling as per (*Rāja*)*dharma* nobody suffered from disease, sorrow or hunger.

A tyrant was done away with as in the case of Vena. SkP exhorts that such a king be thrown into a dark well (IV.i.8.81).

ADMINISTRATIVE DIVISIONS

The kingdom was divided into the following administrative divisions: *Maṇḍala, Deśa, Viṣaya*, towns and villages (*grāmas*). *Maṇḍalas* were big units under semi-independent rulers like *Māṇḍalikas* or *Sāmantas* or Princes (i.e. sons of the kings). Bharata appointed his sons as governors of the nine provinces of Bhāratavarṣa (VII.i.172.6).

TOWN ADMINISTRATION

The head of Town Administration was called *Purapāla*. He was assisted by eight officers.[1] They were masters of the *Smṛti* law. The *Purapālas* were noted for their integrity and stood as the bulwark of the kingdom (VII.i.24.89-82).

1. *aṣṭau pramāṇa-puruṣāḥ paurāṇām kārya-darśinaḥ*||80||
vyavahārān avekṣadhvaṁ smṛtyācāraviśāradāḥ|
vyavasthāṁ matkṛtām etām bhavanto' tra dvijottamāḥ ||81||
dhārayantu mahātmāno diggajā iva medinīm ||82||
SkP VII.1.24.80-82

VILLAGE ADMINISTRATION

SkP notes one king, Kīrtimān of Kāśī, making the following arrangements for village administration:

He posted a Brāhmaṇa well-versed in *Smṛti* Law for a group of five villages. To help them administer justice they were given ten horsemen[1] (II.vii.11.56-57). For the trial of Śāradā, a pregnant Brahmin widow, the *grāma-sabhā* was composed of elderly villagers, Pandits and *Kulavṛddhas*, some well-versed in *Lokavidyā* (SkP III.iii.19.46ff).

Dharma being the dominant force in ancient India, kings, ministers and administrators generally carried out their duties carefully. There were not many political upheavals up to A.D. 1000, i.e. the end of the Purāṇic period, though there had been some temporary and local disturbances due to some foreign invasions which were few and far between. The society was in a way well-established, call it static if you please. *Dharma* and not language or region was the main consideration. Hence we find Kashmiri Pandits at home in the South and South Indian Pandits settling in the North.

GEOGRAPHICAL INFORMATION IN SKANDA PURĀṆA

SkP is a library of *Tīrtha Māhātmyas*. These *Tīrtha Māhātmyas*, as noted by Jan Gonda, give us very valuable information about the topography, legendary history etc. of their particular region. These *Sthala Purāṇas* cover the Himalayan region (as in *Kedāra Khaṇḍa* and *Badarikāśrama Māhātmya*), Uttara Pradesh (in *Kāśī Khaṇḍa* and *Ayodhyā Māhātmya*), Orissa (in *Puruṣottama Kṣetra Māhātmya*), Malwa,

---

1. *vīpraṁ ca dharma-vaktāram grāme grāme nyaveśayat|*
pañcānām api grāmāṇām akarod adhikāriṇaḥ||
daṇḍārthaṁ tyakta-dharmāṇāṁ daśa-vājiniṣevitam|
evam pravṛttaṁ sarvatra sārvabhaumasya śāsanam||
SkP II.vii.11.56-57

Rajasthan and Gujarat (in *Āvantya Khaṇḍa*), the Narmadā Valley (in *Revā Khaṇḍa*), Western India along with Gujarat (in *Nāgara* and *Prabhāsa Khaṇḍas*), South India (in *Veṅkaṭācala Māhātmya* and *Setu Māhātmya*). SkP has thus practically covered the major part of India from the Setu to the Himalayas. Like other Purāṇas it does share the traditional Vedic ideas of cosmology, the philosophical theory of cosmogony hinted in ṚV X.129.1-4 and the creation of a cosmic nucleus, Prajāpati (as in ṚV X.121.7) etc. It shares most of the information about *Bhuvana Kośa* as found in different Purāṇas like VāP (45.109-137), KP (I.47), MtP (chs. 114, 121, 122, 123). It accepts the Sāṅkhya concept of the creation of the universe, the Purāṇic division of *Brahmāṇḍa* into three regions: the heaven, the earth and the nether region (I.ii.37.7-15). The earth consisting of seven *dvīpas* is just in the middle. Above it are seven heavens, viz. *Bhūr, Bhuvaḥ, Svaḥ, Janaḥ, Tapaḥ, Mahaḥ* and *Satyam* (I.ii.38.39-46). There are seven nether worlds or *Pātālas*, viz. *Atala, Vitala, Nitala, Rasātala, Talātala, Sutala* and *Pātāla* (I.ii.39.1-2).

We are interested here in our mother Earth. The Purāṇa knows that the Earth is spherical and moves round the Sun like a potter's wheel (I.ii.38.11-58 and I.i.31-71). Originally the Earth was regarded as consisting of four continents (*catur-dvīpī*) with Mt. Meru as the centre and four *dvīpas, Uttara Kuru Bhārata, Bhadrāśva* and *Ketumāla* to its north, south, east and west respectively—poetically described as a lotus with four petals (VII.i.11.11-12). Later it came to be regarded as consisting of seven continents, viz. *Jambū, Śāka, Puṣkara, Kuśa, Krauñca, Śālmali* and *Gomeda* (I.ii.37.16-22). These *Dvīpas* were believed to be circular, concentric, and each surrounded by an ocean with a different content, such as water, milk, sugarcane juice etc. Like us, ancient Greeks, Chinese and Arabs believed in seven divisions of the world based on climate, habitat etc. Each of our Purāṇic continents has a special representative tree indicating its climatic condition.

The above continents are differently identified by different scholars like N.L. De, V.V. Iyer, D.C. Sircar and S.M. Ali. For example:

Name of the Dvīpa	*Its Location*	*By (Scholar's name)*
1. Jaṁbū	Bhārata	V.V. Iyer A.B.L. Awasthi
2. Śāka	Scythia	V.V. Iyer
	The Oxus and Jaxartes Valley	A.B.L. Awasthi
3. Puṣkara	Turkistan	V.V. Iyer
	Central Asia, North of the Oxus	A.B.L. Awasthi
4. Kuśa	Iran, Arabia	V.V Iyer
	North-Eastern Africa	A.B.L Awasthi
5. Krauñca	Asia Minor	V.V. Iyer
	Region beyond Kuśa	A.B.L. Awasthi
6. Śālmali	Sermatic (?)	V.V. Iyer
	Beyond Kuśa region	A.B.L. Awasthi
7. Gomeda	Tartary	V.V. Iyer
	Unidentified	A.B.L. Awasthi

After all these are mere speculations of the scholars.

Each *Dvīpa* has nine sub-divisions (*Varṣas*). We need not go into the sub-divisions of other *Dvīpas* as we are interested in *Jaṁbū-Dvīpa* ruled by Agnīdhra. Agnīdhra had nine sons among whom he distributed the nine *Varṣas* of Jaṁbūdvīpa. The *Varṣas* are said to have been named after their rulers. They are situated within the boundaries mentioned below (I.iii.37.49-55):

1. Ilāvarta	: Situated between Mt. Gandhamādana and Mt. Mālyavān
2. Bhadrāśva	: Between Mt. Mālyvān and the sea
3. Ketumāla	: Between Mt. Śṛṅgavān and the sea
4. Kurukhaṇḍa (Uttara Kuru)	: Between Śṛṅgavān and the sea
5. Hiraṇmaya	: Between Mt. Śṛṅgavān and Mt. Śveta
6. Ramyaka Khaṇḍa	: Between Mt. Sunīla and Śveta mountain

7.	Harikhaṇḍa	: Between Mt. Niṣadha and Mt. Hemakūṭa
8.	Kiṁpuruṣa	: Between Mt. Himavat and Mt. Hemakūṭa
9.	Nābhikhaṇḍa alias Bhāratavarṣa	: Situated between Hemādri and the sea

Nābhikhaṇḍa became famous as Bhārata after the name of its ruler Bharata, the son of Ṛṣabha (I.ii.37.57). Ṛṣabha as a Jaina Tīrthaṅkara is not mentioned here.

Bharata had eight sons and one daughter. He divided his kingdom into nine divisions, viz. Indradvīpa, Kaseru, Tāmravarṇa, Gabhastimān, Nāgadvīpa, Saumya, Gāndharva, Varuṇa and Kumārī the ninth. The eight islands teeming with towns and villages were 'swamped' (*plāvita*) by the sea. The remaining ninth, Kumārīdvīpa, extending over one thousand *Yojanas*, is situated between the ocean in the south and Bindusaras (a Himalayan lake) in the north (VII.i.172.7-10). This Kumārikākhaṇḍa is the best land, Bhārata Kṣetra (VII.i.11.8-9). The remaining eight Dvīpas were not "lost" in the sea but were separated from each other by the sea and were situated round about India in the sea in south and south-east Asia. But their identification is anybody's guess. For example, Indradvīpa is identified with Madhya Deśa (Alberuni), region between Laṅkā and Mahendra Hills (Abul Fazl in Ain-e-Akbari), Burma (Majmudar), Andamans (V.S. Agrawal), Trans-Brahmaputra region (M. Ali). These are mere speculations of scholars and we need not pursue them.

BHĀRATAVARṢA—LOCATION, SHAPE ETC.

There is a consensus among Purāṇas about the south and north boundary of Bhārata (SkP VII.i.11.8-9; AP. 118.1; VP II.iii.1-2), but there is no consensus about its extent, though SkP states it to be nine thousand *Yojanas* north-south, and eighty thousand *Yojanas* east-west, when actually the distance between east-west is about 1360 miles. SkP poetically yet rightly states that Himālaya in the north has spread like the string of a bow.[1]

1. *himavān uttareṇāsya kārmukasya yathā guṇaḥ|* SkP VII.i.11.13

The configuration of Bhārata conforms to the shape of a tortoise lying outspread facing eastward with its division into nine regions.[1] SkP has obviously borrowed the idea of *Kūrma Saṁsthāna* and distribution of various *Nakṣatras* over it in VII.i.11, from Varāhamihira's *Bṛhatsaṁhitā*, ch. 14 called *Kūrma Vibhāga*.

THE GREATNESS OF BHĀRATA

Like other Purāṇas, SkP glorifies Bhārata as *Karmabhūmi* which enables men to attain all the four objects of human life, viz. *Dharma*, *Artha*, *Kāma* and *Mokṣa* and where people attain the fruits of their acts[2] and which is covetable even to Devas (I.ii.37.57-58).

LIST OF PRADEŚAS IN KUMĀRIKĀ KHAṆḌA*

SkP (I.ii.39.110-125) tells that king Śataśṛṅga divided Bhārata among his nine children including eight sons and one daughter and retired for penance into forest. The eight sons begot nine sons each. The seventy-two princes approached their aunt Kumārī to divide the eight *Khaṇḍas*. Kumārī added her own *Khaṇḍa* and the nine *Khaṇḍas* were sub-divided into 72 *Pradeśas*.

The list of the *Pradeśas* throws light on the political conditions of India in the 7th century as Hiuen Tsang mentions the existence of 70 kingdoms in India. Though SkP states that Bhārata was sub-divided into 72 *Pradeśas*, VP edition gives 75 *Pradeśas* as against the declared 72 *Pradeśas*. The number of villages situated in each *Pradeśa* is a guess of the Purāṇa writer. We give here a list of 75 *Pradeśas*. Some of the names are probably Sanskritization or Sanskrit translation of the place-names in the local dialect:

1. *bhārato yo mahādevi kūrma-rupeṇa saṁsthitaḥ|*
prāṅmukho bhagavān devo kūrmarūpī vyavasthitaḥ||
SkP VII.1.11.18-19

2. *atra dharmārtha-kāmānām mokṣasya ca upārjanam|*
anyatra bhoga-bhūmiś ca|
SkP I.ii.37.58

*Reference to translation of verses and the notes to these verses from 125 onwards is requested for detailed clarification.

LIST OF PRADEŚAS

(1) Nivṛta Maṇḍala
(2) Bālāka
(3) Purasāhanaka
(4) Andhala
(5) Nepāla
(6) Kānyakubja
(7) Gājanaka
(8) Gauḍadeśa
(9) Kāmarūpa
(10) Ḍāhala (Vedasaṁjña)
(11) Kāntīpura
(12) Mācīpura
(13) Oḍḍiyāṇadeśa
(14) Jālandharadeśa
(15) Lohapura
(16) Pāṁbīpura
(17) Raṭa Rājya
(18) Hariāla
(19) Draḍa Viṣaya
(20) Vambhaṇavāhaka
(21) Nīlapūraka
(22) Amala Viṣaya
(23) Narendudeśa
(24) Atilāṅgala
(25) Mālava
(26) Sayaṁbhara
(27) Mevāḍa
(28) Vāguri
(29) Gurjarātra
(30) Pāṇḍu Viṣaya
(31) Jahāhuti
(32) Kāśmīra Maṇḍala
(33) Kauṅkaṇa
(34) Laghu Kauṅkaṇa
(35) Sindhu
(36) Kaccha Maṇḍala
(37) Saurāṣṭra
(38) Lāḍa
(39) Atisindhu
(40) Aśvamukha
(41) Ekapāda
(42) Sūryamukha
(43) Ekabāhudeśa
(44) Sañjāyu Deśa
(45) Śiva Deśa
(46) Kālahayañjaya
(47) Liṅgodbhava
(48) Bhadra
(49) Devabhadra
(50) Ciṭa
(51) Virāṭa
(52) Yamakoṭi
(53) Ramaka
(54) Tomara
(55) Karṇāta
(56) Puṅgala
(57) Strī Rājya
(58) Pulastya Viṣaya
(59) Kāṁboja
(60) Kośala
(61) Bālhīka
(62) Laṅkā Deśa
(63) Kuru Deśa
(64) Kirāta
(65) Vidarbha
(66) Vardhamāna
(67) Siṁhala Dvīpa
(68) Pāṇḍu Deśa
(69) Bhayāṇaka
(70) Magadha Deśa
(71) Paṅgu Deśa
(72) Varendu
(73) Mūlasthāna
(74) Yavana
(75) Pakṣabāhu

In *Aruṇācala Māhātmya*, we get a list of 61 *Śiva Pīṭhas* or *Kṣetras* spread all over India (*Aruṇācala Māhātmya*: *Uttarārdha* ch. 2). There is a list of *Janapadas* on the rivers, i.e. situated in river valleys, in rivers like Gaṅgā, Sarasvatī, Yamunā, Śoṇa, Narmadā, Godāvarī, Gomatī, Haimavatī and Kāverī. The author of that *Māhātmya* seems unacquainted with *Janapadas* in the river valleys of Kṛṣṇā-Veṇī and the Tuṅgabhadrā.

MOUNTAIN SYSTEMS

SkP like other Purāṇas mentions its chief mountain ranges or *Kulaparvatas*. It names Mahendra, Malaya, Sahya, Śuktimān, Ṛkṣa, Vindhya and the Pāriyātra as the *Kulaparvatas* of Bhārata (I.ii.39.112). Mahendra is the chief mountain in Kaliṅga (Orissa); Malaya in Pāṇḍya country; Sahyādri in Aparānta; Śuktimān in Bhallāṭa; Ṛkṣa in the region around Māhiṣmatī; Vindhya in the region of tribals in Madhya Pradesh; and Pāriyātra or Pāripātra in the region of Niṣādas. As different authors probably wrote different books of SkP, we find that SkP gives another list of *Kulaparvatas* where Hemakūṭa and Mālyavān are substituted for Śuktimān and Ṛkṣa (V.iii.17.33). And in another list, Himavān, Gandhamādana and Śṛṅgī (Śṛṅgavān) are substituted for Śuktimān, Ṛkṣa and Pāriyātra (VI.268.11).

RIVER SYSTEMS IN SkP

Since the days of the Ṛgveda (e.g. the *Nadī Sūkta*) all rivers have been regarded as destroyers of sins and conferring blessings (IV.ii.92.3). A region without a river is not worth residing (II.i.32.20). Although hundreds of rivers are mentioned in SkP, the following rivers issuing from the *Kulaparvatas* are mentioned as representative, though many more rivers have risen from these mountains:

Names of mountains	*Rivers rising in these mountains*
Mahendra	— Ṛṣikulyā, Trisamā, Tridivā
Malaya	— Kṛtamālā, Tāmravarṇā, Utpalāvatī
Sahya	— Godāvarī, Kṛṣṇā, Tuṅgabhadrā, Kāverī
Śuktimān	— Ṛṣikā, Palāśinī

Ṛkṣa — Narmadā, Tamasā, Karatoyā
Vindhya — Payoṣṇī, Nirvindhyā, Bhadrā
Pāriyātra — Vedasmṛti, Carmaṇvatī, Śiprā
Himālaya — Gaṅgā, Sindhu, Sarasvatī, Yamunā

These river systems are found in other Purāṇas also like *Brahmāṇḍa*, *Vāyu* etc.

LAKES IN SkP

SkP refers to the following lakes: Acchoda in Kāśmīra (I. iii, Uttarārdha 2.16); Bindusara near Gaṅgotrī (Ibid, 2.15); Indradyumna and Puruṣottama lakes in Orissa (Ibid, 2.17); Puṣkara near Ajmer (Ibid, 2.27); Mānasa in the Himalayas (Ibid, 2.16).

SkP gives the most comprehensive treatment to geographical information. It is of very great importance to researchers in History, Archaeology, Sociology and other disciplines.

THE DATE OF SKANDA PURĀṆA

Though the different *Khaṇḍas* of SkP have been written by different authors at different periods, this is an attempt to determine the date of the last redaction of SkP. We must concede that in such a huge work of more than 90,000 verses interpolations are expected and as such it is difficult to assign a definite date to the text.

Many scholars are tempted to assign to it a date after A.D. 1000, as they believe that the invasion of Asuras and the atrocities depicted to have been committed by them, refer to Muslim invasions and their vandalism. But Muslims were not the first invaders of India. Greeks, Hūṇas, Scythians, Turuṣkas invaded India, and ruled over some parts of it for some centuries before Muslim invaders. And it is against human nature to believe that the pre-Muslim invaders and their occupation armies were too soft and religious-minded to commit the atrocities described as committed by Asuras in SkP.

Secondly our early works on *Dharmaśāstra* quote SkP as an authority like *Smṛtis*. Thus SkP must be in existence for at least a century or two before its attaining the authoritative position of a *Smṛti*.

The following Dharmaśāstra writers quote SkP as authority:

(1) Lakṣmīdhara (A.D. 1100-1180), author of *Kalpataru*, quotes 15 verses on *Vrata*, 92 verses on *Tīrtha* (pp. 36-39, 130-35), 44 on *Dāna*, to mention a few topics.

(2) Aparārka (A.D. 1100-1130) in his commentary on *Yājñavalkya Smṛti* (I.204) quotes 19 verses of *Skanda* on the gift of a cow.

(3) Vijñāneśvara (A.D. 1080-1100) in his commentary *Mitākṣarā* on *Yājñavalkya Smṛti* II.290 mentions it in connection with the status of *Veśyās*.

SkP is still earlier. A Manuscript of SkP written in the 7th cent. A.D. characters is in the Nepal Durbar Library (*Haraprasada Shastri Catalogue of Nepal Palm Leaf MSS*, p. LII). But we are not in a position to trace it earlier. Maybe an interpolation, but we find SkP quoting Bhāravi's *Kirātārjunīya* II.30, *sahasā vidadhīta na kriyām* in I.ii.6.79. *Kāśīkhaṇḍa* (i.7.4-5) mentions *Nāṭya Veda* and *Arthaśāstra*. Dhanvantari and Caraka (ancient authorities on medicine) are mentioned in *Kāśīkhaṇḍa* i.71. Mention of Jhoṭiṅga (a demon) and Barkarikā—though loan words through commercial contacts with the Middle East—show that we cannot locate the present text of SkP earlier than 7th cent. A.D. and not later than 9th cent. A.D.

But the problem becomes somewhat like a riddle when we meet Āma (Nāgabhaṭa II, death A.D. 833) and his son-in-law Kumārapāla (A.D. 1143-1171), Bhoja (A.D. 836-882) in SkP III.ii.36; VII.ii.6.141 and the palm leaf MS of SkP of the 7th cent. A.D. in Nepal Durbar Library. The only way out of this riddle is to regard the accounts of Āma, Kumārapāla and Bhoja as interpolations. We need not consider seriously the palpably unreliable dates in SkP I.ii.40 of the Nanda dynasty (*Kali* 3310), Vikramāditya (*Kali* 3020), Śaka era (*Kali* 3100), and king Pramati (*Kali* 4400).

A critical edition of SkP will help to solve this riddle.

SKANDA PURĀṆA

Book I: MĀHEŚVARAKHAṆḌA

Section I: KEDĀRAKHAṆḌA

CHAPTER ONE

Dakṣa's Insolence

Obeisance to Śrī Gaṇeśa. Om, obeisance to Lord Vāsudeva. Om. After bowing down to Nārāyaṇa[1] as well as to (Sage) Nara,[2] the most excellent one among men, and to goddess Sarasvatī (the goddess of learning), one should narrate the *Jaya.*[3]

---

1. *Nārāyaṇa*—It is significant that a Purāṇa specifically compiled for the glorification of Śiva begins with an obeisance to Nārāyaṇa.

Etymologically 'Nārāyaṇa' means 'one whose abode is waters' (Manu 1.10, Mbh, *Śānti* 328, 25). But Purāṇa-writers ascribed a number of meanings to *Nāra*, e.g. in the *Brahma-Vaivarta Purāṇa* it means 'a form of liberation called *Sārūpya*', 'final beatitude' (*Mokṣa*), 'sins committed'. Thus Nārāyaṇa = Destroyer of sins.

In early Viṣṇuism, Viṣṇu and Nārāyaṇa are not identical. The Vedic god Viṣṇu was later amalgamated with Nārāyaṇa of the *Pañcarātra* system. See J. Gonda, *Aspects of Early Viṣnuism*; G.V. Tagare, Intro. to BhP, pp. XIII-XIV).

2. *Nara* = An incarnation of Viṣṇu, the son of Dharma and Mūrti, a daughter of Dakṣa; a permanent companion of Nārāyaṇa while performing penance at Badarikāśrama. They are supposed to have incarnated as Kṛṣṇa and Arjuna in Dvāpara Age.

3. *Jaya*—Originally this epithet was restricted to the *Itihāsa* called Mahābhārata (Mbh, *Udyoga* 136.18; *Svarrgārohaṇika* 5.51). Later some Purāṇas like BdP (III. iv. 4.47-54), VāP (II.41.48-51) claimed the epithet '*Itihāsa*' to themselves. Some Purāṇas like BhP I.2.4, VāP I.1.1 adopted the verse *Nārāyaṇaṁ namaskṛtya* etc. along with the epithet *Jaya. Kalpataru* (*Brahmacāri-Khaṇḍa,* p. 25) on the strength of *Bhaviṣya Purāṇa* states that the appellation *Jaya* is applied to 18 Purāṇas, *Rāmāyaṇa*, *Mahābhārata* and *Manusmṛti*. Hence our Purāṇa is justified in adopting the epithet *Jaya*.

Vyāsa[1] *said*:

1. Obeisance to that Lord, the wielder of Pināka bow, at whose bidding Viriñci (Brahmā) creates the universe, Hari (Viṣṇu) protects it and the god named Kālarudra annihilates it.

2. There, in the Naimiṣa[2] forest which is the holiest among all holy places and sacred-most among all the sacred spots (in the world), ascetics with Śaunaka[3] as their leader—ascetics who were (usual) performers of sacrifices and whose minds were (always) inclined towards holy rites, started a sacrifice of a long duration.

3. The excessively (highly) intelligent disciple of Vyāsa, an ascetic of great austerities, named Lomaśa[4], came there with an ardent desire to see them.

4. As soon as they saw him coming, all the sages engaged in that sacrifice of long duration, stood up simultaneously with great eagerness to receive him, with materials of worship in their hands.

5. After offering him water for washing his feet and presenting him respectfully materials of worship the sinless sages receiv-

---

1. *Vyāsa*—Kṛṣṇa Dvaipāyana, the son of Satyavatī and Parāśara, out of wedlock. He was dark in complexion and was brought up in an islet in the river Yamunā by Satyavatī (Mbh, *Ādi* 63.86). His great achievement was the arrangement of the floating Vedic *Mantras* into *Saṁhitās*. Hence he came to be known as *Vyāsa* ('The Arranger'). Purāṇas use *Vyāsa* as a title and state that in every Dvāpara Yuga, there is born a *Vyāsa* whose job is to arrange the Vedic *Mantras* and there have been 28 Vyāsas (VP III.3; KP I.52.1-11; VāP II.23.107-213; BdP I.ii. 35.116-126). Some Purāṇas, however, give less than 28 Vyāsas (e.g. KP) while some give more than 28 (e.g. BdP).

2. *Naimiṣa forest*—The ancient site at modern Nimsar at a distance of 20 miles from Sitapur and 45 miles northwest of Lucknow.

3. *Śaunaka*—Name of various authors of important works like *Ṛgveda-prātiśākhya*, *Bṛhad-devatā*. One is identified with the Vedic Seer Gṛtsamada. Mbh states that the Śaunaka at whose sacrificial session Mbh was recited by the Sūta Ugraśravas belonged to the Bhṛgu clan (*Ādi* 1.19) and was the son of Śunaka (*Anuśāsana* 30.65).

Purāṇa-writers have adopted him as the listener of their Purāṇas.

4. *Lomaśa*—A sage from the North who associated closely with Pāṇḍavas during their long stay in forest and narrated ancient legends and importance of sacred places etc. to them (Mbh, *Vana, Anuśāsana*). But Mbh does not regard him as the disciple of Vyāsa as claimed by the SkP here. Our Purāṇa-writer substituted him for the usual Sūta due to Lomaśa's story telling throughout Mbh, *Vana* and automatically Sūta's discipleship of Vyāsa was attributed to him.

ed him with due hospitality. The sages of exalted nobility then asked him to explain in detail *Śivadharma* (pious activities pertaining to Śiva).

The sages said:

6. Recount, O sage of extraordinary intellect, the greatness of the Trident-bearing Lord of Devas. O exalted one, describe everything along with the modes of meditation and worship.

7-11. What is the benefit in sweeping (the temple premises)? What is the benefit in making (mystic diagrams) of various colours, in making gifts of mirror, chowries etc. (or in offering these to Śiva), in constructing canopies as well as fountains? What will be the benefit in offering lamps? What will be the fruit of the worship? What are the meritorious results in worshipping Śiva? Men read and recite the Itihāsas and Purāṇas in front of the idol of Śiva. They study (recite) the Vedas in front of him, and make others do the same. What benefit do those men derive? Let it be mentioned in detail. There is no one else in the world, O sage, more devoted to the narratives about Śiva.

12. On hearing these words of those sages of sanctified souls, the disciple of Vyāsa recounted (to them) the excellent greatness of Śiva.

Lomaśa said:

13. In all the eighteen Purāṇas, Śiva is sung about as the greatest (lord). Hence no one is competent to recount the greatness of Śiva (adequately).

14. Heaven and liberation (from *Saṁsāra*) will be attained by those people who repeatedly utter the two-syllabled name *Śi-va.*[1] Not otherwise.

15. Munificent indeed is Mahādeva (the great god), the lord of Devas, the Supreme Ruler. Since everything has been given by him, he is named *Sarva.*

16-18. Blessed are they, noble-souled are they, who always worship Śiva (or the ever-auspicious god). A person who wishes

1. God's name is regarded as highly efficacious in the *Bhakti*-cult, the roots of which go back to the *Ṛgveda* (See H.D. Velankara, *Bhakti in the Vedas*, pub. in Kauśika Lectures Series in Marathi).

to cross (the ocean) of worldly existence without Sadāśiva, is indeed foolish and confounded. There is no doubt that he, the hater of Śiva, is a great sinner. It was by him that (*Halāhala*) poison was swallowed, Dakṣa's sacrifice was destroyed, Kāla (god of Death) was burnt down and the king was released.

The sages requested:

19. We are very eager. Recount unto us how the poison was swallowed and how Dakṣa's *Yajña* (sacrifice) was destroyed.

Sūta narrated:

20. Formerly at the instance of Brahmā Parmeṣṭhin, Dākṣāyaṇī (Dakṣa's daughter) was given (in marriage) to noble-souled Śaṅkara by Dakṣa, O brāhmaṇas.

21-22. Once, by chance, Dakṣa came to the Naimiṣa forest. On arrival, he was duly honoured by the sages as well as by all Suras and Asuras by means of eulogies and obeisances. Mahādeva who was present there, did not stand up nor did he offer any reverential salutation to him. Therefore, Dakṣa became furious and he spoke these words:

23. "Everywhere all the Suras and Asuras as well as excellent brāhmaṇas repeatedly bow down to me with great eagerness. How is it, then, that, like a vicious fellow, this noble-souled one does not pay obeisance to me now. Accompanied by vampires, goblins and others, he is a shameless permanent resident of the cremation ground.

24. Heretics, wicked people and habitual sinners become haughty and arrogant on seeing a brāhmaṇa. Indeed, people like these deserve killing or excommunication by good people. Hence I am intent on cursing him."

25-27. After saying thus that (Dakṣa) of great austerities, became angry and spoke to Rudra these words:

"May these excellent brāhmaṇas listen to these words of mine. It behoves you all to carry out my words. This Rudra is considered by me as banned out of all *Yajñas* because he has gone beyond the *Varṇas* (castes) and has transgressed the discipline of the *Varṇas*."

Nandin, son of Śilāda, became furious on hearing those

words. He promptly said to Dakṣa who had great refulgence but who uttered that curse:

Nandin said:

28-30. Why is my lord Maheśa excluded from *Yajñas*? Merely by remembering him all these *Yajñas* become fruitful. Sacrifice, charitable gift, penance, different kinds of holy spots of pilgrimage—all these became sanctified by his name. Why has he been cursed now? He has been cursed by you foolishly and improperly due to your brāhmaṇical rashness, O evil-minded Dakṣa. It is by the noble-souled Śarva that this universe is protected. How is it that Rudra has been cursed, O sinful base brāhmaṇa?

31. On being rebuked thus by Nandin, Dakṣa, the Prajāpati, became furious and he cursed Nandin:

32-33. "All of you devoted to Rudra have been completely excluded from the Vedas. You are indeed cursed by the followers of the Vedic path and excommunicated by the great sages. You all cling to heretical doctrines. You are out of the pale of refined breeding and good conduct. All these Kapālins (followers of the skull-cult) are black-faced and addicted to drinking liquor."[1]

34. Thus the servants of Śiva were then cursed by Dakṣa. Then the infuriated Nandin began to imprecate Dakṣa:

35. "O brāhmaṇa, although we, the servants of Śiva, are good and pious, we have been cursed by you improperly (and unnecessarily) out of your brāhmaṇical rashness. Now I shall curse you.

36-39. Arguing that there is nothing else you all adhere to Vedic doctrines. (But) you are lustful, desirous of heaven, greedy

1. Kāpālikas were then beyond the pale of Vedism (like Jainas and Buddhists). This episode reflects the conflict between orthodox Vedism and heterodox followers of Śiva. The obnoxious practices of Kāpālikas offended orthodox Brahmanism so much so that they were not allowed even to have a look at *Śrāddha* food lest it should get polluted. (Vide Gautama DhS 15.25-28, Manu III.239-42, KP II.22.34-35; also G.V. Tagare's Introductions to BdP and VāP.)

The prejudice against Kāpālikas is found even in classical Sanskrit literature.

and deluded. Keeping a follower of the Vedas in front, brāhmaṇas will perform sacrifices on behalf of Śūdras. They will always be impoverished and greedy of monetary gifts. O Dakṣa, some brāhmaṇas will become *brahmarākṣasas* (brahminical demons)."

Lomaśa said:

Those brāhmaṇas were (thus) cursed by Nandin who had become excessively angry.

On hearing the words of Nandin, Sadāśiva smilingly spoke these sweet enlightening words:

Mahādeva said:

40. It does not behove you to be angry always towards brāhmaṇas. These brāhmaṇas, devoted to Vedic doctrines, are always our elders and preceptors.

41. The Vedas are full of *mantras* and of *sūktas* (hymns). The *ātman* of every embodied being is established in the hymn.

42-43. Hence those who have realized the *ātman* should not be censured. I am the *ātman* myself, no one else. Who is this? Who are you? Where am I? Why are the brāhmaṇas cursed? Avoid the concept of diversity, O highly intelligent one, and become enlightened. Manage (everything) through the knowledge of reality. Be established in your own self and avoid anger etc.

44. On being advised and instructed thus by Śambhu, the Supreme Being, Nandin (Śilāda's son) of great austerities, became aware of true knowledge and discernment. Closely associating himself with Śiva, he became immersed in (the ocean of) great bliss.

45. Overwhelmed by anger, Dakṣa went to his abode accompanied by the sages. He entered his abode still indignant.

46. Abandoning his great faith in those who worship Śiva and engaged in censuring them, he bacame the basest of men. Reaching that place along with all the great sages, he continued to censure lord Śiva. He never became calm.

CHAPTER TWO

Satī's Arrival at Dakṣa's Sacrifice[1]

Lomaśa said:

1. Once, a great sacrifice was commenced by him (Dakṣa). All were invited to be present there by the ascetic (Dakṣa) (who was) initiated for the sacrifice.

2-3. A number of sages including Vasiṣṭha and others came there. Agastya, Kaśyapa, Atri, Vāmadeva, Bhṛgu, Dadhīca, holy lord Vyāsa, Bharadvāja and Gautama, these and many other great sages assembled there.

4. Similarly all the groups of Suras (gods), the Guardians of the Quarters and others, Vidyādharas, Gandharvas, Kinnaras and groups of celestial damsels (came there).

5. Brahmā, the grandfather of worlds, was invited from Satyaloka. Similarly Viṣṇu was invited from Vaikuṇṭha to the place of sacrifice.

6. Devendra of great lustre came along with Indrāṇī. Similarly the Moon-god came along with Rohiṇī and Varuṇa came in the company of his beloved.

---

1. Chs. 2 and 3 describe the self-immolation of Satī, the daughter of Dakṣa and the consort of Śiva, in Dakṣa's sacrifice, when she and her husband Śiva were insulted by him. But there is no Vedic evidence to show that Śiva married Dakṣa's daughter (*Rudra-Śiva*, pp. 70-80). Mbh, *Śānti*, ch. 283 describes destruction of Dakṣa's sacrifice by Śiva with Yogic power (*Yoga-balaṁ kṛtvā*—283.32) in order to mollify his consort Umā, the daughter of the King of Mountains (*Śaila-rāja-sutā*—283.7 and 22) and *not* Satī, Dakṣa's daughter. Umā did not know who Dakṣa was and Śiva had to inform her that a Prajāpati called Dakṣa was performing a Horse-sacrifice (*Dakṣo nāma prajānāṁ patiḥ hayamedhena yajate*).

This clearly shows that the story of the self-immolation by Satī, Dakṣa's daughter, in Dakṣa's sacrifice described here is a post-Mahābhārata development. In the next ch. (284) the appeasement of Umā's anger is affirmed as the cause of the destruction of Dakṣa's sacrifice:

devyā manyu-vyapohārthaṁ
hato dakṣasya vai kratuḥ
—Mbh, *Śānti* 284.31

This story of Satī's self-immolation in yogic fire created by herself (*Satī . . . prajajvāla samādhijāgninā*) is however supported in BhP IV. 4; BdP I.ii.13.60-61; VāP I.30.52-55).

7. Kubera came there riding in his aerial chariot Puṣpaka, Wind-god riding on his deer, Fire-god riding on his goat and Nirṛti riding on a ghost.

8. All these came to the sacrificial enclosure of the Brāhmaṇa. All of them were received and honoured by the evil-minded Dakṣa.

9. Great and divine abodes of great value and good splendour were skilfully constructed by the noble-souled Tvaṣṭṛ.

10-13. (The visitors) occupied all those abodes according to their pleasure.

When the great sacrifice commenced in the holy spot Kanakhala,[1] the ascetics beginning with Bhṛgu were appointed as *Ṛtviks* by him. Then Dakṣa underwent due initiation. The solemn, auspicious ceremony was duly performed. Benedictory rites were completed by the Brāhmaṇas for the sake of Dakṣa accompanied by his wife. Always surrounded by his friends, he shone remarkably, thanks to his greatness. In the meantime, Dadhīci spoke these words there:

Dadhīci[2] *said*:

14. These leading Suras (gods), the great sages and the Guardians of the Quarters have come to your (sacrifice). Still the *Yajña* does not shine properly without (the presence of) the noble-souled Pināka-bearing Lord.

15. Great learned men say that everything becomes auspicious and splendid through him. That primordial Puruṣa (person), the bull-bannered, blue-throated lord with matted hair, is not seen here.

16. Presided over and authorized by him, O Dakṣa, even inauspicious things become auspicious. (Without) the Three-eyed Lord, very auspicious things become instantly bereft of their auspiciousness.

17-20. Hence he must be invited only by you immediately through Brahmā, Viṣṇu the powerful lord and Śakra. All of them

1. *Kanakhala*—A village two miles to the east of Haridwar (U.P.), at the junction of Gaṅgā and Nīladhārā.

2. Dadhīci's objection to non-invitation of Śiva and his quitting of the sacrifice (*infra* vv. 31-33) with the prediction (curse) about the non-completion of the sacrifice is found also in Mbh, *Śānti* 284.12-21.

should go where lord Maheśvara is present. Bring him along with Dākṣāyaṇī. Hurry up. Everything shall become extremely sanctified through that Yogin Śaṁbhu by remembering whom and by uttering whose names, merits become well-accomplished. Hence, with all your efforts, the Bull-bannered Lord should be brought.

21-26. On hearing these words of his, the evil-minded (Dakṣa) said laughing (derisively): "Indeed the root cause of Devas is Viṣṇu in whom the eternal virtue (*Dharma*) is present. In him Vedas, *Yajñas* and the different kinds of holy rites are established and that Viṣṇu has come here.

Brahmā, the grandfather of the worlds, has come from Satyaloka along with the Vedas, Upaniṣads and various kinds of Āgamas (scriptural treatises).

Similarly the king of Suras (gods) himself has come along with the groups of Suras. So also you, the sinless sages, have come.

All those tranquil ones who are worthy (of being present) in a *Yajña* have come. All of you are conversant with the Vedas, Vedic expositions and reality. All of you are steadfast in your holy rites and observances.

Of what avail is Rudra to us in this matter? Of course, my daughter has been given to him by me, O Brāhmaṇa, (but that was) when I had been urged by Brahmā.

27. He is not of noble birth, O Brāhmaṇa. He is doomed and he is always a favourite of the doomed. He is the sole lord of goblins, ghosts and vampires. He is unfathomable.

28. He esteems himself very much. He is deluded and stubborn. He is tacitern, jealous and malicious. In this holy rite he is utterly unworthy. Hence indeed he was not invited by me now.

29. Hence, words like these should not be uttered by you again, O Brāhmaṇa. My great *Yajña* should be made successful by all of you collectively."

30. On hearing these words of his, Dadhīci made the following statement:

Dadhīci said:

31. Great injustice has been done to all these excellent sages and Devas of sanctified soul by not having the noble soul with them.

32-33. A great ruin will soon befall all those who are present here.

After saying thus, Dadhīci alone walked out in protest from the sacrificial enclosure of Dakṣa and hurriedly went to his hermitage. When the sage went out, Dakṣa said this laughingly:

34-36. "There, a heroic supporter and friend of Śiva named Dadhīci, has gone out. All those slow-witted rogues whose minds are possessed by evil spirits, who are enamoured of heretic doctrines, who are excluded from the Vedas and whose behaviour and acts are vicious, should leave this holy rite.

You are all devoted to Vedic doctrines having Viṣṇu as your leader. O Brāhmaṇas, make my *Yajña* fruitful ere long."

Then all of them along with the sages performed the worship of the lord.

37-40. In the meantime there on the mountain Gandhamādana[1] the great goddess Dākṣāyaṇī was engaged in various kinds of sports. She was surrounded by her female friends. Sometimes she played beneath in the *Dhārāgṛha* (chamber fitted with fountains and water-jets). Sometimes she moved about in an aerial chariot. Sometimes she stood in the middle of the aerial chariot and indulged in thousands of sports with balls etc.

While engaged in playing the games, the great goddess Satī saw the Moon-god going to the place of sacrifice along with Rohiṇī.

She said to her maid Vijayā, "Where is Candra going now? O Vijayā, go and enquire immediately."

On being thus instructed by her, the gentle lady Vijayā asked him suitably.

41. Everything about Dakṣa's sacrifice and other things were told by him. On hearing it the gentle lady Vijayā became

---

1. *Gandhamādana*—The northern ridge of the great Hindukush arch with its northern extension Khwaja Mohammud range (AGP 58-59). The extent of Purāṇic India was much larger than the pre-partition map of India which was based on the political realities of the 19th century A.D. Soviet Indologists and archaeologists now testify to the existence of Vedic Aryans from the lower reaches of the Dnieper, the area to the north of the Black Sea through the Soviet republics of central Asia. *Vide* for example B.A. Rybakov's *Indo-Aryans in Northern Black Sea Area*, O.N. Trubachev's *Linguistic Periphery of the Ancient Slaves.*

agitated. Hurriedly (she went to Satī) and told her everything exactly as it was said by the Moon-god.

42-43. The goddess began to ponder over the reason thus: 'Why does he not invite (us)? Dakṣa is my father. Why has my mother forgotten me now? I shall ask Śaṅkara now about the reason (thereof).' After deciding thus, she asked the friends to stay there and approached Śaṅkara.

44-49. She saw the Three-eyed Lord in the centre of the assembly stationed there, in an extremely wonderful seat, and surrounded by all his Gaṇas (attendants) beginning with Caṇḍa and Muṇḍa, Bāṇa, Bhṛṅgin, Nandin of great power of penance, the son of Śilāda, Mahākāla, Mahācaṇḍa. Mahāmuṇḍa, Mahāśiras, Dhūmrākṣa, Dhūmraketu and Dhūmrapāda—these and many other Gaṇas, the followers of Rudra, (were present there). Some were hideous and terrifying. Others were mere headless trunks. Some had no eyes. Others were devoid of chests. There were hundreds like these. All of them had elephant-hides for their clothes. Clusters of matted hair were their ornaments. All were adorned with Rudrākṣa beads. They were devoid of attachment. They had conquered their sense-organs. They were antagonistic to objects of sensual pleasure. Śaṅkara, the benefactor of the worlds, was seen by her surrounded by all these.

50-52. Bewildered in her mind, she suddenly went to Śiva's presence. The beloved wife was placed in his lap by Śiva who was pleased. She was addressed with loving words with due respect: "O lady of excellent waistline, what is the purpose of your arrival? Tell me quickly."

On being spoken thus by him, the dark-eyed lady said:

Satī said:

53. O lord, O lord of the chiefs of Devas, how is it that going to the great sacrifice of my father is not approved of by you? Tell (me) everything.

54-55. This is the duty of friends, O Mahādeva, that they (regularly) associate with their friends, thereby increasing the pleasure and love of their friends. Hence make all efforts (to be present there). Oh, go there even if you have not been invited. Go to the sacrificial enclosure of my father today at my request, O Sadāśiva.

56-57. On hearing her words (Śiva) spoke these kind and sincere words:

"O gentle lady, you must not go to the sacrifice of Dakṣa. All those persons who honour Dakṣa, including Suras, Asuras and Kinnaras, have undoubtedly gone to the sacrifice of your father.

58-59. O lady of fine eyebrows, those who go to others' mansions without being invited, meet with insult which is more (painful) than death. Even Indra who goes to the abode of others meets with contempt and disrespect. Hence, O splendid lady, you must not go to Dakṣa's sacrifice."

60. On being told thus by the noble-souled Śiva, Satī, the most excellent one among those who are conversant with modes of expression, spoke these words full of anger:

61. "It is true that you are (the real) *Yajña* in this world, O most excellent lord of Devas. (How is it) that you have not been invited by my father of evil conduct today? Hence I wish to know thoroughly the attitude of that evil-minded one.

62. Hence I shall go to the sacrificial enclosure of my father today itself. Grant me permission, O my lord, lord of the universe, lord of Devas."

63-65a. On being told thus by that goddess, Lord Śiva himself, who has knowledge and vision of everything, the lord who is the sanctifier of all living beings, the lord of Devas, Maheśa, the bestower of all *Siddhis* said to her:

"Go quickly, O gentle lady of holy rites, at my instance, riding on this Nandin and accompanied by various kinds of Gaṇas."

65b-68. At the bidding of Śiva, sixty thousand of the terrifying Gaṇas went (along with her). Surrounded by those Gaṇas, the goddess went to the abode of her father. Observing the entire army, Mahādeva became excessively surprised. Mahādeva, the unperturbed scorcher of enemies, sent very valuable ornaments to her through his attendants. He sent them immediately after her.

Pondering over the departure of the goddess to her father's abode, Lord Maheśa exclaimed:

"On being insulted by her father, Satī, the daughter of Dakṣa, will never come back to her city again."

CHAPTER THREE

Vīrabhadra Comes to the Yajña

Lomaśa said:

1-4a. Dākṣāyaṇī went to the place where the great sacrifice was being performed. After going to the abode of her father, the abode which was full of various wonderful things, she stood at the entrance. The Devas of exalted fortune became delighted. They got down from their seats. After seeing the congregation of the Devas, her parents, friends, relatives and kinsmen, she made obeisance to her father and mother with delight. Then the goddess spoke these words in a manner suitable to the occasion:

4b-9. "Why was Śaṁbhu, the extremely splendid (lord), not invited by you? (He is the lord) by whom this entire universe consisting of the mobile and immobile beings has been sanctified. He is *Yajña* (incarnate), an (important) part of *Yajña*, the sacrificial gift offered therein, the material offered therein, the *Mantras* etc., the *Havya* and *Kavya*—he is identical with all these things. He is the most excellent one among those who are expert in performing *Yajñas*. Everything performed without him will become impure. How can a sacrifice function (at all), O dear father, without Śaṁbhu? How did these come here, O father, along with Brahmā? Don't you know? O Bhṛgu, O Kaśyapa of great intellect, O Atri, O Vasiṣṭha? You are alone, O Śakra, what has been done by you today? O Viṣṇu, you do know the supreme lord Mahādeva. O Brahmā, don't you know the valour of Mahādeva?

10. Formerly you happened to be five-faced. You (spoke) arrogantly to Sadāśiva and you were made four-faced. It is surprising that you have forgotten that miracle.

11. He is the lord Rudra who formerly begged for alms in the forest of Dāruvana,[1] when this mendicant was cursed by you (and) your friends.

1. This refers to Lord Śiva's visit to Dāruvana to teach Pāśupata Yoga to the sages thereof. He adopted the queer behaviour called *Dvāra* (Vide *Pāśupata Sūtra* ch. III.1-19 and Kauṇḍinya's com.). The sages were infuriated at it and they cursed Śiva and suffered disastrous results (BdP I.ii.27 and Tagare's Introduction to BdP on '*Liṅga* worship'). The story is narrated in LP and KP also.

12-14. Even after cursing Rudra, how was (this incident) forgotten by you? He is the lord by whose limb alone the universe including the mobile and immobile beings, has been filled up. The entire universe became the *Liṅga* at that very instant. They call it *Liṅga* because of the dissolution (of the universe in it).[1] All the Devas along with Vāsava (Indra) are born of the Trident-bearing Lord. Such a lord who is to be realized through the Vedāntas, cannot be comprehended by you."

15-19a. On hearing her words, Dakṣa became angry and spoke these words:

"Of what avail is your verbal prolixity. It has no relevance to the present occasion. O gentle lady, (you may) go or stay. Why did you come at all? Your husband is an inauspicious fellow, not conducive to propitiousness, O lady of good waistline.

He is ignoble, excluded from the Vedas. He is the king of goblins, ghosts and vampires. Hence he was not invited to the sacrifice, O gentle lady of sweet speech.

O lady of excellent loins, it is to Rudra who is haughty and evil-minded and of unknown antecedents that you had been given in marriage by me, a dull-witted sinner. Hence, abandon this body (of yours), O lady of pure smiles, and be happy."

19b-23. It was thus that his own daughter Satī who was worshipped by all the worlds, was addressed by Dakṣa then.

On seeing her own father full of contempt (for Śiva), Satī became excessively furious. Then the goddess thought thus: 'Though I am desirous of seeing Śaṅkara, how can I go back to our mansion? What will I say if I am asked (about this incident) by him? He who censures Mahādeva and he who listens when Mahādeva is being censured—both of them go to hell and remain there as long as the moon and the sun (shine). Hence I will abandon this body and enter fire.' Pondering thus and being overwhelmed by insult, she entered fire[2] uttering the words "O Rudra, O Śiva".

---

1. A popular etymology of *Liṅga* from √*li* 'to dissolve'. It is to be derived from √*lig*, √*liṅg*, 'to go'. MW 901 conjecturally traces it to √*lag* 'to adhere', 'to stick'.

2. As contrasted with older Purāṇas mentioned in *Supra* p. 7. fn 1, this text does not bring in 'Yogic fire' for self-immolation.

24-30. The entire quarters became pervaded with the great uproar of "Alas! Alas!". All those (who had come with Satī) climbed on to the platform. Laden with weapons they crowded the place without any gap. They hit and struck themselves with their weapons. They cut off their own bodies. Some of them cut off their heads and eagerly performed the *Nīrājana* (waving of the lights in circles) rites with them. Immediately they were reduced to ash. Then everyone said thus: "Twenty thousand of the Gaṇas roared terrifically. Those dreadful ones cut off their limbs by means of weapons. Thus they all perished there along with Dākṣāyaṇī."[1]

That was a great miracle. All sages, the Devas beginning with Indra, along with the groups of Maruts, Viśvedevas, Aśvins and the Guardians of the Quarters—all these became silent then. Some of them (walked) round requesting Viṣṇu, the most excellent one. This was the end of the *Yajña* of that evil-minded one. The *Yajña* of the unworthy Brāhmaṇa Dakṣa (was ruined) and the sages became afraid.

31. In the meantime, O Brāhmaṇas, all these activities and behaviour of Dakṣa were communicated to Rudra by the noble-minded Nārada.

32. On hearing Nārada's report the supreme Lord Śiva became extremely infuriated. In his anger he as if jumped up from his seat.

33. Uprooting a plait of hair from his (matted hair), Rudra, the cause of the annihilation of all the worlds, angrily dashed it on the top of the mountain.

34. As a result of this dashing, Vīrabhadra of great fame rose up. So also did Kālī surrounded by crores of spirits and goblins.

35. Through the wrathful breath of the noble-minded Rudra a hundred (types of) Fevers and thirteen *Sannipātas* (combined derangement of all the three humours causing deadly varieties of fevers) rose up.

36. Rudra of fierce and dreadful exploits was entreated by Vīrabhadra "O Lord! what task of Your Lordship is to be carried out? Tell me quickly."

---

1. The *Yajña* was disturbed by the *Harakiri* of Satī's attendants. This is not mentioned in VāP and BdP in contexts noted in fn 1 of p. 7.

37. On being requested thus, lord Rudra hurriedly commissioned him, "Destroy Dakṣa's *Yajña.*"

38. Receiving the behest of the Trident-bearing Lord of Devas with his head (i.e. humbly accepting the order), the heroic Vīrabhadra of excessive refulgence, who was kissed (*ā-līḍha*) by Kālikā and was surrounded by all goblins rushed to Dakṣa's sacrifice.

39-40. At that very time, ill-omens occurred suddenly. A rough wind blew carrying with it gravels and sand. The Rain-god showered blood. The quarters were enveloped in darkness. Thousands of meteors fell on the earth.

41. The Devas and others saw such phenomena foreboding evil. Becoming frightened, Dakṣa sought refuge in Viṣṇu.

42. "Save me, save me, O great Viṣṇu. Indeed you are our greatest preceptor and elderly one. You are (identical with) *Yajña,* O most excellent one among Suras. Save me from this fearful danger."

43. On being requested and prayed to by Dakṣa, the slayer of Madhu (Viṣṇu) said: "Protection should be accorded to you by me. There is no doubt about it.

44. Disrespect has been shown by you, O Dakṣa, without understanding genuine *Dharma* (Virtue). Due to the contemptuous disregard of Lord Śiva, everything will become fruitless.

45. Where those who are not worthy of respect are worshipped, where he who is worthy of being worshipped is not worshipped, three consequences, viz. famine, death and fear, prevail there.

46. Hence, the Bull-bannered Lord (Śiva) should be honoured with all efforts. Great fear and danger beset you because the great lord was not honoured.

47. All of us are not powerful enough now, because of your evil behaviour. There is no need to discuss this matter further."

48. On hearing those words of Viṣṇu, Dakṣa became lost in (anxious) thoughts. Turning pale in the face, he remained silent and sat on the ground.

49-51. Expressly commanded by Rudra himself the extremely powerful Vīrabhadra came to the sacrificial enclosure accompanied by the nine Durgās and others.[1] The nine Durgās

1. The legend of destruction of Dakṣa's sacrifice is mentioned in the

were Kālī, Kātyāyanī, Īśānā, Cāmuṇḍā, Muṇḍamardinī, Bhadrakālī, Bhadrā, Tvaritā and Vaiṣṇavī. A big multitude of Bhūtas also entered the sacrificial enclosure of great refulgence. Śākinīs, Ḍākinīs, Bhūtas, Pramathas, Guhyakas, a host of Yoginīs (in circular formation) along with the sixtyfour (*Tantras*)[1]—all these entered the sacrificial enclosure suddenly.

52-55. Hundreds and thousands of Gaṇas who accompanied Vīrabhadra were all the *Pārṣadas* (attendants) of Śaṅkara. All of them had the form of Rudra. They had five faces and blue throats. All had weapons in their hands. They were duly served with umbrellas and chowries. All were as valorous as Śiva. They had ten arms and three eyes. Their hair was matted. They wore the ornaments of Rudra. Bearing crescent moon (on their heads), all of them had (different kinds of) robes and ornaments.

56. Accompanied by these, the noble-souled, three-eyed, dreadful Vīrabhadra of terrible might, who had a thousand arms and was entwined by great serpents, marched towards the sacrifice.

57. His chariot was drawn by two thousand horses and a million lions.

58-59a. The armoured defenders of his sides were many lions, tigers, sharks, fishes and thousands of elephants. He had different kinds of umbrellas and chowries held over the head of everyone everywhere.

Śatapatha and *Kauṣītaki* Brāhmaṇas. But the cause was Dakṣa's illicit relations with his daughter. The destruction of the sacrifice mentioned in Purāṇas (e.g. BhP IV.5, LP I.99 and 100, NP II.5-16, BdP and VāP mentioned above) is caused by the insult of Satī, Śaṅkara's spouse and Dakṣa's daughter.

1. *Tantras* are scriptures promulgated by Śiva. SkP gives a list of 64 Tantras such as *Jñānārṇava*, *Mālinī-vijaya*, *Yāmala* and others. Some of them are still unpublished. They generally contain: (1) Creation of the world; (2) Dissolution of the world; (3) The procedure of worshipping the deity; (4) Penance (*Sādhana*); (5) Repetition of the name of the deity; (6) Six daily sacred duties (*Ṣaṭkarma*); (7) The Yoga of meditation. The *Vārāhītantra* gives the number of verses in each Tantra. Schools of Śaivism such as Trika Śaivism of Kashmir, the Śaktiviśiṣṭādvaita of Liṅgāyatas are based on Śaiva Tantras (Āgamas). Even Vaiṣṇavas had their own Tantras as one finds in Rāmānuja's *Śrībhāṣya* and the ten topics of *Pañcarātra Āgama* have close similarity with these topics.

59bc. Then high sounding *Bherīs* (war-drums), conchs of various (degrees of) sounds, *Paṭahas* (kettle-drums), musical instruments like *Gomukha*, different kinds of horns were sounded.

60. Cymbals, gongs and wind instruments were played. All of them were engaged in singing pleasantly. All of them played on *Mṛdaṅgas* (special drums).

61. The Gaṇas proceeded ahead in front of Vīrabhadra indulging in different kinds of dances. Those Gaṇas of unmeasured power and potency roared along with the martial sounds of the musical instruments.

62-63a. By that great sound the three worlds echoed and reverberated. Thus all those Gaṇas ordered (urged) by Rudra came there to the sacrificial enclosure of Dakṣa and began to smash for the sake of destroying it.

63b-64a. The sky was covered with dust and all the quarters were enveloped in darkness. The earth consisting of the seven islands (continents)[1] shook along with the mountains and forests.

64b-65. Those Devas, Daityas and night-wanderers observed this wonderful spectacle foreboding the ruin of all the worlds. All of them stood up simultaneously. They saw the dreadful army of Rudra advancing.

66-67. Some of them were coming over the earth. Some were coming through the sky. Others covered the quarters and the intervening spaces and rushed on. All of them were of inexhaustible strength; infinite (in number), they were heroic on a par with Rudra in battle. On seeing such an army surrounded by (the followers of) Rudra, all of them said in great surprise and dismay: "Let us advance (against them) with weapons in the hands."

68-70. Indra rode on his elephant. The Wind-god rode on a deer. Yama equipped with the rod of death rode on a buffalo. Kubera drove in the aerial chariot Puṣpaka. Varuṇa rode on a shark. The Fire-god rode on a goat. Nirṛti rode on a ghost.

1. *Dvīpas*—'Dvīpa' originally means a land-mass between two arms of water. According to Purāṇas the earth consists of the following seven continents (*dvīpas*) : (1) Śaka, (2) Kuśa, (3) Plakṣa, (4) Puṣkara, (5) Śālmala (li), (6) Krauñca, (7) Jambū. Scholars differ about their identification with modern parts of the world.

Similarly other groups of Suras, Yakṣas, Cāraṇas and Guhyakas, valorously rode on their respective vehicles.

71. On seeing the preparations of his own people, Dakṣa's face was covered with tears. He prostrated himself on the ground and spoke to all of them:

72. "O (friends) of great lustre, it was on the strength of your support that this great *Yajña* was begun by me. For the accomplishment of this good rite, you are the final authority.

73. O Viṣṇu, you are the protector of holy rites and *Yajñas* as well as the virtue described in the Vedas. O Mādhava, you are the promoter of Brāhmaṇa's rites.

74. Hence, O great Lord, proper protection should be accorded to this *Yajña*."

On hearing the words of Dakṣa, the slayer of Madhu (Viṣṇu) replied:[1]

75-76. "When you say that protection should be accorded by me to maintain holy rites, it is true. But the transgression is of your own doing in regard to this *Yajña*. You said something to Sadāśiva in the Naimiṣa forest, the holy spot of Devas. Is it not remembered by you?

77-78. Rudra, Sadāśiva, who has great splendour, who is of the form of *Yajña*, was excluded from the *Yajñas*, O deluded one. That was the wrong advice of yours. Who is competent to protect you from Rudra's wrath? I do not see anyone, O Brāhmaṇa, who can protect you, the evil-minded one.

79. You do not distinguish between good and evil acts, O evil-minded one. A holy rite alone is not (necessarily) efficacious always (to produce results).

80. Understand that a holy rite with the support of Īśvara (Śiva) is competent to produce results. Excepting Īśvara, there is no other bestower of the fruit of *Karman* (a holy rite).

81. Sadāśiva grants the benefit of the holy rites of those persons who are the devotees of Īśvara, who are calm and whose minds dwell on him.

82. Those people who solely depend upon *Karman* and are

---

1. The author of the Purāṇa takes every opportunity to reduce the gulf between Śaivism and Vaiṣṇavism and to assert the oneness of Śiva and Viṣṇu. Viṣṇu's reply is thus remarkable.

engaged in denying Īśvara, go to hell even if they perform hundred crores of *Yajñas*.

83. Those who put faith in the *Karmans* alone are bound by the fetters of *Karman* in birth after birth. They are roasted and cooked in the hells."

CHAPTER FOUR

A Fight between Vīrabhadra and Viṣṇu and Others

Lomaśa said:

1. On hearing the words uttered by Viṣṇu, Dakṣa spoke these words:

"O slayer of Madhu (Viṣṇu), you have made it appear that Vedas are not authoritative (*pramāṇa*).[1]

2. How can one forsake the Vedic rite and accept the doctrine of the authoritativeness of Īśvara? Let this be explained, O Mahāviṣṇu, by whom *Dharma* has been established?"

3-5. On being asked by Dakṣa, Mahāviṣṇu said to him consolingly: "The Vedas have the three *Guṇas* for their object.[2] They cannot be otherwise. How can the rites mentioned in the Vedas become fruitful without Īśvara? They definitely become fruitless. Hence seek refuge in Īśvara by all means."

Even as Govinda (Viṣṇu) was saying thus, the ocean of an army, similar to Vīrabhadra's came there. All the Suras (Devas) saw it.

6. Indra laughed at Viṣṇu who was engaged in explaining the doctrine of Ātman then. With the Vajra (thunderbolt) in

1. This shows a stage of conflict between the traditional Vedic religion and Śaivism. Vedic tradition prohibited its followers from even speaking with the non-Vedic Śaivas and Pañcarātras. These *Śāstras* were regarded as authoritative so far as they are not opposed to the Vedas (*Sūta-Saṁhitā* IV.4.16-18). *Pārijāta* as quoted in the *Kṛtyaratnākara* (p. 37) states the view of the mediaeval writers on Dharma Śāstra as follows:

pañcarātrapāśupatādīnyapi śāstrāṇi vedāviruddhāni pramāṇam

2. Cf. *traiguṇya-viṣayā vedāḥ*—BG II.45.

his hand, he became desirous of fighting, accompanied by the Suras.

7. He was made to go hurriedly by Bhṛgu who was bent upon routing (the Gaṇas). Then, the Gaṇas in the formation of groups fought with the Suras.

8. They struck one another with arrows, iron clubs and sharp-pointed missiles. In the course of that great festival of war, many conchs were blown.

9. So also drums like *Dundubhis*, *Paṭahas*, *Ḍiṇḍimas* etc., were sounded. Thanks to that great sound, the Suras considered themselves flattered. Accompanied by the Guardians of the Quarters, they killed the servants of Śiva.

10. Some were killed by means of swords. Some were smashed by means of iron clubs. All of the hundreds and thousands of the Gaṇas were entirely routed by the Devas.

11. It was by the power of the *Mantras* of Bhṛgu, that those Gaṇas were instantaneously defeated and driven back by the Guardians of the Quarters headed by Indra.

12. Their extermination was effected by Bhṛgu who performed the *Yāga* as the fire-worshipper. He was initiated in this for the sake of the worship, on behalf of the Devas and for their pleasure too.

13. By that alone did the Devas become victorious at the very instant. On seeing the defeat of his own army, Vīrabhadra became angry.

14-15. He made the goblins, ghosts and vampires go to the rear and the bull-riders advance at the front. The leader of great strength took up a sharp trident and struck down the Devas, Yakṣas, Piśācas, Guhyakas and Rākṣasas in the battle. Striking with spears, all the Gaṇas began to kill the Devas.

16. Some of them were split into two by means of swords. They were smashed with iron clubs. In the course of the battle, some were cut into pieces with battle-axes.

17. Hundreds were pierced with spears; some were torn to pieces. Thus, all of those being defeated, began to run away.

18. Embracing each other, they went back to heaven. Only the guardians of the worlds led by Indra remained there, eager (to fight). They consulted Bṛhaspati, "How can we have victory?"

19-22. Bṛhaspati immediately replied to Indra thus:

Bṛhaspati said:

What had been spoken by Viṣṇu formerly has become true today.

If there is Īśvara as (bestower of) the benefit of a holy rite, he assigns it (the benefit) to the performer (of the rite). He is not powerful over one who does not perform (the rite). Neither *Mantras* nor all the medicinal herbs, neither black magic nor secular rites, neither holy rites nor the Vedas, nor the two systems of Mīmāṁsā are capable of understanding Īśvara. He can be known only through unswerving devotion. By calmness and great contentment, Sadāśiva should (i.e. could) be known.

23. It is through him that the entire universe with happiness and misery as its characteristic features, takes its origin. But I shall speak further with a desire to explain (what are the) right and wrong actions.

24. O Indra, you have been foolish in accompanying the (other) guardians of the worlds here. What can you do further now with the self-same folly?

25. These extremely splendid Gaṇas, the assistants of Rudra, have become infuriated. Those persons of exalted fortune cause nothing to be left over.

26. On hearing these words of Bṛhaspati, all the heaven-dwellers and all those great gods, the guardians of the worlds, became anxious.

27-28. Then Vīrabhadra who was very closely surrounded by the Gaṇas, said:

"On account of your ignorant nature, you have come here for the sake of *Avadāna* (glorious achievement). For the sake of your satisfaction, I shall immediately give you *Avadānas* (cutting into pieces)."

After saying this, he furiously hit them with sharp arrows.

29. Hit by those arrows, all of them fled in all the ten directions.

30. When the guardians of the worlds had left the place and when the Devas had fled, Vīrabhadra came into the sacrificial enclosure accompanied by the Gaṇas.

31. At that time all those sages who were desirous of intimating everything to Janārdana (Viṣṇu), the god of gods, said to him all at once:

32-33. "Protect the *Yajña* of Dakṣa. Indeed, there is no doubt that you are *Yajña* incarnate."

On hearing these words of the sages, Janārdana, the all-pervading lord, the illuminator of spiritual faculties, became desirous of fighting and stood there ready for the battle. Vīrabhadra of powerful arms spoke these words to Keśava (Viṣṇu):

34. "Why have you come here, O Viṣṇu, you who know the great strength (of mine)? How will you be victorious by taking up Dakṣa's side? Tell me that.

35. Did you not observe? What has been done by Dākṣāyaṇī, O sinless one? You too have come for the sake of a share in the course of the *Yajña* of Dakṣa. O lord of powerful arms, I shall give oblation to you also."

36. After saying this, at the very outset, he bowed down to Viṣṇu whose form was similar to his. Vīrabhadra then went in front of Viṣṇu and spoke these words:

37. "You are to me just like Śambhu.[1] There is no doubt about this. Still, O lord of powerful arms, you face me with a desire to fight. If you continue to stay here yourself, I shall give you liberation (*Apunarāvṛtti*)."

38. On hearing those words of the intelligent Vīrabhadra lord Viṣṇu, the lord of all lords, said laughingly:

Viṣṇu said:

39-41. O highly intelligent one, you are born of the splendour of Rudra. You are very pure and holy. I had been requested by this (Dakṣa) before repeatedly for attending this *Yajña*. I am subservient to my devotees. So also is the case of Maheśvara. It is for that reason that I have come to this sacrifice of Dakṣa, O Vīrabhadra, born of the wrath of Rudra. Either I shall restrain you or you shall restrain me.

42. When Govinda said this much, that (Vīrabhadra) of mighty arms laughed and after bowing down humbly said this to Janārdana (Viṣṇu):

1. The Purāṇa reiterates the identity of Śiva and Viṣṇu. Vīrabhadra calls himself the servant of both Śiva and Viṣṇu and bows down humbly to Viṣṇu before fighting (vv 42-43 below).

43. "Just as Śiva, so also you. Just as you, so also Śiva. All of us are servants both of you and of Śaṅkara."

44. On hearing his words, Acyuta, Viṣṇu, the greatest lord, spoke these important words laughingly:

45. "Fight with me unhesitatingly, O lord of powerful arms. I shall go to my own abode when I am surfeited with your arrows and missiles."

46. Saying "so be it", Vīrabhadra, the hero of great strength, took up the greatest of his missiles and roared like a lion.

47. Viṣṇu too blew his conch of loud report. On hearing it, those Devas who had fled away from the battlefield, returned once again.

48-50. All the Guardians of the Quarters including Indra made an array (of their soldiers). Then Nandin was struck by Indra with his Vajra (thunderbolt) that had a hundred spikes. Śakra was hit in the middle of his chest by Nandin with his trident. Bhṛṅgī was struck by Vāyu and Vāyu was struck (in return) by Bhṛṅgī. Standing well prepared with his trident of sharp edge, Mahākāla, endowed with great strength, fought with Yama holding the heavy rod.

51-55. The lord of Kūṣmāṇḍas clashed with Kubera. Muṇḍa of great strength fought with Varuṇa. He fought with such a great strength as surprised the three worlds. The exceedingly powerful Caṇḍa clashed with Nirṛta and fought with a very great missile, mocking his demoniac nature. Bhairava, the great leader, accompanied by the circle of Yoginīs tore through all the Devas and drank their wonderful blood. All the Kṣetrapālas, Bhūtas, Pramathas, Guhyakas, Śākinīs, Ḍakinīs, the terrible nine Durgās, Yoginīs, Yātudhānīs, Kūṣmāṇḍakas and others roared, drank blood and devoured a lot of flesh.

56. On seeing that his army was being devoured, the king of Suras left Nandin behind and challenged Vīrabhadra.

57. Leaving off Viṣṇu, Vīrabhadra engaged Devendra. The battle between them was as terrible as that between Mars and Mercury.

58-61. When Śakra was desirous of killing Vīrabhadra and hastily prepared for the same, Vīrabhadra became furious and filled Indra who was seated on his elephant, with a mass of arrows. The extremely mighty Vīrabhadra who was unrestrainable, was immediately struck by Indra with his Vajra of a hundred spikes. Then he (Vīrabhadra) attempted to swallow Indra along with his elephant and thunderbolt. All the Bhūtas who saw Vīrabhadra like that desirous of killing Indra, raised the loud shouts of "*Hā-Hā*" (Alas-Alas). Seeing Vīrabhadra desirous of killing Indra, Viṣṇu came there in a hurry and stood in front of Vīrabhadra.

62. He pushed Śakra behind and fought with Vīrabhadra. The battle between them was very tough.

63-64. They then fought with various kinds of weapons and missiles. Seeing Nandin once again, Śakra who was an expert in battle, engaged him in a tumultuous duel.

There was a great clash between Devas and Pramathas. Pramathas were smashed by Devas and all of them fled from the battle.

65. On seeing the Gaṇas turning their faces away (from the battle), all those (bacterial) ailments[1] that had originated from the fury of Rudra rushed against Devas.

66. On seeing Devas afflicted with the fevers, Viṣṇu laughingly seized Devas alive separately.

67. He called Aśvinī Devas in order to quell the ailments. The highly intelligent (lord) made them carefully work out and consider the requisite nourishment (medicine) and sustenance, and gave the same to them.

68. Aśvinī gods caught hold of the fevers and *Sannipāta* (fevers) as well as other inimical elements and quelled them. They joyously made Devas free from fever and rejoiced for a long time.

69. The Yoginī Cakra also was subdued by them. With sharp-pointed arrows, they toppled down Bhairava who was highly excited and felled the Gaṇas too.

70. On seeing his army routed by Suras and felled down by them, Vīrabhadra became furious and spoke these words to Viṣṇu:

71. "You are a heroic warrior, O mighty one. Indeed you are the protector of Devas. If you think so, come on, fight with me strenuously."

---

1. An imaginative precursor of modern bacterial warfare?

72. After saying thus, Vīrabhadra of great strength, approached Viṣṇu, the lord of all lords, and showered him with sharp arrows.

73. Then the lord attacked Vīrabhadra with his discus. On seeing the discus coming, it was instantaneously swallowed (by Vīrabhadra).

74-75. On seeing that his discus was swallowed, Viṣṇu, the conqueror of the cities of his enemies, stroked and pressed his mouth. Thus the (discus) was caused to be spitted out by Viṣṇu.

Taking his discus, Viṣṇu of exalted nature, the sole lord of the universe, went to heaven. On understanding everything that had been done and was unbearable to the enemies he became satisfied (of having done his job).

CHAPTER FIVE

Meritoriousness of Devotion to Śiva

Lomaśa continued:

1. When Viṣṇu went away, all those Devas along with the sages and all those who subsisted on that *Yajña* were totally vanquished by the Gaṇas.

2. He (Vīrabhadra) made Bhṛgu fall down and his beard and moustache were plucked and cut.[1] He got the teeth of Pūṣan uprooted after distorting and deforming them.

3. Svadhā was ridiculed and the sages were mocked there. In their fury, they showered the sacrificial fire with faecal matter.

4. The Gaṇas who had become excessively infuriated created unspeakable havoc. Out of great fear, Dakṣa hid himself beneath the altar.

5. After realizing that he was in hiding, he angrily dragged him out. Holding by the cheeks, he struck his head with a sword.

---

1. Cf. BhP IV.5.13-26 for a close similarity in the description of the destruction and humiliation of persons in Dakṣa's sacrifice.

6. Thinking that the head could not be pierced or split through, the valorous Vīrabhadra pressed the shoulder down with his feet and wrung the neck.

7. On being wrenched off from the neck, the head of the vicious Dakṣa was taken away by the intelligent Vīrabhadra and thrown (lit. offered as oblation) into the blazing sacrificial pit instantaneously.

8. Other sages, Devas, Pitṛs, Yakṣas and Rākṣasas who yet stayed on were assaulted by the Gaṇas. All of them fled from the place.

9. The Moon, the groups of Ādityas, all the Planets, Stars and Constellations—all of them were displaced and shaken. They too were attacked by the Gaṇas.

10. Brahmā returned to Satyaloka. He was afflicted with sorrow for his son. He thought without being perturbed: 'What action is to be taken now?'

11-15. As his mind was suffering, the grandfather of the worlds did not derive any happiness. With great effort, he understood all the wicked deeds of that sinner. He decided to go to the Kailāsa mountain.

Riding on his swan, accompanied by all the Devas, the lord of great splendour reached the most excellent mountain. There he saw Śiva, Rudra, accompanied by only Nandin, staying alone.

He had matted hair and possessed great splendour. It was the lord who could not he grasped by the Vedas or their *Aṅgas* (Ancillaries). On seeing such a lord, Brahmā became greatly agitated.

He prostrated himself on the ground like a staff and began to plead for pardon, touching his lotus-like feet with the tips of the four crowns. He began to eulogize Śiva, the supreme soul.

Brahmā said:

16. Obeisance to Rudra, the quiescent Brahman, the supreme soul. You are the creator and sustainer (protector) of the universe; you are the great-grandfather (of the world).

17. Obeisance to the great Rudra, to the blue-throated one, to the creator, to the lord identical with the universe, to the seed of the universe, to the cause of the bliss of the worlds.

18-19. You are *Oṁkāra*; you are *Vaṣaṭkāra*, the prompter of the functioning of all enterprises. You are *Yajña*; you are the *Yājñic* rite. You are the cause of the functioning of *Yajña*; you alone are the protector of all the performers of sacrifice. You are worthy of being the refuge, O great lord, to all living beings. Save me, save me, O lord Mahādeva, I have been afflicted with the grief for my son.

Mahādeva said:

20. O grandfather, listen attentively to my words. The destruction of the *Yajña* of Dakṣa has not been carried out by me at all.

21-22. O Brahmā, there is no doubt about this that Dakṣa was killed by his own deeds. An act (rite) that causes pain to many others, should not be performed at all, at any time. O Parameṣṭhin, what befalls others will befall one too.

23. After saying this, Rudra accompanied by Brahmā and Suras went to the holy spot Kanakhala and to the sacrificial enclosure of the Prajāpati (Dakṣa).

24-26. Rudra saw what had been committed by Vīrabhadra. Svāhā, Svadhā, Pūṣan, Bhṛgu the most excellent one among intelligent beings (all had been injured by the Gaṇas). So also all the other sages and all the manes had been driven to that miserable plight. Many other Yakṣas, Gandharvas and Kinnaras who had been there were wounded, split and torn off. Some died in the battle.

27. On seeing that Śaṁbhu had come, Vīrabhadra prostrated himself like a log of wood by way of obeisance, along with his Gaṇas. Then he stood in front of Śiva.

28. On seeing Vīrabhadra of great strength standing in front, Rudra spoke these words laughingly: "O hero, what is this that has been done here?

29. Immediately bring here that Dakṣa by whom this unusual and inauspicious thing has been committed in the course of a *Yajña*, in consequence of which was (the present) fruit."

30. On being ordered thus by Śaṅkara, Vīrabhadra hurriedly brought the headless trunk and placed it in front of Śaṁbhu.

31-32. Then Vīrabhadra of noble mind was enquired by

Śaṅkara: "By whom has the head of the vicious Dakṣa been removed? Though he is a crooked fellow, O hero, I shall now give him life (revive him)."

On being told thus by Śaṅkara, Vīrabhadra submitted again:

33. "The head was dropped by me into the fire at the very instant, O Śaṅkara. The head that is left, O Śaṁbhu, is that of an animal and the face has been distorted."

34. After knowing (the position), Rudra placed upon the headless trunk the deformed head of the animal. The head had a beard and it was terrible.

35. Thanks to the grace of Śaṅkara, Dakṣa regained his life. On seeing Rudra in front of him, Dakṣa became ashamed. Bowing down he eulogized Śaṅkara, the benefactor of all the worlds.

Dakṣa said:

36. I bow down to the excellent lord, the bestower of boons. I bow down to the most excellent lord of Devas, the eternal lord. I pay obeisance to Īśvara, the lord of Devas. I bow down to Hara, Śaṁbhu, the sole kinsman of the universe.

37. I bow down to the cosmic form of the lord of the universe, the eternal Brahman in the form of one's own soul. I salute Sarva (Śiva) having the existence of one's own mental creation. I pay obeisance to the excellent one, the bestower of boons.

Lomaśa said:

38. Rudra who was eulogized by Dakṣa, spoke laughingly in secret:

Rudra (Hara) said:

39. Four types of meritorious people always worship[1] me. They are: (those who are in misery), those who are thirsting for knowledge, the seekers of wealth and the possessors of spiritual knowledge, O excellent Brāhmaṇa.

40. Hence undoubtedly sages, possessors of true knowledge, are my favourites. Those who strive to attain me without spiritual knowledge are ignorant.

1. An echo of BG VII. 16.

41. Merely by means of *Karman* (holy rites) you wish to cross the (ocean of) worldly existence.

42. Neither by means of the Vedas nor by means of charitable gifts, neither by sacrifices nor by penance at any place can they attain me.[1] But due to the power of *Karman* men get deluded.

43. Hence, be devoted to knowledge and perform holy rites with concentration and purity of mind. Be equally indifferent to happiness and misery and attain eternal happiness.

Lomaśa said:

44. Thus Dakṣa was advised by Śaṁbhu, the greatest god. After establishing Dakṣa there itself, Rudra went back to his mountain.

45. Similarly all the great sages beginning with Bhṛgu were consoled and enlightened by Brahmā. Instantaneously they became endowed with true knowledge.

46. Thereafter Brahmā went to his abode.

47. Dakṣa too achieved the excellent enlightenment through the utterance. Engrossed in the meditation of Śiva, the noble-minded one performed penance.

48. Hence Lord Śiva should be served by means of all possible efforts.

49. Those men who sweep the courtyard of Śiva (i.e. Śiva's temple) attain Śiva's city and become worthy of the praise of the whole universe.[2]

50. Those who offer a mirror of great lustre to Śiva become attendants of Śiva and will be standing in front of Śiva.

51. Those who give chowries to the Trident-bearing Lord of Devas will themselves be fanned with chowries in all the three worlds.

52. The men who offer lamps to the temple of Mahādeva will become refulgent. They will be the illuminators of the three worlds.

53. Those who offer incense to Śiva, the great Ātman, will

1. Cf. BG XI.46.

2. VV 49-62 describe the fruit of different types of services rendered to Śiva. Some of these verses are illustrated by stories of Śiva's devotees, the benefit derived by them by their particular act of devotion.

become famous. They redeem both the families (their own as well as that of their mothers).

54. Those men who offer eatables (*Naivedya*) in front of Hari and Hara with great devotion, attain the fruit of a sacrifice for every lump of boiled rice offered by them (as *Naivedya*).

55. Those excellent men who repair a Śiva temple in ruins attain two-fold benefit. There is no doubt about it.

56. Those who build a new temple by means of bricks or stones rejoice in heaven as long as their spotless fame stays in the world. O excellent brāhmaṇas, no doubt need be entertained about this.

57. Those highly intelligent brāhmaṇas who cause to build a palatial temple of many floors for Śiva, attain the greatest goal (i.e. *Mokṣa*).

58. Those who clean or whitewash a temple of Śiva built by themselves or by others attain the greatest goal.

59. Those who offer a canopy are meritorious men. They go to the world of Śiva and redeem their entire family.

60. Those who tie a ringing bell in a temple of Śiva will become refulgent and well reputed in the three worlds.

61. He who visits (Śiva's temple) once, twice or thrice (a day) attains happiness whether he is rich or poor. He gets released from misery.

62. A religious faithful who offers worships unto Śiva, the great Ātman, redeems ten million members of his family and rejoices in the company of Śiva.

63. In this context they cite this ancient legend,[1] the conversation between the son of Indradyumna and the noble-minded Yama.

64. Formerly, in Kṛtayuga, there was a king named Indrasena. He was a great warrior ruling Pratiṣṭhāna. He was always interested in hunting.

65. Unfriendly to brāhmaṇas, he always indulged in horrible and cruel misdeeds. He was always devoted to worldly plea-

---

1. VV 63-86 narrate the legend of Indrasena to show the efficacy of the syllables *HA-RA* uttered as a part of words of different meaning (e.g. *āhara* 'bring') simply because the name of god Śiva is indirectly pronounced by him.

sures only. That wicked king nourished his own self through the lives of others.

66. Ever-addicted to drinking wine, he very much sought the company of other men's wives. He coveted other men's wealth. Brāhmaṇas were killed by him.

67. He defiled the bed of his preceptor. He always stole gold. All his followers too were of that nature. All the followers of that evil-minded king committed sins like him.

68. Thus that vicious king ruled the kingdom in diverse ways. Then, after a great deal of time, the wicked king died.

69. Then, this evil-minded Indrasena was taken away by the followers of Yama. The sinful king thus came to the presence of Yama.

70. Indrasena who was standing in front there, was seen by Yama. He stood up and bent his head (in honour of) Śiva.

71. Yama, the most excellent one among those who uphold virtue, rebuked his messengers. After releasing Indrasena who had been bound with nooses Dharmarāja (god Yama) spoke:

72-73. "O most excellent one among kings, go to the meritorious worlds and enjoy them as long as Indra stays in heaven, as long as the sun is in the sky. Be happy as long as the five elements exist. O great king, you are a man of meritorious deeds. You are a permanent devotee of Śiva."

74. On hearing the words of Yama, Indrasena spoke: "I do not know Śiva. I am only a person interested in hunting."

75-76. On hearing his words Yama spoke by way of explanation: "The words '*āhara*' (eat), '*praharasva*' (attack) were always uttered by you. As a result of that holy act, O bestower of honour, you are permanently purified. Hence you do go to the Kailāsa mountain, to Śaṅkara."

77-78. Even as the noble-minded Yama was talking thus, the messengers of Śiva came there riding on bulls. They had great refulgence. They were blue-throated, with ten arms, five faces and three eyes. They had matted hair and wore ear-rings. Their heads were markedly adorned with the crescent moon.

79. On seeing them, Yama, the most excellent one among the upholders of virtue, stood up. He worshipped them all who resembled the great Indra.

80. All of them hurriedly spoke to Yama, the son of Vivas-

vān: "O lord of exalted fortune, did Indrasena of unmeasured splendour come here? He is the person who continuously uttered the name of the noble-minded Rudra."

81. On hearing their words, Indrasena was honoured by Yama and placed in an aerial chariot. He was then sent to the abode of Śiva.

82. He was brought in by the excellent attendants of Śiva. Then Indrasena of unmeasured splendour was seen by Śaṁbhu.

83. Rudra stood up to welcome him, approached him and embraced the king. He made Indrasena sit on half of his seat and then said:

84. "O excellent king, what shall be given to you? What is your desire? I shall give you whatever is desired by you."

On hearing the words of the great Śiva the king shed tears of joy. (Overwhelmed) by love, he could not say anything.

85. Then he was made a *Pārṣada* (Attendant) by the noble-minded Maheśa. He became famous by the name Caṇḍa. He was a favourite friend of Muṇḍa.

86. Merely by uttering the name of Rudra, the supreme soul, (former) sinful king Indrasena attained *Siddhi*.

87. By merely uttering 'O Hari', 'O Hara', the names of Śiva, the supreme soul, and of Viṣṇu, the wielder of discus, many men have been saved by Śiva.

88. No other god greater than Maheśa (Śiva) can be seen (found) in the three worlds. Hence Sadāśiva should be worshipped by all the means.

89. He should always be worshipped with leaves, flowers, fruits, even pure water, and with *Karavīra*. And he becomes a bestower of boons.

90. The flower of *Arka* (*calotropis gigantea*) is ten times more efficacious than *Karavīra*. The entire universe consisting of mobile and immobile beings is made with *Vibhūti* (the sacred ash).

91. It is always present in the courtyard of Śiva. Hence one should always besmear oneself with it.

Henceforth, listen to the merit, O excellent brāhmaṇas, of *Tripuṇḍra*[1] (three parallel horizontal lines on the forehead) drawn with sacred ash.

1. VV 91-96 describe the redeeming power of *Tripuṇḍra*.

92. It is meritorious and it dispels all sins. Listen to it, O excellent brāhmaṇas.

There was a certain thief who was a great sinner. He was executed by the servants of the king.

93-95. A certain dog came there to eat him (his flesh) and stood over his head. Some ash sticking between the claws of the dog fell on the forehead of that sinner in the form of an impression similar to *Tripuṇḍra*. His body was without consciousness but the ash fell on it. Therefore the thief was taken to Kailāsa by the messengers of Rudra. Who can specifically describe the greatness of *Vibhūti* (holy ash).

96. The men whose limbs are adorned with holy ash are men of meritorious deeds. The men in whose mouth the five-syllabled (*Mantra*), viz. *namaḥ śivāya* exists are undoubtedly veritable Rudras.

97. Those who have a cluster of matted hair on their heads and those who have *Rudrākṣa* beads as their ornaments, are themselves Rudras in human form. There is no doubt about it.

98. Hence Sadāśiva should be regularly worshipped by men in the morning, at midday and in the evening. The time of dusk is very excellent.

99. By seeing Śaṁbhu during the morning, the sin of (committed at) the night is dispelled. By visiting Śaṁbhu at midday the sin incurred by men in the course of seven previous births becomes quelled. (The merit of seeing Śaṁbhu) at night cannot be adequately calculated.

100. The two-syllabled name *Śi-va* is destructive of great sins. The whole universe is sustained by those men from whose mouths the name issues out.

101. Even heretics and those who cling to false and heterodox doctrines attain the greatest goal and people who are devoted to sinful activities become sanctified if they hear the sound of the *Bherī* (big drum) placed in the courtyard of Śiva's temple by people of meritorious deeds.

102. There is no doubt about this that even that animal attains Śiva's presence, whose hide is used in connection with the *Bherī*, *Mṛdaṅga*, *Muraja* and other types of drums placed in Śiva's temple by men.

103-104. Hence the devotee should offer various things

pleasing to Śaṁbhu in accordance with the injunctions, viz. *Tata* and *Vitata* (stringed musical instruments such as lute etc.), *Ghana* (cymbals, bells and gongs), *Suṣira* (flutes), very valuable chowries, palanquins, beds, (singing) story poems, legends, devotional music etc.

105-108. By offering these things even sinners go to the world of Śiva. (The following people get even better benefits:) Men of good holy rites, noble-souled men proficient in the worship of Śiva, those who are engaged in the worship of Śiva according to the procedure acquired directly from the (oral) instructions of the preceptor, those persons of firm resolve who see the universe as the form of Śiva, persons of good conduct with perfect intellect, men who adhere to the discipline of castes and stages of life as well as others, brāhmaṇas, kṣatriyas, vaiśyas, śūdras and other men. Even a cāṇḍāla (devotee of Śiva) is excellent. He shall be a great favourite of Śaṁbhu. The whole of this universe including mobile and immobile beings is presided over by Śaṁbhu.

109-110. Hence it should be especially understood that everything is identical with Śiva. Śaṁbhu should be known by means of Vedas, Purāṇas, sacred treatises, Upaniṣads and different kinds of Āgamas. Sadāśiva should be worshipped by all people irrespective of their being with or without desires.

Lomaśa said:

111. I shall narrate an old legend describing an event that happened long ago.

Formerly there was a vaiśya named Nandin who lived in the city of Avantī.[1]

112. He engaged himself in meditation on Śiva and performed his worship. Everyday he worshipped a *Liṅga* that was in the penance grove.

---

1. VV 111-193 relate the legend of two devotees—Nandin, a vaiśya, and Mahākāla, a Kirāta (a tribal). Śiva approved of the selfless devotion of the ignorant Kirāta and not the ostentatious worship of Nandin, the vaiśya. It was due to the request of the Kirāta that the rich vaiśya was redeemed by Śiva and absorbed as his *gaṇa* (attendant).

113. He used to get up very early in the morning everyday. Nandī, the lover of Śiva, became excessively devoted to the worship of the *Liṅga*.

114. He bathed the *Liṅga* in *Pañcāmṛta* in the manner prescribed (in scriptures). He was always surrounded by brāhmaṇas who had mastered Vedas and *Vedāṅgas* (ancillaries to Vedas).

115-116. He was devoted to the worship of the *Liṅga* in accordance with the injunctions of the sacred treatises. After bathing the *Liṅga* duly, he always worshipped it with different kinds of wonderful flowers, pearls, aspphires, *Gomedas* (Himalayan gems), *lapis lazuli*, emeralds and rubies.

117. Thus Nandī of exalted fortune worshipped for many years that *Liṅga* stationed in a lonely spot with different kinds of offerings.

118. Once there was a Kirāta (a forester) who was interested in hunting and used to injure and kill animals. Being wreckless he always enjoyed hunting.

119. That wicked fellow of sinful activities used to wander in mountains and caves teeming with beasts of prey, killing the animals here and there.

120. In the course of his wandering that Kirāta, a habitual killer of animals, came by chance where the *Liṅga* had been duly worshipped.

121. He was extremely afflicted with thirst and looked for water (everywhere). He saw a lake in the forest and immediately entered the water.

122. The wicked fellow had placed everything he had got by hunting, on the shore. He gargled, drank some water and came out.

123-126. He saw in front of him the temple that had been wonderfully embellished. The *Liṅga* that had been excellently worshipped by means of different kinds of gems was seen (by him). After seeing the *Liṅga*, when he began to offer his worship, all the gems were tossed about here and there. Bathing of the *Liṅga* was performed by him by means of a mouthful of water. With one of his hands he offered *Bilva* leaves (*aegle marmelos*) for the purpose of worship. With the other hand he offered venison. After prostrating himself like a stick he mentally took the solemn vow to perform worship (as follows):

127. "From today onwards I shall strenuously perform the worship. From today, O Śaṅkara, you are my master and I am your devotee."

128. After having thus become a regular worshipper, the Kirāta returned home.

Nandī saw everything scattered here and there by the Kirāta.

129. Nandī became anxious and worried: 'What flaw is this that has befallen me? Many obstacles have been mentioned in the case of one who is engaged in the worship of Śiva. Owing to my misfortune all those obstacles have beset me.'

130. After pondering thus for a long time, he washed the temple of Śiva. Nandī then returned to his house along the path by which he had gone.

131. The priest approached Nandī (as he was found) dejected in his mind. He spoke these words: "Why have you become dejected in your mind?"

132-133. Nandī then spoke these words to his priest: "O brāhmaṇa, impure things have been seen by me today in the vicinity of Śiva. I do not know at all by whom this has been caused."

134-140. Then the priest spoke these words to Nandin: "The person by whom the offerings of gems etc. have been scattered is a deluded one. There is no doubt. He is a stupid fellow not aware of what should be or should not be done. Hence, O lord, do not worry in the least. Be pleased to go to that temple of Śiva in the morning along with me in order to see that wicked fellow. Thereafter, I shall do what should be done." On hearing these words of his priest, Nandin remained in his house during the night with his mind extremely pained.

When the night passed, he called the priest and went to the temple of Śiva. Nandī went there along with that noble-souled one. Thereafter, what was done by that wicked one the previous day was seen.

Nandī performed the worship elaborately with different kinds of gems for the requisite things. The five *Upacāras* (modes of service in the course of the worship) and recitation of Rudra hymns eleven times while bathing the god were duly performed.

He eulogized Giriśa with various hymns and prayers in the company of brāhmaṇas. Two *Yāmas* (i.e. six hours) were thus spent by Nandī engaged in eulogy.

141. Indeed, at that time, there arrived (the Kirāta called) Mahākāla who was of the same form (as before). He was extremely powerful, very hideous and dreadful like the god of Death. He was valorous and armed with a bow in his hand.

142. On seeing him Nandī was excessively frightened and he cried. The priest too was suddenly struck with fear.

143. Everything was done by the Kirāta scrupulously as before. With the forepart of his foot he kicked aside the (previous) worship by Nandī and offered leaves of *Bilva* (instead).

144. The bathing rite was performed by means of the mouthful of water. The *Naivedya* (food offering) was the piece of flesh. Thus the Kirāta offered everything to Śiva.

145-147. He prostrated himself on the ground like a staff of wood. Then he rose up and went to his abode. On seeing that extremely wonderful incident, he (Nandī) thought about it for a long time. Along with the priest, Nandī was agitated in his mind as he pondered over this. Many brāhmaṇas, expounders of the Vedas, were invited by him. He recounted to them everything performed by the Kirāta and asked them: "What should be done, O brāhmaṇas? Let everything be explained accurately."

148. All of them met together and ascertained the matter from the point of Dharma Śāstra. Then, all those brāhmaṇas spoke to Nandin who was extremely frightened and suspicious:

149. "This obstacle that has sprung up cannot be warded off even by Devas. Hence, O excellent vaiśya, bring that *Liṅga* to your own abode."

150-151. He honoured their suggestion saying, "So be it". Then Nandī dug out that *Śivaliṅga*, brought it to his own house and consecrated it duly after placing it on a golden pedestal rendered splendid by means of the nine precious stones. He then performed the *Pūjā* with various kinds of rites and articles of worship.

152. The next day the Kirāta came to the temple of Śiva and on glancing about could not see the *Liṅga* of Īśa.

153-157. Breaking his silence suddenly he shouted loudly and spoke thus: "O Śaṁbhu, where have you gone? Reveal yourself to me now. If you are not seen now, I will give up my body. O Śaṁbhu, O lord of the universe, O destroyer of Tripura, O Rudra, O Mahādeva, reveal your form yourself."

Thus, by means of sweet words of apparent rebuke Sadāśiva was disrespected by the Kirāta. Then that heroic forester tore up his belly with his nails. Stroking his arms he said angrily, "O Śaṁbhu, reveal yourself. Where will you go abandoning me?"

158. After scolding thus, the Kirāta cut the flesh all round and took out the intestines. With his hand he threw them suddenly into that pit.

159-161. He steadied his heart and took bath in that lake. Similarly he brought water and *Bilva* leaves hurriedly. He worshipped the lord duly and prostrated on the ground stretching himself like a stick of wood. Thereafter the Kirāta remained there in the presence of Śiva engaged in meditation. Thereupon, Rudra surrounded by Pramathas, revealed himself to him.

162. The moon-crested lord Rudra who was white like camphor and who was refulgent with matted hair, grasped him by the hand and assuaged him consolingly.

163. "O heroic one of great intellect, you are my devotee. Choose a boon conducive to your own welfare. O highly intelligent one, (speak) whatever is intensely desired by you."

164. On being addressed thus by Rudra, Mahākāla became joyous. Endowed with great devotion, he fell down on the ground like a stick of wood.

165-167. Then he spoke to Rudra: "I request for the boon. O Rudra, there is no doubt about (the fact) that I am your slave. You are my lord and master. Realizing this, grant me devotion unto you in every birth. You are my mother. You are my father too. You are my kinsman and friend. You are the preceptor. You are the great *Mantra*. You are always worthy of being known through the *Mantras*. Hence in the three worlds there is nothing else than you."

168. On hearing these words of the Kirāta, devoid of desire, Śiva granted him the position of the chief of his attendants and the post of his doorkeeper.

169-173. Then the three worlds were filled with the sound of *Ḍamaru* (a kind of drum), with the booming sound of the big drum *Bherī* and the sound of conchs. Then thousands of *Dun-*

dubhis and *Paṭahas* (different kinds of drums) were sounded. On hearing that sound Nandī was surprised. He hurried to the place in the penance grove where Śiva was present surrounded by Pramathas. The Kirāta too was seen exactly like that by Nandī. Nandī who was surprised much, spoke these words humbly. He became desirous of eulogizing the Kirāta with great intentness: "Śaṁbhu was brought here by you. O scorcher of enemies, you are (his real) devotee. I am your devotee and have come here. Mention about me to Śaṅkara."

174. On hearing his words, the Kirāta grasped Nandī by the hand and hurriedly approached Śaṅkara.

175. Lord Rudra laughingly spoke these words to the Kirāta: "Who is this person brought by you in the presence of the Gaṇas?"

176. Śaṅkara, the benefactor of all the worlds, was then informed by the Kirāta:

Kirāta said:

This is your devotee, O lord. He is always engaged in your worship.

177-178. Everyday you have been worshipped by him with gems and rubies, flowers of various kinds, with his own life as well as wealth. There is no doubt about this. Hence know that he is my friend, Nandin, O lord favourably disposed towards your devotees.

Mahādeva said:

179. I do not know, O highly fortunate one, Nandī, the vaiśya mentioned (by you), (but) O Mahākāla of great intellect, (I shall accept him) because you are my devotee as well as friend.

180. Those who are free from fraud, and are of lofty mind, are dear devotees of mine. They are excellent men.

181. He is your devotee and hence he is a dearer friend to me.

Thus both of them were accepted by Śaṁbhu as his attendants.

182. Then many aerial chariots of great lustre arrived there. That excellent vaiśya was redeemed by that excellent Kirāta of great refulgence.

183. By means of aerial chariots of great speed both of them arrived at Mount Kailāsa. They attained the state of having the same form as that of the noble-souled Īśvara.

184. Waving of the light was performed by Girijā to both of them along with Śiva. Thereupon, the goddess with a graceful gait of an elephant laughingly said to Śiva:

185-188. "Just as you are, so also are these, undoubtedly in form as well as mode of walking. They are well-honoured with smiles and friendliness. Hitherto you alone had been served by me, no doubt."

On hearing the words of the goddess, the Kirāta and the vaiśya turned their faces aside immediately even as Śaṅkara was observing. (They said:) "We are to be sympathized by you alone, O three-eyed lord. We shall perpetually stand at your door. Obeisance, obeisance to you."

189. Knowing their intention, Bhava laughingly said: "On account of your great devotion may your desire be fulfilled."

190. Ever since then both of them became the gatekeepers. They stood at the doorway of Śiva, O brāhmaṇas. They had the vision of Śiva during midday.

191. One was Nandī and the other Mahākāla. Both of them were lovers of Śiva. Both of them joyously talked to Sadāśiva who was one.

192-193. Mahādeva talked to them lifting up one of his fingers. Similarly Nandī said lifting up two of his fingers. Thus with the gestures and signs they stand at the entrance to the abode of the noble-souled (lord) Śaṅkara. O highly fortunate sages, listen.

194-197. Formerly the unlimited pious rites of Śiva had been proclaimed by Śailāda out of sympathy, O brāhmaṇas, for evil-minded living beings, sinners, impious people, blind ones, dumb beings, lame ones, those of ignoble births, evil-minded ones, cāṇḍālas, and other persons whatever their nature may be. If they are endowed with devotion to Śiva, they go to the presence of the trident-bearing lord of Devas. Those learned men who worship a *Liṅga* made of sand, go to Rudraloka undoubtedly.

CHAPTER SIX

Curse to Brahmā and Others

The sages enquired:

1. How did the pre-eminence of *Liṅga*, exclusive of Śiva, come to be established? O highly fortunate sage, let this be narrated to us who are eagerly desirous of learning it.

Lomaśa said:

2-4. Lord Śaṁbhu wandered about in the forest Dāruvana for the sake of begging alms.[1] The sole lord of the worlds with quarters for his garments (i.e. naked), having the cluster of his matted hair loosened, that lord who can be understood only through Vedānta (i.e. Upaniṣads), the great lord, the greatest among leading Yogins, the sole supporter of the group of worlds is greater than the greatest. He is the great lord of the worlds with exalted dignity. That noble-souled Īśvara assumed the form of a mendicant; begged for alms in the Dāruvana forest.

5. At midday the sages, O brāhmaṇas, went to the sacred places (for bath) from their hermitages. At that very time, all the wives of those sages came there.

6-8. On seeing Śaṁbhu they spoke to one another, "Who is this personage of uncommon appearance, who has come here in the form of a mendicant? We along with our friends shall give him alms." Saying, "So be it", they went home and joyously brought various kinds of food as alms. They were fine and delicate. They offered everything in accordance with their capacity but with due honour and gentle behaviour. The alms begged for by the Trident-bearing Lord of Devas were (duly given to him).

9-12. One of the ladies who was struck with wonder asked Śaṁbhu who endeared himself very much to her: "Who are you, O excessively intelligent one? Why have you come here as a mendicant? This is the sacred hermitage of sages. Why do you

1. The story of Śiva's visit to Dāruvana and dropping of his Phallus when cursed by sages, is found in other Purāṇas also (e.g. KP II.3.8-39, BdP I.ii. 27). The peculiar behaviour of Śiva is called *Dvāra* in *Pāśupata Sūtras*.

not sit here in our hermitage?" On being asked thus by her, Śaṁbhu said laughingly:

"I am Īśvara, O lady with excellent tresses; I have come to this holy place." On hearing the words of Īśvara (Śiva) the wife of the sage asked him:

"(You say that) you are Īśvara (Śiva), O gentle Sir, of exalted fortune. You are the lord of the Kailāsa mountain. But, O lord, how does it happen that you are begging for alms alone and single?"

13-14. On being asked thus by her, Śaṁbhu said to her once again these words: "I am bereaved of Dākṣāyaṇī. Hence I wander about nude for the purpose of begging alms, O lady of excellent hips. I am free from any wish or desire or any expectation of advantage from anybody. O beautiful lady, without Satī all the women in the world do not at all appeal to me. I am speaking the truth to you, O lady of large eyes."

15-16. On hearing the words spoken by him, the lotus-eyed lady said: "There is no doubt that women really accord pleasure by their touch unto man. Such pleasurable women, O Śaṁbhu, have been eschewed by a learned man like you!"

17-21. In this manner all young women gathered together at the place where Śaṅkara was (standing). The alms-bowl of Śaṁbhu was filled with cooked food of very good quality. Four types of foodstuffs with all the six tastes filled his bowl.

When Śaṁbhu was desirous of returning to the Kailāsa mountain, all those wives of brāhmaṇas joyously followed him forsaking their domestic duties. With their minds attached to him, they walked on and on (after him).

When all those wives (of sages) had left thus, the excellent sages reached their hermitages and found them empty and vacant. They spoke to one another, "Where have all these women (our wives) gone? We do not know by what damned fellow they have been abducted." Pondering and deliberating thus they searched here and there.

22. Thereupon they saw that they had been following Śiva. On seeing Śiva, the sages angrily closed in upon him.

23. Standing in front of Śiva, all of them said with impetuosity, "What has been done by you, O Śaṁbhu (who profess to be)

detached and noble-souled? You are no doubt the kidnapper of the wives of others, i.e. of us, the sages."

24. Although rebuked thus, Śiva silently went on towards his mountain. Then that immutable Mahādeva was overtaken by the sages. (They then cursed him thus:) "Since you are the abductor of (our) wives, be instantaneously a eunuch."

25. Thus cursed by the sages, his penis fell down on the ground. As soon as it reached the ground, it became very large immediately and it increased in size (enormously).

26-31. From beneath and above, the *Liṅga* covered the seven Pātālas in an instant. Then it pervaded the entire earth and enveloped the firmament. All the heavens were covered. Then it rose beyond the heavens. There was no earth, no quarters, neither water nor fire, neither wind nor ether, neither Cosmic Ego (*Ahṁkāra*) nor the Great Principle (*Mahat*), neither the Unmanifest One (*Avyakta*) nor the Time and no great Primordial Matter (*Prakṛti*). There was no dualistic division. Everything became merged in an instant. Since the entire universe became *Līna* (merged) in that *Liṅga* of the great Ātman (it came to be called so).

Learned men say that it is called *Liṅga* because of *Layana* (merging of the universe). On seeing such a *Liṅga* rising further and further, the celestial sages, Brahmā, Indra, Viṣṇu, Vāyu, Agni and the Guardians of the Quarters and the serpents were filled with surprise in their minds. They spoke to one another:

32. "What is the length (of this *Liṅga*)? What is its girth? Where is its top? Where is its pedestal?" All the Suras who were worried with thoughts like these then said to Viṣṇu:

Devas said:

33. Its root must be seen by you, O Viṣṇu. O lotus-born Brahmā, its head must be seen by you.[1] Then you can justifiably be called protectors.

1. This legend explains why the leaf of Ketakī is not used in Śiva's worship and why god Brahmā is not generally worshipped. This legend has no basis in *Mahābhārata* and Vālmīki's *Rāmāyaṇa*. Here gods requested Viṣṇu to trace the root of the *Liṅga* as he was a Varāha and due to Brahmā's

34. Viṣṇu and the Lotus-born god Brahmā both of whom were (gods) of exalted fortune, heard this. Viṣṇu went to the nether worlds and Brahmā went to heaven.

35. When he reached heaven, Brahmā eagerly looked (everywhere) but that clever (lord) did not see the top of that *Liṅga*.

36. So the Lotus-born (Lord) returned along the path he had gone and reached the top of Meru. There he was seen by Surabhi (Divine Cow).

37. She was standing in the shade of a *Ketakī* plant and spoke to him in sweet words. On hearing her words, the grandfather of all the worlds spoke laughingly to Surabhi in deceptive words:

38-41. "An extraordinarily wonderful *Liṅga* which has pervaded the entire region of the three worlds was seen; I was deputed by Devas to see its top. I am extremely worried as to what I should report in the presence of Devas as the top of that all-pervading *Liṅga* of the noble-souled (lord) was not seen. Though it is untrue, you should tell Devas that the top of the *Liṅga* has been seen. If all the groups of Devas like Indra and others were to ask you, 'Have you witnessed?', you shall say quickly, 'In this matter, O Devas, there are witnesses'. In this matter, O lady of good holy rites, you do be my witness along with the *Ketakī* flower."

42-43. Accepting the suggestion of Brahmā Parameṣṭhin with her head (bent down respectfully), Surabhi in the company of the *Ketakī* flower honoured it. Arriving thus in front of Devas, Brahmā spoke:

Brahmā said:

44. I have seen the wonderful top of the *Liṅga*, O Devas. It was duly worshipped by me with *Ketakī* petals. It is large, soft and spotlessly pure.

45. It is beautiful and fascinating. It is wonderfully lustrous and excessively refulgent.

---

association with swans, the latter was sent to explore the top. In other Purāṇas we are told that Śiva appeared in the form of a column of fire to resolve the conflict between Brahmā and Viṣṇu about personal superiority and showed them that he was superior to them both.

46. Such a *Liṅga* was seen by me. Like that I have not seen anything else anywhere else.

On hearing the words of Brahmā, Devas were struck with wonder.

47-52. Even as the groups of Devas beginning with Indra stood thus filled with wonder, Viṣṇu, the lord of all, the bestower of spiritual illumination, came there from Pātāla. Immediately he reported to all: "(Although) I was eager to see its end, it (the end of the *Liṅga*) has not been seen by me. As I was moving further from Pātāla, I was struck with great wonder. I went through Atala, Sutala, Nitala, Rasātala, Pātāla and Tala and Talātala. Everything appeared empty and void. Even the most vacant place of all was examined well. But it has neither root nor middle nor top. Mahādeva by whom this universe is sustained is the one in the form of *Liṅga*. It was due to his grace that you and the sages were born."

53. On hearing his words Suras and sages honoured him. Then Viṣṇu spoke thus laughingly to Brahmā:

54. "If, O Brahmā, the top has been truly seen by you, who are the witnesses you have had in this matter?"

55-58. On hearing the words of Viṣṇu, Brahmā, the grandfather of the worlds, hurriedly said, "*Ketakī* and Surabhi. O Devas, these two may be known as my eye-witnesses." On hearing the words of Brahmā, all Devas hurriedly sent for Surabhi along with *Ketakī*. The two instantaneously came there for the work of Brahmā.

Thereafter Surabhi was asked by Devas beginning with Indra. She said thus together with *Ketakī*: "Indeed, O Devas, The top of the *Liṅga* was seen by Brahmā and worshipped with the petals of *Ketakī*."

59-60. Even as all of them listened, an ethereal voice was heard from the sky: "Understand, O gods, that what is deposed by Surabhi and *Ketakī* is a false statement. Its top has not been seen (by Brahmā)."

61. Then all Devas along with Indra and Viṣṇu angrily cursed Surabhi who was intent to utter falsehood:

62. "O splendid one, today a lie has been thus uttered by

your mouth. Let your mouth be unholy and impure. Let it be excluded from all religious rites.

63. Even though fragrant, O *Ketakī*, you shall be unsuitable for the worship of Śiva. There is no doubt about it, O good lady, that you have lied."

64-68. Then the ethereal voice cursed Brahmā: "O stupid one, why has falsehood been uttered childishly by you? (Why have you done this) along with Bhṛgu, the sages and the priest? Hence you will never be worthy of worship. You will suffer from pain. The sages (who ought to be) virtuous will be excluded from truthful statements. They will be deluded, engaged in disputes, jealous and unaware of true knowledge. They will be beggars and worthy of being cut to pieces. They will perpetually ruin their own knowledge. They will boast of themselves. They will be stubborn and will censure one another."

Thus Devas beginning with Brahmā, as well as the sages were cursed. All of them, cursed by Śiva sought refuge in *Liṅga*.

CHAPTER SEVEN

Worship of the Liṅga

Lomaśa said:

1. Then all those Suras and even the sages became frightened. Brahmā and others who became perturbed and distressed on account of their knowledge (of their mistake) eulogized the *Liṅga* of Lord Śiva.

Brahmā said:

2. You who have assumed the *Liṅga* form, are of great miraculous power. You who are of the form of the Supreme Soul, are knowable (only) through Vedānta (Upaniṣads). It is by you who is ever engrossed in Bliss that the universe which is rooted in you, has been created.

3. You are the witness unto all the worlds. You are the

annihilator of all. You are the protector, O Mahādeva. You are Bhairava, O lord of universe.

4. This unit of the three worlds has been pervaded by you in the form of *Liṅga.* O lord, we are insignificant creatures whose minds are deluded by *Māyā.*

5. We, viz. I, Suras, Asuras, all the Yakṣas, Gandharvas and Rākṣasas, serpents, Piśācas and these Vidyādharas, are all deluded.

6-7. You are the creator of the creators of the universe. You are indeed the lord and ruler of the universe. You, the Supreme Person, are (both) the creator and annihilator of the universe.

Protect everything belonging to us. O Mahādeva. Obeisance to you, O god of Devas.

Thus the great lord in the form of *Liṅga* was eulogized by Brahmā.

8. The sages who were desirous of eulogizing Maheśvara, the sinless one, eulogized with very great eagerness and respect by means of excellent words recorded in the Vedas.

The sages said:

9. We are all ignorant. On account of lust, we do not recognise your status. Indeed you are the Soul, the Supreme Soul. You are the *Prakṛti*, the evolver (of everything).

10. You are our mother. You alone are our father. You are our kinsman. You alone are our friend. You alone are Īśvara. You are conversant with the Vedas. You are always meditated upon by persons of great magnanimity.

11. You are the immanent Soul of all living beings, like flame of all fuel. Since everything takes its origin from you, you are forever *Sarva.*

12. The lord is called Śaṁbhu because *Śaṁ* (happiness) takes its origin from him.

13. All of us, Devas and others (such as) sages, celestial Gandharvas, Vidyādharas, great serpents have resorted to your lotus-like feet.

14. Hence, with mercifulness, O Śaṁbhu, O lord of the universe, protect us.

Mahādeva said:

15. Listen to my word now. Let it be carried out immediately. May all of you pray to Viṣṇu,[1] O ascetics, with immediate effect.

16. On hearing the word of the noble-souled Śaṅkara, all those Suras bowed down to Viṣṇu and eulogized him.

Devas said:

17. Vidyādharas, groups of Suras, all the sages, everyone has been saved by you today, O sole kinsman of the universe. In that manner, O merciful one, O lord of the three worlds, O lord of the universe, O abode of the universe, protect all the people.

18-19. Lord Viṣṇu laughed loudly and spoke these words then: "Formerly you were oppressed by Daityas and protected by me. But today a great danger of everlasting nature has arisen from this *Liṅga*. It is not possible for me to protect you, O Suras, from the danger from this *Liṅga*."

20. On being told thus by Viṣṇu, Devas became worried. Thereupon an ethereal voice spoke thus, consoling all the Suras:

21. "O Janārdana, choose this *Liṅga* for worship. Becoming a mass of refulgence, O mighty one, protect the mobile and immobile beings."

Saying "so be it" and honouring it, Lord Vīrabhadra worshipped it.[2]

22. At that time, the noble-souled Vīrabhadra, having the moon for his crest and engaged in carrying out the orders of Śiva, was worshipped by the groups of Suras beginning with Brahmā, collectively. Vīrabhadra was a favourite of Śiva and was on a par with Rudra in the three worlds.

23-24. Then Vīrabhadra was absorbed in worshipping the *Liṅga*. It (the *Liṅga*) had the same form wherefrom the entire universe takes it origin, derives sustenance and gets merged with it. The excellent ones among those who are the knowers of the

1. This is how Purāṇas tried to bring together followers of Śaivism and Vaiṣṇavism.

2. Or, was Vīrabhadra worshipped by them? The next verse shows that Vīrabhadra was worshipped by Suras.

Reality call it *Liṅga*, because of its being a place of rest (to the absorbed).

25. The *Liṅga* became pervaded by the spheres of the Cosmic Eggs. It was embellished with *Rudrākṣas*. It grew so large that it could not be surpassed by anyone.

26-27. Then all Devas and sages of great lustre eulogized the great *Liṅga* by means of the Vedic words (*Mantras*) separately:

"O lord, you are minuter than the atom. So also you are greater than the greatest. Hence, O lord Śiva, you must make such arrangements as to make the worship of the *Liṅga* easy for everyone."

28-35. At that time itself, many types of *Liṅgas* were evolved by Sarva (Śiva)[1], viz. the *Brahmeśvara Liṅga* in the world called Satya (god Brahmā's region), *Sadāśiva Liṅga* in Vaikuṇṭha, a well-established *Liṅga* named *Amareśvara* in Amarāvatī (Indra's capital), *Varuṇeśvara Liṅga* in the city of Varuṇa, Lord *Kāleśvara* in the city of Yama, *Nairṛteśvara Liṅga* in the city of Nirṛti, *Pavaneśvara Liṅga* in the city of Vāyu, in the Mṛtyuloka[2] *Kedāra Liṅga* as well as *Amareśvara, Oṁkāra Liṅga* as well as *Mahākāla* in the Narmadā (region), Lord *Viśveśvara* in Kāśī, *Laliteśvara* in Prayāga, *Triyaṁbaka* in Brahmagiri (Nasik District) as well as *Bhadreśvara* in Kali, *Drākṣārāmeśvara' Liṅga* in the place of the Union of Gaṅgā with ocean, the *Liṅga* remembered as *Someśvara* in Saurāṣṭra, *Sarveśvara Liṅga* on the Vindhya, *Śikhareśvara Liṅga* on Śrīśaila, *Mallālanātha*[3] (?) in Kānti, *Siṁhanātha* in Siṅgala (Sīṁhala), so also many *Liṅgas* such as *Virūpākṣa Liṅga, Koṭiśaṅkara, Tripurāntaka, Bhīmeśa, Amareśvara, Bhogeśvara* and *Hāṭakeśvara* in Pātāla. These and many other *Liṅgas* of this sort were installed in all the three worlds by Devas for helping the entire universe.

1. The list of *Liṅgas* and their locations shows that the *Liṅga* is worshipped in the three worlds and by great gods like Brahmā, Viṣṇu, Indra and others.

2. This list covers most of the *Jyotirliṅgas* in India.

3. G.M. (Guru Maṇḍala edition of SkP) reads instead: *kāmadaṁ mallināthaṁ* 'Mallinātha who confers desired objects'.

36. And thus all the three worlds became full of great *Liṅgas*. Similarly, gods created *Vīrabhadrāṁśas* (portions of Vīrabhadra) for worship.

37. There were twenty-eight *Saṁskāras* (consecratory rites) there in the process of worship of *Liṅga*. They were mentioned by Śaṅkara himself.

38-41. There are eternal *Śivadharmas* mentioned by Rudra where Vīrabhadra, Rudra and other Gurus (preceptors) are remembered. The sons of Gurus also have become famous in the three worlds as Gurus. Only Nandī knows factually the greatness of *Liṅga*. So also lord Skanda and those others who bear his names.

All the *Śivadharmas* have been glorified as mentioned by Nandī, the son of Śilāda. Many wonderful persons of exalted nature have been glorified as bearers of *Liṅgas*.[1]

Liṅga is held above a dead body by the ancient people.

42. Living with *Liṅga* and dying with *Liṅga*—these virtuous rites have been established by Śailāda (Nandin).

43-45. The religion of the Pāśupata established by Skanda is the most excellent one. The five-syllabled Mantra (*Na-maḥ-Śi-vā-ya*) is the purest. Then comes the *Prāsādī* (*Oṁkāra*) *Mantra*. The six-syllabled Mantra (*Oṁ, na-maḥ-Śi-vā-ya*) is the illuminator of the *Praṇava*.[2]

From Skanda it was acquired by the noble-souled Agastya. Afterwards due to the difference in the preceptors, many Āgamas were composed.

46. Of what avail is much talk? Those who utter the two

---

1. This is not a reference to the Liṅgāyata cult. Inscriptions from North Karnatak and (western) Āndhra testify to the existence of a Śaiva cult (*Siṁha Pariṣad*) of Kashmira Brahmins who followed *Lakulāgama*. They worshipped Śiva in the *Liṅga*-form and wore *Liṅga* on their persons. They received royal grants for conducting *Pāṭhaśālās* to teach Veda, Vedānta, Yoga. Their temples and Maṭhas along with educational institutes were taken over by Liṅgāyatas in the 13th century. (Vide S.C. Nandimath, *A Hand Book of Vīraśaivism*, Dharwar 1942.) I have dealt with this problem in my work *Śaiva Philosophy* which is being published by MEP (Marathi Encyclopaedia of Philosophy) Council, Pune. (Translator)

2. In *Mantra Śāstra*, *Oṁkāra Bīja* is called *Prāsāda*.

syllables *Śi-va* everyday are Rudras themselves.[1] There is no doubt in this matter.

47. Those who follow the path of good people are all Purāntakas (Śiva). They should be known as heroes of Maheśvara.[2] They destroy the sins of men.

48. Those who perform rites of devotion incidentally, as a consequence of something else, by chance or as an act of faith, attain the goal of the good.

49. Listen. I shall narrate an old legend in this connection. Sweeping was performed formerly by a female bird in a temple of Śiva.

50. It had come (into the temple) for the sake of food. The *Naivedya* was offered by someone. When it fluttered its wings, the dust particles happened to be swept away.

51. As a result of that meritorious deed, she went to the excellent heaven. After enjoying the heavenly pleasures, she came back to the fierce world once again.

52. She was born as the daughter of the king of Kāśī. She became famous by the name Sundarī. Thanks to the previous experience, that girl of auspicious features became a great chaste lady.

53. Early in the morning, the lady of slender limbs was always present at the doorway of the temple of Śiva. With great devotion she used to sweep the premises.

54. The gentle princess, Sundarī, did everything herself. On seeing her in that activity, Uddālaka, the sage, enquired:

55-56. "O girl of splendid features, you are delicate in body. Why do you sweep yourself, O girl of bright smiles? O gentle lady, you have in front of you many men and women servants. At your bidding they will do all the sweeping work etc."

57. On hearing those words of the sage, she laughingly said thus:

58-60a. "The men and women who render service to Śiva, those who are prompted by devotion to Śiva, do go to the

1. The importance of uttering God's name has been emphasized all over India by Saints and Ācāryas even today.

2. *Vīrā Māheśvarāḥ*. Is the term (name of a sect) 'Vīra-Śaiva' derived from this?

world of Śiva. The sweeping must be done by one's own hands. One should go to the temple on one's own foot. Hence, sweeping is done by me unweariedly. I do not know anything else, excepting the single act of sweeping."[1]

60b-62. On hearing her words, the sage pondered: 'Who is she? What has been done by her previously? By whose favour (did she get all these)?' Then everything was understood by the sage through the eye of (the power of his) spiritual knowledge.

63. Struck with wonder, he became silent. After knowing it, he became surprised. Thinking about the power of Śiva, Uddālaka, the most excellent among the learned ones, attained the greatest enlightenment. He became calm and quiescent.

CHAPTER EIGHT

The Story of a Thief: Incarnation of Rāma

Lomaśa said:

1-3. O Brāhmaṇas, once there was a great sinner.[2] He was a thief. He was excommunicated from all religious rites. He was a Brāhmaṇa-slayer, a drink-addict and a thief of gold. He sought the company of excellent women in an illicit way. He was stupid and slow and always engaged in gambling along with gamblers and cunning fellows. Once while playing, he lost wonderfully (large amount). Smashed and hit by rogues and gamblers, he did not speak anything.

4-5. Though he was harassed and tormented, he kept quiet. Then that great sinner was asked thus by them: "You have lost this much wealth in the game of dice. Are you going to give it or not? O wicked fellow, let this be told immediately and

1. The fruit of rendering slightest service to Śiva, even unknowingly, is highly efficacious. The Purāṇa abounds in such legends.

2. Lord Śiva is extremely kind even to wicked robbers. The superb magnanimity of Śiva is illustrated in this story in which a gambler-thief is elevated as his Gaṇa by Śiva.

precisely." Then he said: "What has been lost by me, I shall give at night."

6. Thanks to that statement, he was released by them. Those gamblers and rogues then went away. Then at mid-night he went to the temple of Śiva.

7. Climbing on to the head of Śaṁbhu, he attempted to take the bell. At that time on the peak of Kailāsa, Śaṁbhu said to his servants:

8. "What has been done by this fellow today is far superior to anything done by anyone on the earth. He is the most excellent one among all my devotees, hence he is my great favourite."

9. After saying this, he commanded the Gaṇas beginning with Vīrabhadra to bring him (the thief-gambler). They hurriedly started from Kailāsa, the favourite (resort) of Śiva.

10. The three worlds were filled with the sound of *Ḍamarus* by all of them. On seeing them, the evil-minded thief got down suddenly from the top of the *Liṅga* and took to his heels immediately.

11-14. On seeing him fleeing, Vīrabhadra called him: "Whom do you fear, O stupid fellow? Maheśvara, the lord of Devas, has been pleased with you, as he is very liberal-minded."

After saying thus and placing him in the aerial chariot, he came to Kailāsa. The thief was made an attendant by that noble-souled (lord).

Hence, devotion to Śiva must be preserved and cultivated by all embodied beings. Even animals will be worthy of being worshipped thereby. What to say of men on the earth?

15-16. The followers of *Tarka-śāstra* are engaged in abstract reasoning and arguments.[1] So are the followers of the *Mīmāṁsā* School. They go on arguing and disputing among themselves. And there are others who deliberate on and discuss about the existence, nature etc. of the Soul, but never reach any unanimity, or reconciliation of (their) differences. They are excluded from the worship of Śiva. Without Śiva, of what significance are they, by whom only arguments are forwarded?

17. Of what avail is much talk? All mobile and immobile beings, all animals too, are born bearing the *Liṅga*.

1. Devotion to God is superior to learning. This teaching has been inculcated by all Indian saints since the days of this Purāṇa.

18. Just as the *Liṅga* is placed (and consecrated) in conjunction with the *Piṇḍī* (globular solid pedestal), so also men are endowed with *Liṅgas* and women are *Piṇḍīs*.

19. The entire universe consisting of the mobile and immobile beings is endowed with (the union of) Śiva and Śakti. Those are foolish fellows who, out of delusion, eschew devotion to such Śiva and worship others.

20. Their Dharma is extremely insignificant, perishable and momentary. He who is Viṣṇu should be known as Śiva. He who is Śiva is Viṣṇu alone.[1]

21. The pedestal is the form of Viṣṇu and Maheśvara is in the form of *Liṅga*. Hence the worship of *Liṅga*, O Brāhmaṇas, is excellent for everyone.

22. Brahmā worships a Ruby-*Liṅga* always, Indra worships a *Liṅga* made of gems and Candra (the Moon-god) one of pearls.

23. Bhānu (the Sun-god) always worships a splendid copper (-coloured) *Liṅga*. Kubera worships a golden *Liṅga* and Varuṇa a *Liṅga* red in colour.

24. Yama worships a sapphire *Liṅga*, Nairṛta worships a silver *Liṅga*, Pavana (Wind-god) always worships a saffron *Liṅga* of the lord.

25. Thus, all Guardians of the Quarters including Indra have been characterised as worshippers of *Liṅga*. So are all (persons) in the nether world and also Gandharvas and Kinnaras.

26-27. Among Daityas, O Brāhmaṇas, there are certain devotees of Viṣṇu, the chief of whom was Prahlāda.[2] So also among Rākṣasas, those having Vibhīṣaṇa as their leader. So also (were) Bali, Namuci, Hiraṇyakaśipu, Vṛṣaparvan, Vṛṣa, Saṁhrāda and Bāṇa.

28. These and many others who were the disciples of the intelligent Śukra were engaged in worshipping Śiva. All these Daityas and Dānavas (were devotees of Śiva).

---

1. The identity of Śiva and Viṣṇu is repeated *ad nauseam*. The pedestal which was stated as Śakti above in v. 19, is now stated to be Viṣṇu and the *Liṅga* is Śiva. Thus Śiva and Viṣṇu become identical and therefore Vaiṣṇavas are advised not to express aversion to Śiva.

2. As Viṣṇu and Śiva are united in the *Liṅga* and its pedestal, worship of Śiva-*Liṅga* is automatically the worship of Viṣṇu who is there as the pedestal. So the Vaiṣṇavas need not entertain any aversion to *Liṅga*-worship.

29-32. All the following were Rākṣasas and they were always engaged in the worship of Śiva. They were: Heti, Praheti, Saṁyāti, Vighasa, Praghasa, Vidyujjihva, Tīkṣṇadaṁṣṭra, Dhūmrākṣa of terrible valour, Mālī, Sumālī and the extremely terrible Mālyavān, Vidyutkeśa, Taḍijjihva, Rāvaṇa of great strength, the invincible Kuṁbhakarṇa and Vegadarśī of great valour. These were great Rākṣasas, who were always engaged in worshipping Śiva. After worshipping the *Liṅga* formerly, they had always attained *Siddhi.*

33. A severe penance unbearable to all was performed by Rāvaṇa. Then Mahādeva, the lord of penance, became much pleased.

34-35. He granted him boons very difficult to be achieved by all others. Wisdom with perfect knowledge was obtained by him from Sadāśiva. He further obtained (invinicibility) in battle and twice the number of heads (as those of god Śiva), for Mahādeva had only five faces, whereas Rāvaṇa had ten faces.

36. Thanks to the grace of Maheśa, that powerful (Rākṣasa) defeated Devas, sages and manes by means of his penance and became superior to all.

37. He was made the great king and ruler of Trikūṭa by Maheśa. He occupied the greatest and most excellent position (seat) among Rākṣasas.

38. It was for testing (the enduring capacity of) the sages that he harassed them. Violence towards the sages was indulged in, O Brāhmaṇas, by Rāvaṇa who was himself an ascetic, only because he wanted to test them.

39. Rāvaṇa who made the whole world cry and scream, became great and invincible. Thanks to the grace and favour of Śaṅkara, another creation was evolved by him.

40. The guardians of the worlds were conquered by that ascetic by means of his valour. Brahmā too was subdued by him only through great penance.

41. By becoming the nectar-rayed one, he conquered the Moon, O Brāhmaṇas. Through the power of burning, the Fire-god was conquered and Īśa (himself) was conquered by lifting up Kailāsa (mountain).

42. Indra was conquered by means of his *Aiśvarya* (power and prosperity). So also Viṣṇu, the omnipresent one. By wor-

shipping and propitiating the *Liṅga*, all the three worlds were controlled by him.

43. At that time, all the groups of Suras, with Brahmā and Viṣṇu as their leaders, gathered together on the top of Meru and began their deliberation and discussion:

44-45. "We have been tormented by Rāvaṇa through his penance, very difficult to be performed (by others). O Devas, let this wonderful story be listened to. On the mountain named Gokarṇa, worship of the *Liṅga* itself was performed by that noble-souled (hero). What could be known only through knowledge, what could be achieved only through knowledge, whatever great miracle was there, that which is very difficult to be surpassed by everyone—all these were done by Rāvaṇa alone.

46. He had adopted the greatest *vairāgya* (detachment) as well as liberal-midedness greater even than that (*vairāgya*). The feeling of *mamatā* (mineness) was eschewed by the noble-souled Rāvaṇa.

47. After a period of a thousand years, that (hero) of great arms cut one of his own head and offered it with his own hand, for the sake of worshipping the *Liṅga*.

48. Rāvaṇa's body short of one head stood in front of it in the vicinity. It was endowed with Yogic *dhāraṇā* (steady abstraction) and the greatest *samādhi* (concentration).

49. Fixing his attention deeply on the *Liṅga* after about a *kalā*, he cut off another head and worshipped Śiva with it. Such (performance of) worship was never done by any sage nor by anyone else.

50. Thus many heads were chopped off and offered by him in worshipping Śiva. Again and again he became a headless body. Then Śiva became a bestower of boons.

51. 'Formerly without being myself transformed into a *Piṇḍī*...[1] O descendant of Pulastya, choose boons as you please. I shall grant you the same.'

52-53. Then Śiva of greatest auspiciousness was requested by Rāvaṇa: 'If Your Lordship are pleased, the excellent boon should be given to me. I do not wish to seek any other boon. If you have merciful favour towards me, you should give me such a boon whereby I (always) resort to your feet.'

1. Some lines are missing in the text.

54. Then Rāvaṇa who made the world cry and scream was told by Sadāśiva: 'By my favour, you will obtain everything mentally desired by you.'

55-59. It was thus, O leading Suras, that everything was obtained by Rāvaṇa from Śiva. Hence this Rāvaṇa should be subdued by you all only through great penance. This is what I think."

On hearing the words of Acyuta, the groups of Devas beginning with Brahmā became anxious, because all of them had been addicted to sensual pleasures.

Brahmā was overpowered by sexual desire and he attempted sexual act with his own daughter. Indra was an adulterer. Candra (the Moon-god) defiled the bed of his Guru (preceptor Bṛhaspati). Yama has been avaricious and stingy. Sadāgati (the Wind-god) has been fickle. Pāvaka has been indiscriminate in eating anything and everything. The others among the groups of Devas (had similar defects). Hence, all these were incapable of conquering Rāvaṇa who had become very great by means of penance.

60. Śailāda was an elderly excellent Gaṇa of great splendour. He was intelligent, an expert in adopting the right course of action, highly powerful and very valorous.

61-62. He was a favourite of Śiva and was identical with Rudra. The noble-souled one asked all of them led by Indra, "Why have you all come here in great excitement? Let the whole thing be reported in detail."

On being asked by Nandī, all of them hurriedly said then:

Devas said:

63. All of us along with the sages have been conquered by Rāvaṇa. We have come to propitiate Śiva, the lord of the lords of the worlds.

64. Lord Nandī laughed and said to Brahmā: "Where are you? Where is auspicious Śaṁbhu? (There is a world of difference between you two.) By means of great penance, he should be seen seated in the middle of the heart. He cannot be seen today.

65. As long as the emotional attitudes are too many, the

objects of senses are plentiful and there is the feeling of mineness, so long Īśa is very difficult to be attained.

66. Śiva in the form of the *Liṅga* is easy of access to those noble-souled ones who have subdued the senses, are quiescent and have stabilized themselves in him. He is very difficult to be obtained by you all."

67. Then Brahmā and other Devas as well as the learned sages bowed down to Nandī and said:

"Why do you have the face of a monkey?[1] Tell us everything about it. Tell us about the power of the penance of Rāvaṇa."

Nandīśvara said:

68-70a. Kubera had been made by the noble-souled Śaṅkara the over-lord of wealth and assets. Rāvaṇa came here to see him, riding in his own vehicle. He was in a hurry. On seeing me, he said furiously: "Did Kubera come here? Was he seen by you here? Let this be told immediately."

70b-72. He was asked by me: "What have you to do with Dhanada (Kubera) today?"

Then Rāvaṇa of great splendour, who made the world scream, said: "At the outset he (Kubera) had been indifferent towards me. He did not care for me. Addicted to sensual pleasures, as he is, he has been highly arrogant. He began to teach me saying, 'O lord, it should not be done like this. Just as I am endowed with glory and splendour, just as I am rich and strong, so also you do become, O fool. Do not get into delusion and stupidity.'

73. I have been made a fool and a deluded person by the noble-souled Kubera. On being turned out by me angrily, that Guhyaka (i.e. Kubera) performed penance.

74. Did that Kubera come, O Nandī, to your abode? Let that Kubera be handed over (to me). You need not hesitate in this matter."

75-79. On hearing the words of Rāvaṇa, I hurriedly replied: "You are a *Liṅgaka* (worshipper of *Liṅga*), an exalted one. I too

1. A story to explain why Viṣṇu incarnated in human form as Rāma and with his army of monkeys killed Rāvaṇa. This story, as in SkP, here, has no basis in *Vālmīki Rāmāyaṇa*.

am one like that. Knowing the equality between us both you are prattling in vain, O vicious one."

As he was told thus, he in his arrogance due to his might, asked me about my face in the same manner as I have been asked about my face by you noble-souled ones. The old story was recounted by me about the benefit of the holy rite of the worship of Śiva. "*Sārūpya* (having the same form as that of the lord) was granted by Śiva, but it was not accepted by me then. The face of a monkey was requested by me from Śaṁbhu. It was then granted to me kindly by Śiva who is by nature compassionate.

Those who are devoid of false prestige, those who are free from arrogance and those who have no property or possessions, should be known as favourites of Śaṁbhu. Others are excluded by Śiva."

80-86a. Then Rāvaṇa said to me: "On the strength of my penance, I had been sensible enough to request for ten heads."

At his derisive statement, Rāvaṇa who made the world scream, was cursed by me then:

"When an excellent man of great penance accompanied by those who have faces like this (monkey faces like mine) (comes to your city) keeping me at the head, he will undoubtedly kill you."

Thus, O Brahmā, Rāvaṇa who made the world scream, was cursed by me. Only the *Liṅga* was worshipped by Rāvaṇa without the noble-souled Viṣṇu stationed in the form of the pedestal, O excellent Suras. Hence, O excessively fortunate ones, Maheśvara, Mahādeva, the lord of Devas, in the form of Viṣṇu will carry out everything. May all of you pray to Viṣṇu lying within the cavity of the heart of everyone. Therefore, I shall be at the head of all Devas.

86b. On hearing the words of Nandī, all of them became joyous in their minds. They came to Vaikuṇṭha and began to eulogize Viṣṇu by means of (good) words.

Devas said:

87. Obeisance to you, the lord, O lord of Devas, O lord of the universe. This entire universe consisting of mobile and immobile beings has you for its basis and support.

88. This *Liṅga* has been held by you, O Viṣṇu, in the form of the *Piṇḍī* (globular pedestal). In the form of Mahāviṣṇu (the demons) Madhu and Kaiṭabha were killed by you.

89. Similarly, in the form of a tortoise, the Mandara mountain was held up and supported by you (at the time of churning of ocean for nectar). Assuming the form of a boar, Hiraṇyākṣa was killed by you.

90. Hiraṇyakaśipu, the Daitya, was killed by you by assuming the form of Nṛhari (Man-lion). Bali, the Daitya, was held and bound by you in the form of Vāmana (Dwarf).

91. The son of Kṛtavīrya (Sahasrārjuna) was killed by you after taking birth in the family of Bhṛgus. Hereafter too, O great Viṣṇu, protect us in the same manner.

92. It behoves you to protect us instantaneously from the fear of Rāvaṇa.

93. On being entreated thus by Devas, the lord Vāsudeva, the sanctifier (the creator) of all living beings, who is immanent in the universe, said to all those Suras:

94. "O Devas, let this important statement he heard. It is relevant to this occasion. With Śailādi (Nandin) as your head (leader), all of you immediately take incarnations in the form (bodies) of monkeys.

95. I shall become a human being enveloped by *Ajñāna* (Ignorance). I shall be born in Ayodhyā in the abode of Daśaratha for the attainment of your objectives. I am having *Brahmavidyā* (the knowledge of Brahman) as my assistant.

96. *Brahmavidyā* herself will be born in the abode of Janaka.[1] In fact, Rāvaṇa is (my) devotee as he is directly engaged in the meditation on Śiva.

97. When a man endowed with great penance desires for *Brahmavidyā*, he can be easily managed and won over by means of virtue."

98-100. After saying this, lord Viṣṇu, the highly auspicious one (vanished).

1. *Vālmīki Rāmāyaṇa* I.1. 27-30 compares Sītā to Devamāyā (*devamāyeva nirmitā*) but our text claims her as an incarnation of *Brahma-vidyā* as a suitable consort to Viṣṇu (the future Rāma). The important persons in the *Rāmāyaṇa* are incarnations of various gods.

Vālī was born of a part of Indra. Sugrīva was the son of the Sun. Jāmbavān, the leading *Ṛkṣa* (bear), was born of a part of Brahmā. Nandī, the son of Śilāda, who was a favourite follower of Śiva, incarnated as the great monkey Hanūmān for rendering assistance to Viṣṇu of unmeasured splendour.

101. The monkeys beginning with Mainda were all the excellent Suras. Thus, all Suras incarnated in a befitting manner.

102. Similarly, Viṣṇu was born as one who increased the delight of Kausalyā. He is called Rāma by learned men, because he pleased and gratified the entire universe.

103. Due to his devotion to Viṣṇu, Śeṣa descended on the earth by means of the power of his penance.

104. The mighty arms of Viṣṇu incarnated as the valorous (Princes) named Śatrughna and Bharata well-renowned in the three worlds.

105. She who was mentioned as *Brahmavidyā* by the expounders of the Vedas, incarnated as the daughter of the ruler of Mithilā for the fulfilment of the task of Suras. She was born from a furrow arising from the ploughing of the field with the ploughshare.[1]

106. Hence, she became famous as *Sītā*. She was the Science of Metaphysics (personified). Since she was born in Mithilā, she is called *Maithilī*.

107. She was born in the family of Janaka. Hence, she is well-known as *Janakātmajā* (*Jānakī*). This *Brahmavidyā*, the destroyer of sins, was formerly known as *Vedavatī*.

108-110. She was given by Janaka himself to Viṣṇu, the Supreme Soul. Along with her, the *Vidyā* (incarnated), Viṣṇu the greatest among the auspicious ones, the lord of Devas, the lord protector of the universe, became engaged in a severe penance. As he was desirous of defeating Rāvaṇa for the sake of the fulfilment of the task of Devas, the lotus-eyed Rāma stayed in forest (for the same purpose).

1. *Sītā* means 'a furrow'. In *Ṛgveda* IV.57.6, Sītā is invoked as a presiding deity of Agriculture. In *Vājasaneyī Saṁhitā* XII.69-72 *Sītā* (a furrow) is personified. Here, Sītā is said to be 'born' of the furrow while ploughing. She is called the incarnation of *Ānvīkṣikī* and *Brahmavidyā*.

111. Though the great incarnation of Śeṣa, (Lakṣmaṇa) performed an exceedingly difficult penance by means of his great *Śakti* (power), for the sake of the fulfilment of the task of Devas.

112-115. Śatrughna and Bharata too performed very great penance. Rāma who was thus endowed with the power of penance and was assisted and accompanied by those groups of Devas, killed Rāvaṇa along with his followers within six months. Killed by Viṣṇu by means of weapons, O sages of holy rites, he attained *Sārūpya* (having the same form as the god) of Śiva, along with his kinsmen and followers. By the grace of Śiva, he became (realized) the entire *Dvaitādvaita* (the essence of the philosophy of dualism and non-dualism).[1] Even the sages are deluded in the matter of discrimination between dualism and non-dualism. Men who are engaged in worshipping Śiva derive all those things.

116. Those who continuously worship Śiva in the form of *Liṅga*, whether they be women or śūdras or cāṇḍālas or other low-caste people, do attain Śiva, the destroyer of all miseries.

117-118. Even animals have attained the supreme lord. What then to say about human beings? The twice-born castes who have practised great penance observing the vow of celibacy and who have performed *Yajñas* for many years have attained (merely) *Svarga* (Heaven).

119-123. There are many *Yajñas*[2] such as *Jyotiṣṭoma, Vājapeya, Atirātra* and so on. These *Yajñas* undoubtedly do bestow heavenly pleasures on those who perform them. After enjoying the heavenly pleasures, when their merits become exhausted, those sacrificers come back to the mortal world. Having descended to the world, they are born in the different species with their

1. The Purāṇa-writer has respect for *Dvaitādvaita* philosophy. This school holds the reality of both *Dvaita* (dualism between man and God) and *Advaita* (non-dualism between them). Nimbārka (11th cent. A.D.) in his Com. *Vedānta-Pārijāta-Saurahha* on the *Brahma Sūtra* has advocated this doctrine. But this theory is older than the *Brahma Sūtra* itself, as we find such views of Auḍulomi, Āśmarathya quoted by the author of the *Brahma Sūtra*.

2. VV 119-128 emphasize the *Liṅga*-worship as superior to performance of sacrifices. Sacrifices lead to a temporary stay in *Svarga*, while the *Liṅga*-worship dispels *Māyā* and leads to *Mokṣa*.

intellect of the nature of the three *Guṇas* of *Sattva*, *Rajas* and *Tamas*. Thus, many souls wander about in cycles of birth and death. By chance or as good luck would have it, some of them serve Śiva.

124. Instantaneous removal of *Māyā* takes place in the case of men who are engaged in regular meditation on Śiva and who have restrained their minds and not otherwise.

125. When *Māyā* is dispelled, the three *Guṇas* perish. Then a person transcends the three *Guṇas* and becomes liberated thereby.

126-128. Hence, the worship of *Liṅga* should be thought of and pursued by all embodied beings. Śiva assumes the form of *Liṅga* and protects all mobile and immobile beings.

Formerly I have been asked by you about how Śiva assumed the form of *Liṅga*. Everything has now been truthfully spoken (by me), O Brāhmaṇas.

How Śiva, the great lord of the worlds, swallowed poison (Halāhala), may be listened to, O Brāhmaṇas. I shall recount it to you as it actually took place.

CHAPTER NINE

The Churning of the Ocean[1]

Lomaśa said:

1-2. On one occasion Indra, the lord of Devas, was seated in the middle of the assembly surrounded by the guardians of the worlds, Devas and Sages. He was encircled by bevies of celestial damsels and was honoured by Gandharvas. Songs in

1. This is a favourite topic of Purāṇa-writers as can be seen from its description in Mbh, *Ādi*. 18, VR I.45.17-18, BhP VIII.5.11-18, BdP I.ii.25, MtP 249-250 to mention a few. The background of the churning of the ocean is different in our text. It is for the recovery of the gems of Indra which were sunk into the sea that Devas and Asuras agreed to churn the ocean. In Mbh it was god Nārāyaṇa who advised god Brahmā to churn the ocean for getting *Amṛta* (*Ādi*. 17.10-13).

praise of his conquest were being sung by Siddhas and Vidyādharas.

3. At that time Bṛhaspati who was the scholarly preceptor of the king of Devas and was of exalted fortune and liberal-minded, came there surrounded by his disciples.

4. On seeing him Devas who had been sitting there promptly bowed down to him. Indra too had seen Vācaspati's (Bṛhaspati's) arrival.

5. But the vicious-minded lord did not utter a single word in his honour. No word of welcome, no offer of seat, no formal permission to leave was accorded to him.

6. Knowing that Śakra had become arrogant and evil-minded due to royal authority, Bṛhaspati became angry and he vanished.

7. When the preceptor of Devas had departed, Suras became dejected. Yakṣas, Serpents, Gandharvas and sages also became depressed in mind, O Brāhmaṇas.

8. At the end of the music recital, Indra (as it were) regained consciousness. He asked Suras immediately, "Where has (the preceptor) of great penance gone?"

9-10. At the very same time, Śakra, the lord of Devas, was informed by Nārada: "The preceptor has been insulted by you. There is no doubt about it. O slayer of Bala, your kingdom has gone due to the disrespect (shown by you) to the preceptor. Hence, by all means, you have to plead to him for forgiveness."

11. On hearing these words of the noble-souled Nārada, Śakra suddenly got up from his seat. Surrounded by all of them (Devas etc.), he hastened to the abode of his preceptor promptly (without any slackness).

12. He bowed down to Tārā at the outset and asked her, "Where has (our preceptor) of great penance gone?" Tārā stared at Śakra and said, "I do not know."

13-15. Thereupon, Śakra became worried and returned to his own house. In the meantime, there appeared mysterious ill-omens in heaven, causing misery to everyone including the noble-minded Śakra himself.

All the activities of Śakra were known to Bali who was stationed in the nether worlds. Surrounded by Daityas, he went from

Pātāla to Amarāvatī. Thereupon a great fight ensued between Devas and Dānavas.

16-18. Devas were defeated by Daityas. Instantaneously the whole of the kingdom of Śakra, the deluded and evil-minded one, was conquered by them and everything (belonging to Śakra) was quickly carried to Pātāla. It was by the grace of Śukra that all of them became victorious. Śakra became bereft of glory and splendour. So he was utterly abandoned by Devas. The goddess (of fortune) with lotus-like eyes vanished.

19. The great elephant Airāvata, the horse Uccaiḥśravas and many other precious things and jewels were taken away immediately by Daityas of evil behaviour due to greed.

20. The good ones among them fell into the ocean. Bali who was surprised at this, remarked to his preceptor:

21. "It is mysterious that many jewels brought by us after defeating Devas have fallen into the ocean."

22-23. On hearing the words of Bali, Uśanas (i.e. Śukra) replied to him: "One can attain the heavenly kingdom only through performance of a hundred horse-sacrifices. There is no doubt about it that it will be acquired by one who is initiated in it. Hence, the enjoyer is also he himself. Without performing a horse-sacrifice, heavenly pleasures cannot at all be enjoyed."

24. Understanding the utterance of his preceptor, Bali became quite silent. What was proper and befitting was carried out through and along with Devas.

25. Indra too, on attaining a miserable plight, went to Parameṣṭhin (Brahmā) and informed him of everything, such as the danger to his kingdom and other things.

26-28. On hearing the words of Śakra, Parameṣṭhī said: "We shall gather together all the Suras and go immediately along with you to Viṣṇu, the lord of all lords, in order to propitiate him."

Saying "So be it" all those guardians of the worlds beginning with Śakra went to the shore of the Milk Ocean with Brahmā at their head. After sitting there all of them began to eulogize Hari.

Brahmā said:

29-31. O lord of the universe, O lord of Devas bowed down to by Suras as well as Asuras, obeisance to you, O great Ātman, of auspicious reputation, O infinite one, O immutable one, free from decay.

You yourself are *Yajña*. You are of the form of *Yajña*, O consort of Lakṣmī. Hence, be the bestower of boons unto the Devas.

By insulting his preceptor, Indra has lost (everything) from his kingdom along with the celestial sages. Hence redeem him.

The Lord said:

32. There is no wonder in the fact that everything perishes by insulting the preceptor. Those who are sinners, who are completely engaged in evil activities, who indulge only in sensual pleasures and by whom parents are censured, are undoubtedly godless ones.

33. Immediately he has acquired the fruit, O Brahmā, of what he has committed. Difficulty and misfortune have befallen all due to the act of this Śakra.

34. When a person faces adverse circumstances, they say that, he must be friendly with all living beings in order to achieve all his purposes.

35. For that reason, Indra, do as I suggest. For the realization of your purpose, alliance should be formed by you with Daityas.

36. On being commanded by the lord, the highly intelligent Śakra left Amarāvatī and went to Sutala along with Devas.

37. On seeing that Indra had come, Indrasena became furious. Along with his army, he was desirous of killing Indra.

38. Then by means of different types of (consoling) words, Daityas and Bali, the most excellent one among strong persons, were prevented from killing him by Nārada.

39-40. At the instance of that same sage, Bali controlled (abandoned) his anger. Indra then came in along with his army. He was seen by Indrasena surrounded by the guardians of the worlds. The king of Daityas hastened to tell him laughingly:

41. "Wherefore have you come here to Sutala, O Śakra? Let it be mentioned." On hearing these words, he said smilingly:

42. "We are the descendants of Kaśyapa. All of you are also so. Just as we are, so also you are. Clash and quarrel is meaningless.

43. As fate would have it, my kingdom was seized by you instantaneously. So also many gems were taken away by you. Though brought with very great effort, they too have gone.

44. Hence a learned person must deliberate and ponder. One gets knowledge by means of deliberation and liberation originates from knowledge.

45. But alas! of what avail is my utterance in front of you? I do not know. I have approached you along with Suras as a person seeking refuge."

46. On hearing these words of Śakra, the intelligent (Daitya), the most excellent one among knowers (learned), the most excellent one among those who know what to say, said laughingly to Śakra:

47. "For what purpose, O Devendra, you have come, I do not know."

48. On hearing those words, Śakra's eyes became filled with tears. He did not say anything. Nārada spoke to him the following words:

49. "O Bali, don't you know the difference between right and wrong activities? This is the virtue of great men. They protect those who seek refuge in them.

50. Those who do not protect the one who seeks refuge, a Brāhmaṇa, a sick man and an old man, are (really) slaughterers of Brāhmaṇas.

51-52. He has come to your presence with words asking for refuge. He is worthy of being protected by you. There is no doubt in this matter." On being told thus by Nārada, the lord of Daityas himself pondered over everything with great understanding regarding what was right and what was wrong. With great respect, he honoured Śakra along with the guardians of the worlds as well as the groups of Devas.

53. For the sake of credence, Puranadara performed many good holy observances of the *Sāttvika* quality which created confidence in Bali.

54. Thus Śakra entered into an agreement with Bali in order to further his selfish ends. That great lord stayed with Bali solely devoting himself to the (precepts in the) science of political economy.

55. Thus Indra passed many years living in Sutala. Remembering the words of Viṣṇu and pondering over them again and again, he thought of a plan.

56. Once the king of Devas himself was sitting in the middle of the assembly (of Bali). Conversant with the right policy, he spoke laughingly these words to Bali:

57-58. "Many gems and jewels, elephants etc. have dropped into the ocean, while you were bringing them here. They belonged to us then. They should be recovered from the ocean by you as well as by us, O heroic one.

59. We must hurry up in exerting ourselves to recover those jewels from the ocean. Hence, it must be churned by you for the purpose of achieving the desired result."

60. Induced thus by Śakra, Bali, the slayer of Suras, spoke to Śakra immediately, "By whom and with what should the churning be done?"

61-63. Then an ethereal voice with the majestic rumbling sound of cloud said: "O Devas, O Daityas, do churn the Ocean of Milk. There is no doubt about this that your strength will increase. Make the Mandara mountain the churning rod and Vāsuki the requisite rope. Afterwards, O Devas and Daityas, join together and let the ocean be churned."

64. On hearing the words of that ethereal voice, all Suras exerted themselves along with Daityas.

65. Those Suras and Asuras came out of Pātāla. They all came to the matchless, excellent mountain Mandara.

66. Daityas were ten million in number. So also were Devas undoubtedly. Preparing themselves, they came to Mandara having golden lustre.

67-68. It abounded in gems and precious stones. It was globular in shape. It was very big and exceedingly lustrous. Many gems were (lying scattered) all round. It had many trees such as sandal tree, Pārijāta, Nāga, Punnāga and Campaka. It was full of various kinds of animals and deer, lions and tigers.

69. On seeing such a great mountain, all the excellent Suras joined their palms in reverence and said:

Devas said:

70. O mountain, all of us, the Suras have come here to submit to you. Listen to it, O great mountain, the helper of others.

71-72. On being requested thus by Devas and Daityas then, the mountain Mandara came out in an embodied form and in that form the mountain Mandara said: "What for have all of you come to me? Let that be mentioned."

73. Then Bali said these words befitting the occasion. Indra too hurriedly spoke these courteous and sincere words:

74. "O mountain Mandara, you cooperate with us in a great undertaking. O observer of holy vows, you should be the churning rod for the production of nectar."

75. Saying "So be it" and honouring their words, because it was for the accomplishment of the task of Devas, he spoke these words to Devas and Asuras and particularly to Indra:

76. "My wings have been cut (by you) with the thunderbolt of hundred spikes. How is it possible for me to go for realizing your purpose?"

77. Then all Devas and Asuras praised the mountain. They then uprooted that incomparable and wonderful Mandara mountain.

78. But, though they were desirous of taking it to the Milky Ocean, they proved incapable of doing it. The mountain fell on Devas and Daityas.

79. Some were crushed. Some died. Some fell into a swoon. Some of them began to blame and censure and some suffered great pain.

80. Thus, Asuras, Suras and Dānavas failed in their attempt. When they regained consciousness, they eulogized the Lord of the universe:

81. "Save us, save us, O great Viṣṇu, O lord compassionate to those who seek refuge. The entire world, mobile as well as immobile, is pervaded by you."

82-83. Then Hari appeared before them for the accomplishment of the purpose of Devas. Viṣṇu who was seated on Garuḍa, saw them and suddenly and sportingly lifted up the excellent mountain and placed it on Garuḍa.[1] Then, the lord granted all of them protection from fear.

84. Rising from there (and taking leave of) those Devas, he took the old mountain to the northern shore of the Ocean of Milk. After placing it in the waters, he went away from that place.

85. Then all those groups of Suras arrived there along with Asuras, taking Vāsuki with them. Then they made the agreement.

86. After making Mandara the churning rod and Vāsuki the rope, all of them, Suras and Asuras, churned the Ocean of Milk.

87. As the Ocean of Milk was being churned, the mountain sank deep into Rasātala. At that very instant, the Lord of Ramā, Viṣṇu, became a tortoise and lifted it up. That was something really marvellous.

88. When the mountain rotated, it was further pulled and pushed by Suras and Dānavas. Now it rotated without any basis, like the understanding without a preceptor.

89. Viṣṇu, the supreme soul, then became the basic support of the Mandara mountain. With his four hands he gathered it up and churned pleasantly.

90. Then all Suras and Asuras churned the Ocean of Milk after uniting together. Very powerful themselves, by uniting together, they became all the more powerful.

91. The excellent mountain had adamantine strength. It rolled on the back, neck, thighs and the space between the knees of the noble-souled tortoise. Due to the friction of these two, submarine fire was generated.

92. The Halāhala poison too emerged and it was seen by Nārada. Thereafter, the celestial sage of unmeasured splendour spoke these words:

93-94. "The churning of the ocean should not be carried on by you all now. O Devas, all of you pray to Śiva.[2] Have you

1. In Mbh, *Ādi* 18.8 it was the serpent Śeṣa who carried Mt. Mandara to the sea. Here the credit is given to Garuḍa, Viṣṇu's vehicle.

2. Our text is a propagandist of Śiva. In the Mbh it is Nārāyaṇa who

forgotten the sacrifice of Dakṣa and what Vīrabhadra did there?

Hence, let Śiva be immediately remembered, O Devas. He is greater than the greatest; he is beyond the greatest. He is the embodiment of supreme bliss. He is worthy of being meditated upon by Yogins; he has no form. (As a matter of fact) however, he is formless and unmanifest (or without diversity)."

95. Devas were eager to achieve their purpose. Therefore, they hurriedly went on churning the ocean. All those who are overwhelmed by desires do not listen (to the advice of others), because they become irrational and stupid.

96. They should not be given many pieces of advice and instructions. They are subject to *Rāga* (desire) and *Dveṣa* (hatred). All of them are averse to Śiva.

97. With their sheer continuous exertion, they churned the Ocean of Milk. Due to excessive churning, the poison called Halāhala was generated from the Ocean of Milk.[1]

98. It was strong enough to burn down the three worlds. It came up to kill the heaven-dwellers. It went up still further and spread to all quarters. The entire sky was pervaded by it. The Kālakūṭa poison advanced to consume all the living beings.

99. They observed the huge king of serpents grasped by their own hands. They left him there along with the mountain and then went (immediately) away. They fled along with Asuras.

100. So also the sages beginning with Bhṛgu, sages in hundreds (fled in all directions). It was like what happened at the sacrifice of Dakṣa.

101. Earnestly urged by Bhṛgu, all of them went to Satyaloka: "This poison Kālakūṭa will be quelled by means of various Vedic Sentences. O Devas, there is no doubt in this matter. It is true; I am speaking the truth unto you."

---

guides Devas and Asuras in churning the ocean. Śiva is not mentioned at all in this context (Mbh, *Ādi* 18).

1. VV 97-113 describe the disastrous effect of the poison Kālakūṭa, viz. burning down of the entire three worlds. The author's object is to heighten the greatness of Śiva in drinking the poison (see the next chapter). Mbh sums it up in one line:

prāgrasal loka-rakṣārthaṁ brahmaṇo
vacanāc chivaḥ (Ādi 18.42b)

'At the instance of god Brahmā, Śiva consumed it (the poison) for saving the world.'

102. On hearing these words uttered by Bhṛgu, all of them distressed by the poison Kālakūṭa went to Satyaloka and sought refuge in Brahmā.

103. Brahmā saw the blazing Kālakūṭa with sparkling lustre. He found that Suras and Asuras were ignorant of their duties. He was about to curse them, but he was prevented by Nārada.

Brahmā said:

104. O Devas, what a wrong thing has been committed by you? Why has this explosive thing cropped up? It is Īśvara's anger. My speech cannot be otherwise.

105. Thereupon, surrounded by Devas, the Vedas, the Upaniṣads and the different kinds of Āgamas, he proceeded ahead out of fear of the Kālakūṭa.

106. Then, Devas who were worried said to to one another, "We are enveloped in *Avidyā* (nescience) and lust. How can we do anything to Śaṅkara?"

107. Then Devas kept Brahmā at their head and hurriedly went to Vaikuṇṭha, because they were afraid of Kālakūṭa.

108. Brahmā and others as well as the groups of sages sought refuge in the great lord Viṣṇu, the primordial Puruṣa, the mighty lord who had resorted to Vaikuṇṭha, Mādhava, Adhokṣaja. The groups of Suras and Asuras sought refuge in lord Viṣṇu.

109. By that time, the great poison Kālakūṭa came there. After burning Brahmā's world at the outset, it burned Vaikuṇṭha.

110. Viṣṇu who dwells in the cavity of the heart of everyone, was burned by the fire of Kālakūṭa also with his attendants. Immediately he acquired the colour of Tamāla.

111. Vaikuṇṭha also became blue in colour. It was surrounded by all the worlds. Hence, all the worlds became encircled by the poisonous substance from the waters.

112. The wonderful poison of the waters reduced to ash the whole of the Cosmic Egg with its eight outer coverings and along with Brahmā.

113. There was no earth, no water, no fire, no wind, and no ether. There was neither *Ahaṁkāra* (Cosmic Ego), nor *Mahat* (the Great Principle). There was no *Mūlāvidyā*. On account of Śiva's wrath, the entire universe became reduced to ash.

CHAPTER TEN

Śiva Swallows the Poison

The sages said:

1. O holy Sir, you said that the Cosmic Egg including the mobile and immobile beings was entirely reduced to ash by the fire of Kālakūṭa on account of the wrath of Rudra.

2-4. But, we consider Rudra to be within the Cosmic Egg. Then the mobile and immobile beings with Brahmā and Viṣṇu as leaders were destroyed and reduced to ash through the wrath of Rudra. How was creation resumed and made to function? Wherefrom did Brahmā, Viṣṇu and other Suras and Asuras with the Moon at their head (originate again)? Where did they get merged? Where were they reduced to ash? What happened after that? It behoves you to recount everything.

5. By the grace of Vyāsa you know everything. No one else knows it. Hence you understand the holy scripture full of knowledge as no one else does.

6. Asked thus by all those sages of sanctified souls, Sūta bowed down to Vyāsa and spoke these words:

Lomaśa said:

7. When Devas beginning with Hari and Brahmā, stationed in the middle of the Cosmic Egg, as well as the guardians of the worlds including Indra were enveloped by the fire of poison, Śaṁbhu was informed by the noble-souled Heraṁba (Gaṇeśa):

Heraṁba said:

8-9. O Rudra, O Mahādeva, O Sthāṇu, the lord of the universe, an obstacle very difficult to be surmounted has been created for them by me by way of amusement.[1] There are persons who start an enterprise, but either because of their fear or through the delusion of their minds, they do not worship you or me. The distress unto them will be very great.

---

1. The destruction of the universe by Kālakūṭa is a 'diversion' (*vinoda*) to god Gaṇeśa, because people do not worship him and Śiva through delusion.

10-11. On being requested thus by the over-lord of Gaṇas, who dispels obstacles like the sun dispelling darkness, the Pināka-bearing Lord with a bull for his emblem, the Lord Nīlalohita with matted hair, the lord devoid of ailments, the lord in the form of *Liṅga*, the unsullied lord without form or features, the sky-haired lord Śiva, Śaṁbhu spoke thus:

Maheśvara said[1]:

12-14. O Heraṁba, listen to my words with great faith and attention. This universe consisting of the mobile and immobile beings is of the form of *Ahaṁkāra* (Cosmic Ego). This *Ahaṁkāra* creates, sustains and destroys. At the beginning of the universe, O Gaṇapati, *Vijñapti* (Intelligence, Consciousness) alone (remained). It was devoid of *Māyā*. It was quiescent and of the form of *Dvaita* and *Advaita* (duality and non-duality). It was in the form of intelligence alone characterized by existence and eternal bliss.

Gaṇapati said:

15. If you are the sole Ātman, characterized by supreme bliss, O Scorcher of foes, then there is nothing other than you.

16. Then how did the different forms originate, differentiated as Suras and Asuras? It is of variegated form observed by the three Devas. It is the cause of delusion.

17. The cycle of worldly existence originated as different from *Nitya* (eternal) and *Anitya* (transient). It consists of four types or species of living beings endowed with many distinctive features etc.

18. People are deluded by various doctrines and tenets of knowledge antagonistic to one another. Some are devoted to the doctrine of *Karman*. Some resort to their (intrinsic) qualities.

19. A few are adherents of the path of knowledge but they are opposed to one another.

O Bull-bannered Lord, thus I have been overwhelmed by doubts. Save me (by dispelling the doubt).

1. One wonders whether this was the proper occasion for expounding the *Dvaitādvaita* philosophy when the entire universe was being burnt down by Kālakūṭa.

20. Where do I and the Gaṇas belong to? Whence is this bull, O Lord? From where are these and many others born? Where (do they go)?

21. Whence are all these exceedingly fortunate ones made into *Sāttvikas*, *Rājasas* etc.?

Lord Śambhu laughed and began to speak to Gaṇeśa:

Maheśvara said:

22. *Rajas*, *Sattva* and *Tamas* are produced by *Kālaśakti* (Power of Time). The entire universe including Devas, Asuras and human beings is enveloped by them.

23. This (world) that is being seen is imperishable ultimately, but, understand that as an evolved effect it is perishable. It is evolved by means of all *Siddhis*.

Lomaśa said:

24-25. While Sadāśiva of Cosmic Form and in the form of the Liṅga was conversing with Gaṇeśa, His Power (*Śakti* called Śiva), the source of the universe of the nature of cause and effect was born of Sadāśiva. At the same instant, the Lord in the form of the *Liṅga* became submerged.

26. The single supreme *Śakti*, characterized as the *Ātman* of *Brahmavidyā* abided (there). Overwhelmed by wonder, Gaṇeśa became engrossed in looking (at that form).

The sages asked:

27. If this entire universe consisting of the mobile and immobile beings is included within *Prakṛti*, how is it then that Gaṇeśa was able to preserve his separate entity? Let this be explained.

Lomaśa replied:

28. Lord Gaṇeśa was directly born of *Prakṛti* herself.[1] Gaṇeśvara has the same form as that of Śiva himself.

29-30. A battle ensued between Śiva and that noble-souled one who had been *Prākṛta* (born of *Prakṛti*) due to ignorance. That battle continued without a break for a long time.

1. VV 28-38. This is another version how Gaṇeśa became elephant-headed and why he is called 'the king of obstacles and difficulties.'

On observing that he was invincible as long as he was riding an elephant, Śaṁbhu hit him with his trident and toppled him down along with the elephant.

31. Then Mahādeva the scorcher of enemies, was eulogized by the Supreme Power (*Prakṛti*). The lord then said to the great *Śakti*, "O splendid lady, choose your boon."

32-33. Then an excellent boon was chosen from Mahādeva: "O lord, he who was killed by you was undoubtedly my son. Being born of a part of *Prakṛti*, he is deluded. Hence he does not know you. In order to gratify me, resuscitate this son of mine."

34. Lord Rudra laughed loudly and revived the son of *Māyā*. He fixed the head of an elephant to his body.

35. Thus the elephant-faced lord was born by the grace of Śaṅkara. Although he was the son of *Māyā*, he was free from the clutches of *Māyā* and became endowed with (spiritual) knowledge.

36. He was perpetually contented with the nectar of the knowledge of *Ātman*. He was free from ailments. Sitting in deep meditation, he became very fierce and then destroyed Kāla (god of death) of black complexion.

37. He pulled out his own huge tooth for the sake of *Yogadaṇḍa*[1] (the mystic wand of Yogic practice) and held it in his hand. He was the presiding deity of the Gaṇas. He surpasses the *Śabdabrahman* (the Vedas or the supreme spiritual knowledge expressed in words). Though accompanied by both *Ṛddhi* and *Siddhi*, he shines in his aloneness.

38. The groups of Gaṇas and *Vighnas* (obstacles) and many others superior to these—whatever there was on the earth, he became the lord thereof. He was made so by Śaṁbhu then.

39. Hence he was able to see *Prakṛti* which has the Cosmic form. He remained separate and was able to realize the *Liṅga* as well as the *Prakṛti*. He saw the pure *Liṅga* naturally abiding in the *Prakṛti*.

40. Heraṁba who was equipped with perfect knowledge

1. In BdP Paraśurāma is said to have cut down one of Gaṇeśa's tusks with his axe (II.iii.41.2-4). Here it is self-extraction of the tusk by Gaṇeśa himself.

saw himself along with the Gaṇas as well as the three worlds entirely merged in the *Liṅga*.

41. Though he was endowed with perfect knowledge, he lost his consciousness. He regained it with very great effort. The lord of the Gaṇas bowed down his head to those two supreme powers.

42. Then he saw there itself Brahmā, Rudra, Viṣṇu and Sadāśiva in the form of the annihilator of the worlds.

43-45. He saw some beings resembling ghosts. They were the *Liṅgaśaktis*. He saw crores of spherical Cosmic Eggs like so many atoms. They were getting merged and dissolved in Maheśa who was in the form of a *Liṅga*.

The *Liṅga* was inside the *Prakṛti* and the *Prakṛti* was within the *Liṅga*. The whole of the *Liṅga* was seen covered by *Śakti*. The *Śakti* was covered by the *Liṅga*. Thus the two encompassed each other.[1]

46. The whole world consisting of the mobile and immobile beings stayed supported by both Śivas (i.e. Śiva and Śakti). Only Gaṇeśa and none else, though great, had that knowledge.

47. The presiding deity of the Gaṇas (Lord Gaṇeśa), of great splendour, accompanied by the Gaṇas eulogized with great strength, the Lord accompanied by Śakti.

Gaṇeśa prayed:

48. I bow down to the god accompanied by His Śakti (Power)—the Lord who is the embodiment of knowledge, who is kindly disposed (but) beyond the ken of knowledge and of the form of supreme Light, who transcends forms, is the Supreme Reality incarnate, who is beyond the principles (categories of Sāṅkhyas), supremely auspicious, who is called Bliss undivided and uncontaminated by sorrow.

49-50. The fire in (a ball of) iron is beyond smoke (smokeless), but it appears as though filled with smoke. You who are the source of knowledge, appear to be within *Prakṛti*. You who are present within the *Prakṛti* by *Māyā*, are spoken of as manifested.

You whose nature is such, O lord, create, annihilate and protect the universe by your *Māyā*. On account of this

1. This peculiar mutual relation between Śiva and Śakti shows the influence of Trika Śaivism of Kashmir.

poison, the entire universe consisting of the mobile and immobile beings and accompanied by Brahmā, Viṣṇu and Indra, has been destroyed.

51. You are lord Maheśa. You are the lord of the three worlds. You are the immanent soul of the mobile and immobile beings. The mobile and immobile beings along with the vestures of individual souls, have been completely burnt down. Please revive them quickly and make it (the world) as it was before.

Lomaśa said:

52-54. On being eulogized thus by Gaṇeśa, the Lord (Śiva), the sanctifier of all living beings, assumed the form of a *Liṅga* and consumed the Kālakūṭa that arose there and caused the destruction of all the worlds. He made everything free from impurities. Since the lord was endowed with great compassion and considerateness, all Devas, Asuras and human beings and all the three worlds were instantaneously saved.

Brahmā, Viṣṇu, Surendra, the Guardians of the Quarters along with the sages, Yakṣas, Vidyādharas, Siddhas, Gandharvas and groups of celestial damsels—all of them got up as though from sleep.

55. They were struck with wonder. They were agitated and frightened. All Devas and Asuras said in dismay:

56-62. "Where is that immense Kālakūṭa by which we had been compelled to flee and made almost dead along with the Guardians of the Quarters?" So said they, but Daityas remained silent. The Guardians of the Quarters beginning with Śakra, who were able to regain strength and happiness with god Brahmā as their leader, said this after honouring Viṣṇu, the lord of all lords:

"By whom has this been caused? We do not know as we are deficient in intelligence." Then Viṣṇu laughed at Brahmā and all those (Suras). All of them then began to meditate with great concentration of their minds. O Brāhmaṇas, that dispelled base emotions such as lust and anger as well as other feelings by means of the knowledge of Reality. Then Devas and others saw the *Liṅga* present in their own *Ātman* (Soul). Keeping Viṣṇu at their head, they eulogized the Lord for the attainment of the ultimate truth:

"Yogins worship the Supreme Soul through their own souls. The *Liṅga* alone is the greatest knowledge. The *Liṅga* alone is the greatest penance. The *Liṅga* alone is the greatest Dharma. The *Liṅga* alone is the greatest goal. Hence, there is nothing at all which (can be called) greater than the *Liṅga*."

63. After saying thus, Suras and Asuras along with the Guardians of the Quarters and sages kept Viṣṇu whose complexion is dark like the Indian cinnamon, at their head. They then sought refuge in Śambhu who is worthy of being resorted to:

64. "Save us, save us, O Mahādeva, O merciful lord, O Supreme God. It behoves you to save us as we had been saved before (by you).

65. O Lord of Devas, your lotus-like feet possess greatness befitting our repeated service. They have infinite forms. We have resorted to them. (Save us) with the greatest mercy. Obeisance to you, O excellent one among Devas. Be pleased."

66. Lord Ramāpati (Viṣṇu), the sanctifier of the living beings, stood in the middle of the form of *Liṅga* along with all the groups of Suras and spoke thus:

67-69. "You are the Lord in the form of the *Liṅga*. You bestow protection from fear on all the worlds. All those who died on account of the poison, have been saved. Hence, O Lord, the conqueror of Mṛtyu (Death), save us, save us. O Mahākāla, the destroyer of Tripura, obeisance to you."

On being eulogized by Viṣṇu, Lord Maheśvara in the form of the *Liṅga* appeared before them along with Ambā (goddess Pārvatī). He appeared to awaken (i.e. enlighten) those Suras:

70-74. "O Viṣṇu, ye all Suras and Sages, let this be heard. Ordinary people think that the worldly existence is eternal, while it is only transitory. Thereby, they are agitated. O Devas and others, of what avail are the *Yajñas*, austerities and activities connected with holy rites, if one does not perceive the (Supreme) *Ātman* by means of (his individual *Ātman*)? There is no benefit therefrom, whether they are performed collectively or separately. All of you joined together and carried out a very difficult task, namely the churning of the ocean. That you did for the sake of getting nectar. But why was it performed after rejecting Mṛtyuñjaya and always disrespecting me? Hence all of you undoubtedly fell into the mouth of Death.

Lord Gaṇeśa has been created by us for the purpose of achieving success in an undertaking.

75. Those who do not bow down to Gaṇeśa as well as Durgā of similar nature will be victims of distress. There is no doubt about this.

76. All of you are sinful and stubborn. You profess to be learned without knowing what is right and what is wrong. You are deluded by mere false prestige.

77-78. All of you, groups of Devas beginning with Indra, are devoted to the Vedas. All those beginning with Indra are mediocres, pleasure-seekers, praise-mongers and useless ones. O consort of Śacī (i.e. Indra), you do not understand yourself on account of delusion.

79. A great effort has been made by you for getting nectar, O rogue. You attained a kingdom by performing a hundred horse-sacrifices. Even that is under the control of your enemies now. O vicious one, you do not know that.

80. O deluded one, you have been eulogized by ascetics through the Vedic statements (*hymns*). Those ascetics are fools. They propitiate you, because they are prompted by different passions.

81. O Viṣṇu, on account of your partiality you do not know what is good and what is otherwise. Some persons are killed by you, O Viṣṇu, and some have been protected.

82. You are desirous of certain things in this matter. You are always childish in your activities. Why talk of all the other Guardians of the Quarters?

83. If a matter is pursued in a way other than what is proper, the result is bound to be in a way other than (what is expected). You all forgot that thing whereby your efforts are crowned with success.

84-85. It is he by whom all (of you) have been saved from the great fear of Kālakūṭa today. It is he by whom you have been saved from a poison by which Viṣṇu is turned blue (dark-complexioned), by which all of you were defeated and by which all the worlds have been reduced to ash. Hence, the worship of that noble-souled Gaṇeśa should be performed by you.

86. If at the beginning of any holy rite, people do not wor-

ship Gaṇādhipa (Gaṇeśa), they will never realize their objectives as in your own case."

87. On hearing these words of Maheśa, Suras, Asuras, Kinnaras and Cāraṇas asked Girīśa about the method of worship in the proper manner.

CHAPTER ELEVEN[1]

Procedure of Gaṇeśa Worship: Manifestation of Lakṣmī

Maheśvara said:

1. In every fortnight Gaṇeśa should be worshipped on the fourth day. (But) in the bright half of the month a devotee, after taking bath, should worship always with white sesamum seeds.[2]

2. After finishing all necessary daily routine religious duties, the devotee should perform the worship of Gaṇeśa with great care, by means of scents, garlands, *akṣatas* (raw unbroken rice grains) etc.

3. At the outset, meditation on Gaṇeśa should be performed in accordance with scriptural injunctions.

---

1. The chapter consists of two topics:
   (i) The procedure of worshipping Gaṇeśa.
   (ii) The emergence of various "Gems" during the churning of the ocean.

2. VV 1-18 describe the procedure of worshipping Gaṇeśa. It may briefly be outlined as follows:
   (1) Special day—every fourth day in a fortnight (vv 1-2).
   (2) Materials of worship (v 3).
   (3) Names of Gaṇeśa (v 5).
   (4) The five faces of Gaṇeśa—their different complexions etc. (vv 7-8).
   (5) Weapons in Gaṇeśa's ten hands.
   (6) Three types of Gaṇeśa image for meditation:
      (A) *Sāttvika*(vv 11-12a).
      (B) *Rājasa* (vv 12b-13).
      (C) *Tāmasa* (v 14).
   (7) Offering of twenty-one Dūrvā grass blades—one pair of blades per name of Gaṇeśa and *Modakas* (sweet eatables) (vv 15 and 16).
   (8) Ten names of Gaṇeśa for worshipping as above (vv 17-18).

4. As the worshippers are of various types having *Tāmasa*, *Sāttvika* and *Rājasa* traits, the names also (of Gaṇeśa) became many in number according to their class (characterized by a particular *Guṇa*).

5. They are as follows: *Pañcavaktra* (Five-faced), *Gaṇādhyakṣa* (Chief of the Gaṇas—Śiva's attendants), *Daśabāhu* (Ten-armed), *Trilocana* (Three-eyed), *Kāntasphaṭika-saṅkāśa* (Resembling a shining crystal), *Nīlakaṇṭha* (Blue-throated), *Gajānana* (Elephant-faced).

6. I shall describe his five faces correctly.

7. The middle face is fair in colour with four teeth and three eyes. It is beautiful with a long trunk. In the trunk he keeps a *modaka* (a round piece of sweetmeat).

8. The other faces of Gaṇeśa are yellow, auspicious blue, tawny and grey. The faces are splendid and characterized by good features.

9-10. I shall tell you the weapons in the ten hands (of Gaṇeśa). They are: noose, axe, lotus, goad, tusk, rosary, ploughshare, pestle, *varada*(*mudrā*—gesture) (the hand indicating bestowal of boons) and a vessel containing *modakas*. One should meditate that he is holding the vessel in his hand.

11-14. The meditation is of three types. In *Sāttvika* meditation contemplate thus: (He is) *Lambodara* (Pot-bellied). *Virūpākṣa* (of uneven eyes = three-eyed), *Nivīta* (sacred thread worn like a garland). He is having a girdle. He is seated in the Yogic posture; the crescent-moon adorns his head.

Rājasa meditation is as in the case of men. The deity has pure golden complexion. (He is) elephant-faced and super-natural. He has four hands, three eyes, one tusk and huge belly.

In *Tāmasa* meditation he holds a noose and a goad (in his hands). The lord holds a tusk and a vessel of *modakas*. He is blue in colour.

Thus there are three types of *Dhyāna*. Thereafter, the worship should be begun quickly by you all.

15. Twenty-one Dūrvā grass-blades are (to be) taken. Two blades of grass are offered after uttering one name. (Thus ten names are uttered and twenty blades of grass are offered.) In the end, all the names are uttered and one blade of grass is offered to the Lord of Gaṇas.

16. Similarly twenty-one *modakas* should be offered. I shall mention the ten names intended for worshipping separately.

17-18. The names are: 1. *Gaṇādhipa* (Lord of Gaṇas), 2. *Umāputra* (Son of Umā), 3. *Agha-nāśana* (Destroyer of sins), 4. *Vināyaka*, 5. *Īśaputra* (Son of Lord Śiva), 6. *Sarva-siddhi-pradāyaka* (Bestower of all *Siddhis*), 7. *Ekadanta* (One-tusked), 8. *Ibha-vaktra* (Elephant-faced), 9. *Mūṣaka-vāhana* (Mouse-vehicled) and 10. *Kumāra-guru* (The elder brother of Kumāra). At the end of every word *namastestu* (Obeisance to you) should be added. In the case of the last, the words *Kumāragurave tubhyaṁ namo'stu*, 'Obeisance to you, O Kumāraguru' should be uttered. Thus Gaṇeśa should be worshipped with care.

19-20. After speaking thus to Suras, Sadāśiva, Śaṁbhu, the highly splendid lord, eagerly embraced Viṣṇu who abides in the cavity of heart, as well as Brahmā, and (he) immediately vanished. All of them bowed down to Śaṁbhu and then became engaged in worshipping *Gaṇādhyakṣa* (Gaṇeśa).

21. After worshipping him in accordance with the injunctions, they became engaged in honouring him with various *Upacāras* (ways of service) and the Dūrvā grass blades separately.

22. Gaṇeśa who was contented and delighted (by their worship) bestowed boons on Devas. They circumambulated him, bowed down to him and propitiated him.

23. Asuras who possessed only *Tamas Guṇa* did not worship Gaṇeśa.[1] The excellent Asuras were engaged in ridiculing Devas.

24-25. Devas finished worshipping the son of Śaṅkara and went to the Milk Ocean once again. Brahmā, Viṣṇu, the excellent Suras, Devas, Daityas and sages made Mandara the churning rod and Vāsuki the churning rope. Keeping Viṣṇu near them, Devas began the churning.

26. When the ocean was being churned, it was the Moon that came out at the outset,[2] for the purpose of realizing the objectives of all Devas. He was full of nectar.

1. Due to their negligence in worshipping Gaṇeśa, Asuras did not get the fruit (*Ratnas*—jewels) of their labour of churning the ocean.

2. The following is the serial order of the 'Gems' that were churned out from the ocean:

1. The Moon

Śaunaka said:

27-29. O sage of holy rites, was the Moon formerly placed in the ocean? By whom was he placed? It was told by you formerly that the excellent gems like the elephant etc. (had been cast into the ocean). O lord, tell me all these things briefly in the beginning. After understanding these, all of us shall later describe them.

On hearing their words, Sūta began his narrative:

30. Candra (the Moon) is watery by nature, O Brāhmaṇas. He was born as the son of Atri. He was endowed with all good qualities. He was born of Anasūya from a part of Brahmā. Durvāsas was born from a part of Rudra and Dattaka (i.e. Datta) was born from a part of Viṣṇu.

31. On seeing the Milk Ocean being churned, Candra became delighted. On seeing the Moon, the Milk Ocean too became extremely attached to him.

32. Since both of them liked each other, Candra entered the Ocean. Let this be heard, O excellent Brāhmaṇas. In front of and in the presence of Devas, Candra became filled with nectar.

33. On seeing the splendour of Candra, the *Nīrājana* rite (waving light around the face) was immediately performed by the groups of Devas with respect to Candra, along with the loud and tumultuous sounds of musical instruments, drums of many types and conchs.

34. They all then bowed down to him along with Suras, Asuras and Dānavas. Then they asked Garga about the genuine inherent power of Candra.[1]

35-37. Thereupon, Garga told them, "All the Planets are powerful today. All the excellent Planets are in their central

2. Surabhi—Wish-yieiding cow and other cows
3. Kalpavṛkṣa (Wish-yielding divine trees)
4. Kaustubha, Cintāmaṇi
5. Uccaiḥśravā horse
6. Airāvata elephant
7. Wine and intoxicants
8. Lakṣmī

1. This is known as '*Candra-bala*'. All Planets became favourable due to this.

positions. (Therefore they are beneficial) to you. Guru (Jupiter) has come in conjunction with Candra (the Moon). Budha (Mercury) has also come in his contact. So also the Sun, Śukra (Venus), Śani (Saturn) and the great Planet Aṅgāraka (Mars). Hence the power and influence of Candra is very excellent for the realization of your objectives. This *Muhūrta* (auspicious time) named *Gomanta*[1] is the bestower of victory."

38. At this encouraging assurance of the noble-souled Garga, the mighty Devas began to churn the ocean vigorously and roared (lustily in their eagerness).

39. Remembering Maheśa and Gaṇeśa again and again, those noble-souled (Devas) of firm holy rites attained double strength.

40. During churning, Surabhi (divine cow) came out directly for the sake of the accomplishment of the tasks of Devas, from the ocean that was roaring with a rumbling sound on all sides.

41. Tawny in colour and with quite heavy udders, the cow, in a contented mood, came very slowly floating over the waves.

42. On seeing Kāmadhenu (Wish-yielding Cow) coming up, all Suras and Asuras showered flowers on that (cow) of unmeasured splendour.

43. Various kinds of trumpets and musical instruments were played and drums were beaten. She was brought from the middle of the waters (though) surrounded by hundreds of cows.

44. Among them there were cows of various colours such as blue, black, tawny, partridge-coloured, smoke-coloured, dark-coloured, red ones, wood-apple-coloured and reddish-brown ones. Surabhi was seen accompanied by these cows.

45. Sages who were delighted instantly entreated Devas and Asuras (to give to them) Kāmadhenu which was closely surrounded by them (Devas and Asuras).

46. "These cows along with Surabhi should be given to all Brāhmaṇas belonging to various Gotras. There is no doubt about it."

47. On being requested by them, Suras and Asuras gave those cows to them in order to gratify Śiva. Those Surabhis

1. *Gomanta*—It may mean at the time of sunrise.

(cows) were accepted by the noble-minded sages of great auspiciousness and excessive merit.

48. Then *Puṇyāhavācana*[1] (the formal religious declaration 'This is an auspicious day') was performed for Suras by all those sages in order to enable Devas to achieve their objects and to cause the destruction of Asuras.

49-50. All of them once again exerted themselves very well and churned the Milk Ocean. From the ocean that was being churned rose up Kalpavṛkṣa, Pārijāta, Cūta and Santānaka. They set apart those trees on one side, like the city of Gandharvas. Immediately those wise (Suras and Asuras) resumed the churning of the Milk Ocean powerfully in all earnestness.

51. From the ocean that was being churned emerged a highly refulgent, extremely bright, most excellent gem having the brilliance of the Sun. It was called Kaustubha.

52-53. With its brilliance, it illuminated the three worlds. Keeping the Cintāmaṇi (a miraculous stone) in front, they saw the Kaustubha brightening the worlds. All those Suras gave the Kaustubha to Viṣṇu. Suras and Asuras of enhanced strength lustily roared again and began to churn the ocean keeping Cintāmaṇi in the middle.

54-58. From the ocean that was being churned rose up Uccaiḥśravas, the wonderful gem of a horse, and then Airāvata, the gem of an elephant, along with sixty-four other white elephants each with four tusks and in the rut. They set apart all these in the middle and churned once again. Many precious things then arose from the ocean that was being churned, viz. the wine Vijayā, Bhṛṅgī, garlic, turnip, the poisonous and highly intoxicating Dhattūra (Datura Alba) which causes too much of madness, and Puṣkara. All these were placed on the shore of the ocean without any hurry. Again those great Asuras churned the ocean along with the excellent Suras.

59-61. As the ocean was being churned once again, that

1. *Puṇyāhavācana*—When a person intends to perform an auspicious rite, he invites Brāhmaṇas, honours them, requests them with palms folded: "May you declare the day auspicious for such and such a rite", and the Brāhmaṇas respond "*Om*, may it be auspicious." Each of the Brāhmaṇas is to repeat it with words, '*Svasti*', '*Puṇyāham*' and '*ṛddhim*' (*Āpastamba Dh. S.* I.4.13.8; cf. *Baudhāyana Gr. Seṣa Sūtra* I.10).

divine Lakṣmī,[1] the sole protector of the worlds, rose up from it. Those who are the knowers of Brahman call her *Ānvīkṣikī* (Metaphysics). Others praise her as *Mūlavidyā*. Some competent persons call her *Brahmavidyā*. Some call her *Siddhi* (Success), *Ṛddhi* (Prosperity), *Ājñā* (Command) and *Āśā* (Hope). Some Yogins call her *Vaiṣṇavī*. Some exponents of Māyā always engaged in Yogic practice call her *Māyā*. All people call her *Kenasiddhāntayuktā* (the one associated with Brahman—the Principle spoken of in the *Kenopaniṣad*). Those who are equipped with the power of knowledge call her *Yogamāyā*.

62-69. They saw Mahālakṣmī coming slowly. She was very fair, youthful and tender with the filaments of the lotus for her ornaments. She was sweetly smiling with beautiful teeth. A lady of slender shade, she had the fresh youthfulness as an adornment. Her garments and ornaments were variegated with the refulgence of many gems. Her lips were red like the Biṁba (Momordica Monadelpha) fruits; the nose was very beautiful and the neck and the eyes were very splendid. She was very slender with fine waistline and splendid buttocks. The hips were large. Her lotus-like face was brilliantly illuminated by means of a number of gems that served the purpose of the lights in a *Nīrājana* rite for her face. Her face was fascinating and delightful. She was remarkably splendid with her necklaces and anklets. An umbrella was gorgeously held above her head. She was being fanned with chowries gently shaken by the waves of Gaṅgā. She was riding a white elephant and was being eulogized by great sages. With the ends of her hands, she held a garland of the flowers of heavenly trees along with jasmine flowers.

On seeing her Devas were eager to look at her at close quarters. But she, Mahālakṣmī, the chaste lady, looked at Devas, Dānavas, Siddhas, Cāraṇas and Serpents in the same manner as a mother looks (affectionately) at her children.

70. Devas were glanced at by that Lakṣmī. So they became

1. Lakṣmī is identified with *Brahma-vidyā, Ānvīkṣikī, Vaiṣṇavī, Ṛddhi, Siddhi* and also with *Umā* as in the *Kenopaniṣad* 25 (*umāṁ haimavatīm*). She, being the mother-goddess looked with affectionate glance at all beings but married Viṣṇu.

prosperous instantaneously and were characterized by those indications of attainment of the kingdom. Daityas who were not glanced at by Lakṣmī became devoid of splendour (royal glory).

71-72. She glanced (lovingly) at Mukunda who was blue in complexion like Tamāla (Xanthochymus Pictorius), whose cheeks and nose were very handsome, who shone brilliantly with his superior person and was characterized by *Śrīvatsa* and looked (at everyone mercifully).

On seeing him, Lakṣmī suddenly got down from her elephant with the garland of forest flowers (still in her hands). With a broad smile, she put round the neck of the Supreme Being Viṣṇu, the garland that was wreathed by Śrī herself and wherein bees swarmed together.

73. She then sat there leaning on the left side of the great *Ātman*. On seeing them both, Suras and Daityas experienced a wonderful joy. So also Siddhas, Apsarās (celestial damsels), Kinnaras and Cāraṇas.

74. At that union of Lakṣmī and Nārāyaṇa, the delight of everyone was very great. All the worlds, all the people everywhere were simultaneously happy and joyous.

75. Mahāviṣṇu was sought and wooed by Lakṣmī. Lakṣmī was wooed by him alone. Thus through mutual love they became absorbed in looking at each other.

76. The sound of the various musical instruments and drums such as *Paṭahas*, conchs, *Mṛdaṅgas*, *Ānakas*, *Gomukhas*, *Bherīs* and *Jharjharīs* was very tumultuous.

77-79. The songs of the musicians were immensely splendid. With the four types of musical instruments, viz. *Tata*, *Vitata*, *Ghana* and *Suṣira*, the groups of Gandharvas and celestial damsels propitiated the all-pervading Lord Hari in every way. Gandharvas, being proficient in the art of music delighted the lord. Nārada, Tumburu and other Gandharvas and Yakṣas then sang sweetly. The groups of Suras and Siddhas served thus lord Nārāyaṇa who is in the form of the Supreme Ātman and whose enlightenment was boundless, deep and profound.

CHAPTER TWELVE

Devas Taste the Divine Nectar[1]

Lomaśa said:

1. After bowing down to Janārdana, the Supreme Being, along with Ramā, the groups of Suras and Asuras once again churned the ocean for the sake of Nectar.

2. From the ocean that was being churned, came out a youthful person of very great fame, well-known as Dhanvantari.[2] He was the great conqueror of *Mṛtyu* (Death).

3-4. He held in his hands a pot filled with nectar. While all Suras were (gladly) looking at the fascinating Lord Dhanvantari, Daityas wanted to attack him in a body and snatch away the pot (of nectar) that had been held in the hands of Dhanvantari.

5. The excellent physician surrounded by a series of waves was advancing slowly when he was seen by Vṛṣaparvan.

6. The pot that was in his hand was forcibly taken by him (Vṛṣaparvā). Thereupon, Asuras roared in a terrific manner.

7. Seizing and taking the pot filled with nectar, the impatient Daityas came down to Pātāla. Then Devas became confused and embarrassed.

8. They (Devas) who were well-prepared and ready for a battle, pursued them with a desire to fight. Turning towards Devas, Bali spoke thus:

Bali said:

9. O Devas, we are contented and gratified with the nectar only. You excellent Suras do go back quickly.

10. Please go back to Triviṣṭapa (Heaven) joyously. Of what avail are we to you? Formerly we entered into a friendly alliance

---

1. This chapter describes how Asuras were cheated by Viṣṇu by assuming the form of an enchantress and were deprived of their share of *Amṛta*.

2. Dhanvantari: Mbh, *Ādi* 18.38 also states that Dhanvantari came out of ocean along with a pot of *Amṛta*. He is regarded as an incarnation of Viṣṇu. This divine physician Dhanvantari is different from Dhanvantari, the physician-king of Vārāṇasī. He learnt *Āyurveda* from sage Bharadvāja and composed a systematic work of eight parts on *Āyurveda* and taught it to different disciples (BdP II.3, 67.1-24).

with you only because we wanted to realize our common objectives. Now it has been known to you. Do not have any doubt in it hereafter.

11. Thus rebuked and repulsed by Bali, those excellent Suras went back to Lord Nārāyaṇa along the path by which they had come.

12. On meeting him, all the Suras whose desires were frustrated, were consoled by Viṣṇu with various kinds of words capable of pacifying them:

13-14. "In this matter, do not be afraid unnecessarily. I shall bring back the nectar", said Lord Viṣṇu, the refuge of those who are helpless. The slayer of Madhu (Viṣṇu) having asked all the Suras to stay there itself, assumed the form of a charming lady, Mohinī, and appeared before Daityas.

15. By that time Daityas had become highly excited and agitated. They spoke to one another (about this). For the sake of nectar, all the Daityas began arguing with one another.

16-17. While this was going on, fortunately they saw a woman fascinating the minds of all living beings (who had assumed the form of Mohinī). They were struck with wonder and with covetous eyes (they staied at her). Honouring her, Bali, the king of Daityas, said:

Bali said:

18. O highly fortunate lady, this nectar should be (properly) distributed by you, so that it can reach all. Be quick about it. Do as I request.

19. On being requested thus, she smilingly said to Bali: "Women should never be trusted by a wise man.[1]

20. The following are the inherent natural defects of women: Falsehood, daring, deception, foolishness, excessive greed, uncleanliness and ruthlessness.

---

1. These traditional verses are meant for creating disaffection about *Saṁsāra*. Mohinī (Viṣṇu) cleverly uses them to create confidence about her in the gullible Asuras. The whole chapter shows how Mohinī cunningly appeals to the noble qualities of Asuras and cheats them.

21. Lack of genuine affection as well as mischievous cunningness should also be known as existing in them, in fact. These defects should undoubtedly be known as existing (even) in one's own wives.

22. Just as wolves among beasts of prey, crows among birds and foxes among wild animals are given to killing, so also women among human beings should always be understood by the wise as exceedingly mischievous and cunning.

23. How can there be friendship and alliance between me and you all. Should this not be considered? Who are you and who am I?

24. Hence everything should be done by you after careful consideration with your keen intellect. Of course, you are very efficient in knowing what should be done and what should not be done, O excellent Asuras."

Bali said:

25-26. The women mentioned by you are the uncivilized ones of the rural area. They have no culture and they are the favourites of the vulgar and the rustic people. But, O splendid lady, you are not one among those women mentioned (by you). Why do you talk much? Do according to our directions.

After Bali had spoken, Mohinī said this:

27-29. "O lord, I shall follow your instructions whether they are good or bad."

Bali said:

Today distribute the nectar among all in a befitting manner. We shall take what is given by you. It is true. I am speaking the truth.

On being told thus, goddess Mohinī who was auspicious in every respect, spoke to all the Asuras desirous of following the conventional propriety:

The Lord (*i.e. Mohinī*) *said*:

30-32. By a stroke of good luck, all of you have become blessed and achieved your desired objective, O excellent Asuras.

Do observe fast today and let the preliminary consecratory rite of the nectar be performed. Something is yet (to be observed) with a desire for your welfare. Tomorrow you can have the *Pāraṇā* (ceremonial breakfast). Your desire for observances and worships (is commendable). For the sake of propitiating Īśa, the *Viniyoga* (ceremonious disposal) rite should be performed by an intelligent (devotee) with a tenth part of the amount legally and justifiably earned by him.

33. Saying "So be it", they all honoured whatever was said by Devamāyā. Deluded and not being very proficient and experienced, they did everything advised by Devamāyā.

34. Very big, fascinating, lustrous and rich mansions were built by the Asura, Maya.

35. They sat in those abodes after taking bath and adorning themselves befittingly. Excited much, they placed the full pot (of nectar) in front of themselves.

36. With very great joy, all of them kept vigil during the night. At dawn, they engaged themselves in taking early morning ablutions.

37. After finishing all necessary daily routine duties, Asuras, the chief of whom was Bali, sat in rows in due order. They were eager to drink (the nectar).

38-41. The following were the important ones among Daityas etc.: Bali, Vṛṣaparvan, Namuci, Śaṅkha, Sudaṁṣṭra, Saṁhlādī, Kālanemi, Vibhīṣaṇa, Vātāpi, Ilvala, Kuṁbha, Nikuṁbha, Pracchada, Sunda, Upasunda, Niśuṁbha, Śuṁbha, Mahiṣa, Mahiṣākṣa, the valorous Biḍālākṣa, the mighty-armed Cikṣura, Jṛṁbhaṇa, Vṛṣāsura, Vibāhu, Bāhuka, Ghora, Ghoradarśana, Rāhu and Ketu. These and many other Daityas, Dānavas and Rākṣasas sat there in due order.

42-43. There were rows and rows of those Daityas numbering crores and crores. Now, O Brāhmaṇas, listen to what happened thereafter and what great things were done by that goddess in the matter regarding (the distribution of) the nectar.

44-45. All were informed by her immediately (to be ready). She took up the pot. That Viśvumohinī was endowed with the greatest splendour. The goddess appeared splendid with the pot resting in her hands. The (goddess) conducive to the auspiciousness of all auspicious things in the universe shone with the greatest lustre.

46. At the very same instant, all the Suras who had halos around them, came to the place where those excellent Asuras were present.

47. On seeing them, Mohinī, the most excellent one among young women, said immediately:

Mohinī said:

48. These (people) should be known as guests. They are conducive to the accomplishment of every thing virtuous. If you keep the promise given to me, something should be given to these in accordance with your capacity. You are the authority in this regard. Do everything now. Do not delay.

49. Those who render help to others in accordance with their capacity are blessed ones. They should be known to be very pure and protectors of the worlds.

50-51. Those who endeavour only for (filling in) their belly should be known as destined to suffer. There is no doubt about this. Hence, O (friends) of auspicious rites, this should be divided by me. You give Devas whatever you like or dislike.

52. When these words were spoken by the goddess, the energetic and alert Asuras did so. The Asuras invited all Devas including Vāsava.

53. All of them sat, O Brāhmaṇas, for the sake of receiving the nectar. While they were occupying their seats, Mohinī who was conversant with all holy rites and virtuous acts, smilingly said to the Asuras these great words:

Mohinī said:

54-55. The Vedic Text prescribes that the guests should be honoured at the very outset. Hence, you who are all devoted to the gods and the Vedas speak out immediately. So whom shall I give the nectar at the very outset? Indeed, let those whose leader is Bali, let those persons of exalted fortune say.

56. Then the goddess was told by Bali. "(Do) what appeals to your mind. O lady of beautiful face, you are our mistress. There is no doubt about it."

57-58. On being honoured thus by that Bali of pure soul, the goddess hurriedly took up the pot for the purpose of serving.

A silk cloth shone over her thighs resembling the trunk of a royal elephant. She walked rather slowly on account of the (huge) buttocks. Her limbs were agitated and excited due to inebriation. With the tinkling of the golden anklets, she appeared to be cooing (like a cuckoo). Her breasts resembled pitchers. With the pot (of nectar) in her hand, she entered (the place where they were seated).

59-60. Then the goddess Mohinī proceeded serving the group of Devas directly. She showered on Devas the juice of the nectar again and again as though their sole diet consisted of this nectar. The groups of Devas, the chief among whom was Devendra, and the groups of Gandharvas, Yakṣas and celestial damsels along with Guardians of the Quarters swallowed again and again the juice of nectar served by that great (goddess) of cosmic form.

61. All Daityas, the chief among whom was Bali, O leading Brāhmaṇas, continued to be seated there. They were anxious and afflicted with hunger. The resolute Daityas kept quiet and were engaged in meditation.

62-63. On seeing those Daityas in such a plight after resorting to a delusion, the two leading Daityas Rāhu and Ketu assumed the forms of Devas and hurriedly sat in the row of Devas for receiving the nectar.

64-65. The exceedingly invincible Rāhu was desirous of drinking the nectar. When this was reported to Viṣṇu of unmeasured splendour by the Sun and the Moon, the head of Rāhu of deformed body was cut off. The head went up into the sky. The headless body dropped down on the earth. Rolling down, it crushed many mountains into small particles.

66-68. The entire world including the mountains was reduced to fine dust. On seeing that the entire universe consisting of mobile and immobile beings was smashed to fragments by her (i.e. Mohinī) through that body (of Rāhu), Mahādeva stood above it. The abode of all Devas was at the soles of her feet. The affliction (?) was near her, hence the name *Nivāsa*[1] (abode) (*obscure*).

1. The name *Nivāsa* reminds one of Nevāsā, a village in Ahmednagar District in Maharashtra where the incident is traditionally said to have taken

69. Since her lotus-like feet had been the abode (*ālaya*) of great ones (*mahatām*), the enchantress of the three worlds became reputed as *Mahālayā*.

70. Ketu vanished into the sky in the form of smoke. It was after handing over the nectar to the Moon that he vanished thus.

71. Vāsudeva is the origin of the universe. He is the supreme cause of all the worlds. It was due to Viṣṇu's grace that everything took place favouring the realization of Devas' objectives.

72. Since the fate was adverse, the enterprise of Mohinī was conducive to the destruction of Asuras. Understand that all exertions without (favourable) fate are useless.

73. The churning of the ocean was conducted by all of them simultaneously. But, it ended in the success of Devas, while Asuras failed (in their objective).

74. Therefore, they were furious at the excellent Devas. Daityas who were deluded took up many weapons and missiles. When Viṣṇu went away they began to roar.

CHAPTER THIRTEEN

The Fight between Devas and Asuras

Lomaśa said:

1-2. Then (those Asuras) roared at the Suras, the chief among whom was Indra, and whose strength and valour was great. They challenged them for a fight. The noble-souled son of Virocana got into his aerial chariot. He was accompanied by Daityas who were very powerful and who came in various (groups). With his entire army he rushed at Suras in a terrible way.

3. They had assumed their (original real) forms. They

place. There is an old temple of Mohinī (Mahālasā, Oyā). Archaeologically that is a very ancient site in Maharashtra. If the conjecture be correct, the author might have probably belonged to this part of the country. But vv 66-68 mention the name of Somanātha (Saurashtra).

attacked (the enemies) in thousands. Some of them rode on tigers and others on buffaloes.

4-6. Some of them rode on horses, others on elephants; while some others rode on lions, panthers and śarabhas (eight-footed mythical animal), peacocks, royal swans, cocks, horses, elephants, camels, mules and asses. Some drove in carts. Many Daityas came on foot with swords, javelins and daggers in their hands.

7-8. There were demons with iron bars as weapons. Others had nooses, javelins and iron clubs in their hands. Some had thin-bladed swords. Others had *bhuṣuṇḍī* (a sort of missile) and iron bolts as their weapons. Others came on horses, chariots and elephants and began to strike. Thousands of Asuras, the chief among whom was Bali, rode in aerial chariots.

9. They vied with one another roaring frequently. Vṛṣaparvan then said to Bali, the leading Daitya:

10. "O mighty one, an alliance was entered into with Indra by you. One should not place too much of faith in an evil-minded person.

11-12. By no means should one trust and enter into an alliance with a base person, even if one happens to be weak and inferior. Friendship must be formed with an intelligent person. In case of emergency (he will help one) to make the mishap ineffective.

One must not believe in a person who has been an enemy previously. It is because of you, O Bali, that we have been defeated now! Why should those chronic rogues not try to undo what has been agreed upon?"

13. Those (sturdy Asuras) who could not be thwarted and were desirous of fighting said thus and arrayed themselves suitably. They adorned the battlefield with banners, umbrellas and flags.

14-15. They covered all the quarters with chowries. The battlefield was completely covered up.

Similarly all Suras were also eager to (fight with) Daityas. Those persons of exalted fortune drank the nactar, put on the coats of mail and got on their respective vehicles. Mahendra, the valorous one with vajra (thunderbolt) in his hand, rode on his elephant. The Sun was seated on Uccaiḥśravas and the Moon rode on a deer.

16. They were equipped with umbrellas and chowries. They were rendered splendid by the martial glory born of victory. Desirous of victory, all those persons beginning with Indra bowed down to Viṣṇu.

17-18. Permitted by Viṣṇu, they angrily (rushed at) Asuras. Asuras of huge body, terrible eyes and dreadful exploits (withstood them). The fight of Devas with Dānavas was very terrible, tumultuous and exceedingly dreadful, instilling fear into all living beings.

19-20. Arrows were continuously showered. Everything became excessively wonderful. The rough and harsh noise like *Caṭacaṭā* reverberated in all the ten directions.

Within a moment, they were wounded by arrows. Struck and hurt by arrows, iron clubs, javelins and iron-tipped missiles, they fell on the ground.

21-22. Even as they were being split and pierced, they split and tore others in the battle. They were shattered with *Bhalla*,[1] arrows and smashed to pieces by *Nārācas* (iron-tipped arrows). Some of the Daityas, Dānavas and Rākṣasas were hit with many *Kṣurapras* (arrows with horseshoe-shaped tips) and they appeared to be torn with them. Some Dānavas were shattered and killed by *Śilīmukhas* (sharp-pointed arrows).

23. On seeing the army of Dānavas broken up thus, Devas roared and moved all round. Delighted, they assembled together and celebrated the victory they had gained.

24-26. The three worlds were filled with the sounds of conchs and musical instruments. Dānavas of great strength became furious with Devas. Bali and all the others rose up once again with great excitement. They were equipped with many aerial chariots resembling the sun. With a desire to conquer each other Devas and Dānavas engaged themselves in tumultuous duels.

27. Mahendra fought with Bali, the lord of Dānavas. Similarly, Yama of great and powerful arms met Namuci in combat.

---

1. *Bhalla, Nārāca, Kṣurapra, Śilīmukha* are different kinds of arrows.

28. Nairṛta fought with Praghasa. Varuṇa clashed with Kuṁbha. Sadāraya (Wind-god) fought with Nikuṁbha.

29. Rāhu fought a very terrible combat with Soma (the Moon). The *Amṛta* (nectar) arising from the body of the Moon was imbibed by Rāhu. Due to the contact with nectar (another figure) like Rāhu rose up.

30-32. All these things were seen by Śaṁbhu, the great lord. "There is no doubt about this that I am the base and support of all living beings. I am affectionate and dear to all, Asuras as well as Suras." On being told thus Rāhu bowed down to Śiva. The Moon stationed on his crest discharged nectar out of fear. On account of it, many such heads were produced simultaneously. Śaṁbhu made them into a beautiful garland and tied it to his head like a (decorative) head-ornament.

33. By swallowing Kālakūṭa for the purpose of accomplishing the objective of Devas, he became blue-throated with a garland of skulls (thus) made.

34. Maheśvara wore the garland of skulls.

35. By means of that garland shone the noble-souled Hara, the primordial lord of Devas, the destroyer of Tripura. He is the lord by whom the great demon Gaja (Elephant) was struck down and the huge (demon) Andhaka was reduced to dust.

36-37. It was Śiva by whom Gaṅgā was held in the middle of his head. He, the dispeller of fear, kept the Moon on his crest. *Vedas*, *Purāṇas*, *Āgamas*, different kinds of *Śrutis* and scriptures argue and discuss variously in accordance with difference in their respective texts. In the course of their discussion they become dumb. Śiva, the sole friend of the universe, is being investigated and described differently according to the opinion of the preceptors of different Āgamas.

38. Abandoning the eternal lord Śiva, the supreme spirit that could be comprehended only through the Vedas, deluded people commit blunders. They do not realize Śiva of the form of the Great Spirit.

39. Śiva is the Paramātmā (Supreme Soul) by whom everything is created and sustained. He pervades everything and evolves everything. The entire universe is a part of this Lord. He may, perhaps, be comprehended through the *Vedānta*.

40. A person always engaged in devotion to Śiva is undoubtedly Śiva, whether he is rich or poor, noble or base.

41. If a person becomes delighted on seeing the splendid worship of Śiva performed by others, he gets a gift (i.e. merit) equal to his (i.e. that of the worshipper).

42. People should offer rows of lamps in the month of Kārttika with great faith. A devotee who offers lamps thus is honoured in heaven for as many thousands of *Yugas* as the number (of hours) during which those lamps burn in front of the *Liṅga*.[1]

43. If the lamps with safflower oil are offered in the temple of Śiva, those who offer them rejoice in Kailāsa in the presence of Śiva.

44. If the lamps with linseed oil are offered in the temple of Śiva, those who offer them rejoice in Kailāsa in the presence of Śiva.

45-46. As a result of the offering of lamps, people become *Jñānins* (endowed with perfect knowledge).

If the lamps with gingelly oil are offered in the temple of Śiva, they (the offerers) go to Śiva in the company of a hundred members of their family.

47. Those by whom lamps are filled with ghee and lit in the temple of Śiva, go to the highest abode in the company of a hundred thousand members of own family.

48. Those who worship Śiva always with camphor, aloe and incense and those who perform the rite of waving lights everyday along with camphor, attain *Sāyujya* (identity with the Divinity). There is no doubt about it.

49. Those who worship the *Liṅga* once, twice or thrice a day with care are Rudras (themselves). There is no doubt about it.

50. If the devotees wear Rudrākṣa beads[2] at the time of the

1. It is an age-old practice to illuminate temples with oil-lamps in the month of Kārttika (November-December). VV 42-47 describe the 'fruit' of using different kinds of oil for these lamps.

2. Rudrākṣa is the 'berry' of *Elaeocarpus Ganitrus*. It is of different kinds, 'one-faced', 'five-faced' etc. Genuine 'one-faced' Rudrākṣa is rare and is

worship of Śiva, when charitable gifts are offered, when penance is performed, in the holy spots and during festive occasions with care, their merit is infinite, O Brāhmaṇas.

51. Listen, O excellent Brāhmaṇas, to what Śiva has said about Rudrākṣa beads. There are Rudrākṣas with one face, two faces etc. up to sixteen faces. Among these, two should be known as the most excellent ones, O Brāhmaṇas, which redeem (devotees).

52. They are the five-faced Rudrākṣa and the single-faced Rudrākṣa. Those men who always wear the single-faced Rudrākṣa, go to the world of Rudra and rejoice in the presence of Rudra.

53. *Japa*, penance, holy rites, yogic practice, holy bath, charitable gift, worship etc.—if these splendid rites are performed while wearing Rudrākṣa beads, these rites yield infinite results.

54. If a Rudrākṣa bead is tied round the neck of even a dog, it will be redeemed thereby. There is no doubt about it.

55. Due to the association of the Rudrākṣa bead one's sin will be destroyed. Knowing this one should perform auspicious rites after wearing a Rudrākṣa bead.

56. If the devotees have *Tripuṇḍra* (three horizontal parallel lines on the forehead) (marked) with *Vibhūti* (sacred ash) sanctified by Mantras, they will undoubtedly become Rudras and (rejoice) in the world of Rudra.

57. The dung of a tawny-coloured cow should be gathered before it touches the ground. It must be dried and burned by the devotees of Śiva for preparing *Vibhūti*.

58-59. It is called *Vibhūti*. It destroys all sins. At the outset, a single line should be drawn carefully with the thumb on the forehead. Then, two lines should be drawn, one above and one below the previous line by means of two fingers avoiding the middle finger. If the three lines are clearly visible on the forehead, that person is a devotee of Śiva. He should be known as the destroyer of sins by (his) mere sight, like Śiva.

60-61. Those devotees of Śiva who keep matted hair, keep five, seven or nine such clusters. Those who do so in accordance

valued highly. VV 50-55 describe the spiritual importance of wearing Rudrākṣa.

with the injunctions in Śaiva treatises, do attain Śiva. There is no doubt about this. Rudrākṣa beads should be worn particularly by Śiva's devotees.

62. Sadāśiva can be worshipped with a very little quantity (of materials) or with profusely rich material. The devotee redeems thereby ten million members of his family and rejoices with Śiva.

63. Hence, O excellent Brāhmaṇas, there is nothing greater than Śiva. When this is told in the scripture (it must be known that), everything has Śiva for its cause.

64. Indeed Śiva is the bestower of the worlds. He is the maker of the worlds. He rejoices along with (his devotees). Know, O excellent Brāhmaṇas, that the whole universe consists of both Śiva and Śakti.

65. The two-syllabled name *Śi-va* saves one from very great danger. Hence, O excellent Brāhmaṇas, let Śiva be contemplated upon and remembered.

The sages said:

66-68. The greatness of Somanātha has been understood. It was due to his grace that all were saved from the fear of the heads of Rāhu by Parameṣṭhin. Suras beginning with Indra and others (were saved by the lord) in that dreadful battle. Thereafter, what did all those Suras do? Let it be narrated. Everything about the greatness of Śiva as narrated by you was heard directly (while) uttered by you orally. Let the narration of the battle be made exactly as it happened.

Lomaśa said:

69. When Suras were defeated by Daityas, all of them sought refuge in Śaṁbhu. The excellent Suras bowed down to Śiva. All of them immediately decided to fight.

70. Similarly, all Daityas who were very powerful and enthusiastic began to fight. Equipped with great missiles, they came into contact with Devas and fought again and again.

71. Thus, all Suras and Asuras who were desirous of victory and who were exceedingly furious, fought with one another with javelins, swords, spears, iron bars and axes. Being struck down and hit by Suras with many great arrows and missiles combined

with one another Asuras (though) indomitable fell down in the same manner as lions falling into Gaṅgā.

72. They made the entire earth muddy with flesh and blood. They made the entire earth including oceans, forests, mines, trees and mountains (full of blood and flesh).

73. Deep rivers of blood lashed and swept heads, headless bodies, great armours, flags, chariots, banners and heads of elephants and horses.

74. These rivers instilled fear into the minds of cowards. Brahmarākṣasas crossed these bloody rivers and made the other goblins, ghosts, Pramathas and Rākṣasas cross them.

75. There were groups of female devils such as Śākinīs, Ḍākinīs etc. and thousands of Yakṣiṇīs. Rejoicing in the company of each other, they were engaged in various sports.

76. Thus, in that highly dreadful battle Devas and Asuras clashed directly with one another. There Bhūtas, Pramathas and Rākṣasas continued their sports.

77. Devendra of wonderful exploits fought with Bali. The infuriated son of Virocana (Bali) struck Devendra with a javelin.

78-79. Mahendra of quick and nimble steps dodged that javelin. He struck Bali, the lord of Daityas, with great effort and force with his great thunderbolt of sharp edges The valorous (lord of Devas) cut off his (Bali's) arms. (Thereupon) he fell down dead on the ground from his aerial chariot resembling the sun.

80-81. On seeing Bali fallen, Vṛṣaparvan furiously showered Mahendra and his elephant with a volley of arrows like the cloud showering a mountain. Mahendra bore the sharp arrows. Then a terrible battle ensued between Mahendra and Vṛṣaparvan.

82-85. Indra, the tormentor of the enemy's army, caused Vṛṣaparvan to fall down. Then he killed Dānavas in the battle with his great thunderbolt. Some were pierced through the head. Some were hit in the neck. Some were rendered bewildered and afflicted by the furious Indra. Similarly, Dānavas were killed by Yama, Vāyu and Varuṇa. Others were killed by Kubera and Nairṛta. Some were killed by Agni and torn asunder by Īśa.

86. Thus the powerful Asuras of great exploit were killed by Suras and the guardians of the worlds. It was due to the favour of Śiva that they were killed then.

87. Then the great and excellent Daitya who was equipped with excellent missiles and weapons came in to kill the excellent Suras. The evil-minded demon who was very cruel in his heart advanced alone.

88. Armoured and armed with a trident, he rode on a lion surrounded by one hundred millions of Daityas, all riding on lions.

89. All those lions of great strength and exploit were equipped with coats of mail. The great Daityas riding on those lions were also equal to them.

90. On seeing the entire army of Daityas, that was adorned by lions and led by Kālanemi, advancing, the Devas with Indra, their leader, became exceedingly frightened. Then they began to ponder.

91. 'What shall we all do now? How will we conquer this wonderful and countless army surrounded by lions?'

92-93. When they were thinking thus, Nārada happened to come there. The old story of Kālanemi's power of penance was told to Mahendra by Nārada. He told him about his invincibility in battle, by virtue of the power of boons granted to him.

94. "O Devas, we are not competent to conquer (this army) in the battle ground without Viṣṇu's help. Hence, let the great lord Viṣṇu, the lord dark in complexion like the Tamāla leaves, the bestower of boons, be remembered by (all of you) desirous of conquest."

95. On hearing the words of Nārada, Devas hurriedly meditated on Mahāviṣṇu, the tormentor of the enemy's army, the Supreme Soul. Remembering the lord, they prayed to him thus:

Devas said:

96. Obeisance to you, the lord, the cause of the auspiciousness of the universe. O Śrīnivāsa (Abode of Śrī), obeisance to you. O Śrīpati (Consort of Goddess Lakṣmī), obeisance, obeisance to you.

97. Today we are exceedingly frightened. We are oppressed by the fear of Kālanemi. It behoves you, O lord, the bestower of freedom from fear to Devas, to save us from the Daitya.

98. On being meditated and remembered thus, the dark-

complexioned Hari, the bestower of freedom from fear to all the worlds, appeared before them riding on Garuḍa.

99. The lord with the discus in his hand came there for the victory of Devas.

They all saw Mahāviṣṇu seated on Garuḍa and stationed in the firmament, the invincible lord Śrīvāsa (the resort of Śrī) who was desirous of fighting.

100. On seeing the lord like that, Kālanemi who was very mighty and highly infuriated, said laughingly (loudly): "Who are you, O exalted one of great fortune? You are excellent in form and features. You are young and dark-complexioned and possess the valour of an elephant in rut. A sharp-edged brilliant discus is held by you in your hand. Why? Let me know, O Lord."

The Lord said:

101. I came here for the purpose of fighting, for the fulfilment of the cause of Devas. Be steady, O stupid one, I shall undoubtedly burn you now.

102. On hearing the words of the Lord, the valorous Kālanemi became angry and said to lord Adhokṣaja (Viṣṇu):

103. "You are the lord and root-cause of Devas. You are highly proud of your ability to fight. If you are a brave warrior, fight with me now."

104-107. Lord Mahāviṣṇu of great lustre laughed and said: "Either you be stationed in the sky, or I shall be stationed on the earth. O mighty one, fight [either in the sky or on the ground, so that the battle will not be on uneven planes and blameworthy."

Saying "So be it" the Daitya of great mangificence, surrounded by one hundred million Daityas who were dignified and glorious and seated on lions, who were powerful and ruthless, rose up in the sky slowly. He was accompanied by the groups of Asuras. He was desirous of killing (Viṣṇu) the lord of cosmic form. He took up another fierce trident with a desire to fight with Hari. His mouth and face had a hideous form due to his (curved ferocious) teeth as well as (his desire to send) an oral message (to his followers).

CHAPTER FOURTEEN

Resuscitation of Dead Daityas

Lomaśa said:

1-2. Then the fight between Asuras and Viṣṇu became exceedingly terrific. The exceedingly wonderful winged lions equipped with armours and ridden by Asuras tore up Garuḍa. The lions too were pierced and torn to pieces by him.

3-4. Then Daityas were cut into pieces by Viṣṇu with his discus. On seeing Asuras killed, the valorous Kālanemi, with his eyes full of wrath, struck Viṣṇu with his trident. Mukunda (Viṣṇu), the support of those who are helpless, caught hold of the trident as it rushed at him.

5. Viṣṇu playfully caught hold of Kālanemi, the Asura of great power with his trident, by his left hand sportively. Being struck with the self-same trident, he suddenly fell down senseless.

6-7. The fallen Daitya came to senses again and slowly opened his eyes. Regaining consciousness, he saw Viṣṇu standing in front of him—Viṣṇu, the lord abiding in the cavity of the heart of everyone. Kālanemi of great strength then spoke these words:

"I will not offer to fight with you. I have no desire for worlds (and worldly pleasures).

8-9. According to the words of Brahmā, those Asuras who are killed in the battle will attain the *Akṣaya* (Everlasting) world. Immediately they will come into contact with Indra. Enjoying various kinds of worldly pleasures, they will roam about like gods along with Indra. Then they will fall down to the earthly world.

10. Hence, I do not desire death in battle. It is of a momentary nature. O heroic lord, it behoves you to grant me *Kaivalya* (salvation) alone, the great benefit, in the course of my next birth, of course, as a result of an inimical attitude."

11. Saying "So be it", the Supreme Being, the bestower of the greatest benefit, caused the excellent Daitya to fall down. Having given *Sudhā* (nectar) to Devas (before) and having granted freedom from fear to Devas (now) (the lord saved them).

12. Kālanemi, the great Daitya who was like a dart, was

killed by Viṣṇu, the powerful lord. Devas became rid of thorns (enemies).

13-14. The lotus-eyed Lord vanished immediately.

Having caused extremely wonderful (terrific) havoc among Daityas, Indra also continued the slaughter of Daityas who were fallen, cowardly like eunuchs, broken (in spirit) and frightened in mind, and had their garments and tufts of hair loosened.

15. The liberal-minded consort of Śacī (Indra), who was like the god of Death unto Daityas and who could never be conquered (did all these things), because, he was devotedly following the (instructions laid down in the) *Arthaśāstra.*[1]

16. While Asuras were being killed like this, the holy lord Nārada came there in order to make Indra desist from it.

Nārada said:

17. Many heroic Asuras have been killed fighting in the battlefield. Why do you kill the frightened ones after that?

18. The haughty and arrogant ones who cause the death of those who are afraid and those who seek refuge should be known as murderers of Brāhmaṇas. They are guilty of great sins.

19-20. Hence, even mentally injury should not be caused by you.

On being told thus by the noble-souled Nārada, Indra immediately came back to Triviṣṭapa (heaven) accompanied by the armies of Suras. Then all the groups of Suras, all the Yakṣas, Gandharvas and Kinnaras became joyous. Along with their friends, they enjoyed the company of one another.

21-26a. Then Indra was crowned in Amarāvatī along with Śacī by leading celestial sages and leading Brāhmaṇa sages. It was due to the favour of Śaṅkara that Śakra attained victory.

Then, O Brāhmaṇas, there was a great celebration in the world of Devas. Then conchs and different kinds of drums like

1. *Arthaśāstra*—A treatise on political economy. It is the title of a famous work of Kauṭilya or Ārya Cāṇakya who masterminded the revolution in Pāṭalīputra (Magadha), uprooted the Nanda dynasty and installed Candragupta Maurya as the King. Kauṭilya refers to many predecessors. Hence the *Arthaśāstra* mentioned here may be a more ancient work than that of Kauṭilya.

Paṭahas, Mṛdaṅgas, Murajas, Ānakas, Bherīs and *Dundubhis* were sounded simultaneously. Gandharvas and Kinnaras were the musicians. The groups of celestial damsels danced. Siddhas, Cāraṇas and Guhyakas sang praises.

Thus Śakra, the lord of Devas, attained victory.

26b-27a. At that time, the noble-souled Daityas, the chief among whom was Bali and who had been killed by Devas, fell down lifeless on the surface of the earth.

Formerly the Brāhmaṇa Bhārgava (accompanied by his disciples) had gone to mount Mānasottara for performing penance. Hence he was not aware of that battle.

27b-29. Those Daityas who had survived approached Bhārgava. The news of the great destruction of Asuras was conveyed to him. On hearing it, the son of Bhṛgu became furious. He returned surrounded by his disciples. With the *Vidyā* (magic formula) called *Mṛtajīvinī* ('Resuscitator of the dead'), he revived the Asuras who had fallen dead.

30. Then those Asuras got up as though they had awakened from sleep. Bali who rose up, said to Bhārgava of unmeasured splendour:

31. "Of what avail is it to me today to be revived back to life? There is no benefit to me. I have been struck down by the lord of Devas like a mean contemptible wretch."

32-33. On hearing the words uttered by Bali, Śukra spoke these words: "Those heroic persons who are high-souled and intelligent, who are learned, and who fall down dead in battle on being struck by a weapon go to heaven. This is undoubtedly the statement of the Vedas."

34. Thus, the son of Bhṛgu consoled Bali. He then performed various kinds of penance conducive to the achievement of *Siddhis* by Daityas.

35. All the Daityas urged by Bhṛgu went to Pātāla. All the Daityas, the chief among whom was Bali, stayed in Pātāla in happiness.

CHAPTER FIFTEEN

Nahuṣa and Yayāti: Their Indrahood and Fall

The sages enquired:

1-2. It has been mentioned by you that Devendra regained kingdom without his preceptor. It was on account of disrespect to his preceptor that he had been dethroned from his kingdom. Urged by whom did he retain his position for a long time? Do tell us all these things quickly. We are very eager to hear it.

Lomaśa replied:

3-4. The consort of Śacī (Indra) ruled over the kingdom (of heaven) without his preceptor (Bṛhaspati). The great Indra (could) continue (to rule) over the kingdom due to the (religious) performance in accordance with the injunctions of Viśvarūpa.

5-6. O Brāhmaṇas, Viśvarūpa,[1] a great king, was the son of Viśvakarmā. He became the preceptor and performer of sacrifices for Śakra.

In that *Yajña*, Triśiras (one with three heads) performed the worship with partial oblations separately for Asuras, Suras and human beings.

In the direct presence of Indra everyday he used to give ladles (full of Soma) to Devas with a loud shout, to Daityas silently, and to human being in a fallen middle tone.

7-8. Once he was detected due to his partiality (regarding relative importance of oblations) by Indra who remained concealed and unobserved. Then the desired object (of Triśiras) was understood (by Indra).

(Devendra thought) 'He is making this piecemeal offering for the sake of accomplishing the task of Daityas. He is our preceptor, but gives the benefit to (our) enemies.'

9. After thinking thus, Śakra cut off his heads instantaneously by means of his *Vajra* (thunderbolt) of hundred spikes. The death was instantaneous.

10-11. The Kapiñjala (a sort of partridge) birds were born

1. Viśvarūpa alias Triśiras was the son of Tvaṣṭṛ. He was killed by Indra for his fraud described here. *Vide* also Mbh, *Udyoga* 9.

from the face with which he drank Soma juice. Then from the other face with which he drank liquor, the Kalaviṅka (sparrow) birds were born. From the other (third) face, the Tittira birds of various forms were born. Thus, Viśvarūpa was killed by Śakra, the ill-fated one.

12-14. The female fiend (born of and called) *Brahmahatyā* ('Brāhmaṇa-murder') manifested there. She was terrific and unthwartable. She was evil-faced, wicked, full of Cāṇḍāla impurity and could not be blocked or defeated.

The terrible sinners are those who slay Brāhmaṇas, those who drink liquor, those who steal (gold etc.) and those who defile and outrage the modesty of the preceptor's wife. The means of expiation for these sinners is the utterance of the names of Viṣṇu, since the mind has him for its object.

The three-headed fiend with smoke-coloured hands rushed forth to swallow Indra.

15. Thereupon (Indra) fled from there out of great fear. On seeing him fleeing, the terrible (devil) chased him.

16-17. Wherever he ran, she too ran after him. If he stood anywhere, she too stood beside him. She behaved in the manner of a shadow of one's own body. When she came so close as to envelop him, Indra sank beneath the waters suddenly, O Brāhmaṇas, like an old aquatic being.

18-19. Thus three hundred divine years passed since the consort of Śacī (Indra) began staying (beneath the waters) with great misery. A terrific state of anarchy spread throughout heaven. Thereupon Devas, sages and ascetics became anxious and worried. All the three worlds were overwhelmed by adversity, O Brāhmaṇas.

20. Even if there is a single Brāhmaṇa-slayer in a kingdom staying there with impunity, untimely death of good men will take place there.

21. The king of the state wherein he (the Brāhmaṇa-slayer) lives, becomes contaminated by the sin. There will be (prevalence of) famine, death and calamities.

22. There will be many misfortunes causing the destruction of the subjects. Hence, *Dharma* should be practised by a king with great faith.

23. Similarly, the ministers of the king too should be

installed with purity. Sin was committeed by Indra and due to that sin, O Brāhmaṇas, the whole of the universe met with calamities along with great distress of diverse kinds.

Śaunaka enquired:

24. It was by performing a hundred horse-sacrifices that the great realm of Devas was acquired by him, O Sūta. Why then did Śakra meet with obstacles, O highly fortunate one? Do tell us exactly as it happened.

Sūta replied:

25. In the case of Devas, Dānavas and particularly that of human beings, *Karman* alone is undoubtedly the cause of happiness and misery.

26-27. An immensely reprehensible act has been committed by Indra, O Brāhmaṇas. He insulted his Guru (preceptor Bṛhaspati). Viśvarūpa was slain. The wife of Gautama, his Guru (preceptor, elderly one), was carnally approached. It was the fruit of all these sins that was reaped by Mahendra for a long time. There was no way of atonement for the same.

28. If persons committing wicked and sinful deeds, do not perform expiatory rites (for the same), they do incur miseries just like Indra, (though) he had performed a hundred sacrifices.

29. If sins are committed, atonement should be performed instantaneously in accordance with the injunctions, O Brāhmaṇas, for the sake of quelling all the sins.

30-32. If minor sins are repeatedly performed, they turn into major sins. Those men who steadfastly cling to their duties of the morning, midday and dusk can get their sins destroyed. They attain the excellent world. There is no doubt about it. Hence, this person of evil conduct (i.e. Indra) reaped the fruit of his *karman*.

33. All the Guardians of the Quarters hurriedly deliberated together. They approached Bṛhaspati and reported to the preceptor about Indra everything they had in their mind.

34. On hearing the words uttered by Devas, Bṛhaspati, the intelligent (preceptor), thought about the anarchy that had begun to spread.

35-36. 'What shall be done now? How will they secure

welfare—Devas, the worlds and sages of sanctified souls?' In his mind, he thought over the details of what should and what should not be done. Accompanied by Devas, the preceptor of great fame went to Indra.

37. They reached the lake where Purandara (Indra) was lying (hidden) and on the bank of which was staying the (devil of) Brāhmaṇa slaughter terrible like a Caṇḍālī.

38. All the Devas, accompanied by the groups of sages sat there. Then Śakra was called by the preceptor himself.

39. Thereupon, Indra got up and saw his preceptor. With tears flowing over his face, he spoke to Bṛhaspati.

40-41. He bowed down to all the persons assembled there. He pondered over the great (blunders) committed by himself before, as a result of ignorance. He joined his palms in reverence and with a piteous face spoke: "O Lord, tell me what should be done by me just now?"

42-43. The holy lord Bṛhaspati of liberal mind laughed and said: "O Indra, this is the result of that act of yours committed previously against me. Only by experiencing its result, can it be annihilated. But, no atonement for Brāhmaṇa-slaughter has been seen (i.e. laid down) by the authors of *Smṛti* texts.

44. Expiation has been prescribed by those conversant with *Dharma Śāstras* (Code of Laws) for the sin committed unknowingly. There is no atonement for an offence wilfully committed.

45. A sin committed by a person intentionally does not become one committed unintentionally. Expiation is laid down for both based on the differences in the objects.

46. If a sin is committed wilfully (deliberately), the expiation is to be performed up to death. Atonement is laid down in case of sins committed unknowingly.

47. Since this has been intentionally done by you, since the twice-born, the learned priest has been killed, there is no atonement.

48. Stay in the waters here and wait for your death.

49. The meritorious deed of yours termed 'performance of one hundred horse-sacrifices', O evil-minded one, has already been destroyed at the very moment when the twice-born was killed by you.

50. Just as not a drop of water remains in a pot with holes,

similarly meritorious deeds of a sinner go on reducing every moment.

51. Hence, by good luck, if heaven etc. are attained, those can be retained only by really righteous ones. There is no doubt about it."

52. On hearing his statement, Indra spoke these words: "Undoubtedly this has fallen to my lot through my own misdeeds.

53. Hasten to Amarāvatī along with the celestial sages, O Bṛhaspati. For the purpose of accomplishing the tasks of the worlds as well as of Devas, O sage of great fortune, crown as Indra, anyone whom you approve in your mind.

54. Enveloped by the great devil of *Brahmahatyā*, I am just like one who is dead. I have been overwhelmed by the sin arising from *Rāga* (attachment) and *Dveṣa* (hatred).

55. Hence hasten all of you to make someone king of Devas. You have my permission for the same. I am speaking the truth to you."

56. On being told thus, all those (Devas) with Bṛhaspati at their head came to Amarāvatī immediately and coolly told Śacī everything about Indra's activities as they had taken place.

57. They consulted one another and began to deliberate thus: 'What should be done for the sake of the kingdom?'

58. While Devas were thus deliberating, Nārada, the celestial sage of unmeasured splendour, came there by chance.

59. On being honoured, he asked Devas: "Why are you all sad and perplexed?"

On being enquired (thus) they spoke everything about Śakra's activities:

60. "Indra's status of being the lord (of Devas) has come to an end on account of a great sin."

Thereupon Nārada, the celestial sage, spoke these words to those Devas:

61-62. "You are omniscient Devas endowed with the power of penance and valour. Hence Nahuṣa,[1] born in the Lunar race,

1. Nahuṣa—Son of Āyu of the Lunar race. He was elected as Indra by gods (Mbh, *Udyoga* 11.9, *Śānti* 342.44-52). He wanted Indra's wife Śacī and went to her in a palanquin borne by Seven Sages. When he prodded Agastya to go quickly '*sarpa*' he was cursed by Agastya to be a python (*sarpa*) and he fell from heaven (Mbh, *Udyoga* 17.14-18).

should be made Indra. He should be established in this realm, O Devas, immediately. Ninety-nine horse-sacrifices have been performed by that noble-souled Nahuṣa, O highly fortunate ones. Nahuṣa was a regular performer of *Yajñas*."

63-67. That statement coming out of the mouth of Nārada was heard by Śacī. With her eyes filled with tears and not engaged in anything (seriously), she went into the inner apartment.

On hearing the words of Nārada, all the Devas congratulated him. They approved of his suggestion to make Nahuṣa the ruler of the realm unanimously. Then, king Nahuṣa was brought to Amarāvatī and the kingdom of Mahendra was given to him by all the Suras and great sages.

Then all of them served Nahuṣa. Agastya and others (sages), Gandharvas, Apsarās, Yakṣas, Vidyādharas, the great serpents, Rākṣasas, the birds of bright wings (*suparṇas* like Garuḍa) and other heaven-dwellers (served him).

68. Then in the city of Devas, there was a continuous grand celebration. Conchs, musical instruments, *Mṛdaṅgas* and *Dundubhis* sounded simultaneously.

69. In that grand celebration of the kingdom of Devas, musicians sang songs, players of instruments played on them and dancers danced.

70. Then he was coronated there by the sages, of whom Bṛhaspati was the foremost.

71. He was worshipped with *Deva-Sūkta* and was made to perform the worship of Planets in due procedure and with formalities.

72. The great king Nahuṣa was duly honoured and respected by the learned sages of sanctified souls and by all others also. As the king of Suras, he sat on the throne of Indra. He had the same features as those of Indra. Endowed with the greatest splendour, he was eulogized by all.

73. Dressed in excellent sweet-scented bright garments and with his person adorned excellently with ornaments and articles of enjoyment, Nahuṣa appeared resplendent as he was being eulogized by prominent sages and leading Devas.

74. Thus the great king Nahuṣa who was endowed with great ingenuity and worshipped by groups of great Devas and sages, became severely tormented at heart by intense passion (lust).

Nahuṣa said:

75. How is it that Indrāṇī does not come near me? Call her quickly. It does not behove you to delay.

76. On hearing the words of Nahuṣa, the liberal-minded Bṛhaspati went to Śacī's abode and spoke in detail:

77. "It was on account of the calamity fallen on Indra that Nahuṣa was brought here for the sake of the kingdom. O beautiful lady, occupy half of his seat."

78-79. Śacī laughed and spoke to sinless Bṛhaspati: "He has occupied the seat of Indra without completing the quota of (hundred) *Yajñas.* Only ninety-nine horse-sacrifices have been performed by him. Hence, he is not qualified enough to obtain me. Let this be thought over truthfully. If this senseless fellow still continues to be desirous of me, wife of another person, let him obtain me by coming here by means of a vehicle that is carried by undeserving carriers."

80. Saying "So be it", Bṛhaspati returned hurriedly to Nahuṣa who had been distressed through intense lust. He reported to him what was spoken by Śacī in her own words.

81-84. Saying "So be it", Nahuṣa who was deluded by lust, thought over it. He deliberated on this intelligently: 'Who can be the carrier not worthy of being so?' After thinking about it intelligently and trying to remember for a long time (he decided thus): "The Brāhmaṇas and the ascetics are not usually thought of as carriers. I shall make two of them bear me in order to reach her. This is my decision." So (the king) who was deluded by lust gave the palanquin to two Brāhmaṇas.

Seated in that palanquin with great concentration, he urged them on with the words "*Sarpa, sarpa*" (Move on, move on). (*Sarpa* means 'serpent' also.)

85. Agastya who had been one of the palanquin-bearers became infuriated and cursed the king. "You are a lunatic and despiser of Brāhmaṇas; you be a python."

86. Immediately, after the utterance of the curse by the Brāhmaṇa, the king became a python and fell from there itself. Indeed the curse of a Brāhmaṇa is untransgressable.

87. Just as Nahuṣa became (a python), so also all like him fell into dirty hell by disrespecting Brāhmaṇas.

88. Hence, in order to attain benefits here and hereafter, a wise, circumspect person who has achieved a position of importance, should refrain in all possible ways from committing blunders.

89. Nahuṣa became a serpent in a very dreadful forest. Hence there prevailed anarchy in the world of Devas.

90. Similarly, all the Devas were struck with consternation. "Alas! What a wretched condition the king has fallen into!

91. This evil-minded fellow has obtained neither the mortal world nor the heavenly world. His (fund of) merits has been instantaneously burnt down.

92. If there is any other person who has performed (many) *Yajñas*, let him be named, O great sage."

Then the excellent sage Nārada of great splendour said:

93. "O highly fortunate ones, hasten to bring Yayāti.[1]"

Messengers of Devas went immediately and brought Yayāti quickly.

94-95. The noble-souled (Yayāti) got into an aerial chariot, and went to heaven accompanied by the messengers of Devas. He was then honoured and received by the excellent Devas as well as Serpents, Yakṣas, Gandharvas and Siddhas. He arrived at Amarāvatī and was then propitiated by Devas. He seated himself on the throne of Indra and was immediately addressed.

96. He was told thus by Nārada: "You are a king who has performed *Yajñas*. By insulting good people Nahuṣa attained the status of a venomous serpent.

97-98. Those virtuous persons who attain the highest position by means of good luck, become deluded too, on account of previous *Karman*. They do not see (distinguish between) auspiciousness and inauspiciousness. Those stubborn persons fall into terrible hell. There is no doubt about it."

---

1. Yayāti—Son of Nahuṣa. Married to Śukra's daughter Devayānī and Daitya King Vṛṣaparvā's daughter Śarmiṣṭhā. Out of jealousy of Śarmiṣṭhā, Devayānī insisted upon Śukra to curse Yayāti with old age. The latter was condemned but was empowered to borrow the youth of his son. He realized the folly of carnal enjoyment and returned his youthfulness to his son Pūru. He was a pious king but fell from heaven due to his boastfulness (Mbh, *Ādi* 88). But neither Mbh nor VR knows of the offer of Indrahood to him as mentioned in this Purāṇa (vv 94-95). The boast of Yayāti in one verse in Mbh, *Ādi* 88.2 is expanded here in vv 99-107.

Yayāti said:

99. Obstacles beset those persons too who have performed unmeasured and limitless meritorious deeds. They were by no means in small measures, O celestial sage. Know that everyone of those deeds of mine was very great.

100. Great charitable gifts have been offered along with the gifts of food. Many gifts of cows have been made along with the gifts of lands too.

101. Similarly, all excellent (religious) gifts mentioned by learned persons have been given by me then and there at the proper time, and in accordance with the great injunctions.

102. The sacrifices *Vājapeya*, *Atirātra*, *Jyotiṣṭoma*, *Rājasūya*, Horse-sacrifice etc. as mentioned in the *Śāstras*—all these have been performed by me. The earth has been adorned all round with sacrificial posts.

103. The Lord of the universe, the Lord of Devas has been worshipped in many ways. This daughter Mādhavī[1] was given to Gālava in the city.

104. Daughters were given to four persons as wives, O sage, for the sake of the intelligent preceptor of Gālava, viz. Viśvāmitra.

105. These and many other meritorious rites have been performed by me formerly. They are great and numerous. It is impossible to recount all of them."

106. That king was again asked by all the Devas: "Were all these holy rites performed secretly by you and properly too? We all wish to hear the truth. O Yayāti, we are all desirous of hearing too."

107. On hearing the words of Devas, Yayāti of unmeasured splendour described everything regarding the remaining part of his meritorious deeds.

108. Everything was described without leaving anything. Everything was severally mentioned in detail. Recounting his own merits, Yayāti fell down on the earth.

109. At that very instant, even as all the Suras went on watching (Yayāti fell down). Thus anarchy was produced and spread quickly.

---

1. Mādhavī became an ascetic. She gave half of her merit of penance to her father Yayāti when he fell from *svarga* (Mbh, *Udyoga* 120, 5-11, 25).

110-111. None else was seen by them deserving to be crowned in the place of Śakra on account of his being a *Yajña*-performer. Let this be heard, O excellent Brāhmaṇas.

All the Suras, Sages, great and leading serpents, Gandharvas, Yakṣas, Khagas (Birds), Cāraṇas, Kinnaras, Vidyādharas, groups of Suras and celestial damsels—all these became full of anxiety. So too were the human beings.

CHAPTER SIXTEEN

Dadhīci's Gift of His Body

Lomaśa said :

1-9. Thereupon Śacī spoke to them the following words full of virtuous advice : "O Devas with Bṛhaspati as the head, do not get despondent. All of you hasten to the place where the excellent Sura (lies hidden) on being attacked by the devil of Brāhmaṇa's slaughter. Hurry up, O clever ones, to see Śakra. It was for the sake of many (i.e. all gods etc.) that the dull-witted Viśvarūpa was killed by Mahendra. But, he was banished by all (of you). Hence, all of you should go to the place where the lord (is lying hidden). O sinless one, previously Mahendra had disregarded you. On account of that disrespect you became agitated and cursed Purandara. Similarly, O Bṛhaspati, you have been cursed by me. Though (Śakra) has been dismissed, you be loyal (to him) till the end. Just as two persons were brought for my sake even though Śakra is alive, so also, O Brāhmaṇa, even while you are alive (someone else) will do your job. Some person of exalted magnificence and felicity will procreate a son of great renown in your wife.[1] There is no doubt about this. Go immediately along with Suras. Bring Indra. Do not delay. If you do not hasten to go, I will curse you once again."

10. On hearing the words uttered by Śacī, he went there

1. Seduction of Tārā (Bṛhaspati's wife) is attributed to Śacī's curse in the text.

along with Suras. All of them went to Purandara (Indra) who had been afflicted with the devil of Brāhmaṇa's slaughter.

11. After reaching the shore of the lake, they made obeisance to Śakra. All of them were seen by Śakra who was staying in the waters.

12. The lord of Devas spoke to them : "Why have you all come here? I am staying here in the waters being overwhelmed by the sin of Brāhmaṇa's slaughter, alone and engaged in penance, O Devas."

13. On hearing these words of Indra, all the Devas became perturbed. They spoke to the king of Devas (these) amazing (words) :

14. "Words like these should not be uttered by you. Such of your activities as killing of Viśvarūpa had been done for the sake of helping others.

15. A mysterious sacrifice was performed by the son of Viśvakarmā, whereby Devas and the illustrious sages would be ruined.

16. It was for this reason, O lord, that he was killed by you for the sake of helping others. Thereupon, all of us have come to you to take you to Amarāvatī."

17-19. While Devas were discussing this matter, the devil of Brāhmaṇa's slaughter hurriedly said: "I am chaiming Devendra."

Then suddenly Bṛhaspati spoke these words:

Bṛhaspati said:

We shall now make arrangement of dwellings for your stay.

Thus the devil of slaughter was pacified by Devas on account of the importance of that matter.

20. All those Suras, the intelligent sages, Yakṣas, Piśācas, serpents, birds as well as all the celestial Siddhas and Cāraṇas deliberated on this matter and divided the sin of slaughter into four parts.[1]

21. At the outset, all the heaven-dwellers spoke to *Kṣamā* (the Earth): "O Earth, for the sake of realizing (our) objectives a

1. The distribution of the sin of Brahmin-slaughter among women, fire, trees and cows as briefly mentioned in Mbh, *Śānti* 342.53 (*vanitāgnivanaspati-goṣu*) is expanded in vv 21-41 here but the sin is distributed among the earth, trees, waters, and women in our text.

portion of the sin of Brāhmaṇa-slaughter should be accepted by you."

22-23. On hearing those words of Suras, *Dharitrī* (the Earth) trembled and said: "Let it be pondered as to how a part of the sin of Brāhmaṇa-slaughter can be taken over by me? I am the mother of all living beings. I sustain this universe. But, if I come into contact with sin, I will become exceedingly impure."

24. On hearing those words of the Earth, Bṛhaspati said to her: "Do not be afraid, O lady, beautiful in every limb. You are sinless. It cannot be otherwise.

25. When Vāsudeva[1] of great glory is born in the family of Yadus, you will become free from sins when his feet are placed (upon you).

26. Do carry out our request. You must not hesitate in this respect."

27. On being told thus, the Earth devoid of sins did according to their instructions (i.e. accepted a part of the sin).

Then all those Devas called Trees and spoke these words:

28. "A part of the (sin of) slaughter should be taken up by you for the purpose of realizing the objectives (of all the Devas)."

On being told thus, all the Trees who had come there said to Devas:

29-30. "We are all of this nature that we regularly provide ascetics with fruits. If we are tainted by the (sin of) slaughter, all the ascetics too, of great fortune, will become sinners. Hence, let everything be thought of."

Thereupon, all the Trees that had come there were told by the preceptor Bṛhaspati:

31-32. "None of you need worry about this. If you are cut off into several parts, you will grow further with many branches by the grace of Indra. Then you will be permanently endowed with (possession of branches)." On being told thus, all of them partially accepted the (sin of) the slaughter.

33. Then they called the Waters and all the heaven-dwellers spoke thus to the Waters: "Let a part of the (sin of) Brāhmaṇa's slaughter be taken up by the Waters for the sake of realizing the objectives (of Devas)."

---

1. The influence of Kṛṣṇa cult is obvious.

34-35. Then all the Waters joined together and said to the priest (Bṛhaspati): "All the living beings enveloped by sins sanctify themselves by dispelling whatever sins and evils they are tainted with, by coming into contact with us, through ablutions, cleansing processes and drinking."

36-38. On hearing their words, Bṛhaspati said: "O Waters, do not be afraid of the sin, though it is difficult to be crossed. Let the Waters sanctify all living beings, mobile and immobile."

Then Bṛhaspati called women and said: "Now itself a part of the (sin of) Brāhmaṇa-slaughter should be taken up for the sake of realizing the objectives of all."

On hearing the words of Guru (Bṛhaspati), all the women said:

39-40. "This is the injunction of the Vedas that if a woman commits a sin, other (many) members of her family become tainted with it and not otherwise. O priest, has this not been heard by you? Let it be pondered over."

On being told thus by the women, Bṛhaspati said:

41-42. "Do not be afraid of this sin, O ye ladies of beautiful eyes. This (act of yours) will bestow benefits on other ladies of the future. The part of the (sin of) slaughter will benefit everyone. (Further) you will have *Yathākāmitva* ('ability to love to the heart's content')." Thus, four parts of the sin of slaughter were allotted by Suras. The sin of slaughter stayed in those beings, O excellent Brāhmaṇas.

43. Mahendra then became free from sins and he was crowned in the city of Devas by the groups of Devas along with the sages.

44. Accompanied by Śacī, the noble-souled Purandara became the overlord of the universe. He was accompanied by Devas, the leading sages of great magnanimity and groups of Siddhas too.

45. Then, fires and winds became splendid. All the planets were lustrous and quiescent. The earth shone with great splendour; so also the mountains yielded gems and jewels.

46-48. The minds of learned men became delighted. Rivers flowed with nectarine waters. Trees yielded fruits perpetually. Planets and medicinal herbs grew and matured without being cultivated. They were comparable to nectar (in taste and effect).

The inhabitants of Indra's world were all enthusiastic and exceedingly joyous.

Lomaśa said:

49. In the meantime, Tvaṣṭṛ who witnessed the celebrations in honour of Indra became exceedingly infuriated and was afflicted with sorrow for his (dead) son.

50-51. With great dejection, he went (to forest) for performing a severe penance. Brahmā, the grandfather of the worlds, became pleased with that penance. Being delighted he said to Tvaṣṭṛ, "O (Tvaṣṭṛ) of good holy rites, choose your boon."

Thereupon, Tvaṣṭṛ chose a boon that caused fear to all the worlds:

"A son who will be terrifying Devas should be given as boon."

52. Saying "So be it", the boon was granted by Brahmā Parameṣṭhin. No sooner had the boon been granted than a person appeared there.

53. He was a wonderful Daitya named Vṛtra. Everyday, the Asura increased by a hundred *Dhanus* (1 *Dhanus* = about 2 metres) in stature and size.

54. Those Daityas who had been killed by the groups of Suras at the time of the churning of the Milk Ocean and were resuscitated to life quickly by Bhṛgu, came out of Pātāla.

55. The whole of the earth was pervaded by that Asura of great soul.

56. Then, all the sages who had been hurt and injured and all the ascetics hurriedly reported to Brahmā about the calamity that had befallen them. So also did Indra and other Devas and Gandharvas along with the groups of Maruts.

57. Everything that Tvaṣṭṛ intended to do was told by Brahmā.

58-59. "By performing very severe penance, a great overlord of all Daityas called Vṛtra, of great refulgence, has been created for killing you (all).

Still endeavour may be made to see that this Daitya is killed."

On hearing the words of Brahmā, Devas including Vāsava spoke these words:

Devas said:

60. When Indra was absolved of the sin of Brāhmaṇa-slaughter and established (as a ruler) in the heaven, something which should not have been done and which is hard to be born, had been done by us.

61. Many weapons and missiles had been foolishly thrown in the hermitage of Dadhīca. What shall we do now, O Brahmā?

62. On hearing those words, Brahmā laughingly said to Devas: "They have remained there for a long time. Enquire and return, O Suras."

63. All the Devas went there, but could not see their respective weapons. They asked Dadhīci and he replied: "I do not know."

64-65. Again they came to Brahmā and all of them told him what the sage said.

Brahmā then said to Devas: "Request him for his bones for the sake of accomplishing the objectives of all (of you). He will undoubtedly give (them)."

66-67. On hearing the words of Brahmā, Śakra spoke: "O lord, for the sake of accomplishing the objectives of Devas, Viśvarūpa was killed. But I alone was made the most (condemned) sinner by Suras, O Brahmā.

68. Further, at the very same instant, I was made *niḥśrīka* ('devoid of glory and splendour') by my preceptor. It was indeed a good luck that I have now entered my mansion.

69. Even if, after getting Dadhīci killed, many of his bones (are taken) and weapons are made from them, those (bone-made) weapons will be inauspicious, O Lord.

70. Thus, I am perpetually in fear of sin. How can I kill this king of Daityas named Vṛtra who has been begotten by Tvaṣṭṛ?"

Hearing the words of Śakra who was perpetually in fear of sins, god Brahmā spoke thus: He enlightened (Indra) through the instruction of *Arthaśāstra*.

71. "One can withstand and even kill a desperado whether he be a Brāhmaṇa or an ascetic in case he rushes at one and desires to kill one. One does not become a Brāhmaṇa-slayer thereby."

Indra said:

72. I am afraid of causing the death of Dadhīca, O Brahmā. There is no doubt about this that a great sin will result from that Brāhmaṇa-slaughter.

73. Hence, Brāhmaṇas should not be slighted or insulted by us. Many defects result from insulting (them). It cannot be otherwise.

74. Only that which brings about great merits should be done by a wise man. Only such acts should a learned man think of doing (and plan).

75-77. On hearing his disinterested words, Brahmā spoke to him:

"O Śakra, make use of your own intelligence. Go to Dadhīci quickly. Request for Dadhīci's bones in view of the gravity of the matter." Saying "So be it", Śakra, accompanied by his preceptor and Devas, went to the auspicious hermitage of Dadhīca, which contained different kinds of animals devoid of their natural animosity.

78-80. Cats and mice were joyous in each other's company. Lions and she-elephants along with their young ones found joy in remaining in the same place. Different species of animals were engaged in sports in one another's company. Serpents and mongooses were playing about in one another's company. Devas who saw these and many other miraculous things in that hermitage were surprised very much.

81-82. They saw the pre-eminent sage seated in his excellent seat. He was shining with great splendour like the sun or like a second fire. The excellent sage was accompanied by (his wife) Suvarcā, just as Brahmā is accompanied by Sāvitrī.

83-85. After bowing down to him Devas spoke these words:

"You are a donor (famous) in the three worlds. (Hence) we have come to you."

On hearing the words of those Devas, the sage spoke: "O excellent Suras, tell me what for have all of you come. I shall give it. There is no doubt about it. My word cannot be otherwise."

Then all those Suras in a body said to Dadhīci, as they were seekers of their own selfish interests:

86-88. "We have been desirous of seeing you as all of us are (mortally) afraid of dangers, O Brāhmaṇa. Hearing about you as a saviour, Brahmā has urged us. So we have come. Understand all these things. O sage of good holy rites, it behoves you to give us."

On hearing their words (the sage said): "Let it be mentioned what should be given?"

89-90. Then Devas said: "O Brāhmaṇa, give us your bones for the sake of making weapons in order to destroy Daityas."

Then the Brāhmaṇical sage laughed and said: "Wait for a moment, O Devas. I shall myself give up my body today."

91-93. After saying this to them, he called his wife Suvarcā. The sage of great splendour said: "Listen, O gentle lady of pure smiles. I have been requested by Devas for my bones. I am forsaking this body. I shall go to the world of Brahmā by means of profound meditation. There is no doubt about this that when I have gone to the world of Brahmā, you will also attain me there by means of your own virtue. Do not become worried over this unnecessarily."

94. After saying this to his wife, he sent her to his own hermitage. Then, the Brāhmaṇa went into a state of concentration in the presence of the Devas.

95. By means of the greatest concentration of mind, he cast off his own body. Immediately he went to the world of Brahmā from where no one returns.[1]

96. The most excellent one among the groups of sages, named Dadhīci was a favourite (devotee) of Śiva. He was initiated (in the cult) of Śiva. It is for the sake of helping others that the Brāhmaṇa quickly abandoned his body at that time.

---

1. The supreme sacrifice of Dadhīca in giving his bones for making a weapon (*Vajra*) out of them for killing Vṛtra is mentioned in Mbh, *Śalya* 51 but it does not mention his wife Suvarcā. As a propagandist of Śaivism, our text claims Dadhīca as Śiva's devotee.

CHAPTER SEVENTEEN

Vṛtra Killed: *Bali Prepares for War*

Lomaśa said:

1-3. Then on seeing him absorbed (in the Supreme Spirit), the groups of Suras began to think: 'How do we make (the weapons out of this body)?' Then the consort of Śacī called Surabhi (the divine cow) and said: "At my instance lick up the body of Dadhīca." Saying "So be it" and honouring his words, Surabhi licked the body at the same instant. The body was immediately made rid of all flesh by that cow.

4-5. Suras picked up those bones and made weapons out of them.[1] The weapon *Vajra* (thunderbolt) was made out of his backbone and the weapon *Brahmaśiras* was made out of his skull. Suras picked up many other bones of that sage (and made weapons out of them). Similarly, Suras who were naturally inimical to Daityas, made nooses out of his clusters of nerves and veins.

6. After making the weapons, all Suras of great strength and exploit hurried back, eager to kill Vṛtra.

7. Then Suvarcā, the wife of Dadhīci, who had been sent away for the purpose of accomplishing the objectives of Suras, came back to that place and saw the dead body of her husband.

8. On coming to know that everything had been the work of Suras, the chaste lady became immediately infuriated. The chaste lady Suvarcā, the wife of the excellent sage, became extremely enraged and pronounced a curse:

9. "O Suras, all of you are very wicked. All of you are weak and greedy. Hence, from today onwards all the heaven-dwellers shall be issueless."

10. Thus, that ascetic lady cursed those Suras and then came to the root of an *Aśvattha* tree. (the Indian fig tree) There she tore up her belly.

11. From the belly, the foetus of the noble-souled Dadhīca

1. VV 4-5 describe the different weapons made out of the bones of Dadhīci.

came out. It was Pippalāda[1] of great lustre. He was a direct incarnation of Rudra.

12-13. With eyes (flared up) with wrath, the mother Suvarcā laughed (in derision) and spoke to Pippalāda, the foetus: "Stay here for a long time near this *Aśvattha*, O highly magnificent son. Be fruitful unto all." Speaking thus to her son, that chaste lady Suvarcā followed her husband by means of the greatest *Samādhi* (concentration).

14. Thus, that wife of Dadhīca went to Heaven along with her husband.

15. After making the missiles and the weapons, Devas of great might and exploits, who were eager to (fight) with Daityas, returned with Indra at their head.

16. Honouring Guru and abiding by his bidding, the many groups of Suras, of great strength and exploit—all of them equipped with great weapons and missiles, came to the earth, the Middle Land (world), and spoke (among themselves).

17. On hearing that Devas with Indra as their leader had come, Vṛtra[2], the great Daitya, went (there) accompanied by the groups of Daityas.

18. Just as the peak of Meru is completely visible, so appeared that great son of Viśvakarman, with great refulgence.

19. Mahendra was seen by him. The great Asura was seen by Mahendra. The meeting of Devas and Dānavas was exceedingly wonderful.

---

1. Pippalāda—There are different persons—sages—of this name. One is a teacher of *Brahma-vidyā* in *Praśna Upaniṣad* (I.1); another in *Atharvaśikha* mentioned along with Sanatkumāra. This may be the same mentioned in the *Guru-Paraṁparā* (Teachers' list) of the *Atharvaveda*. The Pippalāda of our text is different. He is the son of Dadhīci and Suvarcā. Mbh, *Śānti* 47.9 mentions one Pippalāda, but he seems to be a different person.

2. Vṛtra—The Vedic Vṛtra is transformed beyond recognition in Purāṇas. In his previous birth he was Citraketu (according to BhP VI.14.10), a Gandharva who, due to his criticism of Śaṅkara's public dalliance with Pārvatī, was cursed by her to be an Asura. He was born of Tvaṣṭṛ who got the boon from god Brahmā of having an *Indra-śatru* as his son. But due to his wrong accent, he, instead of asking 'Killer of Indra' as his son requested *a son whose killer is Indra.* Both Mbh (*Vana* 101.15, *Śānti* 283.59-60) and our text send him to the higher world (Vaikuṇṭha as per Mbh and Śiva-loka as per our text) after his death.

20. Devas and Daityas who had harbored bitter hatred for one another became furious with one another.

21. During that encounter between Suras and Asuras, terrible, high-sounding instruments of martial music were played everywhere and their majestic loud report was heard everywhere.

22. As the instruments were being played, all of them hurriedly and powerfully struck one another with many groups of weapons.

23. In that war between Devas and Asuras, all the three worlds including mobile and immobile beings, were overwhelmed by great fear and became unconscious.

24. Some were cut and broken into two with the weapons. Some were injured by means of arrows and some cut into pieces with *Nārāca* arrows, weapons and missiles.

25. Some of the heaven-dwellers were maimed and crippled with *Bhallas* (arrows with crescent-shaped heads). They moved about like the streaks of lightning from clouds that shine in the sky.

26-27. Many heads fell from the sky like stars as though the great confusion and consternation of *Mahāpralaya* (the great annihilation) had overrun the Middle World, causing the destruction of all living beings. Then Namuci fought with Śakra.

28-29. The king of Devas himself hit Namuci with great force by means of his *Vajra.* But not even a single hair of the Asura Namuci was cut by that *Vajra.* All the Asuras and Suras were much surprised at this. Mahendra became ashamed.

30. He struck Namuci with his club, but as soon as that club came into contact with Namuci's body, it was smashed into pieces and fell down on the earth.

31. Similarly, Purandara struck him with a great spear. That spear colliding with Namuci's limbs split into a hundred pieces.

32-33. Thus, the slayer of the enemies of Suras struck him with various kinds of weapons. But, Namuci went on smiling and laughing. He did not strike Purandara.

Beset with great worry and thought, Indra kept quiet. He did not know what should be done or what should not be done.

34. In the meantime, during that terrific great battle, an ethereal voice was heard immediately, addressing Indra:

35-36. "Kill this Daitya today immediately, O Mahendra.

He is getting terrible and striking terror into the heaven-dwellers. Kill this great leader of Asuras quickly by means of the foam which is near the waters and which is hard to be borne. If struck with any other weapon, he can never be killed. Hence, O lord of Devas, make all possible endeavour to kill this evil-minded Namuci."

37. On hearing the divine speech that was characterized by truth, that caused perpetual delight and was conducive to auspiciousness, (Indra) who was the most excellent one among those who endeavour, went to the other shore of the ocean and attempted (to kill Namuci) as he had infinite fund of vigour.

38. On seeing him to have come there, Namuci became exceedingly angry. He struck Devendra with his spear and laughingly asked:

39. "Why have you resorted to the shore of the ocean? You have left the battlefield. You have even abandoned your weapon.

40. O evil-minded one, what (harm) has been done to me even by your own *Vajra*?

41-42. Similarly many other missiles and weapons had been taken up by you previously to kill me, O dull-witted one. Now what will you do to kill me? You have come here to fight, but, O fool, with what weapon do you wish to fight in this battle?

43. I will kill you today itself, if you stand here in the battle. If not, go, being set free by me. Live long and be happy."

44. On hearing these arrogant words of that (Daitya) who shone in the battle, Mahendra too became furious. He took up the mysteriously wonderful foam.

45. On seeing the foam in his hand, Asuras laughed.

46. Namuci said (to himself), 'He has exhausted his weapons. Therefore, Purandara wishes to kill me today by means of this foam alone. Indeed Śatakratu (Indra) is liberal-minded.'

47-48. He thus slighted Purandara laughingly. Namuci, the great Daitya, stood in front of him displaying his contemptuous disregard. At that very moment Indra killed him quickly with the foam.

49. When Namuci was killed, all the Devas became delighted. The sages honoured (Indra) with the words "Well done, well done."

50. After the killing of Namuci in the battle, all Devas became victorious. Daityas were excited with anger. They were furiously desirous of fighting (with Devas).

51. The battle was resumed. Devas fought with Dānavas equipped with many kinds of weapons and missiles. Both were desirous of killing one another.

52. When those Asuras were being struck down again and again, Vṛtra, of great refulgence, approached Śatakratu (Indra).

53. On seeing Vṛtra, all of them including Suras, Asuras and human beings were overcome by great fear. They fell on the ground and lay there.

54. When all the Suras and Siddhas became frightened, the valorous Indra (came there) riding on Airāvaṇa (i.e. Airāvata) (armed) with the thunderbolt in his hand.

55. He shone by an umbrella that was held (over him) and the chowries (by his side) too. He was accompanied by all the Guardians of the Quarters. He was endowed with great power of exploit.

56. On seeing Vṛtra, all the great Devas and the Guardians of the Quarters became terrified. All of them sought refuge in Śiva.

57. All of them mentally contemplated Śaṅkara, the benefactor of the worlds. Mahendra who was desirous of victory, duly worshipped the *Liṅga*.

58. This was understood immediately by Guru (Bṛhaspati). With great confidence, the highly intelligent Bṛhaspati said to Śakra:

Bṛhaspati said:

59-60. The bright half of the lunar month of Kārttika (October-November), Saturday and Trayodaśī (thirteenth day)—when all these are concurrent, it is undoubtedly conducive to the accomplishment of everything. On that day, at the time of dusk, Sadāśiva should be worshipped in the form of *Liṅga*, O Devendra, for the accomplishment of all desired objectives.

61. The devotee should take his bath at midday and worship Śiva with sweet scents, fragrant flowers, fruits etc. together with gingelly seeds and emblic myrobalan.

62. Afterwards, at the time of dusk, he should worship an immobile *Liṅga*, whether it is self-existent or an installed one, whether it is man-made or of divine origin.

63. The devotee should worship that *Liṅga* with great devotion, whether in the midst of people or in a lonely place, in a forest or in a penance-grove. He should particularly worship at the time of dusk.

64. If the *Liṅga* is stationed outside a village, it is a hundred times more efficacious than when it is in the village. The merit of the worship of the wonderful *Liṅga* in a forest is one hundred times more than when it is outside the village.

65. If the *Liṅga* is worshipped on a mountain, it is a hundred times more efficacious than when it is worshipped in a forest. If the *Liṅga* installed in a penance-grove is worshipped, it yields a great benefit. It is ten thousand times more efficacious than the *Liṅga* stationed on a mountain.

66. Hence the worship of *Śivaliṅga* should be performed efficiently by wise men on the basis of this difference. A holy dip in the sacred spot and other similar rites should also be diligently performed.

67. If the devotee offers five *piṇḍas* (rice balls) accompanied by holy dip alone, it is splendid. One should perform the holy ablution in a well especially with the water drawn.

68. One should perform the holy dip in a lake after offering ten *piṇḍas*. The holy dip in a river is especially superior and particularly so in a great river.

69. The holy dip in Gaṅgā is superior to that in all the other holy spots and waters. If the holy dip is performed in a *Devakhāta* (natural pond or reservoir) it is equal in efficacy to a dip in Gaṅgā. The devotee should perform the rite of holy ablution in a praiseworthy manner.

70. Illumination should be offered to god Sadāśiva with a thousand lamps or a hundred lamps or a series of thirty-two lamps.

71-72. For the sake of Śiva's gratification, the devotee should illuminate the lamps with ghee. For the attainment of all desired objects Sadāśiva should be worshipped at the time of dusk, in the form of a *Liṅga*, by men with fruits, lamps, food-offerings, sweet scents, incense and all the sixteen *Upacāras*[1] (i.e. modes of rendering service during worship) for the fulfilment of all objects.

73. The devotee should circumambulate (Śiva) one hundred and eight times. He should as well exert himself to perform as many prostrations (before Śiva).

74. Sadāśiva should be honoured and worshipped by means of circumambulations and prostrations. Rudra should be eulogized by reciting his hundred names.

75. "Obeisance to *Rudra*, to *Bhīma* (the terrible one), to *Nīlakaṇṭha* (blue-throated god), to *Vedhas* (the creator), to *Kapardin* (one having matted hair), to *Sureśa* (the lord of Devas); obeisance indeed to *Vyomakeśa* (sky-haired);

76. to *Vṛṣadhvaja* (bull-bannered god), to *Soma* (one accompanied by Umā), to *Nīlakaṇṭha*, to *Digambara* (one with the quarters for garments), to *Bharga* (refulgent one), to *Umākānta* (the husband of Umā), to *Kapardīn*;

77. to *Tapomaya* (one who is of the nature of penance), to *Vyāpta* (one who is pervaded). Obeisance indeed to *Śipiviṣṭa* (one who is pervaded by rays), to *Vyālapriya* (one who is fond of serpents), to *Vyāla* (one who is identical with serpents); obeisance to the lord of serpents,

78. to *Mahīdhara* (one who supports the earth), to *Vyāghra* (the tiger); obeisance to the lord of *Paśus* (individual souls), to *Trīpurāntakasiṁha* (leonine destroyer of Tripura), to *Śārdūlogra-rava* (one whose roaring sound is as dreadful as that of a tiger);

79. to *Mīna* (fish), to *Mīnanātha* (to the lord of fishes), to *Siddha*, to *Parameṣṭhin*, to *Kāmāntaka* (the destroyer of Kāma), to *Buddha* (the enlightened one); obeisance to the lord of the intellect,

80. to *Kapota* (pigeon), to *Viśiṣṭa* (superior one), to *Śiṣṭa* (of good discipline), to *Paramātman* (the Supreme Soul), to *Veda*, to *Vedabīja* (seed of the Vedas); obeisance indeed to *Devaguhya* (secret known only to gods);

---

1. They are: *Āvāhana* (invitation), *Āsana* (offering seat), *Pādya*, *Arghya*, *Ācamanīya* (offering water to wash feet, to sip etc.), *Snāna* (bath), *Vastra* (offering clothes) and *Yajñopavīta* (sacred thread), *Gandha* (ointment, sandal etc.), *Puṣpa* (flowers), *Dhūpa* (incense), *Dīpa* (lamp), *Naivedya* or *Upahāra* (food, eatables), *Namaskāra* (bowing), *Pradakṣiṇā* (circumambulation), *Visarjana* (send-off).

81. to *Dīrgha* (long one), to *Dīrghadīrgha* (longer than the long one), to *Dīrghārgha* (one of long respectable offering), to *Maha* (festival); obeisance to *Jagatpratiṣṭha* (one who is established in the universe); obeisance indeed to *Vyomarūpa* (one in the form of the firmament);

82. to *Gajāsuravināśa* (one who has destroyed the demon in the form of an elephant), to *Andhakāsurabhedin* (one who has split the demon Andhaka), to *Nīlalohitaśukla* (one of blue, red and white colours), to *Caṇḍa-Muṇḍapriya* (one who is fond of Caṇḍa and Muṇḍa);

83. to *Bhaktipriya* (one who is fond of devotion), to *Deva* (resplendent lord), to *Jñānajñāna* (knowledge of knowledges) to *Avyaya* (the immutable), to *Maheśa*(the great lord), O Mahādeva. Obeisance to you, to *Hara* (the destroyer);

84. to *Trinetra* (the three-eyed god), *Triveda* (one who is eulogized in the three Vedas); obeisance, obeisance to *Vedāṅga* (the embodiment of Vedas), to *Artha* (wealth), to *Artharūpa* (one who has the form of wealth); obeisance indeed to *Paramārtha* (the Ultimate Reality),

85. to *Viśvarūpa* (one who has the cosmic form), to *Viśva* (the universe). Obeisance indeed to *Viśvanātha* (lord of the universe), to *Śaṅkara* (the benefactor), to *Kāla* (god of Death), to *Kālāvayavarūpin* (one who is in the form of the units of time);

86. to *Arūpa* (formless), to *Sūkṣma* (the subtle one). Obeisance indeed to the subtler than the subtlest. Obeisance to you who reside in the cremation ground; obeisance to you, wearer of the elephant hide,

87. to *Śaśāṅka-śekhara* (one who has the moon as the crest-jewel), to *Rudra*, to *Viśvāśraya* (the support of the universe), to *Durga* (unattainable), to *Durgasāra* (the essence of the unattainables), to *Durgāvayavasākṣin* (one who is witness unto the limbs of Durgā);

88. to *Liṅgarūpa* (one who is in the form of the *Liṅga*), to *Liṅga*; obeisance to the lord of *Liṅgas*; obeisance to *Oṁkāra*; obeisance indeed to *Praṇavārtha* (the meaning of *Praṇava*).

89. Obeisance, obeisance to you, the cause of the causes, to *Mṛtyuñjaya* (the conqueror of Death), to *Ātmasvarūpin* (one who is in the form of the Soul), to *Bhava-svarūpīn* (one who is

of the form of the world), to *Triyaṁba* (one who has three eyes), O Asitakaṇṭha (dark-throated), O Bharga (refulgent one).

O Gaurīpati (Consort of Gaurī), obeisance to *Sakalamaṅgala-hetu* (the cause of all auspiciousness)."

Bṛhaspati said:

90. The hundred names of Maheśa should be repeated always by a *Vratin* ('observer of holy vows') along with circumambulations and prostrations of that number with great effort. This should be done at the time of dusk for the sake of gratifying Śaṅkara.

91. Such is the holy observance fully explained to you, O Śakra, of great intellect. Perform this quickly. O lord of exalted fortune, fight only afterwards, O Lord.

92. By the grace of Śaṁbhu, victory etc. will come to you.

93. This highly refulgent Daitya has formerly propitiated god Śiva by (performing) penance on mountain Gandhamādana.

94. There was a king named Citraratha. Know, O Indra, that his park was near the city of Śiva. His park was named Caitraratha.

95. O Indra of exalted fortune, the six infirmities of human beings (viz. grief, delusion, old age, death, hunger and thirst) do not find a place in that park. Hence that park named Caitraratha was exceedingly auspicious.

96. A wonderful vehicle had been given to that king by Śiva himself. The vehicle could go wherever one desired to go. It was fitted with small ornamental tinkling bells and was attended upon by Siddhas and Cāraṇas. It was rendered resplendent by Gandharvas, Apsarās, Yakṣas and Kinnaras.

97. Once he was wandering round the earth, big mountains, different kinds of islands etc.

98-99. Once in the course of his wanderings, the great king named Citraratha came to Kailāsa. There he saw an exceedingly wonderful assembly hall of Maheśa, that shone on account of the Gaṇas. He saw Maheśvara also who looked splendid with the goddess adhering to half of his body.

100-101. When he saw Sadāśiva accompanied by the goddess (as well as closely joined to the goddess), he spoke these words: "We, the ministers etc. and others, O Śaṁbhu, cling to worldly pleasures. Others there are who are enslaved by (and enamoured of) women. We are indeed ignorant too, but out of shyness we do not enjoy the company of women in the midst of people."

102-104. On hearing these words, Maheśa laughingly said in a just and proper manner, even as all were listening: "All are afraid of popular censure and not otherwise. The poison Kālakūṭa which could not be digested by anyone was swallowed (by me). Still a mocking criticism about me was made by this king. This is difficult to be digested by me."

Girijā called Citraratha and spoke these words:

Girijā said:

105. O evil-minded one, O ignorant fellow, why was Śaṅkara mocked at and ridiculed along with me? O dull-witted one, you will see the consequences of your action.

106. He who mocks and ridicules equanimous and even-minded good people, whether he is a Deva or a human being, should be known as the meanest of all mean people.

107. These leading sages of great magnanimity, those anchorites steeped in the Vedas and these (philosophers) Sanaka and others, worship Śiva. Are they ignorant ones?

108. O confounded one, among all the people (you suppose that) you alone are *Abhijña* (one with rich experience and profound knowledge) and not other people. Therefore, I shall make you a wiseacre Daitya excluded (excommunicated) by Devas and Brāhmaṇas.

(*Bṛhaspati continued*:)

109. On being cursed thus by goddess Bhavānī, the excellent king Citraratha, immediately fell from heaven.

110. He took birth in the race of Asuras and came to be known by the name Vṛtra. He was gradually made to perform penance by Tvaṣṭṛ.

111-112. It is said that Vṛtra became invincible on account of that great penance. Hence worship god Śaṁbhu now during the time of dusk in accordance with the prescribed method. Then kill Vṛtra, the great Daitya, for accomplishing the cause of Devas.

On hearing these words of his preceptor, Indra said: "Tell me the mode of the performance of the worship of (Śiva) during *Pradoṣa* (dusk time) along with its *Udyāpanavidhi* (the concluding rites)."[1]

Bṛhaspati said:

113. In the month of *Kārttika* when *Saturday* and *Trayodaśī* (13th day) coincide, all the requirements are complete for the sake of getting the benefit of the entire holy rite.

(*Procedure of worshipping god Śiva*)

114-115. A silver bull should be made. There must be a good *Pīṭha* (seat) upon its back. The devotee must keep the Three-eyed Lord, the consort of Umā, upon it. The lord must have five faces and ten hands. Half of his body must be the chaste daughter of the Mountain. Thus both Umā and Maheśa should be made of gold by the learned devotee.

116. All these (the bull etc.) must be placed in a copper plate and covered with a cloth. The *Liṅga* must be placed along with Umā with all the necessary offerings of enjoyment (food offerings, scents, incense etc.).

117. During the night the devotee should keep a vigil in accordance with the injunctions and with great faith.

At the outset the bathing rite should be performed with *Pañcāmṛta* (five sweet ingredients in fluid form). (Then the following Mantras should be recited in offering each.)

(*The Mantra at the time of bathing the god with cow's milk*:)

118. "O lord of Devas, O lord of the chiefs of Devas, bathing is offered by me with cow's milk. Accept it, O Parameśvara (great Lord)."

(*The Mantra while bathing the god with curds*:)

119. "O Lord, bathing is performed by me now with curds. Accept what has been offered by me. Be highly delighted now."

1. VV 112-135 give details of Śiva-worship on the 13th day of the bright half of Kārttika. The success of Indra is attributed to Indra's observance of this *Vrata* and Vṛtra's negligence of the same. The whole episode is meant to glorify the *Vrata* of god Śiva.

(*The Mantra at the time of bathing with ghee*:)

120. "O Lord, bathing is performed by me now with ghee. Accept what has been offered with faith for the sake of gratifying you."

(*The Mantra for bath with honey*:)

121. "This honey is given by me for the sake of your pleasure. Accept it, O Lord of Devas. Be the bestower of tranquillity on me."

(*The Mantra while offering bath with sugar*:)

122. "O lord, bathing is performed by me now, O lord of the chiefs of Devas, with sugar. Accept this which has been offered with faith. O Lord, be delighted."

123. Thus the Bull-bannered Lord must be bathed in *Pañcāmṛta*. Afterwards *Arghya* (materials of worship) must be offered by the intelligent devotee in a copper vessel with this following Mantra for the gratification of the consort of Umā:

(*Mantra for offering of Arghya*:)

124. "You are the most befitting person for being worshipped by this *Arghya*, O consort of Umā. Accept this, O Lord, offered by me. Be pleased, O Śaṅkara."

(*Mantra for offering Pādya*:)

125. "Accept, O Lord of the chiefs of Devas, the *Pādya* (water for washing the feet) offered by me to you along with fragrant flowers and sweet scents. Be pleased. Be the bestower of boons."

(*Mantra for offering a seat*:)

126. "A seat along with another seat has been offered by me, O Lord, for the sake of your peace and calmness. O Lord of Devas, always be the bestower of boons on me."

(*Mantra at the time of offering Ācamanīya*:)

127. "*Ācamanīya* (i.e. water for the ceremonial sipping) has been given to you. O Lord Viśveśvara, accept; O great Īśāna, be delighted with me today, O Lord."

(*Mantra while offering the sacred thread*:)

128. "A golden sacred thread which consists of *Brahmagranthi* (knot) and which causes all holy rites to function is offered by me to you, O Lord."[1]

(*Mantra while offering sandal paste* :)

129. "Sweet scents and sandal paste have been offered by me, O Lord, with great devotion. O Śaṁbhu, Bhava, make me fragrant."

(*Mantra while offering a lamp*:)

130. "O Śaṁbhu, an excellent lamp[2] kindled with ghee has been offered by me. Accept it, O Lord of Devas. Be the bestower of knowledge on me."

(*Mantra while offering incense* :)

131. "Excellently superior lamp[3] invigorated with all medicinal herbs (has been offered by me). Accept it, O great Īśāna, for the sake of my peace and calmness."

(*Mantra before Āratī—Waving of lamps*:)

132. "O Parameśvara, accept the row of lamps offered by me. By virtue of my offering of waving of lights, be the bestower of splendour on me."

133. By persons who are conversant with injunctions (regarding worship) the Lord should be (carefully and) deligently worshipped on that night (by offerings) in the following order: fruits, lights etc. food-offering, betel-leaf etc.

---

1. V.L.

Yajñopavītaṁ sauvarṇam mayā dattaṁ ca Śaṅkara|
gṛhāṇa parayā tuṣṭyā, tuṣṭo bhava tu sarvadā||

"O god Śaṅkara, a golden sacred thread has been given by me. Please accept it with great satisfaction. Please be for ever gratified."

2. Offering incense precedes the offering of a lamp in *Pūjā*. Verse 131 should have come here.

3. *Dhūpam* is the correct reading and not *Dīpam* as the offer of incense precedes the offer of lamps.

134. The devotee must keep awake thereafter whether in a house or in a temple. The canopy over the dais must be put up with various, wonderful decorations. God Sadāśiva should be worshipped by means of songs, musical instruments and dance.

135. It is in accordance with these injunctions that the concluding rites in the worship at *Pradoṣa* should be performed duly for the sake of the fulfilment of all objects.

136. Śatakratu (Indra) performed everything mentioned by Guru (Bṛhaspati). With him as his main help, Indra engaged himself in the battle.

137. Śatakratu fought against Vṛtra along with Suras. The fight between Devas and Dānavas was fierce.

138. In that exceedingly fierce battle that caused destruction among Devas and Daityas, the duels were extremely terrifying and tumultuous:

139-142. Vyoma fought with Yama. Tīkṣṇakopana fought with Agni. Mahādaṁṣṭra fought with Varuṇa and Mahābala fought with Vāyu. All those engaged in duels were desirous of (suppressing) the strength of one another. The excellent Devas of powerful arms were heroic in battle. They became victorious then. All the leading Daityas met with very great defeat on all fronts. On seeing the leading Daityas defeated by Suras, running away as fugitives, Vṛtra of great strength spoke these words with extreme wrathfulness:

Vṛtra said:

143. O Daityas, why are you greatly distressed? Why are you so frightened? All of you are running away abandoning the war of wonderful (events).

144-145. O heroes, resolve to fight. Display your respective valour. O mighty ones, kill the groups of Suras with maces, spears with sharp edges, swords, javelins, iron clubs, mallets, swords with thin edges, small javelins hurled at the enemies, nooses, maces and even your fists.

146. Then Devas fought Asuras with great weapons and missiles made out of Dadhīci's bones. They tore up Asuras.

147. This was repeated often. Again and again Daityas were killed by Devas. They met with defeat. Again and again, they were urged by Vṛtra to fight Suras.

148. The excellent Daityas were being killed by the leading Suras. They fled in all directions. Some of the Dānavas were frightened so much that they appeared to be eunuchs.

149-153. The leading Daityas were rebuked and censured by furious Vṛtra: "O Puloman of great fortune; O Vṛṣaparvan, obeisance to you. O Dhūmrākṣa, O Mahākāla, O Vṛkāsura, the great Daitya, O Sthūlākṣa, the eminent Daitya, O Sthūladaṁṣṭra, obeisance to you. The excellent battlefield is the gateway to heaven for Kṣatriyas of great magnanimity. Why do you abandon it and run away? Those who meet death in the battlefield attain the greatest position. A learned man must desire to die in battle. Those who forsake the battle(field) certainly go to hell.

154-155. If men who have committed great sins fight in a battlefield with weapons in their hands for the sake of Brāhmaṇas, their servants or for their own sake and get killed being hit with weapons in the battle, they go to the highest region. There is no doubt about it.

156. Those whose bodies are cut off by means of weapons for taking up the cause of cows or their own masters, those who die or those who are wounded in war do attain the greatest goal (heaven).

157. If persons of great heroism are killed in battle, they attain the greatest region even if they be sinners. They attain the region not easy of access even to the learned men.

158-159. Pilgrimage to holy places, study of the Vedas, worshipping of the deities, performances of *Yajñas* and other different kinds of holy rites conducive to welfare—all put together do not deserve even a sixteenth part of the holy action of those who fall in battle. This has been laid down in all the sacred treatises.

160. Hence the valorous and glorious act of fighting should be carried out by you without suspicion or fear. It should not be otherwise, because the Vedic statements are authoritative.

161. All of you belong to the profession of heroes. You are magnanimous and dignified due to nobility of birth and

course of conduct, but if you run away from the war-zone like cowards, you are sure to go to those worlds of cowards like them.

162. According to *Smṛtis*, all of them (cowards) certainly go to the world of sinners (i.e. hell).

163. Those worst sinners who adhere to unrighteous things, the slayers of Brāhmaṇas and the defilers of the preceptors' bed go to hell. In the same manner those who stray away (desert) from war, incur the same sin and go to hell.

164-165. Hence you people who are capable of bearing the burden of the work of your master must fight."

On being told thus by the noble-souled Vṛtra, the Asuras carried out his words. They fought a furious battle with Suras terrifying all the worlds.

166. When that tremendous and tumultuous battle ensued, Vṛtra, the sole lord of the great Daityas, who was overwhelmed by extraordinary wrath, said to Indra accompanied by the excellent Devas:

Vṛtra said:

167. Listen to the words uttered by me. It is conducive to your welfare. It is connected with virtuous objects. Although you are the lord of Devas, you do not know what is good and what is not.

168. What were your objectives for which Viśvarūpa was killed by you?

169. Whatever these persons do for the accomplishment of their tasks is futile: Those who do not see far into the future, those who are foolish and confounded, those who are excluded from piety and virtue and those who are incompetent. Know all these, O Devendra. Let it be pondered over mentally.

170. Hence be virtuous and free from the taint of sin. Then fight with me. You are the slayer of my brother, O Indra. Hence I will kill you.

171. Be steady. Do not run away surrounded by Devas.

On being told thus by Vṛtra, Śakra became exceedingly furious. He mounted on the elephant Airāvata and went ahead with a desire to kill Vṛtra.

172. On seeing Indra coming, Vṛtra, the most excellent one

among the powerful persons, said laughingly even as all the others were listening (to it):

173. "Strike me at the outset. Then I shall kill you."

174. On being told thus, Devendra hit hard with his mace Vṛtra of great strength and the most excellent one among those who possess power at the knee.

175. Seeing that mace coming, Vṛtra caught hold of it sportively. With that very same mace, he struck back immediately Indra, the king of heaven.

176. That *Gadā* (mace, iron club) knocked down Purandara, along with his *Vajra*. On seeing Śakra fallen, Vṛtra spoke to Suras:

177. "O Devas, take your lord to your own city Amarāvatī."

178-179. On hearing these truthful words of the noble-souled Vṛtra, all the Suras did so. Eagerly they removed him even while he was seated on the elephant, from the battlefield and surrounded him with fear. All those Suras left the battlefield and went to heaven.

180. When Devas had departed, the great Asura Vṛtra danced and laughed loudly and thereby the quarters were filled with that (sound).

181. The entire earth including the mountains, parks and forests shook and trembled. All mobile and immobile things became agitated.

182. On hearing that Devendra had gone (from the battlefield), Brahmā, the grandfather of the worlds, came near him. With the water from his *Kamaṇḍalu*, he touched (sprinkled) Devendra. At that very same instant, Purandara regained consciousness.

183. Seeing Brahmā in front of him, Indra became ashamed. Brahmā, the grandfather, said to Mahendra who felt ashamed:

Brahmā said:

184. Vṛtra is endowed with the power of penance (done by himself). He is endowed with the power of penance of Tvaṣṭṛ also. He abides by the holy rite and vow of celibacy. This Vṛtra of great fame has become invincible due to his severe penance. Hence conquer him by means of penance.

185. Vṛtrāsura, the lord of Daityas, can be conquered only through great penance, O Śakra.

On hearing the words of Brahmā, Hari (i.e. Indra) remembered the Bull-bannered Lord.

186. The noble-souled Purandara urged by his (preceptor) Bṛhaspati began to eulogize (Lord Śiva) with a prayer.

Indra prayed:

187. Obeisance to lord Bharga, who is very difficult to be approached by Devas. O lord of Devas, be the bestower of boons for the sake of the accomplishment of the tasks of Devas.

188. The liberal-minded consort of Śacī was thus engaged in eulogy. Indeed he was very prompt and skilful in matters concerning himself. He was slow-witted but was certainly devoted to worldly (pleasures).

189. Deluded persons devoted to worldly pleasures do not attain the highest region of Īśa, even if they are engaged in devotion to Śiva (as) they are passionate and sensualist.

190-192. Those people who are free from impurities, egotism and arrogance and who worship Mṛḍa (the Gracious), Īśa (the Supreme Lord), Śaṁbhu, the greatest lord, who bestows perfect knowledge are really great people. Śaṅkara is the bestower of boons on them both here and hereafter.

Mahendra was a great sensualist. Śarva had been eulogized by Mahendra who was passionate.

There is no doubt that Śaṁbhu can rarely be approached by sensualists. Hence Sadāśiva can always be visualized directly by non-sensualists.

193. Indeed the king of Suras was exceedingly passionate. He (professed to be) very efficient in accomplishing his own tasks. Hence Śacīpati (Indra) (had) always to strain and exert himself. He was perpetually indulgent in his own lust and similar emotions of the heart.

194-195. On account of the seriousness of the matter, Maheśa, of the form of the *Liṅga*, who was the seer and vision of all, understood (everything) and spoke to Indra who was eulogizing: "O Indra, go to Vṛtra, the Dānava, along with Suras. O

Śatakratu (Indra), he can be conquered in the battle only through the power of penance."

Indra said:

196. By what means can this great and excellent Daitya be conquered? O Śaṁbhu, let that be mentioned immediately whereby my success can be (achieved).

Rudra said:

197. He cannot be killed in battle even by the excellent Devas. Hence a mean act (of trickery) must be performed by you today.

198. Formerly this (demon) had been cursed by Pārvatī in my presence. (At that time) he had been a king named Citraratha, well reputed in all the three worlds.

199. He was wandering (here and there) in an excellent refulgent aerial chariot given by me. The leading Daitya had to be born of this womb (of a Daitya) because of his satirical ridicule.

200-201. Hence, O excellent one among those who are expert in wars, know him to be invincible in war.

Thus Mahendra was told by Śaṁbhu, the greatest Yogin. Saying "So be it" and honouring it, Śakra took up devout observances and restraints.

202. O highly fortunate sages, he made up his mind to stay near Vṛtra for a thousand years waiting for a weak and vulnerable point in order to kill Vṛtra.

203. With the permission of Guru (Bṛhaspati), his priest, the thunderbolt-armed Indra stood out of *Antaredī* and carried on his activities vigorously.

204. Once Vṛtra, the Daitya Chief, surrounded by all Daityas casually came to Narmadā.

205-206. Vṛtra endowed with manliness, always thought thus: 'Indra has met with defeat and discomfiture. He has been taken to heaven by Devas. All my enemies have been struck down. There is no one like me.' Thinking thus, O Brāhmaṇas, he came to Narmadā at the time of dusk.

207. At that time of dusk, the very great (Daitya) Vṛtra, the

most excellent one among powerful persons, surrounded by Asuras, was seen by Indra.

208. On that day, *Trayodaśī* (thirteenth day) was in conjunction with Saturday. Bṛhaspati caught hold of the hand (of Indra). Indra was urged by Guru (to perform the worship of Śiva).

209. At that time, the *Liṅga*-form *Oṁkāra* (a famous *Jyotirliṅga*) on the bank of Narmadā was worshipped by Indra by means of circumambulations, prostrations (etc.) in accordance with the injunctions (of sacred scriptures).

210. Due to the greatness of the holy rite during the dusk hours as well as the grace of Śaṅkara, the valorous (lord) armed with the thunderbolt became (very powerful) instantly.

211. Though he was endowed with the (power of) penance, the great Vṛtra was overcome by sleep during the time of dusk. He was roused (from sleep) by Śuṇḍa.

212. Since he slept during the time of dusk, the merit that had been earned through penance was ruined at the very same instant. He became devoid of splendour.

213-215. On account of the curse of the goddess too, Vṛtra became disappointed in his desired object. (More than) a quarter of the duration of the dusk had passed, when Vṛtra entered the holy waters surrounded by different kinds of Daityas with diverse kinds of weapons. Śatakratu, the consort of Śacī, who was seeking the weak and vulnerable points, understood the same and so slowly approached him to kill his enemy.

216-217. By that time all the excited and terrible Daityas of horrifying exploits stood up simultaneously unable to bear (the attack of) Śatakratu. Thereafter ensued a battle with them as they had a very strong army. Then all Devas came there for rendering assistance to Indra.

218-220. With very great speed and force Daityas and Devas fought (one another). The battle that was fought during the night resulted in the crushing and destroying of both, Suras and Asuras. The battle became extremely terrible as many weapons and missiles were used by them. When the war of exceedingly severe and terrible nature went on thus, Vṛtra took up his exceedingly powerful spear and got ready. He faced Indra and roared terrifically. The reverberation of the loud shout frightened all the three worlds.

221-222. Mahendra mounted on (his elephant). Airāvaṇa shone then with the umbrella that was refulgent like the disc of the moon, being held high up above him. Even as he was being fanned by chowries, he spoke to the great Daitya:

Indra said:

223. O Vṛtra, you are surrounded by a great army (although) you are the hero of heroes on account of your great penance. Fight with me.

224. On being told thus by him, Vṛtra spoke these words: "O Indra, strike me first. Afterwards I shall kill you."

225. Saying "So be it" and thinking about it, Purandara was desirous of discharging the exceedingly unbearable thunderbolt of a hundred sharp edges. But he was prevented by that priest of great lustre, the most excellent one among the intelligent persons. Thinking that it should be so, Indra did accordingly.

226-227. The lord of Devas took up an iron club and struck Vṛtra with it. Vṛtra warded it off like a miser dodging a guest. On observing that his iron club had been futile, Indra became full of anxiety.

228. As he was thinking thus, Vṛtra spoke to him rebukingly: "O Śakra, has the wonderfully contemptible vulgar act performed by you been forgotten? It was on account of it that you have become a thousand-eyed one due to the curse of the great sage Gautama.

229-230. Those heroic persons who restrain their different sense-organs do attain victory and not others like you. Undoubtedly the battlefield is extremely terrible unto sinners."

231. Thus the great Daitya rebuked Devendra. The lord of Devas then shook his trident that was on a par with lightning.

232. With that great spear, Vṛtra of wonderful exploits shone like Rudra, the destroyer of (creation at the end of) *Yugas*, by means of his penance.

233. On observing him in that posture, Śatakratu, the lord of Devas, rushed at Vṛtra, the great Dānava, with a desire to kill him.

234-236a. On seeing Purandara rushing at himself with a desire to kill him (Vṛtra) laughed loudly instilling fear in Śakra. Opening his mouth very widely, the lord of Daityas with great splendour came there suddenly to swallow Śakra. He grabbed into his mouth, Śakra along with his elephant, thunderbolt and crown. He then danced and roared.

236b-238. Within a moment, Purandara was (completely) swallowed.

There was a great shout of Alas! Alas! from the Devas who watched it. There was an earthquake and thousands of meteors fell. The entire universe consisting of mobile and immobile beings was enveloped in darkness. Vṛtra who was dancing then became exceedingly brilliant.

239. Being pierced (in the heart), all the Devas came to Brahmā and reported to him everything that was done by the Asura Vṛtra.

240-241. On hearing it lord Brahmā became distressed and surprised very much: 'How has this wonderfully serious crisis in the case of Mahendra taken place?' Then, along with Devas, Brahmā, the grandfather of all the worlds, eulogized Lord Giriśa with great concentration of mind.

Brahmā eulogized:

242-247. Om, obeisance to Mahādeva whose form is *Liṅga*. I bow to the lord of cosmic form. Obeisance to Virūpākṣa (of uneven three-eyes). Save, O lord of the three worlds. Save Purandara who has been swallowed by Vṛtra.

At that time a very clear, fine, ethereal voice spoke even as all were listening. It referred to the process of the worship of *Liṅga*. It was addressed (to everyone) desirous of his welfare: "What has been done by Indra who has undertaken the holy *Pradoṣa* rite is incomplete and imperfect in regard to *Nirmālya* (remainder of the previous worship), *Pīṭhikā* (pedestal), *Chāyā* (shadow) and *Prāsāda* (palace). The pedestal has been crossed by him as he was circumambulating.

Those confounded persons who cross it are undoubtedly worthy of being punished by Caṇḍa, the chief of Gaṇas.

Hence circumambulations and prostrations should be carefully performed along with the worship of the *Liṅga.*

Indeed the worship of the *Liṅga* should be carefully performed by those who have had the initiation for the sake of quelling all the sins. It should be performed with the sole intention of attaining spiritual (welfare)."

248. On hearing those words not originating from any embodied being, Suras beginning with Brahmā asked with palms joined in reverence to the ethereal voice, the cause of everything auspicious:

249. "How are we to worship the *Liṅga*? By what method or procedure? (When should it be:) in the morning, at midday or in the evening?

250. What are the flowers to be used in the evening as well as at midday? Are they the same as in the morning? Say exactly as it is."

251-254. Then the ethereal voice said in detail: "The following flowers can be used on all the three occasions: Karavīra (oleander, nerium odorum), Arkapuṣpa (gynandropsis pentaphylla), Bṛhatī Puṣpa (solanum indicum) Dhattūra (the white thorn-apple), Lotus, Āragvadha (cathartocarpus fistula), Punnāga (calophyllum inoplyllum), Bakula (mimusops elengi), Nāgakesara (mesua roxburghii), white Lotus, Kadamba and Mandāra (erythrina indica). Many other excellent flowers and many varieties of lotuses should be known as always sacred by learned men.

255-256. Jātī, Mallikā (Jasmine varieties), Mogaraka flowers, Nīla flower (blue flower), Kuṭaja (wrightia antidysenterica), Karṇikāra (cassia fistula), Kausumbha (wild safflower) and red lotus. These are the flowers for the worship of the *Liṅga* during midday. They are mentioned as the best by me. Now I shall tell you about the evening (worship).

257. Campaka flowers are undoubtedly sacred on all the three occasions. At night Mogaraka flowers are very sacred. There is no doubt about it.

258. After knowing these differences in the modes of worshipping the *Liṅga,* the due process of worship, should be followed by those who are conversant with the injunctions. The worship shall always be in the temple of Śiva.

259. One shall not perform circumambulation through the

space between the bull and *Liṅga*. Nor should one go beyond the *Pīṭhikā*. If that is done, one shall incur a sin.

260. Further the circumambulation was performed by Śakra with *Rājasa* trait of character. Hence it has become fruitless.

261. Purandara has been swallowed today by Vṛtra along with his elephant. That action whereby Indra is released should be performed by you people.

262. You must perform the rite in accordance with the injunctions in *Mahārudra*. He shall become liberated at the same time. O Devas, Purandara will thus become liberated. There is no doubt about it."

263. Following those words, Devas scrupulously worshipped Rudra as per the injunctions (and reciting) *Rudra-sūkta*.[1]

264. Suras worshipped Rudra with eleven recitations of the *Rudra-sūkta*. They performed *Havana* (fire offerings) rites to the extent of one-tenth (of the recitations), O excellent Brāhmaṇas.

265. Desirous of setting Purandara free suddenly, Devas performed *Japa*, *Pūjā* and *Havana*. Then the king of Devas, by the grace of Śaṁbhu, came out after breaking open his belly.

266-268. On seeing that the lord of Devas had come out by means of his prowess, along with his elephant, thunderbolt, crown and ear-rings and Purandara of great prowess had regained his great glory, many of the celestial wardrums and conchs were sounded. Gandharvas, celestial damsels, Yakṣas and the sages became joyous. Immediately after Purandara got liberated, all the heaven-dwellers became extremely delighted.

Then Śacī came to the place where Purandara got liberated.

269. There he was crowned along with Śacī by the great sages. The auspicious rite of *Puṇyāhavācana* (repetition of the words 'Today is an auspicious day' etc.) was performed with great effort by everyone.

270. Thus Mahendra was crowned by the sages then. The earth became extremely auspicious then, O excellent Brāhmaṇas.

271. The quarters became clear. The sky was rid of its impurities. Then the fires became tranquil, so also the minds of exalted souls.

272. When Śatakratu was liberated, these and many other miraculously wonderful auspicious omens occurred.

1. Tait. S. IV. v and vii corresponding to Vāj. S. chs. XVI and XVIII.

273. When the great festivities of those exalted persons were taking place, Vṛtra's dreadful body fell down.

274-277. There itself the extremely sinful *Brahmahatyā* fell on the ground. The space between Gaṅgā and Yamunā is called *Antarvedī*. It is well-known as a sacred land (*Puṇyabhūmi*). It is famous as the sanctifier of the worlds. The land where the Vṛtra-hatyā (Brahma-hatyā) fell dead is a sinful region. Since there was a great deal of impurity (*Mala*) that place is glorified as Mālava.[1] The great head of Vṛtra fell on that ground of impurity within six months after being cut off by all the Devas including Vāsava. Thus by slaying Vṛtra Śakra attained victory.

278. The consort of Śacī sat on the throne of the overlord without any mental worry or agony.

In the meantime Daityas approached Bali who was staying in Pātāla and recounted to him all the activities of Śakra.

279. On hearing their words the son of Virocana became angry. He asked Śukra how Indra could be won over.

280. This was said to Bali by him: "O king, perform a great *Yajña* today for the acquisition of the chariot of victory. Your victory will be achieved by means of that."

281. Bali who was making preparations for the *Yajña*, was told by Bhṛgu thus. The liberal-minded son of Virocana quickly gathered together whatever materials were required for the *Yajña* and kept them in store.

282. The great *Yajña* was started by the noble-souled son of Bhṛgu. Bali took up the *Dīkṣā* (initiation) and performed the *Homa* in the sacred fire.

283. When the *Homa* was duly performed in the sacred fire in the course of the holy rite in accordance with the injunctions, a miraculously wonderful chariot came out from that fire for Bali.

284. It was yoked with four horses. The emblem was that of a lion of great lustre. It was adorned by means of white horses. The chariot was glorious and equipped with weapons and missiles.

285. Then, urged by Śukra, he performed the *Avabhṛtha* (Valedictory) bath. After worshipping the chariot, Bali rode in it.

1. A popular etymology of *Malwa*, a part of Madhya Pradesh. As a matter of fact, the land where the tribe or people called Mālavas settled is Malwa.

286. Surrounded by Daityas and desirous of fighting Purandara, Bali, the great son of Virocana, immediately went to heaven.

287. After coming there along with his army, he laid siege to Amarāvatī. On seeing that their city had been besieged, all the excellent Suras pondered and deliberated on it for a long time and said to Bṛhaspati:

288. "What shall we do now? O highly fortunate one, the chief Daityas have come. All of them are exceedingly terrible, very efficient in war and desirous of fighting."

289. On hearing their words Bṛhaspati said:

290. "O Suras, these terrible (Daityas) beginning with Ghṛta (?) have been incited by Bhṛgu. All of them have become invincible by penance as well as valour."

291. On hearing these words full of good qualities, all the Suras became ashamed. Indra too lost his sense on account of worry. He became ashamed on being openly rebuked.

CHAPTER EIGHTEEN

Vāmana's Arrival at Bali's Sacrifice

Lomaśa said:

1. Overwhelmed by his own *Karman*, Mahendra spoke to Bṛhaspati, his preceptor: "What is that rite whereby we can surmount a distress without any very great effort? May it (please) be explained".

2. Bṛhaspati said thus: "We shall abandon Amarāvatī. Desirous of victory, we shall go elsewhere along with our families."

3. All the Suras did so. Assuming the form of a peacock Purandara left Amarāvatī and went away immediately.

4. Yama assumed the form of a crow. The lord of wealth (Kubera) himself became a chameleon. Agni became a small pigeon and Maheśvara became a frog (and went away).

5. Nairṛta became a dove at that very instant and then

went away. Pāśī (Varuṇa) became a Kapiñjala bird and Vāyu became a turtle-dove.

6-7. Assuming various bodies, they thus abandoned heaven and went away. In their great fright, they went to the holy hermitage of Kaśyapa.

All of them informed their mother Aditi of the activities of Daityas.

8-9. On hearing that unpleasant news, Aditi who was very fond of her sons, spoke to Kaśyapa about the critical danger of the Suras. "O great sage, let my words be listened to. After hearing them it behoves you to do (what should be done about) them. Devas have been defeated by Daityas. They have abandoned Amarāvatī and have come to your hermitage. Protect them, O Prajāpati."

10. On hearing her words, Kaśyapa spoke these words: "O slender-bodied beautiful lady, understand that Asuras are unconquerable on account of their great penance. O chaste lady, they are being approved and encouraged by Bhṛgu.

11-12. Indeed their conquest (is possible) only through first undertaking a severe penance, O beatiful lady. Observe this holy rite and vow as quickly as possible, O lady of exquisite fortune, for the accomplishment of the tasks of Suras. I shall explain (the rite) conducive to the realization of your object. Perform it, O splendid lady, with great effort and care, in accordance with the injunctions mentioned.

13. In the month of Bhādrapada (August-September), O gentle lady, on the *Daśamī* (tenth) day, be pure (in body and mind) with self-restraint.[1] The rite of *Ekabhakta* (taking only one meal a day) should be performed for propitiating Viṣṇu.

14. Lord Hari who himself is the direct granter of everything that is desired, should be requested prayerfully by his devotees with the following *Mantra*, O lady of excellent complexion and good fortune:

15. *Mantra*: 'I am your devotee, O lord. I shall perform this holy rite over three days beginning with *Daśamī*. O Viṣṇu, it behoves you to grant (me) permission.'

16-17. The lord of the universe should be prayed to only

1. VV 13ff. This is *Ekādaśī Vrata* to be observed for full one year.

Atri said:

36-39. At that time, what did all those Asuras do? Let it be mentioned:

Lomaśa said:

Then, all those Asuras beginning with Bali, desirous of fighting with Purandara, besieged the beautiful city in heaven. All those Asuras were not aware that Devas had gone away from heaven towards the hermitage of Kaśyapa assuming different forms.

They climbed the rampart wall with great excitement. When Daityas, desirous of killing Sureśa, entered Amarāvatī, they found it vacant. They became delighted in their minds.

40. Then Bali was crowned in Indra's throne by Śukra in accordance with the injunctions regarding the ceremony of coronation. He was surrounded by all the Asuras.

41. Bali, the great son of Virocana, established in the realm in that manner, shone with the greatest prosperity in the authoritative position of Mahendra.

42. He was served by Nāgas and groups of Asuras. Like Mahendra, the divine tree (*Kalpaka*), the divine cow Kāmadhenu and the jewel were all won over by him.

43-44. Those people who have gained the title of a *Dānī* (Donor) have done so with limited donations. But Bali the great was a donor unto all living beings. Whatever anyone desired was immediately given by him. The overlord of Dānavas distributed liberally to everyone what he sought.

Śaunaka said:

45. O excessively fortunate one, Devendra never gave anything to anyone. How is this that Bali became a donor? Describe it truthfully.

Lomaśa said:

46. Whatever man does after exerting himself yields either good or bad results. This should be known by a learned person.

47. Indeed Śakra who performed a hundred horse sacrifices and gained the realm in Amarāvatī was addicted to worldly pleasures only.

48-49. A man seeks something and gains his object. Know that immediately (after getting the result) a sort of niggardliness besets him. Afterwards he dies and his merit becomes exhausted. As a result of this, Indra may turn into a worm and a worm may become Indra. Hence there is nothing more conducive to liberation than charitable gifts.

50. From charitable gift knowledge is acquired and from knowledge liberation is achieved undoubtedly. Devotion unto the Trident-bearing Lord (Śiva) is greater than liberation, O Brāhmaṇas.

51. Sadāśiva, the lord of all, gives away everything when his mind is pleased. Śaṅkara becomes satisfied with even a very little thing that is offered, say, even water of a very little quantity.

52. In this connection they cite this ancient legend. This has been undoubtedly done by the son of Virocana.[1]

53. There was a roguish gambler, a great sinner. He used to censure Devas and Brāhmaṇas. He indulged in great fraud and dishonesty. He was an adulterer.

54-59. Once much wealth was earned by him through great sins and gambling. He took with him flowers, betal leaves and sandal paste for giving them to a prostitute. (On the way robbers took away all his garments and ready cash.) The gambler was left with only a loin cloth. Scents, garlands etc. which he had taken with him to be offered to the courtezan, were still with him. He clasped his shoulders with crossed hands, thereby making a Svastika sign to cover the nakedness of his body. Taking the scent etc. he was running towards the house. He stumbled on the way and fell on the ground instantaneously. After the fall he swooned. After some time he regained consciousness. Although he was a sinner causing unpleasantness (trouble) to others and though he was dull-witted, suddenly his intellect was directed towards good thoughts. Evidently it was the result of his previous deeds. The gambler was exceedingly disgusted with worldly objects. He was repentant and miserable for what he had done so far. The scent, the flowers etc. that had fallen on

1. VV 52-81. This story of the previous birth of Bali as a gambler-donor is given to explain Bali's nature of thoughtless liberality, his *atidāna*. The story however glorifies the liberality of the gambler to the detriment of god Yama.

the ground were dedicated to Śiva by that gambler unconsciously and unintentionally.

60-64. By this meritorious deed (something good happened). He was taken to the abode of Yama by the attendants of Yama. Yama who is dreadful unto all the worlds said to him after calling him a sinner: "O stupid fellow, you are to be cooked in the great hells." On being told by Dharmarāja thus, the gambler spoke these words: "O lord, no evil conduct has been practised by me. O Yama, let my meritorious deeds be truly considered."

Citragupta spoke:

Something had been given by you to Śiva, the great soul. What fell on the ground was given to Śiva at the time of your death. Due to that meritorious deed, understand, you will attain the position of Indra undoubtedly for three *Ghaṭikās* (1 *Ghaṭikā* = 24 minutes).

65. At that time the lord came there accompanied by all the Suras. Riding on Airāvata, this gambler was taken to Śakra's abode. Śakra was them enlightened and advised by Bṛhaspati of sanctified soul:

66. "O Purandara, for a period of three *Ghaṭikās* this gambler should be installed in your seat at my bidding."

67. On hearing the words of his preceptor, he betook (respected) them on his head (i.e. bowed down his head to signify assent). Śakra went elsewhere and the gambler was ushered into the wonderfully furnished abode of the king of Devas.

68. He was crowned and installed on the throne of Śakra. He attained the kingdom of Śatakratu, because he had offered scents to Śaṁbhu along with flowers and betel leaves.

69-70. What then in the case of those people who are actuated by faith to offer large quantities of scents, flowers etc. always with great devotion to Śiva, the Supreme Spirit? (I.e. they deserve much greater reward.) They will attain *Śivasāyujya* (identity with Śiva). They will be accompanied by Śiva's army (*Gaṇas*) and acquire great joy. Indeed Śakra is the servant of such people.

71-72. The happiness that people of quiescent minds engaged in the worship of Śiva attain is very great. It is rare and difficult of achievement even by Brahmā, Śakra etc. Those who are covetous of sensual pleasures are deluded. They are poor and pitiable. They do not know (these things).

Mahādeva is (i.e. deserves) to be saluted and Sadāśiva to be worshipped.

73. Mahādeva is to be worshipped and adored by all living beings knowing the truth. Thus the gambler attained the status of Indra for a period of three *Ghaṭikās*.

74. On being crowned by the priest, he occupied the seat of Purandara. At that time, this gambler of great fame was told by Nārada:

75. "Bring Indrāṇī by whom the kingdom is rendered very splendid." Then the gambler, the lover of Śiva, laughed and said:

76. "I have nothing to do with Indrāṇī. This ought not to have been mentioned by you, O highly intelligent one."

After saying thus, the gambler began (to give) charitable gifts.

77-80. The lover of Śiva gave Airāvata to Agastya. The gambler of liberal-minded nature gave Viśvāmitra the horse named Uccaiḥśravas. The gambler of great fame gave Kāmadhenu and Cintāmaṇi of great lustre to Vasiṣṭḥa. The gambler of great splendour gave Gālava the divine tree Kalpataru. The gambler of great fortune gave Kauṇḍinya a house.

Joyously he gave these and many other jewels of diverse kinds to sages. He gave everything for the pleasure of Śiva.

81. The lord continued his charitable gifts over a period of three *Ghaṭikās*. After the period of three *Ghaṭikās* was over, the previous lord arrived.

82. Purandara was seated on his own throne in Amarāvatī. He was being eulogized by the sages. He was accompanied by Śacī also.

83. The evil-minded one said to Śacī: "O splendid and beautiful lady, you have been enjoyed by that gambler; were you not? Tell me the truth fully."

84-86. Then the lady without blemish said to Purandara: "Everywhere you see things and persons on the analogy of your own self, O Purandara. He is a noble soul in the form of a gambler. By the grace of Śiva, he has been the knower of the reality and ultimate truth. He is high-minded and detached (from worldly pleasures). He forsook for the sake of others the kingdom and other things that had come to him. All those great things were considered binding nooses causing delusion. Hence he gave them to others. (Hence) he has become victorious."

87. On hearing the words of Indrāṇī, Purandara, the lord of Devas, became ashamed. He sat silently in his seat.

88-91. The most excellent one among those conversant with arguments said to Bṛhaspati: "Airāvata is not to be seen. So also Uccaiḥśravas, the horse. By whom have Pārijāta and other objects been taken away?"

Then Guru (Bṛhaspati) said to him the great thing done by the gambler. As long as he had power, he gave away (those) to the sages. Those who are not influenced by and not attached to their own great power and position, those who are continuously engaged in meditation on Śiva are the favourites of Śaṅkara.

Abandoning the fruits of the *Karmans*, they attain the greatest region by resorting to *Jñāna* (knowledge) alone."

92-93. On hearing the words of Bṛhaspati, Indra said these words: "Mostly these things Yama will say, for the sake of his own prosperity."

Thinking that to be so, Śakra, the king of Suras, suddenly went accompanied by Bṛhaspati. Purandara who desired his own objectives, went to the city of Saṁyaminī.

94. On being welcomed and honoured by Yama, Śakra said these words: "My position and region was given to the evil-minded gambler by you.

95. But this highly despicable action has been committed by him. All jewels and fine things belonging to me were given to different persons by him. O Dharma, know this exactly.

96. Your name is Dharma. How did you give the gambler (this position)? Everything has been done by you for destroying my kingdom.

97. O highly fortunate one, fetch the elephant and other things back quickly. Other things, jewels etc. have been given to different persons."

98. On hearing the words of Śakra, Yama spoke these words to the gambler furiously: "What is this that has been done by you, a great sinner?

99-102. Śakra's kingdom was given to you for your enjoyment. But it has been given to Brāhmaṇas. A great thing has been done otherwise. What should not be done has been committed by you, (viz.) the removal (stealing) of other people's wealth, O foolish one. You will go to hell because of this sin." On hearing the words of Yama, the gambler said: "The fact that I am to go to hell does not deserve anxiety. As long as I had the possession of Śakra's throne, something was given to the Brāhmaṇas."

Yama said:

103-104. Charitable gift is commended on the earth where the fruit of *Karman* is had. In heaven charitable gift should never be given to anyone by anyone at any place. Hence, O stupid one, you are worthy of being punished. What is opposed to the injunctions of the scriptures has been perpetrated by you. The preceptor is the chastiser and guide of those who are wise and self-possessed. The king is the chastiser of evil-minded persons. I am undoubtedly the chastiser of all persons of sinful conduct.

105. After rebuking that gambler thus, the lord of Dharma (i.e. Yama) himself spoke to Citragupta: "Let him be cooked in the hell."

Then Citragupta laughed and said to Yama:

106-108. "How can this gambler be sent to hell? The great elephant Airāvata has been given to Agastya by him. The horse that came out of the ocean (Uccaiḥśravā) has been given to the noble-souled Gālava. Welfare unto you, Cintāmaṇi of great lustre has been given to Viśvāmitra.[1] These and other jewels have been given away by this gambler. As a result of that *Karman*, he is worthy of being praised and worshipped in all the three worlds.

109. Everything that is given away with Śiva in view either in heaven or in the mortal world by men is, it should be known, everlasting. It is called a flawless *Karman*. Hence there is no question of this gambler falling into hell.

110-111. Whatever sins the gambler committed have all been reduced to ash by remembering Śaṁbhu. He has become a noble soul. Thanks to the grace of Śambhu, many merits have been acquired by him at the same instant." On hearing these

1. Cp. vv 77-80 which state it differently.

words of Citragupta, the king of the departed spirits bent down his head. He laughed and said this to Śatakratu (Indra):

112-114. "Indeed you are the king of the leading Suras. (Though) old you are too covetous of the kingdom. One good thing of the whole of your life has been earned by you by means of a hundred sacrifices. There is no doubt about it.

You have to request all those sages, Agastya and others, particularly by falling at their feet or offering them monetary compensation in order to get back the elephant and other jewels, whereby you can become happy. You are to hasten."

115. Thinking that it should be so (after hearing) those words, Purandara of indiscriminate vision went back to his city. With his neck bent down in humility, he requested the sages. Then he got back (the tree) Pārijāta.

116. In the same manner, Purandara got back the whole of the kingdom. He became (once again) the king in Amarāvatī along with noble-souled (persons).

117. A rebirth was granted to the gambler by Yama. As a consequence of some noble action, he became the son of Virocana.

118. Suruci, the daughter of Vṛṣaparvan, the principal queen of Virocana, became the mother of the gambler. He remained in the womb of that noble-souled lady.

119. From the son of Prahlāda and from Suruci, he inherited the great inclination for virtue and charitable gifts.

120. Even as he was staying in the womb, his own mind was made excellent by the gambler. What is difficult of access even to learned men, O Brāhmaṇas, has been accomplished by that gambler.

121. Śakra once went to Virocana, the lord of Daityas, in the guise of a Brāhmaṇa beggar.[1] He was desirous of killing him.

122. After reaching Virocana's abode, Indra spoke these words on assuming the guise of an old Brāhmaṇa: "O king of good holy rites, O lord of Daityas, you are (the most celebrated) learned man and donor in the whole of the three worlds. Give me (what I am going to ask).

1. VV 121-136 describe how Bali's father Virocana offered his own head to Indra in the guise of a Brāhmaṇa.

123. Standing in the midst of assemblies, O king of excellent fortune, Brāhmaṇas extol your wonderful life-story and spotless fame. I am a beggar, O lord of Daityas of good holy rites; it behoves you to give me (what I beg)."

124. On hearing his words, the lord of Daityas spoke these words: "O holy lord, what should be given (to you). Tell me quickly."

125-126. Indra in the form of a Brāhmaṇa spoke to Virocana: "It is a humiliating thing, yet I beg of you. Whatever is highly pleasing and dear to you, should be given to me. There is no doubt about it."

The Asura, the son of Prahlāda, laughingly spoke these words:

127. "If you desire, O Brāhmaṇa, I shall give you my head. Even this kingdom (I shall give) without any strain. This glory and prosperity shall not go to others. I shall undoubtedly offer everything to you."

128. On being told thus by the Daitya, Indra pondered over it and said: "Give me your own head adorned with the crown."

129. When these words were spoken by Śakra in the form of a Brāhmaṇa, the Asura, the son of Prahlāda, joyously hurried up and cut off his own head with his own hand and gave it to Mahendra.

130. The virtuous action performed by Prahlāda previously was (of course) very difficult to do, but by resorting to *Bhakti* (devotion) alone of Viṣṇu, it was done by him with his mind devoted to him.

131. There is nothing greater than a charitable gift anywhere. That charitable gift offered to persons in distress is highly meritorious.

132. Anything whatsoever within one's capacity, (if offered) is capable of infinite results. There is nothing greater than charitable gift in all the three worlds.

133. There are three types of charitable gifts, viz. *Sāttvika*, *Rājasa* and *Tāmasa*. That charitable gift which is characterized as *Sāttvika*, was performed by him.

134-135. The head was cut off and given to Indra who was in the guise of a Brāhmaṇa. The crown fell down there. So also the gems and jewels of great lustre fell down simultaneously for the purpose of the groups of Daityas, kings and serpents.

136. That charitable gift of Virocana became well-known in all the three worlds. Even today poets sing about (the charitable gifts) of the noble-souled king of Daityas.

137-138. This gambler of great refulgence became the son of Virocana. He was born after the father had died. His mother, a chaste lady, forsook her body and attained the world of her husband. Then in the very same throne of his father, he was crowned by Bhārgava (Śukra).

139. He earned great fame and he became well-known by the name Bali. All the groups of Suras of very great strength were terrified by him.

140. It has already been mentioned that they went to the auspicious hermitage of Kaśyapa. At that time Bali of great fame became Indra in the city of Devas.

141. By means of his penance, he became the Sun-god himself and blazed. The Asura became Īśa himself and stayed in the north-eastern quarter protecting it, keeping watch over it.

142. Similarly he himself became Nairṛta and Varuṇa, the lord of the waters. Bali then stayed in the north as the lord of wealth (Kubera). Thus Bali directly enjoyed the three worlds himself.

143. Thus, O Brāhmaṇas, Bali became eagerly devoted to and engaged in munificent charitable gifts due to the previous practice which the gambler had, because he was engaged in the worship of Śiva.

144. Once he was seated in the middle of the assembly along with Bhṛgu. The glorious lord was surrounded by the leading Daityas. He spoke these words to Śaṇḍa and Marka:

145. "Take up your residence along with the Asuras here itself near me. Leave off Pātāla today itself. It does not behove you to delay."

146-147. On hearing it, Bhārgava laughingly said: "One is honoured in the heavenly world only through different kinds of *Yajñas*. Heaven can be enjoyed, O great king, only by those who perform *Yajñas*. O king, my words cannot be otherwise."

148. On hearing the words of the preceptor, the lord of

Daityas spoke these words: "Let all the great Asuras live in heaven for a long time, by virtue of the *Karman* performed by me. There is no doubt about this."

149. Thinking that Bali was childish, Śukra, the holy lord of Bhṛgu clan, whose power of penance was very great and who was the most excellent one among the intelligent people, laughed and said:

150-151. "O Bali, the words uttered by you do not appeal to me. If you wish to come here itself and stay, O Daitya of good holy rites, worship the Fire-god with a hundred horse-sacrifices after going to the land of *Karman* (i.e. the earth). It does not behove (you) to delay."

152. Thinking that it should be so, the noble-souled Bali abandoned heaven. The learned leader of Daityas went to the earth accompanied by Daityas, the preceptor and all attendants.

153. On the banks of the river Narmadā there is a great holy spot of exalted refulgence named Gurukulya. After conquering the entire surface of the earth, the noble-souled lord of Daityas went there.

154. Urged by his preceptor, Bali, son of Virocana of great fame, who was very efficient, had the great initiation. He who was the most excellent one among truthful persons worshipped through many horse-sacrifices.

155. He kept a Brāhmaṇa as his *Ācārya* (preceptor). He had sixteen *Ṛtviks*. All of them were well-tested by the noble-souled Bhārgava.

156. Bali, who was readily initiated, performed ninety-nine *Yajñas*. He decided to complete the hundredth horse-sacrifice too.

157-158. By the time the full merit of the hundred sacrifices was to accrue, the excellent *Vrata* of Aditi as mentioned by me before, was also completed. The powerful lord Hari was delighted at that *Vrata*. He became Aditi's son in the form of a great religious student.

159-162. The sacred thread ceremony of the lord was performed by Kaśyapa himself. When the rite was completed, Brahmā, the grandfather of the worlds, also came there. A sacred thread was given by Brahmā, Parameṣṭhin. A staff was given by the noble-souled Soma (Moon). A girdle was brought and a wonderfully potent deer-hide too. Similarly two sandals were given to the noble-souled boy by the Earth. Alms were brought by Bhavānī for the sake of the realization of his desired object. Thus (everything) was given to Viṣṇu who was in the form of a *Baṭu* (religious student).

163. The lord of Śrī, in the form of Vāmana (Dwarf), bowed down to Aditi and Kaśyapa. The lord of great refulgence went to the sacrificial chamber of Bali for the sake of deceiving Bali, it is said.

164. Then that great lord went to heaven shaking the earth with the weight of the forepart of his foot. That Lord Vāmana, Viṣṇu himself in the form of the religious student, the Supreme Soul (did so) for the cause of Suras.

165. The noble-souled lord was eulogized by means of truthful words by the people, leading sages and groups of Devas. Proceeding quickly the lord, the sole kinsman of the universe, reached the sacrificial chamber.

166. Since the lord was in the guise of a *Baṭu*, he sang the Sāman hymns loudly. It was the lord himself, lord Hari who can be realized only through the Vedāntas, who was being sung about in those Sāman hymns.

167. Vāmana whose refulgence was very great had assumed the form of a *Baṭu*. He stood at the entrance and saw that great horse-sacrifice of Bali.

168. The whole of the cardinal points were pervaded by the great Brahminical splendour of the noble-souled Vāmana, the *Baṭu*, the sanctifier of everything.[1]

169. On hearing it, the intelligent Bali told Śaṇḍa and Marka: "Let it be looked into as to how many Brāhmaṇas have come."

170. Thinking that it should be so, both Śaṇḍa and Marka hurriedly got up. They came to the entrance of the hall erected for the performance of the sacrifice.

171. They saw the noble-souled Śrī Hari in the form of a *Baṭu*. They returned quickly in order to intimate it to Bali.

172. "A certain *Brahmacārin* (a religious student) alone has

1. Or by the loud sound of the Vedic *Pavamāna* hymn recited by the noble-souled Vāmana.

come. There is no one else. He has come to your presence, O great king. (He is engaged) in reciting etc. Why he has come to you, we do not know. Know it yourself, O highly intelligent one."

173. When these words were spoken by both of them, that high-minded (Daitya) stood up immediately for seeing that *Baṭu*.

174. The great son of Virocana, of excessive refulgence, prostrated himself on the ground like a rod on seeing the *Baṭu*. He bowed down to the *Baṭu* with his head.

175. He immediately took the *Baṭu* in and made him sit on his own throne. After offering *Arghya*, *Pādya* etc. duly, he honoured and worshipped the *Baṭu*.

176. With his neck drooping down due to modesty, he spoke in polished soft words: "Whence have you come, Sir? What for have you come? Whose (son) are you? O lord, let these things be mentioned."

177. On hearing the words of the son of Virocana, Vāmana was delighted. He began to speak.

The Lord said:

178. You are the king and overlord of the three worlds. No one else deserves to be so. If on account of a person the family becomes weaker and deficient, that person is remembered as *Kāpuruṣa* ('contemptible one').

179. If on account of a person the family continues to be in the same position or becomes better and superior, that person is a true man. The *Karman* performed by you has never been done by your ancestors.

180. Hiraṇyakaśipu and others were the most excellent ones among Daityas. Hiraṇyakaśipu performed great penance for a period of a thousand divine years.

181. As he was engaged in the great penance his body was eaten by many ants and covered with biting gad-flies.

182. On coming to know of it, Surendra formerly went to his city and besieged it with a great army.

183-184. In his presence all the Asuras were killed by the enemy of Daityas. His queen Vindhyā[1] was being taken away,

1. Kayādhū according to BhP.

but, O King, was prevented by Nārada who was desirous of doing something. By the grace of Śaṁbhu, all those things which had been desired mentally by the lord of Daityas were won over by means of penance alone.

185-186. Her son was that person of great splendour (i.e. Prahlāda) by whom his own son, i.e. your father who was a favourite of his father, was led to the Assembly, O King of great fortune. Your father was known by the name Virocana. It was by that noble-souled (Daitya) that the learned Indra was propitiated by the offer of his own head. O King, you are his son. Great fame has been earned by you.

187. By the great lamp of your fame, Suras have been burnt like locusts and fireflies. There is no doubt about this that even Indra has been conquered by you.

188. All your activities have been heard by me, O Daitya of good holy rites. I am a small insignificant person clinging to my vow of celibacy.

189. For the sake of a hut give me some ground, O most excellent one among the kings of earth.

On hearing the words of that *Baṭu*, Bali spoke:

190-191. "O *Baṭu*, you are a scholar. What you have spoken before, you yourself do not know, because you are only a child. On hearing it, I think that it is truthful.

Speak quickly, O highly fortunate one, how much ground shall I give you? Ponder over it quickly in your mind."

192. Then Vāmana spoke these sweet words smilingly:

"Those Brāhmaṇas who are not contented are undoubtedly doomed.

193-194. Those are Brāhmaṇas who are contented, not others. They are Brāhmāṇas in disguise. They (i.e. real Brāhmaṇas) are engaged in their own duty, O King. They are devoid of arrogance. They have no hindrance (of any kind). They are free from jealousy. They have conquered anger and are liberal-minded, O highly intelligent one. They are real Brāhmaṇas, O highly fortunate one. This earth is sustained by them.

195. You are lofty-minded. You have plenty. You are the sole donor in the three worlds. Still the ground measured up to three paces should be given to me.

196. I have nothing to do with plenty of earth, O slayer of Suras. It will serve as a hut with a mere entrance.

197. Three paces of ground are enough for our purpose. There is no doubt about it. I shall take the steps and give me the ground as much as I cover. Only that number (of steps) need be given to me if you are a real donor."

198. Bali, the son of Virocana, laughed and said this:

"I shall give you the entire earth including mountains, parks and forests.

199-202. O highly fortunate one, take this which belongs to me and given to you by me. See, O *Baṭu*, you are the person who is an entreater and that you are begging of a Daitya. Whether the beggar is insignificant or not, the donor sees himself (i.e. considers his capacity) and gives away things to those who seek them. He is the real liberal-minded person who gives away commensurately with his own status. Hence a suppliant who is unfortunate should not go abegging. O *Baṭu*, I shall give you the entire earth today, including the mountains, parks and forests and oceans. My statement cannot be otherwise."

203. The *Baṭu* said once again to the son of Virocana: "My (need) is fulfilled, O great Daitya, by taking land covered in three steps."

204. On hearing those words, Bali, the lord of Asuras, spoke these words laughingly: "Let the space adorned by three steps and given by me, be accepted."

205. On being told thus, Vāmana laughingly said to the Asura: "Intending the whole of the earth (for *dāna*), it behoves you to give it, O Daitya of good holy rites."

206. Thinking that it should be so, Vāmana, the great son of Kaśyapa, was adored well by Bali. Bali was then eulogized well by the sages and leading ascetics.

207. While after worshipping Vāmana, Bali was about to give (the gift), that great son of Virocana was prevented by his preceptor.

208. "This gift should not be offered by you to Viṣṇu in the form of a *Baṭu*. He has come here for the sake of Indra. He will create obstacles in your *Yajña*. Hence Viṣṇu, the illuminator of spiritual life, should not be worshipped by you.

209-211. Formerly much has been done by this one assuming

the form of Mohinī, the enchantress. Nectar was given to Devas and the great Rāhu was killed. Daityas were routed. The powerful Kālanemi was killed. Such is he. He is the noble-souled *Puruṣa*. He is *Īśvara*. He alone is the lord of the universe. Ponder over everything, O highly intelligent one, mentally. It behoves you to do what is conducive to your welfare or otherwise."

CHAPTER NINETEEN

Śukra Curses Bali: Vāmana Grants Boon to Bali

Lomaśa said:

1. On being addressed thus by his preceptor Bhārgava, the Daitya laughed and spoke these words in a voice as majestic as the (thundering) sound of the cloud:

2. "I have been moved by those words with which I have been addressed by you for the sake of my welfare. Your statement may be for my happiness and welfare. But it is sure to go against my welfare.

3. I will surely give what has been begged of (me) to Viṣṇu in the form of a *Baṭu*. This Viṣṇu is the lord of the fruits of all *Karmans*.

4-6. Certainly, those people in whose heart Viṣṇu is stationed, are the most deserving persons. Everything seen in this world, is called holy by his name. This Hari is the lord of the universe. Vedas, *Yajñas* and these things beginning with *Mantras*, *Tantras* etc., become perfect and complete on account of him. Lord Hari, the soul of everyone has come here out of sympathy for me, in order to redeem me. There is no doubt about it. Understand this truthfully."

7. On hearing these words of his, Bhārgava became furious.[1] He began to curse the lord of Daityas, fond of virtue and piety:

---

1. Śukra, Bali's preceptor, warned that Vāmana, the *Baṭu*, was Viṣṇu and the proposed gift of three paces of land should not be given. When Bali refused to obey, Śukra cursed him. In the end Vāmana committed a disin-

8. "O suppressor of foes, you wish to offer the gift, transgressing my directives. Hence, O stupid one, become devoid of good qualities; be rid of all your glory."

9. Thus (Śukra) cursed his noble-souled disciple, conversant with the ultimate truth and possessing unfathomable knowledge and understanding. Mahā Kavi ('the Great Śukra'), the most excellent one among those who know virtue and piety, hastened to his own hermitage.

10. When Bhārgava had departed, Bali, the son of Virocana, worshipped Vāmana and began to offer the earth.

11-12. Vindhyāvalī, the resplendent better-half of Bali, came there and washed the feet of the *Baṭu*. He (Bali) gave the earth to Viṣṇu along with the rite of *Saṁkalpa* ('ritualistic proclamation of the intention') as he was an expert in the procedure (for holy rites). By his determination, the unborn Lord increased in size.

13. When the lord increased in size, the whole of the earth was covered with one of his steps by Viṣṇu who was powerful. All the *Svargas* (Heavens supposed to be twenty-one in number) were covered with the second step by that Supreme Soul.

14. The foot of Viṣṇu that went as far as Satyaloka, was washed by Parameṣṭhin (i.e. Brahmā) with the water from his *Kamaṇḍalu* ('water-pot').

15-16. From the water that came in contact with his feet was born (the sacred river) Bhāgīrathī who was auspicious unto all, by whom all the three worlds were rendered sacred and pure, all the Sagaras were uplifted and the matted hair of Śaṁbhu was filled. By Bhagīratha the first and foremost of all the holy waters named Gaṅgā was made to descend. It was connected with Viṣṇu's foot by Brahmā.

17. The greatest Ātman came to be known by the name *Trivikrama*, because of his three steps. Then all the three worlds were covered up by the steps taken by Trivikrama.

18-19. Or (it is better to state that) the whole of this universe including mobile and immobile beings was completely covered up by means of two steps.

---

genuous fraud of demanding three paces of land of his *Viśvarūpa*, when the promise was made of the *Baṭu's* small three paces and Bali was bound down for non-fulfilment of the pledge.

Janārdana, the lord of Devas, cast off that form (i.e. the cosmic size) and again assumed the form of the *Baṭu*. He took his seat (as before). At that time Devas, Gandharvas, Sages, Siddhas and Cāraṇas came to the place of Bali's *Yajña* in order to see the lord, the presiding deity of *Yajñas*.

20. Brahmā came there and eulogized the Supreme Spirit. Other leading Daityas also hastened to the place of Bali.

21. Vāmana sat there in the abode of Bali surrounded by all these. Then he said to Garuḍa:

22-23. "In his childish ignorance, sufficient ground to be covered up by three steps was offered by him to me. Two steps have been taken by me. One step that had already been promised, this evil-minded fellow does not give me. Hence the third step must be taken up by you."

24. On being told thus by Vāmana of great soul, Garuḍa rebuked the son of Virocana and spoke these words:

25. "O stupid Bali, why is this despicable thing committed by you? When you do not have sufficient material what will you give to the Supreme Soul? Of what avail is a (show of) liberal-mindedness by you, an insignificant person now?"

26. On being told thus, Bali was overcome (by grief) but smilingly he spoke to Garutmān, the lord of birds, the following words:

27-28. "I am (really) capable, O (bird) of huge wings. I am not a miser. What can I give him by whom all these have been created? O dear one, I have been made incapable by this noble-souled lord."

Then Garuḍa of noble mind spoke to Bali:

29. "Indeed you know (everything), O lord of Daityas. You were prevented by your preceptor. Yet you offered the earth to Viṣṇu. Is this important thing forgotten by you?

30. That step, the third one that has been promised to Viṣṇu must be given to him. How is it that you do not give it, O hero? You will fall into hell.

31. How is it that you do not give the third step to my master? I will take it forcibly, O foolish one." Saying this he bound the great Asura, the son of Virocana, by means of nooses of Varuṇa.

32. Garuḍa, the most excellent one among conquerors, be-

came very ruthless (and did like this). On seeing that her husband had been bound, Vindhyāvalī came there.[1]

33. She placed (her son) Bāṇa on one side and stood in front of Vāmana. It was enquired by Vāmana, "Who is this (lady) standing in front of me?"

34. Then Prahlāda of great splendour, the lord of the Asuras, spoke: "This is Vindhyāvalī, the chaste wife of Bali. She has come to you."

35. On hearing the words of Prahlāda, Vāmana spoke these words: "Say, O Vindhyāvalī, what shall I do for you?" On being told thus by the lord, Vindhyāvalī spoke:

Vindhyāvalī said:

36. What for has my husband been bound by the noble-souled Garuḍa? Let it be explained immediately, O Janārdana of exalted fortune?

Then Hari of great splendour, who had assumed the guise of a *Baṭu* said:

The Lord said:

37. Ground measured by three steps had been offered to me by him alone. The whole of the three worlds has been covered up by me with two steps.

38. The third step has to be given to me by this (Daitya) your husband. Hence, O chaste lady, he has been bound by me through Garuḍa.

39. On hearing the words of the lord, she spoke these great words:

"What has been promised by him, O lord, is not given to you.

40-41. All the three worlds have been covered up by you of valorous form. Therefore (everything) that we had in heaven as

---

1. Vindhyāvalī, the Queen of Bali, who saw through Viṣṇu's fraud, rose to the occasion and told Viṣṇu (Vāmana) to take still three paces by placing them on the head of Bali, of herself and of her son Bāṇa. The great Viṣṇu was vanquished. He restored Bali to his kingdom in Sutala and became his doorkeeper.

well as on the earth has been hindered and obstructed by you. That was why something has not been given to you, O Lord, O Lord of the universe, O Lord of Devas."

Then the lord laughed and said to Vindhyāvalī:

42. "Three steps have to be given to me today. Why (were they not given) now? Tell me quickly, O lady of large wide eyes, what have you in your mind?"

Then that chaste lady stood steady and said to Urukrama ('one of large step' i.e. Vāmana):

43. "Why was the whole of the three worlds, O lord of the universe, occupied by you with large steps? Therefore, O sole kinsman of the universe, has everything to be given to you of matchless form by us?

44. Hence leave it off, O Viṣṇu and do thus now. Three steps had been promised by my husband now. My husband will give (those promised steps) now to you. You need not worry about it.

45-46. Place a step on my head, O lord, the most excellent one among Devas. Place the second step, O lord of the universe, on the head of my child (Bāṇa). Place the third step, O lord of the universe, on the head of my husband. Thus I shall give you three steps, O Keśava."

47. On hearing her words, Janārdana became delighted. He spoke these gentle and soft words to the son of Virocana:

The Lord said:

48. Go to Sutala, O lord of Daityas. Do not delay. It does not behove you to delay. Live long and be happy along with all the groups of Asuras.

49. I am delighted and contented, O dear one. What shall I do for you? You are the most excellent one among all donors, O highly intelligent one.

50-51. Choose a boon. Welfare unto thee. I shall give you everything you wish.

On being told thus by Trivikrama, the son of Virocana was released (from bondage) and embraced by the Discus-bearing Lord of Devas. Then Bali, an expert in the use of words, spoke these words:

52. "It was by you that the whole of this universe consisting

of mobile and immobile beings was created. Hence I do not wish for anything except your lotus-like feet, O Lord.

53. Let my devotion be to your lotus-like feet, O lord Janārdana. Let it flourish again and again, O lord of Devas. Let my devotion (unto you) be everlasting."

54. Thus requested by him, the lord, the sanctifier of all living beings, became exceedingly pleased then and spoke to the son of Virocana:

The Lord said:

55. O Bali, go to Sutala surrounded by kinsmen and relatives.

On being told thus by him the Asura spoke these words:

56. "What have I to do in Sutala, O lord of Devas? Tell me. I shall stay near you. It does not behove you to say otherwise."

57. Then Hṛṣīkeśa, the merciful (lord), said to Bali: "O King, I shall always be near you.

58. O lord, I shall stand at the entrance to your (abode) and stay there perpetually. O Bali, the most excellent one among Asuras, be not afflicted and distressed. Listen to my clear and open statement. I shall be the bestower of boons on you. Along with the residents of Vaikuṇṭha, I shall betake myself to your abode."

59. On hearing those words of Viṣṇu of matchless splendour, the Daitya went to Sutala surrounded by Asuras.

60. He stayed there along with his hundred sons, the chief (eldest) of whom was Bāṇa. The (Daitya) of great might was the greatest among all donors, their ultimate resort.

61. All the beggars and mendicants of the three worlds went to Bali. Viṣṇu who stood at the entrance to his abode, granted to them whatever they desired to get.

62. Some of them were desirous of worldly pleasures. Others were desirous of liberation. He gave them everything. He gave it to those persons in whose *Yajñas* they officiated as the Brāhmaṇa priests.

63-65. It was by the favour of Śaṅkara that Bali became thus.[1] In his former birth as a gambler, fragrant flowers, scents

1. One fails to understand where Śiva's favour comes in this episode.

and other great things that had fallen on dirty ground were offered by him to the great *Ātman*. What had fallen down was dedicated to Śiva, the great spirit by him. What then in the case of those who worship Maheśvara with the greatest devotion? Those who devoutly offer sweet scents, flowers, fruits or even water go to Śiva's presence.

66-67. There is no greater (deity) worthy of being worshipped than Śiva. Those who are dumb, blind, lame and sluggish, those who are devoid of nobility of birth, Cāṇḍālas, dog-eaters and even low-born mean fellows, always attain the greatest goal if they are engaged in devotion to Śiva.

68. Hence Sadāśiva should be worshipped by all learned men. Sadāśiva should be worshipped, adored and venerated.

69. Those who are aware of the ultimate truth think about Maheśa stationed in the heart. Wherever there is the individual soul, Śiva too dwells there.

70. Everything without Śiva becomes inauspicious instantaneously. Brahmā, Viṣṇu and Rudra—these carry on their activities through the *Guṇas*.

71. Brahmā possesses *Rajas Guṇa*. Viṣṇu has *Sattva Guṇa*. Rudra resorts to *Tamas Guṇa*. Maheśvara is beyond all the *Guṇas*.

72. Mahādeva should be worshipped in the form of *Liṅga* by those who desire salvation. There is no greater bestower of worldly pleasures and liberation than Śiva.

The author, a propagandist of Śiva, however, gives Śiva the credit of Bali's ultimate victory.

CHAPTER TWENTY

The Nirguṇatva of the Śiva Liṅga: The Manifestation of Bhavānī

The sages said:

1. Brahmā, Viṣṇu and Rudra were mentioned by you as (deities) possessing *Guṇas*. Similarly Īśa has *Liṅga* for his form. How is he beyond *Guṇas*? Tell us.

2. This universe consisting of mobile and immobile beings is pervaded by the three *Guṇas*. Whatever is great, pervasive or small—everything is of the nature of *Māyā* and appears so. Whence and through what does it appear without the *Liṅga*?

3. Whatever is visible whether great or small is perishable, O Sūta, because it is created.

4. Hence, O Sūta, it behoves you to ponder over everything, critically examine it and dispel our doubts. By the grace of Vyāsa you and none else, know everything.

Sūta said:

5. In this matter everything has been told (explained) by Vyāsa to Śuka.

Śuka enquired:

Śaṁbhu has *Liṅga* as his form. How is he described as free from *Guṇas* by you? O dear father, it behoves you to dispel this doubt of mine completely.

Vyāsa explained:

6. Listen, O dear one. I shall tell it. It was formerly explained by Nandī to Agastya who asked about it. O Śuka, everything was heard by him.

7. Know that the Great Ātman is devoid of *Guṇas* but it is in the form of *Liṅga*. Similarly Satī, the greatest and eternal *Śakti*, should also be known as devoid of *Guṇas*.

8. It is by her that this ultimately perishable universe consisting of mobile and immobile beings and evolved out of the three *Guṇas*, has been created.

9. The Ātman alone, the greatest unsullied Lord in the form

of *Liṅga* (is eternal). Those three *Guṇas* got merged into it (the Supreme *Ātman*) along with *Prakṛti*.

10. It was hence called formerly *Liṅga* because of *Layana* ('merging'). Even the *Parā Śakti* gots merged into the *Liṅga*. What of others?

11. At the instance of Rudra, the *Guṇas* whereby mobile and immobile beings are bound, become merged, O highly fortunate one. Hence one should worship *Liṅga*.

12. Know, O excellent Brāhmaṇas, that *Liṅga* is devoid of *Guṇas*. It is on account of the merging of the *Guṇas* that the *Liṅga* is glorified.

13. Śaṅkara is described by learned men as the bestower of happiness. He is called *Sarva*, O Brāhmaṇas, as he is indeed the support of all.

14-15. O Brāhmaṇas, he is called *Śaṁbhu* because he is one from whom auspiciousness originates. Thus all the names of the great Ātman are meaningful. The entire universe is enveloped by that Śaṁbhu, Parameṣṭhin (the Supreme God).

The sages enquired:

16-17. Satī of great fortune, the daughter of Dakṣa, fell into the sacred fire of the holy rite of *Yajña* of Dakṣa. When did she appear again, O Sūta? Let it be described now by you. How did the greatest Śakti rejoin Maheśa?

18. All these incidents of yore, O (Sage) of great fortune, should be described to us truthfully. There is no other person to recount it.

Sūta replied:

19-21. O Brāhmaṇas, when Dākṣāyaṇī got her limbs (i.e. body) burnt in (the fire of) the *Yajña*, Maheśa was left without Śakti.

Hence he performed a great penance on the Himālaya mountain with a body playfully assumed by him. He was surrounded by Bhṛṅgī, Viśva, Nandī, Caṇḍa, Muṇḍa and other *Baṭus*[1] (young boys in the stage of religious students). He was surrounded by ten crores of Gaṇas (i.e. attendants).

22. The Bull-bannered Lord was surrounded by other Gaṇas numbering one crore and sixty thousand.

1. V.L. *Bahubhiḥ* ('by many others').

23. The Supreme Ātman thus engaged in penance suddenly went to the top of Himālaya surrounded by his Gaṇas, the chief of whom was Vīrabhadra. He was alone, being bereft of the *Mūlavidyā*.

24-26. In the meantime, Daityas were born of Avidyā. Bali was bound by Viṣṇu. Then those powerful Daityas became tormentors of Indra, O Brāhmaṇas. They were Kālakhañjas, the exceedingly terrible Kālakāyas (? Kālakeyas) and others. There were Nivātakavacas and those named Ravarāvakas. There were many other Daityas causing the massacre of the subjects.

27. Tāraka, the son of Namuci, propitiated Brahmā by means of a great penance. Brahmā was pleased with him.

28. He granted to the evil-minded Tāraka boons just according to his wish. He said: "Choose your boon. Welfare unto you. I shall give you all that your desire."

29. On hearing those words of Brahmā Parameṣṭhin, he chose a boon that instilled terror in all the worlds:

30. "If you are pleased with me, grant me freedom from old age and death and give me invincibility too as you know it."

31-32. On being told thus by the evil-minded Tāraka, (Brahmā) laughingly spoke these words:

"Wherefrom can you have immortality? Know it as a fact that certain indeed is death unto one who is born." Then Tāraka laughed and said: "Then give me invincibility."

33. Brahmā then said to the Daitya: "Invincibility has been granted to you, O sinless one, except from an infant. An infant will defeat you."

34. Then Tāraka bowed down and said to Brahmā: "O lord, O lord of Devas, I am blessed and contented by your grace now."

35. Having acquired the boon thus, Tāraka, the Asura of great strength, challenged Devas for war and fought with them.

36-38. Resorting to Mucukunda,[1] Devas became

1. Mucukunda: Son of King Māndhātā of the Solar Race. He helped Indra to defeat Asuras. He wanted a boon of sound sleep and the ability to burn whosoever disturbed his sleep. Kṛṣṇa while pursued by Kālayavana entered the cave of Mucukunda and lay concealed. Kālayavana, thinking Mucukunda to be Kṛṣṇa, kicked him and got burnt (BhP X.51.14-23). When Kṛṣṇa came forward, he praised him and went to Badarikāśrama for penance (BhP X.52.1-4).

victorious. Although Devas were repeatedly attacked and tormented by Tāraka, they gained victory through the power of Mucukunda. 'What is to be done by us? We are being continuously attacked and dragged into war.' Thinking thus, Suras including Vāsava (Indra) went to Brahmā's region. Going in front of Brahmā, they spoke thus:

Devas said:

39-40. Madhusūdana is staying in Pātāla along with Bali. Without Viṣṇu, all those, Vṛṣa and others have fallen on account of the enemies, the leading Daityas. O highly fortunate one, O lord, it behoves you to save us.

Then an ethereal voice spoke to them consolingly:

41-46a. "O Devas, let my suggestion be carried out exactly and immediately. O Devas, when an exceedingly powerful son is born to Śiva, he will undoubtedly kill Tāraka in battle. Take such a course of action that lord Śaṁbhu, dwelling in the cavity of the heart of everyone, takes a wife unto himself. Let a great effort be made by you all. These words cannot be otherwise. Know this, O ye Devas." So said the unembodied voice. Struck with wonder, Devas spoke to one another. After hearing the ethereal voice, all the Devas of great fortune came to Himālaya keeping Bṛhaspati at their head. They spoke these words to Himālaya on account of the seriousness of the matter:

46b-47. "O Himālaya of great fortune, let our words be heard now. Tāraka terrorizes us. Render assistance in killing him. Be refuge unto us and to all the ascetics. It is for this that we have come here accompanied by Mahendra, O lord."

Lomaśa said:

48-51. On being requested thus by Devas, Himavān, the most excellent among mountains spoke these words laughingly to Devas. Himavān, the most excellent one among those conversant with the (use of) words, was full of satirical laughter against Mahendra: "O Suras, it was by Mahendra himself that we have been made incapable of anything. What task of Suras can we do in this matter of killing Tāraka? If only we had our wings, O excellent Suras, we would have killed Tāraka along with his kinsmen. I am an *Acala* (immobile; mountain). I am a *Vipakṣa* (devoid of wings; belonging to the opposite side); what shall I do unto you all?"

52-53. On hearing his words, all the Devas spoke to him: "All of you and all of us are incapable of killing Tāraka, O highly fortunate one. Let the means whereby Tāraka, our enemy of great power, can be brought under control, be thought off."

Then the highly refulgent Himavān spoke to Suras:

54. "By what means, O Devas, do you wish to kill Tāraka? Be pleased to tell me quickly so that I can understand the matter on hand."

55. Then everything that had been previously declared by the (ethereal) voice in regard to their duty was mentioned by Suras. When it was heard by the Mountain, the Himālaya mountain spoke these words:

56-57. "When Tāraka, the Daitya of great soul, is to be slain by the intelligent son of Śiva, every objective of Suras shall be auspicious. What has been said by the ethereal voice shall become true. Hence let that be done by you, which makes Maheśa take up a wife unto himself. Who is that girl suitable to Śiva? Let that be ascertained by Suras now."

58. On hearing his words, Suras laughed and said: "For the sake of Śiva and for accomplishing our task, a daughter has to be begotten by you.

59. O Mountain of great intellect, carry out the suggestion of Suras. You will undoubtedly become the support of Devas."

60-63. On being told thus by Devas, the lord of mountains went to his house. He said to his wife Menā: "The task of Suras has become our responsibility. For the accomplishment of the task of Devas a good daughter has to be begotten. It is for the benefit of Devas, sages and ascetics. (Of course) the birth of a daughter may not be pleasing to women. Still, O lady of splendid face, a daughter has to be procreated."

Menā laughed and spoke to her husband Himālaya: "What has been spoken by you (is true). Let my words be heard by you now.

64. O my lord, a daughter is the cause of misery unto men. So also, O highly intelligent one, she causes sorrow unto women. Hence ponder over this for a long time yourself with your keen

intellect. Let what is conducive to our welfare be told, O lord of Mountains."

65. On hearing the words of his wife, the intelligent Himavān spoke these words motivated by a desire to help others:

66. "By an intelligent person, that whereby others can sustain themselves, should be done.

67. The same should be done by a woman also, viz. that which helps others." Thus his queen was made to comply by the Mountain. Then the lucky Menā conceived a girl in her womb.

68. She was the great Vidyā, the great Māyā, the embodiment of the highest intellect. She was Aṁbā, the great daughter of Dakṣa, Rudrakālī, Satī.

69. The chaste lady of beautiful eyes and excellent fortune, Menā, bore in her womb that highest glory of large eyes.

70. Then Devas, sages, Yakṣas and Kinnaras eulogized Menā of excessive fortune and the Mountain Himavān.

71-74. In the meantime, their daughter named Girijā was born. When the goddess, the bestower of happiness on all, manifested herself, divine drums were sounded; celestial damsels danced; lords of Gandharvas sang; Siddhas and Cāraṇas eulogized (her); Devas showered plenty of flowers. Then everything, the entire unit of the three worlds became delighted. When the great Satī, Girijā, incarnated herself, Daityas became excessively frightened. The groups of Devas, the great Sages, Cāraṇas and the groups of Siddhas attained great joy.

CHAPTER TWENTYONE

Pārvatī's Penance

Lomaśa said:

1. The chaste girl grew up day by day and shone very much. Living in the house of Himālaya, she reached the age of eight years.

2. At that time Maheśa was performing a great penance in a

valley of Himālaya. He was surrounded by all the groups of Gaṇas, Vīrabhadra and others.

3. Accompanied by Pārvatī, the intelligent Himavān went to Maheśa engaged in this penance, in order to see his sprout-like feet.

4. When he arrived thus in order to see (the Lord), he was stopped by Nandin who was standing at the entrance. Then for a moment he stood steady.

5. The mountain Himavān informed through Nandin. Śambhu (i.e. Śiva) was informed by Nandin that the Mountain had come to see him (i.e.Śiva).

6. On hearing his words, Parameśvara spoke these words to Nandin: "Bring the Mountain here."

7. Saying "So be it" and honouring (his words) Nandin brought the Mountain Himācala to Śaṅkara, the benefactor of the worlds.

8-10. He saw (Śiva) the lord of everyone engaged in penance with his eyes closed. He had matted hair with the digit of the moon as an ornament. He could be understood only through the Vedānta and was stationed in the Supreme Soul. On seeing him, Mountain Himācala of unimpaired inherent strength, bent down his head and saluted him. He then attained the greatest joy. Himālaya, the foremost among those conversant with the use of words, spoke these words to the Lord who is the sole cause of auspiciousness to the universe:

11-13. "I am lucky, O Śaṅkara, the great lord, thanks to your grace. I shall come here everyday, O lord, to pay a visit along with this (daughter of mine). It behoves you, O lord of Devas, to grant me permission."

On hearing his words, Maheśvara, the lord of Devas, (said): "O Mountain, you may come here everyday to meet me after keeping this girl in the house. Otherwise there would be no audience with me."

14. With his neck bent down the Mountain replied to Giriśa: "Why should I not come along with this (girl)? Let that be told."

Śambhu who was performing the holy rites, laughingly spoke these words to the Mountain:

15. "This slender-bodied girl of good lips and exquisite

speech should not be brought near me. I am forbidding it repeatedly."

16. She heard Śaṁbhu's harsh words, devoid of blemishes and free from any desire. On hearing the words uttered by that ascetic, Gaurī laughed and spoke to Śaṁbhu:

Gaurī said:

17-18. O Śaṁbhu, you are endowed with the power of penance. You are performing a great penance. This inclination for performing penance you have because you are noble-souled. But let this be pondered over: Who are you? Who is the subtle *Prakṛti*, O holy lord?

On hearing those words of Pārvatī, Maheśa spoke these words:

19. "I am destroying *Prakṛti* by means of the greatest penance itself. In fact, O lady of good eyebrows, I will stay without *Prakṛti*. Hence nothing that has been evolved out of *Prakṛti* should be accumulated together at any time by Siddhas."

Pārvatī said:

20. What has been said by you, O Śaṅkara, by means of '*Parā*' speech, is it not *Prakṛti*? In that case how are you beyond it?

21-22. O lord, of what avail is our disputation and argument? Whatever you hear, whatever you see and whatever you eat, O Śaṅkara, is entirely the evolute of *Prakṛti*. An untrue speech is meaningless. Why should penance be performed after going beyond *Prakṛti*?

23. O Lord Śaṁbhu, just now on this mountain Himālaya you have met *Prakṛti*. But you cannot understand it, O Śaṅkara. What have we to do with (i.e. What is the propriety of) oral dispute and argument, O Lord?

24. If your statement that you are beyond *Prakṛti* be true, you need not be afraid of me now, O Śaṅkara.

25. Then Lord (Śaṅkara) laughed and replied to Girijā:

Mahādeva said:

26. Serve me everyday, O Girijā of excellent speech.

27. After saying thus to Girijā, Maheśa spoke these words to Himālaya: "Here itself, on this very ground, I shall perform a great penance with concentration on the ultimate truth.

28. Permission should be granted to me for performing the penance, O Lord of Mountains. Without (your) permission it is not possible to perform penance."

29. On hearing these words of the Trident-bearing Lord of Devas, Himavān laughed and spoke these words to Śaṁbhu:

30. "The entire universe along with Devas, Asuras and human beings belongs to you. I am an insignificant person, O Mahādeva. What can I give you?"

31. On being told thus by Himavān, Śaṅkara, the benefactor of all the worlds, laughed and respectfully said to the Lord of Mountains: "You may go."

32. Permitted to go by Śaṅkara, Himavān went to his abode. Everyday he came there along with Girijā to pay a visit.

33-35. Thus some time passed when the father and the daughter continued their visits and service. But Śaṅkara was difficult to be tackled and won over. Suras began to worry about Pārvatī. 'How will Śaṅkara join Girijā?' was the thought worrying the minds of Suras. They asked: "O Bṛhaspati, what should we do now? Tell us. Do not delay."

36-37. Bṛhaspati spoke the following good words (of advice) to Mahendra: "O Mahendra, this must be done by you. Let it be heard. This task can be carried out only by Madana (the god of Love), O King. None else will be competent for it in all the three worlds. The penance of many ascetics has been upset by him. Hence Māra (god of Love) should be requested (in this matter) immediately."

38. On hearing the words of Guru (Bṛhaspati, the preceptor) Indra sent for Madana. Madana who accomplished (his) tasks came there on receipt of the call.

39. Accompanied by Rati and Mādhava (i.e. the Spring season) the flower-armed deity came to the assembly in front of Mahendra and spoke these proud words in a manner captivating the minds of the people:

40. "Why have I been called today, O Śacīpati (i.e. Indra)? Tell me what work should I do? Do not delay.

41. The moment they think about me, the ascetics meet

with their downfall. You do know, O Indra, my valour and prowess.

42. Parāśara, the son of Śakti, knows my power and vigour. Thus many other sages such as Bhṛgu do know it.

43-44. Bṛhaspati too knows it, as well as the wife of Utathya.[1] Bharadvāja was born of her begotten by Guru and was thus illegitimate. Guru had then said, *Bharadvāja* ['Bear two (sons) simultaneously (conceived)']. Prajāpati (Brahmā) knows my heroism and powerful valour.

45. *Krodha* (Anger) is my kinsman. He has great strength and valour. By both of us, this great universe consisting of mobile and immobile beings has been conquered (and liquidated, i.e. excited and stirred up). Everything beginning with Brahmā and ending with a blade of grass, the whole world of mobile and immobile beings, has been (flooded and) overwhelmed by us."

Devas said:

46. O Madana, you are capable of always conquering us. (But) go immediately to Maheśa for accomplishing the task of Suras. Unite Śaṁbhu with Pārvatī, O highly intelligent one.

47. On being requested thus by Devas, Madana, the enchanter of the universe, went away (from that place) immediately in the company of celestial damsels.[2]

48. That wielder of a great bow made the twanging sound of his flowery bow. He took with him charming and fascinating arrows. That hero, the sole conqueror of the worlds, the most excellent one among warriors, Smara, was then seen on the grounds of the mountain Himavān.

49-50. Then all these celestial damsels came there, viz. Raṁbhā, Urvaśī, Puñjikasthalī, Sumlocā, Miśrakeśī, Subhagā and Tilottamā. There were others also to render different kinds of assistance to Madana. These damsels were seen by Gaṇas (attendants of Śiva) along with Madana.

51-53. All the Gaṇas were suddenly enchanted by Madana. Raṁbhā (was approached) by Bhṛṅgi, Urvaśī by Caṇḍa, Menakā

1. This refers to Bṛhaspati's rape of his pregnant sister-in-law (brother Utathya's wife).

2. VV 47-58 give a beautiful description of the romantic transformation of Śiva's penance-grove.

by Vīrabhadra and Puñjikasthalī by Caṇḍa(?). Tilottamā and others were surrounded by the Gaṇas then, who had become mad and abandoned all shame although they were high-minded and learned.

The whole of the earth was pervaded by cuckoos, though it was not the proper season (i.e. the spring).

54-55. *Aśoka, Caṁpaka,* mangoes, *Yūthīs* (jasmine), *Kadaṁbas* (Nanclea Cadamba), *Nīpas* (Ixora Bandhucca), *Priyālas* (Buchamania Latifolia), *Panasas* (jack fruit trees), *Rajavṛkṣas, Carāyaṇas* (?), vine creepers, and *Nāgakesaras* (Mesua Roxburghii), plantains, *Ketakīs* (Pandanus Odoratissimus) etc.—all these trees were in full bloom and they were rendered beautiful by bees.

56-58. By the contact of Madana *Kalahaṁsakas* (swans) became intoxicated in the company of female swans, he-elephants with she-elephants and peacocks with peahens. Though all these had been free from lust due to the qualities arising from contact with Śiva, they now became excited.

The highly refulgent Nandī, the son of Śailāda and of immeasurable (infinite) valour, pondered over this: Why have these become so all of a sudden? This must be the working of Rākṣasas or of gods.

59. In the meantime Madana took up his bow and fixed five arrows to it, O Brāhmaṇas. He resorted to the shade of a *Devadāru* tree.

60-62. He saw Śaṁbhu performing his penance. The Lord was seated on an excellent seat. He was the lord of all Parameṣṭhins (creators). He kept Gaṅgā (within his matted hair). His throat was blue in colour like *Tamāla* (dark-barked Xanthochymus Pictorius). He had matted hair. He had the crescent moon (as an embellishment). All his limbs were marked by the coiled bodies of many serpents. He had five faces. His gait was in long strides like that of a lion. He was fair in complexion like camphor. He was accompanied by *Parā*. Madana was desirous of piercing the fierce ascetic Maheśa, very difficult of access and the most excellent among highly refulgent ones. In the company of Mādhava (Spring) he was about to hit Śiva with his arrow when Girijā, the mother of the universe, came there. She was surrounded by her friends. She approached Sadāśiva, the most auspicious of all auspicious ones, for the sake of worship.

63. She placed a garland of golden flowers on Nīlakaṇṭha. At that time she had a rare splendour. She appeared very beautiful with white rays (diffused all round). The mother of all people looked (lovingly) at the handsome face of Śiva. Then her eyes bloomed and expanded widely as she smiled.

64. At that time Śaṁbhu was hit and pierced with the arrow called *Mohana* ('the Enchanter') suddenly. On being hit, Śaṁbhu opened his eyes slowly. The lord saw Girijā like the ocean viewing the digit of the moon.

65-67. She had a beautiful delightful face. Her lips were like the *Biṁba* fruit (Momordica Monadelpha). Her eyes brightened with her smile. Her teeth were fine and excellent. She appeared as though she had come out of fire (i.e. she was resplendent). She had a slender body with a beautiful and wide face. Gaurī had all the signs of pleasure (within). She was capable of enchanting the entire universe. It was she who created the three worlds along with Brahmā and others. Making use of the qualities of *Rajas, Sattva* and *Tamas*, she caused the origin, sustenance and annihilation (of the worlds). That enchanting goddess, the sole cause of auspiciousness of all auspicious things, was seen in front by Hara who was awakened.

68. On seeing Girijā, the sanctifier of all the worlds, lord Bhava became fascinated. At her sight he was afflicted by Madana. Śiva's eyes suddenly became expanded due to surprise.

69. The lord of the universe, the lord of Devas (began) to look around. With the mind pained much, Sadāśiva said thus:

70. "I am engaged in penance. I am devoid of blemishes. Yet how was I enchanted by this girl? Whence, why and by whom was this done causing my displeasure?"

71-72. Then Śaṁbhu looked in all directions earnestly. Madana was seen by him in the south with the bow lifted up. The god of Love bent his bow like a circle; kept it ready, drawn in order to pierce and wound Sadāśiva. But by the time he was able to discharge the arrow, O Brāhmaṇas, he was stared at by Maheśa angrily.

73. He was looked at with the third eye by the greatest lord.

Madana was instantly encircled by clusters of flames. There was a loud wailing among Devas who stood there watching.

Devas said:

74. O Mahādeva, lord of Devas, be the bestower of boons on Devas. It was to help Girijā that Madana had been sent now.

75-81. In vain was Madana of great lustre burned by you. It is by you alone, the sole kinsman of the universe, that the task of Suras should be carried out by means of your great splendour. O lord Śaṁbhu, (a son) will be born of her and by him alone can our objective be achieved. O Mahādeva, Devas are very much afflicted by Tāraka. For that purpose grant life unto this (Madana) and woo Girijā, O lord of exalted fortune. (Please) be capable of accomplishing the task of Devas. All of us, the heaven-dwellers, were protected by you from the demon in the shape of an elephant. Certainly we have been saved from the Kālakūṭa poison (by you), not otherwise (by anyone else). Undoubtedly we have been protected from Bhasmāsura by you, O Lord of everyone. This Madana came here for accomplishing the task of Suras. Hence he should be protected. That will be a great help to us (also). Without him, O Śaṅkara, the entire universe will be ruined. How can you also be devoid of *Kāma* (Love)? Let this be pondered over by your own intellect.

82-88. Then Maheśvara who was overwhelmed by anger, spoke to Devas: "You must all be without *Kāma*. It cannot be otherwise.

It was when *Kāma* was kept at the head, that all the Devas including Vāsava had a fall from their positions. They were overwhelmed by misery and became wretched.

Certainly *Kāma* is the cause of a fall into hell in the case of all living beings. This *Anaṅga* ('Bodiless one') is an embodiment of misery, understand what I say. Tāraka too whose conduct of life is very bad will be devoid of *Kāma*. How can a man commit a sin without *Kāma*? Hence for the sake of peace and calmness unto everyone, *Kāma* was burned by me. Let the mind be directed towards penance by you all, Suras, Asuras, the great sages and other living beings. The entire universe has been rendered by me rid of love and anger. Hence I will not resuscitate this sinner, the cause of misery, O Suras; keep waiting for that sole form which is not other than (you all), which yields spiritual pleasure and enlightenment and which is characterized by bliss. It is difficult to guage its depth."

89. On being told thus by Śaṁbhu Parameṣṭhin, all the great sages spoke to Śaṅkara, the benefactor of all the worlds:

90. "What has been said by Your Honour, O Śaṁbhu, is indeed exceedingly conducive to our welfare. But we shall say (something) which may be listened to attentively and comprehended fully.

91. This universe was permeated by *Kāma* and *Krodha* (anger) even while it was being created. Indeed the whole of it is in the form of *Kāma*. That *Kāma* is not killed.

92. O Mahādeva, it was by *Kāma* that the four (aims in life) named *Dharma* (Virtue), *Artha* (Wealth), *Kāma* (Love) and *Mokṣa* (Salvation) have been given a single (composite) form. That *Kāma* is not killed.

93. It was by *Kāma* that the universe of the nature of everything from Brahmā to an immobile being has been united together. How was that *Kāma*, very difficult to be tackled indeed, burned by you?

94. The universe decays and declines due to *Kāma*. The universe is protected and sustained by *Kāma*. The universe is produced by *Kāma*. Hence *Kāma* is very powerful.

95. It is from *Kāma* that the fierce *Krodha* (anger) takes its origin. You yourself have been won over by *Krodha*. Hence, O Mahādeva, it behoves you to resuscitate Kāma.

96. Indeed, O lord, the mighty Madana has been brought under control by you. Only a man of power can exercise his power because of being powerful."

97. Though he was entreated thus by the sages, Hara's anger became doubled. He became desirous of burning (everything) by means of his third eye.

98. The Pināka-bearing, Bull-emblemed Rudra, Sadāśiva was bowed to and eulogized by the sages, Cāraṇas, Siddhas and Gaṇas.

99. On account of his anger, after burning Madana and

leaving off that Mountain named Himavān, he vanished immediately.

100. The lofty-minded goddess Girijā saw that the Lord had vanished and that Manmatha had been burned along with the cuckoos, mango trees, bees and *Campaka* flowers.

101. On seeing Madana burned down, Rati began to cry for a long time shedding tears. The goddess pondered over this with great dejectedness. She was anxious as to how to win over Rudra.

102. After pondering over this for a long time, the chaste lady Girijā fainted. Rati saw Girijā whose beauty was very great, who was high-minded and crying, and spoke:

103-104. "Dear friend, do not get dejected. I shall resuscitate Madana to life. For your sake, O wide-eyed lady, by means of penance I shall propitiate, Hara, Rudra, Virūpākṣa, the lord of Devas, the sire of the universe. Do not be anxious, O lady of beautiful lips and buttocks. I shall revive Madana back to life."

105. After consoling thus the daughter of the Mountain the chaste lady Rati immediately (proceeded to) perform a great penance. The lady of excellent waistline performed the penance in order to get back her husband.

106. She performed the penance at the very same place where Madana was burned by Rudra, the Supreme Soul. Nārada saw her performing the penance.

107-108. He hastened to the side of the beautiful lady Rati and said: "Whom do you belong to, O lady of wide eyes? What for are you performing the penance? You are a young woman richly endowed with beauty and great conjugal felicity."

On hearing the words of Nārada, she became very angry. She spoke these harsh words in a sweet manner:

Rati said:

109. You have been recognized by me; you are Nārada.[1] Undoubtedly you are a bachelor. O (sage) of holy rites, it behoves you not to show your form (V.l. you desire to have a look at the women of others).

---

1. Rati rebukes Nārada for his overtures (vv 109-111). Nārada takes revenge by instigating Śambara, King of Daityas, to abduct Rati. He made her the chief of his kitchen under the name Māyāvatī (vv 113-125).

110. Go back along the path you have come by. Do not delay. O *Baṭu*, you do not know anything. You are only a great quarrel-monger.

111. You are a leader among the following groups of people: Those who are passionately devoted to other men's wives, insignificant persons, libertines, those who indulge in vices, those who are stubborn and those who do not perform any holy rites.

112. On being rebuked thus by Rati, the excellent sage Nārada himself hurriedly went to Śaṁbara, the leading Daitya.

113-114. He intimated to the king of Daityas that Madana had been burned by Rudra who had become furious. Then he continued: "His wife is a noble-minded lady. Bring her here, O highly fortunate one. Make her your wife, O mightly one. Among all those beautiful ladies who have been brought by you, that Rati, the wife of Madana, will be the most beautiful one."

115. On hearing these words of the celestial sage of sanctified soul, he went to that place where the highly splendid lady was staying.

116. On seing Rati, the large-eyed enchantress of Madana, Śaṁbara, the cause of the grief of Devas, laughingly said these words:

117. "O slender-bodied lady, come along with me. Enjoy my kingdom and its pleasures as much as you wish, O gentle lady, by my favour. Of what avail is the penance?"

118. On being told thus by Śaṁbara of great soul, that slender-bodied queen of Madana spoke these words in sweet voice:

119. "I am a widow, O mighty one. It does not behove you to speak thus. You are the king of all the Daityas with all the (royal) characteristics."

120. On hearing these words, Śaṁbara who was deluded by lust, became desirous of catching hold of her hand. He was prevented by Rati.

121-122. She pondered over his invincibility mentally and said: "O foolish one, do not touch me. You will be burned (by the fire) arising from my contact. My words cannot be otherwise." Then Śaṁbara of great splendour said laughingly:

123. "O proud lady, do you want to terrify me with many

threats (like these)? Go ahead to my abode quickly. Of what avail is so much talk?"

124. The slender-bodied, lofty-minded lady was forcibly taken to his great city by Śaṁbara who was addressed thus (by Rati).

125. She was made the head in charge of his kitchen, under the name Māyāvatī.

The sages asked:

126. Was everything authorized by Pārvatī regarding bringing Madana back (to life)? The slender-bodied beloved of Madana was abducted by Śaṁbara. Subsequent to this, O Sūta, what happened there? Let it be described.

Sūta said:

127. On seeing that Śiva had gone away after burning Madana with his great prowess, the beautiful lady Pārvatī stayed there itself and engaged herself in penance.

128. The slim lady was enquired[1] by her father and mother: "O girl, come back to our abode quickly. Do not exert yourself. It does not behove you to strain yourself."

129-132. On being told thus by both of them, Girijā spoke these words:

Pārvatī said:

I am not coming home, O mother, O father. Listen to me clearly. This is a true statement of mine full of *Dharma* (virtue) and *Artha* (prosperity), whereby you will be contented and delighted.

Śaṁbhu is greater than the greatest. The mighty Madana was burned by him. I shall bring that Śiva to my presence here itself. Śaṁbhu is difficult of access to those beings who wish for a home (and homely comforts). Hence, O mother, I am not coming home. Let all these things be pondered over.

133. Himavān of great refulgence then said to his daughter:

1. If the reading *Vicāritā* is emended as *Nivāritā*, the meaning would be "was prevented".

"Śiva who is bowed down to by Devas themselves cannot easily be propitiated. Indeed it is impossible for you to attain him. Hence you go back to your own abode."

134. With her throat choked up by and filled with tears Menā said to her daughter: "O slim girl, proceed homewards quickly."

135-136. Then Pārvatī laughed and said to her mother: "Listen to my vow, dear mother. Indeed, with my great penance I shall fetch that clever (lord) here itself and woo him. O lady of excellent complexion, I shall destroy the *Rudratva* (dreadfulness) of Rudra."

137. Abandoning all pleasure, the lofty-minded daughter of the Mountain performed the propitiation of Śaṁbhu by means of profound meditation.

138-140. Many of Girijā's friends attended upon her, viz. Jayā, Vijayā, Mādhavī, Sulocanā, Suśrutā, Śrutā, Śukī, Pramlocā, Subhagā, Śyāmā, Citrāṅgī, Cāruṇī, Svadhā and many others such as the beautiful lady Devagarbhā etc.

For performing the great penance, the lady of sweet laughter built an altar exactly at the place where Madana was burnt by the noble-souled Rudra. She established herself upon it.

141-142. She refrained from drinking water and subsisted on leaves. Thereafter, she avoided green leaves and took up only dried ones. Later on she stopped eating the dried leaves too when the lady of slender waist became famous as *Aparṇā*.[1]

143. After a lapse of a great deal of time, the chaste daughter of the Mountain gave up drinking water and became engaged in subsisting on air only. Then she supported her body on a single big toe.

144. With the greatest contentment, the chaste lady propitiated Śaṅkara by means of austere penance, for the sake of the delight of Śaṅkara too.

145. Resorting to the noblest of mental feelings, (the goddess) the cause of the auspiciousness of all auspicious things, performed the greatest penance for the delight and pleasure of Maheśa.

---

1. Explanation of Pārvatī's epithet '*Aparṇā*.' Cf. Kālidāsa's *Kumārasaṁbhava* V. 28.

146-147. Thus she performed the penance for a thousand divine years. Then, accompanied by his wife, Himālaya came there to his daughter Pārvatī who had determined (to practise penance). (In the capacity of a) trustworthy adviser, he spoke to Mahāsatī (i.e. Girijā):

"Do not get afflicted and don't strain yourself, O Mahādevī, O beautiful one, by performing this penance.

148-150. Where is Rudra seen? O girl, undoubtedly he is devoid of love and attachment. You are very young and slim. Due to this penance you will become confounded undoubtedly. I am speaking the truth. Hence, O lady of excellent complexion, get up and go home immediately. What have you to do with that Rudra by whom formerly Madana has been burnt because he was devoid of any feeling? O sinless one, how will (i.e. can) you solicit him (as a husband)?

151. Just as the moon stationed in the sky cannot be grasped, so also Śambhu is difficult to be attained. O girl of pure smiles, understand this."

152-153. Similarly, the chaste lady was told so by Menā, Sahya Mountain, Meru, Mandāra and Maināka.

On being urged thus by these, the slim girl Pārvatī of pure smiles, who was engaged in the penance, spoke to Himavān laughingly:

154. "Has what had been said by me before been forgotten by you, father? O mother, has it been forgotten by you? O my kinsmen, listen to my vow now itself.

155-158. By means of my penance, I will gratify Śaṅkara, the benefactor of the worlds, (although) this great lord is detached and devoid of attachment because Madana has been killed by him. All of you go. You need not worry in this matter. By means of my penance I will bring him here; I will bring (that lord) by whom Madana was burnt and by whom the forest of the mountain was burnt. Indeed Sadāśiva can be conveniently served through the great power of penance. Understand him, O exceedingly fortunate ones. It is true. I am saying the truth."[1]

---

1. Pārvatī, being Śakti, speaks so confidently, as she knows her close relation of being identical with Śiva.

159. That daughter of the king of Mountains—she who habitually spoke very little—conversed thus with her mother Menā, (father) Himālaya and also with Meru and Mandāra.

Then those Mountains went away the way they had come while glancing (this way and that).

160. When all of them had gone, the chaste lady with the greatest being as her object of desire, performed the penance surrounded by her friends.

161. By that great penance the entire universe consisting of mobile and immobile beings became scorched. At that time all Suras and Asuras sought refuge in Brahmā.

Devas said:

162-164. O lord, the whole of this universe, mobile and immobile, has been created by you. It behoves you to save us, Devas. None other than you can be capable of protecting us.

On hearing these words, Brahmā pondered over them mentally. He understood that a great fire had been produced by the great penance of Girijā. Having realized it, Brahmā immediately went to the wonderful Ocean of Milk.

165-171. There he saw Lord Viṣṇu sleeping on his excellent and exceedingly splendid couch named Śeṣa. The pair of his feet was continuously served (kneaded) by Lakṣmī. He was served by Tārkṣya (Garuḍa) with stooping neck and standing a little away. He was also served by Śrī, Kānti, Kṣānti, Vṛtti, Dayā and others. Viṣṇu was accompanied by the nine Śaktis. He was surrounded by his Pārṣadas (attendants). Kumuda, Kumudvān, Sanaka, Sanandana, Sanātana of exalted fortune, Prasupta, Vijaya, Arijit, Jayanta, Jayatsena, Jaya of great lustre, Sanatkumāra of excellent power of penance, Nārada, Tuṁburu and others served him and attended upon him. The great conch of Viṣṇu, named Pāñcajanya, his iron club Kaumodakī, the discus Sudarśana and the exceedingly wonderful bow Śārṅga—all these were seen in embodied form by Parameṣṭhin.

All the Suras and the Dānavas came very near Viṣṇu, the great Ātman. On the shore of the Ocean of the great Ātman, they spoke to Viṣṇu, the lord of all Parameṣṭhins:

172. "Save, save us, O great Viṣṇu, save us who have been scorched and who have sought refuge in you. We have been

scorched by the severe and dreadful penance of Pārvatī." The great Lord sat up on his couch Śeṣa and said:

173-174. "I shall go to the Supreme Lord Śiva along with you all. O Suras, we shall pray to Mahādeva in the matter of Girijā. There itself, we shall do something so that the Pināka-bearing Lord of Devas will be led to grasp her hand and marry her.

175. Hence we shall go to that place where the great Lord Rudra is seated, where the greatest cause of auspiciousness (viz. Śiva) is engaged in a severe penance."

176-177. On hearing the words of Viṣṇu, all Suras and Asuras said: "We will not approach the Uneven-three-eyed god (Virūpākṣa) of great lustre. He will burn us in the same manner as he has burnt the unconquerable Madana formerly. There is no doubt in this matter."

178-180. Lord Viṣṇu, the great lord, laughed and said: "All of you need not be afraid. Sadāśiva is the embodiment of auspiciousness. He is the destroyer of fear of all Devas. He will not burn (you). Hence, O clever ones, all of you must go along with me.

I seek refuge in Śambhu who is the ancient Puruṣa, is the overlord of excellent form, who is greater than the greatest and is engaged in penance. His form is the greatest one and he is greater than the greatest."

CHAPTER TWENTYTWO

Śaṅkara's Revelation of Himself to Pārvatī: Their Dialogue

Sūta said:

1. On being told thus by Viṣṇu, the Parameṣṭhin, all of them went ahead desirous of seeing the Pināka-bearing Maheśa.

2. On the other shore of the Ocean, Śambhu was engaged in supremely profound meditation seated in the pedestal of Yogic posture. He was surrounded by the Gaṇas.

3. As a sacred thread he was wearing Vāsuki, the king of serpents, as well as the Nāgas Kaṁbala and Aśvatara on his chest.

4. Karkoṭaka was worn by him in the ears as ear-rings and Pulaha as bangles round his arms.

5. He appeared brilliantly shining with Śaṅkhaka and Padmaka as his anklets. Suras saw the blue-throated mysterious lord, the most excellent one among Devas, white in complexion like camphor and accompanied by the bull.

6. Then Brahmā, Viṣṇu, the Sages, Devas and Dānavas eulogized him with various hymns from the Vedas and the Upaniṣads.

Brahmā said:

7-9. Obeisance to Lord Rudra, the destroyer of Madana; to Bharga of plenty of excellence and fortune; to the three-eyed lord of heaven; to Bhīma (the terrible one) enveloped in rays. O Śeṣa-śāyin (lord identical with Viṣṇu lying on the serpent Śeṣa), obeisance, obeisance to you.

Obeisance to the three-eyed creator of the universe having cosmic form. You are the creator of all the worlds. You are the father, mother and the lord. You are endowed with the greatest mercy. O Supreme Lord, protect us.

10-11. While Devas eulogized thus, Nandin asked them: "What have you come for? What is in your mind?"

They said: "We have come to request Śaṁbhu regarding (accomplishing) the task of Devas." In order to accomplish the task of Suras, Mahādeva who was engrossed in meditation was informed by Nandin, the noble-souled son of Śilāda:

12-14. "The groups of Suras beginning with (headed by) Brahmā, the groups of gods and Siddhas, O most excellent one among Suras, are particularly desirous of seeing you. They are seeking (your help) in their task. They are being threatened by the excellent Asuras and are being tormented by enemies. They have come here.

Hence, O lord of Devas, Suras must be protected now by you." Thus, O Brāhmaṇas, Śaṁbhu was informed by Nandin.

Śaṁbhu of excessively furious nature, gradually came back (to normal state) from his spiritual trance.

The great lord, the Supreme Ātman said:

Mahādeva said:

15. O highly fortunate ones, what have you come here for? These Devas beginning with Brahmā have come near me. Tell me the reason for the same now (itself).

16-18. Then Brahmā spoke about the great task of Devas: "O Śaṁbhu, an extra-ordinarily painful and distressful situation has been created by Tāraka for Devas. O lord, we have come here to respectfully inform you about it. O Śaṁbhu, he can be killed by a son born of you. Tāraka, the enemy of Devas, can be killed only thus. My word cannot be otherwise. So, O lord Śaṁbhu, Girijā should be held by you with your right hand (in marriage) when offered by the Lord of the Mountains. Make her (your wife) by marriage, O lord of great magnanimity."

19-20. On hearing the words of Brahmā, Śiva said laughingly: "(If and) when the most beautiful daughter of the Mountain is made my wife by me, all the leading Suras, sages and ascetics will become passionate and lustful. They will be incapable of traversing the great path (of salvation).

21-22. Indeed Madana has been burnt by me for the purpose of accomplishing the task of all. The slim daughter of the Mountain, Pārvatī of excellent waistline, has been already authorized by me then. O Brahmā, she will revive Madana back to life. There is no doubt about it.

23. Having this in view deliberation on what is to be done should be had, O Devas. A great and important work of Suras was accomplished by Madana when he was burnt.

24-25. All of you have been undoubtedly made free from lust by me. By putting in effort, all of you, O Suras, can become endowed with the greatest power of penance, just like me. We can accomplish even difficult tasks (thereby). All of us shall become happy and blessed with the greatest bliss.

26. You (can achieve everything) through penance. This has been forgotten by Madana. *Kāma* leads to hell. It is from it (*Kāma*) that anger is produced.

27. Confusion and bewilderment result from anger. The mind whirls on account of this bewilderment. Both lust and anger

should be avoided and abandoned by you all, excellent Suras. All of you should honour and abide by my advice and not otherwise, anywhere."

28. Announcing thus the Bull-emblemed Lord enlightened Suras, the groups of sages and ascetics.

29. Śaṁbhu became silent and resumed his meditation once again. As before, he remained there surrounded by the Gaṇas.

30. On seeing (the lord) engrossed in meditation, Nandin dismissed all those Devas including Brahmā and Indra, saying to them laughingly:

31. "All of you go along the path you have come by. Do not delay." Thinking that it should be so, all of them went back to their respective abodes.

32. When all of them had gone away, Bhava (Śiva) engaged himself in meditation keeping the Ātman within the Supreme Ātman and starting his thoughtful concentration.

33. The Lord identified himself with the Supreme Being that is greater than the greatest, that is very clean, free from all impurities, that has no hindrance whatsoever, that is unsullied, commits no fallacies and in which even poets and learned men lose their sense and become confounded.

34. No sun illuminates it, nor the fire nor the moon nor any other luminous body.[1] No wind (blows over it). It is not the object of thought or deliberation. It is beyond the subtle ones and the subtler ones.

35. It cannot be specifically pointed out. It is unimaginable. It is devoid of all aberrations. It is free from ailments. It is in the form of pure knowledge. Those who set aside (and renounce everything) go there (i.e. attain it).

36. It is beyond all words and sounds, having no *Guṇas* or decay and decline. It is (of the form of) the pure existence comprehensible through perfect knowledge. It is not easy to attain. It is that real thing which is mentioned by the Āgamas that are superior to the Vedas and constitute the Mantras.

37. The Pināka-bearing Lord, the Bull-bannered Īśvara, by whom the Shark-bannered (god of Love) was directly killed and

1. Cf. *Kaṭha Upaniṣad* 5.15.

who was Īśvara performing the penance, identified himself with the Supreme Being.

Lomaśa said:

38. At that time the goddess Girijā performed a very great penance. By that penance even Rudra reached the height of fear.

39. By means of her great penance goddess Pārvatī conquered Śaṁbhu, the bestower of all wealth, Sthāṇu, the sole being having his own form.

40-44. When the Bull-bannered Lord was won over by means of her penance by the goddess, the Pināka-bearing Lord of Devas became shaken from his spiritual meditation. He hastened to the place where Pārvatī was staying. There he saw the goddess surrounded by her friends and attendants. She was seated on an altar. She resembled the digit of the moon. Immediately after seeing her, the god became a *Baṭu*.[1] In the form of a *Brahmacārin* (young celibate) Lord Bhava, the great Lord went in the midst of the attendants (of Pārvatī). The Lord in the form of a *Baṭu* spoke to them: "Why is this lady of slender body, beautiful in every limb, seated in the middle of the attendants? Who is she? Whom does she belong to? From where has she come? Why is this penance being performed? Let everything be described to me now, O friends, exactly as it has happened."

45-47. At that time Jayā told Rudra about the ultimate cause of the penance: "This is the daughter of the Himālaya Mountain. She is desirous of getting Lord Rudra as her husband by means of penance. She sat here and performed a very great penance which cannot be excelled by anyone else. O *Baṭu*, understand my words. They cannot be otherwise (i.e. are perfectly true).

48. On hearing her words, Maheśa in the form of a *Baṭu* laughed and said thus, even as all the attendants were listening:

49. "O friends, this Pārvatī is foolish indeed. She does not know what is beneficial and what is not beneficial. Why should a penance be performed for the attainment of Rudra?

50. That Skull-bearing fellow is inauspicious. He has the

1. Cf. The dialogue between Śiva, the *Baṭu*, and Pārvatī in Kālidāsa's *Kumārasaṁbhava* V. 30-86. This does not mean that Kālidāsa borrowed it or based it on SkP as Kālidāsa lived before the compilation of SkP.

cremation ground as his abode. He is *Aśiva* (inauspicious) but he is spoken of as *Śiva* (the auspicious one) in vain.

51. If Rudra, wooed by her were to join her, O friends, this slim lady will undoubtedly become inauspicious.

52. By Dakṣa's curse, he has already become deformed. This rogue has been excluded from *Yajñas*. Highly poisonous serpents have become the very limbs of Śarva.

53. Rudra (smears himself) with the ashes of dead bodies; he wears the hide of an elephant as a cloth. He is very inauspicious. He is always surrounded by Piśācas (vampires), Pramathas (ghosts) and Bhūtas (goblins).

54. What has this lady of delicate features to do with Rudra? She is as though desirous of putting an end to her life like a Piśāca. Let her be prevented by (you, her) friends.

55-56. She is setting aside Indra who is charming, Yama who has great lustre, Nairṛta of large eyes, Varuṇa the lord of waters, Kubera, Pavana (the Wind-god) and Vibhāvasu (the Fire-god)."

Parameśvara said these and many other similar words in the place where she (Girijā) was engaged in penance even while her friends were listening.

57. On hearing these words of Rudra, in the form of a *Baṭu*, the chaste lady Śiva became angry with Maheśa who had assumed the form of a *Baṭu*.

58. "O Jayā, O chaste lady Vijayā, O beautiful Pramlocā, O highly fortunate Sulocanā, what has been done to me is not proper indeed!

59. What have you all to do with this *Baṭu*, here now? A censurer of Devas has assumed the form of a *Baṭu* and come here.

60. Let this boy be dismissed, dear friends. Of what avail is he?"

(After saying this) she angrily spoke to Rudra who was in the form of a *Baṭu*.

61. "O *Baṭu*, go away quickly. You must not stay here now. Of what use is your non-sensical talk? It does not serve any purpose."

62-63. Even after being rebuked by her thus, the *Baṭu* stood there itself steadily, laughed and spoke these words to Vijayā slowly and truthfully without delay:

"O slim lady, why is she angry? What is the reason thereof?

64. Only that should be spoken to all which is nice, pleasing. Why was that slender-bodied lady rendered furious by the aforesaid (true) words?

65. He who is called Śaṁbhu in this world is a mendicant, fond of mendicants. The anger would have been justified if a lie had been uttered by me.

66. This girl has lovely features but Sadāśiva has ugly and hideous features. This lass has (lovely) large eyes but Bhava has deformed (uneven-three) eyes.

67. How can she be fascinated by Rudra of such features as these? The husbands of women should be fortunate and always fond of love-making.

68. This girl has all good qualities in her. How is she charmed by one devoid of any quality? By whom has not Śiva been heard, seen or understood?

69. Sadāśiva is difficult of access to all living beings who are swayed by love. This lady of excellent waistline has become rather proud of her great penance.

70. Sthāṇu is always devoid of restraint. How will she attain him as her husband? O lady of large eyes, what has been said by me for which you are furious now?

71. As long as there is anger in men and particularly in women, the whole of the merit acquired by them will become reduced to ash on account of that anger.

72-73. O slim and chaste lady, what is said is true. *Kāma* (love), *Krodha* (anger), *Lobha* (greed), *Daṁbha* (arrogance), *Mātsarya* (jealousy), *Hiṁsā* (violence), *Īrṣyā* (envy) and *Prapañca* (fraud)—everything (good) perishes on account of these bad qualities. Hence it is proper on the part of ascetics to avoid love, anger etc.

74. If at all Īśvara is to be meditated on, he should be meditated on in the middle of the heart by learned men in the form of pure knowledge. Then he should be adored strictly adhering to the regular practice of sages by the ascetics. He should not be thought of otherwise."

75. On hearing these words of Śaṁbhu, Vijayā spoke to Śarva: "Go away. There is nothing to be done here by you. O childish one, do not speak any other word."

76. Thus Vijayā who was efficient in the use of words dis-

missed Sadāśiva who had assumed the form of a *Baṭu* and was engaged in arguments and disputes.

77-80. Maheśa suddenly vanished from there. But he appeared again to Girijā alone without being seen by any of those friends and attendants. Parameśvara assumed his own form and appeared in front of her suddenly. When the goddess meditated upon him in her heart, the lord of Devas stationed in her heart appeared in front of her, before her physical eyes, in the same form as she meditated upon. That chaste lady opened her eyes. Girijā of large wide eyes saw the lord of the chiefs of Devas, the great lord of all the worlds, with a single face and two arms. He was wonderfully clad in elephant's hide. He had matted hair with the crescent moon above it. He had covered his body with the skin of an elephant.

81. The great serpents Kaṁbala and Aśvatara were stationed in his ears (as ear-rings). The lord of great lustre had Vāsuki, the king of serpents, as a necklace.

82. Even the bangles were made with serpents. These bangles of great value were made by Rudra very splendid and refulgent.

83. Śaṁbhu who appeared like this in front of Pārvatī, hurriedly spoke to her: "O beautiful lady, choose your boon."

84-86. Overcome by great shyness, the chaste lady said to Śaṅkara: "O lord of Devas, you are my husband. Has this been forgotten by you that formerly you had destroyed Dakṣa's *Yajña* and the reason why it had been destroyed, O lord? I am the same woman now born of Menā for the sake of the accomplishment of the task of Devas,[1] regarding the slaying of Tāraka, O lord of the chiefs of Devas. A son will be born of me to you.

87. Hence, O Maheśvara, my suggestion should be carried out by you. You must go to Himavān. You need not hesitate in this matter.

88. Accompanied by the sages, you request him for my hand,[2] O Mahādeva. There is no doubt about it that my father will act according to your request.

1. One is amused to hear Pārvatī telling this to the *omniscient* Śaṅkara.

2. This is called '*Vara-preṣaṇa*'. This custom was in vogue since the Vedic times (vide RV X.85.8-9).

89. Formerly when I was Dakṣa's daughter, when I was given to you by my father, the marriage rite was not performed by you in accordance with the injunctions laid down (in scriptures).

90. The Planets were not worshipped by the noble-souled Dakṣa. As it had been a matter concerning the Planets, the defect therein was very great.

91. Hence, it behoves you, O lord of good holy rites and great fortune, to perform the marriage rite in accordance with the injunctions for the accomplishment of the tasks of Devas."

92-96. Then Mahādeva said to Girijā laughingly: "The entire great universe consisting of mobile and immobile beings, that is born was by its very nature deluded by you and enveloped by the three *Guṇas*.[1]

O Pārvatī, the principle of *Mahat* was born of *Ahaṁkāra* (i.e. Cosmic Ego), *Tamas* was born of the principle of *Mahat*. Ether was enveloped by *Tamas*.

Vāyu was born of Ether; Agni was born of Vāyu. Waters were born of Agni and Earth was born of waters. The earth and other (elements) are mobile as well as immobile, O lady of excellent face. Everything that is visible is perishable. Know this, O proud lady.

The one being has become many. The being devoid of *Guṇa* has become enveloped by *Guṇas*. The self-luminous one that blazes always, has become joined with *Parajyotsnā* (great Moonlight). The independent one has become dependent. O goddess, a great thing has been achieved by you.

97-102. The entire universe has become pervaded by Māyā. By means of the great intellect, it has been thoroughly comprehended. It had been covered up by groups of *Indriyas* (sense-organs) by persons of good deeds, the souls of all oriented towards the highest good. (*obscure*)

What are those planets? What are those groups of stars? What things created by you are affected? Everything has been set free, O lady of excellent complexion, for the sake of Śarva. Our manifestation takes effect in the context of the *Guṇas* and their effects (products). Indeed, you are the *Prakṛti* of the nature of *Rajas*,

1. VV 92-105. The Sāṅkhya-Vedānta theory of creation etc. seems here just out of place.

Sattva and *Tamas*. Hence you are capable of action continuously (i.e. are ever active). O lady of excellent middle, I am not. I will not go to Himavān. I will not request at all. By uttering the word 'give' a man attains insignificance and disrespect immediately. Understand these things, O gentle lady, and say what should be done by us at your bidding. O gentle lady, it behoves you to say everything."

On being told thus by him, the lotus-eyed chaste lady said:

103. "You are the *Ātman*. I am *Prakṛti*. There is no doubt about it. Still, O Śaṁbhu, the great rite of marriage alliance should be performed.

104. The physical body is produced by *Avidyā*. You are the great Being devoid of physical body, indeed. Still adopt a covering in the form of a physical body in this manner.

105. At my instance, O Lord Śaṁbhu, create diversity and manifoldness. Request for me (my hand) and grant me (conjugal) felicity."

106. On being told thus by her to follow (the conventions of) the world, the noble-souled Maheśvara accepted (her suggestion) saying "So be it" and laughingly went to his own abode (where) he was adored duly by the excellent Devas.

107-108. In the meantime, Himavān who was in a hurry to see Pārvatī came there along with Menā, his wife, surrounded by his sons and (other) Mountains.

109. Then Himavān was seen by Pārvatī along with the Mountains. The chaste lady stood up to honour him. She bowed down her head to her parents, brothers and all kinsmen.

110-111. The Mountain Himālaya of great fame embraced his daughter and placed her in his lap. With tears in his eyes he spoke these sweet words: "What is being done by you, O chaste lady of great fortune? Let everything be told to us who desire to hear it." On hearing those sweet words, she spoke to her father:

112. "With great penance the destroyer of Madana has been solicited. My great task has been concluded, which is rather difficult for all to carry out.

113-114. Mahādeva was satisfied. He came to woo (to grant the boon). Then Śaṁbhu was told by me, 'How is my marriage being performed, O Śaṁbhu, without my father now?' Then the slayer of Tripura went away along the path he had come by."

115. On hearing those words of hers, he attained great joy. The virtuous-souled one spoke to his daughter once again, in the company of his own kinsmen:

116-117. "We shall all go to our own abodes—we and all the Mountains. The Pināka-bearing, Bull-emblemed Lord has already been propitiated by her." So said all the Suras with Himālaya at their head. All of them together eulogized Pārvatī with glorious and reverential words.

118. Even as she was being eulogized, Himālaya placed that lady of excellent complexion on his shoulders. All the Mountains eagerly surrounded her and brought her to his (Himālaya's) abode.

119. The divine *Dundubhi* drums were sounded. Conchs and many musical instruments were played.

120. With a great shower of flowers she was brought home by him.

121. She was duly worshipped by many of them. The ascetic lady shining with great splendour, was worshipped by Devas, Cāraṇas, the great sages and all the groups of Siddhas.

122. On being worshipped, the goddess said to Brahmā, Devas, Pitṛs, Yakṣas and all others who had come:

123. "All of you who have come here, go to your respective abodes. Let Parameśvara be served to your fullest satisfaction."

124. Thus then, Pārvatī who had gone to her father's abode, shone splendidly with great refulgence. She was adored by the excellent Devas—she who ever remained thinking of Sadāśiva mentally.

CHAPTER TWENTYTHREE

Śiva's Marriage[1]

Lomaśa said:

1. In the meantime, the sages deputed by Ma
to Himālaya suddenly.[2]

2. On seeing them, the Mountain Himālaya
diately. With a delighted mind, he worshipped all of them and with his neck bowed down, he spoke to them respectfully:

3-4. "Why have all of you come? Tell me the reason for your visit." Then the Seven Sages said: "We have been sent by Maheśa. We have come to you in order to see the girl. O Mountain, understand us. Show us your daughter immediately."

5. Saying "So be it" to the group of Sages, Pārvatī was brought there. Himavān, the lord of Mountains, who loved his children, placed Pārvatī in his lap[3] and said laughingly:

6-9. "This is my daughter indeed. But listen to my words again. Śiva is the most excellent one among ascetics. The destroyer of Madana is devoid of attachment. How does he by whom Smara (Madana) has been made *Anaṅga* (bodiless), seek a marriage alliance?

Offering the daughter in marriage to the following persons is not recommended : one who is very near (i.e. closely related), one who is very far off, one who is extremely rich one, one who is devoid of wealth, one who is unemployed and a foolish fellow.

One shall not offer one's daughter in marriage to a stupid person, to a person who is devoid of attachment, to a self-esteeming person, to a sick man and to a madcap. Hence, O excellent

---

1. This chapter throws immense light on the customs in marriage ceremony prevalent at the time of the last redaction of the SkP.

2. This is called *Vara-preṣaṇa* (sending persons to negotiate for the hand of the girl). This was prevalent at the time of the *Ṛgveda* (RV X.85.8-9), *Gṛhya-sūtras* (e.g. *Baudhāyana* I.1.14-15, *Āpastamba* II.16, IV.1-2 and 7). This practice is noted by Bāṇa (6th cent. A.D.) in *Harṣacarita*, 4th *Ucchvāsa*. This old practice is still preserved among non-Brahmins in Maharashtra.

3. Evidence of child-marriage at the time of our text. Pārvatī who performed penance for a long time, must have been too old to sit in the lap of her father.

[Sa]ges, I must exchange ideas with you and then only I should give her to Maheśa. This is my excellent vow."

10. On hearing those words of the king of Mountains, those great Sages laughed and immediately spoke to Himālaya:

11. "A severe penance has been performed by her. Śiva has been propitiated by her. Being pleased with her penance, Sadāśiva is kindly disposed today.

12. O Mountain, you do not know anything about her or him, anything about their greatness. Hence give her (in marriage).

13-14. Give Girijā to Śiva (in marriage); carry out our suggestion."

On hearing these words of those Sages of sanctified souls, the Lord of Mountains hurriedly addressed the other Mountains: "O Meru, O Niṣadha, O Gandhamādana, O Mandāra, O Maināka, all of you say specifically what should be done today."

15. Menā who was an expert in the use of words, spoke these words: "Of what avail is a deliberation now? The matter has been decided then itself (already).

16. This girl of great fortune is born for accomplishing the task of Devas. She should be given to Śiva because she has incarnated for the sake of Śiva.

17-19. She has been propitiated by Rudra. She has been in the mind of (i.e. liked by) Rudra. Let this Satī (chaste lady) of great fortune be given to Śiva. In worshipping Śiva, what she has done is a mere means (to this end)."

On hearing these words uttered by Menā, Himavān became completely satisfied and spoke these words to the sages glancing at her: "This daughter of mine now (shall be given to Śiva)."[1]

20. Then they brought Gaurī there. She had complexion like heated gold and beautiful eyes. Splendid as she was, she wore a girdle round her hips. She was wearing bangles studded with lapis lazuli and pearls. She had dazzling refulgence like the digit of the moon.

21. Gaurī, the splendid lady of bright face, had glittering garments. She was as though a tank of the nectar of beauty. On seeing her even the Sages became deluded. They were confounded

1. VV 13-20 describe *Vāgdāna* or betrothal.

and excited. They did not utter a word. On seeing the very beautiful beloved of the lord of the three worlds, having splendid lustre, they appeared to be stunned and crazy.

22-23. Thus those Sages too were enchanted by her beauty. What then in the case of Devas?

So, after seeing the lady of slender frame, the daughter of the Lord of Mountains, who was the beloved of Śiva, they approached Śiva once again. Then those Sages, the favourites of Śiva, spoke to him:

The Sages said:

24. His (Himālaya's) daughter has undoubtedly been well-adorned by the Lord of Mountains. O Lord of Devas, go (there) in order to marry (her). Go there surrounded by all the Devas.

25. Go quickly, O great Lord, to Pārvatī for the sake of a son.

On hearing their words, he laughed and said:

26. "O Sages of great fortune, marriage has never been seen or heard of by me before. Let its special points be mentioned."

27-30. Then all the Sages spoke to Sadāśiva laughingly: "O Lord, invite Viṣṇu, Brahmā and Indra. Similarly send for the groups of sages, Yakṣas, Gandharvas, Serpents, Siddhas, Vidyādharas, Kinnaras and groups of celestial damsels. Bring these and many others immediately." On hearing these words uttered by the Sages, the lord, an expert in the use of words, spoke to Nārada: "Bring Viṣṇu quickly. Bring Brahmā, Mahendra and others too."

31. Honouring the words of Śaṁbhu with great humility, the sage Nārada who sanctified the worlds and who was a devotee of Viṣṇu, hurried to Vaikuṇṭha.

32-33. He saw Lord Viṣṇu who was seated on the excellent couch and was being served by goddess Śrī. The Lord was the most excellent one among Devas; his lustre was very great and he was four-armed, with a body dark in complexion like a blue lotus. He wore beautiful ear-rings set with gems and jewels of great value. He was refulgent with the excellent gems of his great crown and had the excellent garland of sylvan flowers named Vaijayantī. He was the sole handsome person in the whole world.

34. Nārada approached him and spoke to him the words of

Śaṁbhu. The most excellent one among the sages, the omniscient one playing on his lute called Brahmavīṇā, spoke to him with great respect:

35. "Come, come, O Mahāviṣṇu. Come quickly to (meet) Mahādeva. You are the only one to manage the affairs efficiently in the matter of the marriage of Śaṁbhu."

36. The Lord laughed and said to Nārada: "How did the idea of marriage occur to the Trident-bearing Lord?" Although the lord had understood the matter, he asked Nārada about it.

Nārada said:

37. By means of a great penance, Rudra was gratified by Pārvatī. He himself went to the place where the chaste daughter of the Mountain was seated.

38-40. Śaṁbhu who was gratified by Pārvatī, said to her "I am your servant." He requested Pārvatī: "O lady of great splendour, choose (me) in marriage quickly." So spoke Śaṁbhu. He calls you now.

On hearing his words, Janārdana, the lord of Devas, prepared himself to go to Śiva. He was accompanied by Nārada and surrounded by his *Pārṣadas*. The great soul Acyuta, the great Lord of leading Yogins, mounted on Suparṇa (Garuḍa) and went through the path of the sky. Hari was accompanied by Nārada and excellent Devas.

41-42. On seeing the Śārṅga-bearing Lord (i.e. Viṣṇu), the Lord Śiva whose lotus-like feet are worthy of being meditated upon by Yogins, stood up joyously and embraced Viṣṇu.

Then the lords Hari and Hara stood up in the same place and enquired of the welfare of each other.

Īśvara said:

43-48. O Viṣṇu, I have been undoubtedly won over by the penance of Girijā. It is for the purpose of marriage that I am going to Himālaya.

I shall tell the exact position to you. Formerly when Satī was given to me by Dakṣa, the marriage rite was not performed by me in accordance with the injunctions. It is only now that all the rites should be very elaborately performed by me. I do not know all those rites connected with marriage alliance. I do not know anything that should be performed by me.

After hearing those words of Śaṁbhu, the slayer of Madhu laughed. When he was about to say something, Brahmā came there hurriedly along with Indra and all the Guardians of the Quarters.

Similarly Devas, Asuras, Yakṣas, Dānavas, serpents, birds, celestial damsels and the great sages, all these gathered together to speak to the Lord. Then they bowed down their heads and spoke to Īśa:

49. "Go ahead, go ahead, O Lord Mahādeva, along with us." Then Viṣṇu spoke these words appropriate to the occasion:

50-52. "O Śaṁbhu, it behoves you to perform the rites in accordance with the injunctions laid down in the *Gṛhyasūtras.*[1] Perform the holy rite of *Nāndīmukha.*[2] Fix the *Maṇḍapa.*[3] Perform all the religious rites connected with them. Some of the men learned in the Vedas perform this rite avoiding the confluence of great rivers. O Lord, let the *Maṇḍapa* be fixed now."

Śaṁbhu who was told thus by Viṣṇu, did so for the sake of his own welfare.

53. Everything conducive to prosperity was performed by him along with Brahmā and others. Kaśyapa accompanied by Brahmā performed the worship of the Planets.

54-56. Similarly Atri, Vasiṣṭha, Gautama, Guru, Bhṛgu, Kaṇva Bṛhaspati (?), Śakti, Jamadagni, Parāśara, Mārkaṇḍeya, Śilāvāka, Śūnyapāla, Akṣataśrama, Agastya, Cyavana, Garga and many others came to the presence of Śiva. Directed by Brahmā there, they performed the rites in accordance with the injunctions.

---

1. Though the name of the *Gṛhyasūtra* is not given, the general items of the ceremony are common. It is difficult to pinpoint the Sūtra followed by the author.

2. The *Śrāddha* rite offered to the manes before the festive rites of marriage. This is mentioned only in the *Baudhāyana Gṛ. S.* I.1.24. Other *Gṛhyasūtras* are silent about it.

3. *Maṇḍapa-karaṇa* or creating a pandal for social ceremonies like *Upanayana* (thread ceremony), in marriage is prescribed in *Pāraskara Gr. S.* I-4.

57. All of them who were masters of the Vedas and the Vedāṅgas (i.e. ancillary subjects) tied an amulet (round the arm) of Maheśa in accordance with the injunctions of the Vedas. They tied the marriage thread also (round his wrist) for the sake of auspiciousness.

58-60. The sages who knew the reality performed various auspicious rites reciting the *Sūktas* (hymns) of Ṛgveda, Yajurveda and Sāmaveda. They made Śiva, the great Ātman, take the ceremonies of oil bath etc. The famous matted hair of Śiva, the Supreme Soul (assumed the form of fine tresses). The garland of skulls turned into a fine necklace fitted with many pearls. Those serpents that had been round his limbs instantaneously turned into ornaments of gold.

61. Maheśvara, the lord of Devas, richly endowed with all ornaments and surrounded by Devas went to the city of the king of Mountains.[1]

62-64. The terrible deity, Caṇḍikā, became *Varabhaginī*[2] ('sister of the bridegroom'). Caṇḍī who was adorned with serpents as ornaments and who was seated on a ghost went ahead taking a gold pot of great lustre and filled (with water) on her head. She was accompanied by her retinues. Mahācaṇḍī had a brilliant face and terrible eyes. There were thousands of hideous Bhūtas (goblins). Accompanied by them Caṇḍī of deformed face went ahead.

65. All the exceedingly terrible Gaṇas went behind her. The terrible Rudras numbering eleven crores also went behind them. They were the great favourites of Rudra.

66. Then all the three worlds became pervaded by the loud sound of *Ḍamaru*, the sounds of *Bherīs* and *Bhāṅkāras* (varieties of drums) and the sound of conchs.

67. So also there was a tumultuous sound of *Dundubhi* drums. All over-eager Devas and all Siddhas accompanied by the Guardians of the Quarters followed close behind the Gaṇas.

68-70a. Mahendra seated on his Airāvata was proceeding ahead in the middle (of the group) with a white umbrella held

1. This is called *Vadhūgṛhāgamana* (bridegroom's going to the bride's house). *Śāṅkhāyana Gr. S*, I.12.1 mentions it.

2. The author's sense of humour becomes obvious in describing Caṇḍī as the '*Vara-bhaginī*' (bridegroom's sister) and her antics during the marriage ceremony.

aloft. He was being fanned by chowries and surrounded by many Suras. O Brāhmaṇas, many of these sages, Bharadvāja and others, were also going ahead towards (the place) of the marriage of Śiva.

70b-73. Śākinīs, Yātudhānas, Vetālas, Brahmarākṣasas, Bhūtas, Pretas, Piśācas and others such as Pramathas etc. followed Caṇḍī and asked about her, "Where has Caṇḍī gone?" Running at a very great speed, they came up to her. Even as she was proceeding ahead, they bowed down to her. They said to Caṇḍī who was accompanied by Bhairava and whose lustre was very great, "Where are you going, O Caṇḍī, without us? Say specifically."

74-76. That Caṇḍī laughed and said to the Bhūtas who were listening: "Mounted on a ghost, I am going (to attend) the marriage ceremony of Śaṁbhu. I am holding this golden pot on my head (for the same purpose)." Then Caṇḍī changed herself into the form of Śīva's nearest female relative.

Surrounded by all the Bhūtas, she went ahead of all. Gaṇas followed her and Suras were behind Gaṇas.

77. The Guardians of the Quarters beginning with Indra and the sages were leading those who followed behind. Behind the sages were the *Pārṣadas* (Attendants) of great lustre.

78-80. They were fully conversant with the unfathomable nature of Viṣṇu. They were more charming than Mukunda. All of them resembled clouds (in colour). They had garlands of sylvan flowers. All of them had the body-mark Śrīvatsa. All were clad in yellow robes. They had four arms. They wore ear-rings. All of them appeared splendid by means of crowns, bangles, armlets, necklaces, anklets, threads, waist-bands and rings. They had the characteristic features of great men. In their midst was Viṣṇu, the slayer of the enemies of Suras. He was accompanied by Śrī.

81. Hari, the greatest Soul, the sole kinsman of the universe, who had rendered the three worlds completely auspicious, who is established in the heart by persons of great magnanimity and who is the bestower of the greatest objectives and aims (in life), shone in the company of Śiva.

82. Hari, the great Lord, was seated on Garuḍa. The great Lord was accompanied by Lakṣmī. The sole Lord of all the worlds was being fanned by chowries. He was accompanied by all the leading sages.

83. Viriñci (i.e. Brahmā) was seated on his own vehicle. Accompanied by the Vedas along with the six ancillary subjects, he, Hiraṇyagarbha, was surrounded by *Āgamas* along with *Itihāsas* and *Purāṇas*.

84-86. Maheśa was thus accompanied by Brahmā and Hari. He was surrounded by the leading Suras. He was encircled by the sages. The Bull-bannered Lord who cannot be attained by all, who is difficult of access even to leading Yogins, was seated on a bull that resembled a pure crystal, that was given to virtue and that was characterized by cows (? that had all the fine characteristics of bulls). He was accompanied by the Mothers also. Accompanied by these and Asuras and Dānavas and adorned by learned scholars, Maheśa then went to Himālaya, the most excellent one among Mountains, for the marriage with the most excellent young woman.

CHAPTER TWENTYFOUR

The Marriage Ceremony of Śiva: The Arrangement for Accommodating Devas and Others

Lomaśa said:

1. Similarly, the Lord of Mountains with the greatest joy, made all arrangements for the sake of his daughter. (The Mountain) of exalted magnanimity made Garga (the priest) in-charge and decorated the place for the auspicious ceremony with the greatest magnificence.

2. He sent for Viśvakarman and eagerly made him build the hall (for the ceremony of marriage). It was very extensive and exceedingly fascinating with raised seats.

3. It extended to ten thousand *Yojanas*, O excellent Brāhmaṇas. The hall was of very fine quality with various specimens of wonderful workmanship.

4-7. Everything mobile and immobile was equally charming.[1]

1. This description reminds us of the Maya-sabhā in Mbh, *Sabhā*, 3.

The mobile one was excelled by the immobile one and the immobile one was excelled by the mobile one. There dry ground was excelled by water. There people did not know clearly which was water and which was dry ground. In some place there were lions and in some other places there were swans and cranes of great lustre. In some place there were very beautiful artificial peacocks. So also there were artificial elephants, horses and deer.

8. (People could not find out) which were real (animals) and which were unreal (i.e. artificial) ones created by Viśvakarman. Similarly wonderful gatekeepers were made.

9. There were men drawing bows. They were immobile but appeared (life-like) like mobile ones. Similarly, there were (statues of) horses with horsemen and elephants with elephant-riders.

10. There were some men holding flowers and sprouts and being fanned by chowries. Some persons shone there, wearing garlands.

11. There were many artificial banners made there. (The statue of) Mahālakṣmī, born of the Ocean of Milk, was stationed at the gateway.

12. There were well-caparisoned artificial elephants and horses along with elephant-riders and horsemen. They appeared like real ones.

13. There were artificial chariots with charioteers. They were like real ones. In order to confuse everyone, assembly halls and courts of justice were created.

14. At the main gate of the hall (a statue of) Nandin was made by him. It was as white as the pure crystal just like Nandin (in real life).

15. Above him there was a great divine aerial chariot embellished with gems and jewels. It shone and it was rendered splendid by means of sprouts, umbrellas and chowries.

16. On the left side there were two elephants resembling those made of pure saffron. They had four tusks. They were sixty years old. They were noble-souled and exceedingly refulgent.

17. Similarly on the right side two horses had been made. They had armours on. Viśvakarman had made Guardians of the Quarters too endowed with gem-set, jewel-studded ornaments.

18. The sixteen Prakṛtis were realistically made by that

intelligent one. All the Devas were depicted (by way of statues) by Viśvakarman (in life-like) poses.

19-21. Similarly all the sages and ascetics, beginning with Bhṛgu, Viśvedevas, along with their *Pārṣadas* (retinues) and Indra in his true form (were made by him). All those noble-souled ones were realistically depicted by the intelligent (Viśvakarman). Such a *Maṇḍapa* of a divine form was made by him. It was divine and divinely fascinating with many wonderful features. In the meantime there came Nārada in front of him.

22-25. It was directed by Brahmā that Nārada came to the house of Himavān. Nārada saw in front of him (a statue of) himself depicting him as one endowed with humility and modesty.

Seeing that artificial (statue) Nārada became confused. The sage of great fame then became engaged in viewing (the various things) made by Viśvakarman.

He entered the *Maṇḍapa* of Himavān, studded with gems of various colours. There were (statues of) Rambhā and golden pitchers. The *Maṇḍapa* was rendered splendid by them. It had a thousand columns.

Then Mountain Himālaya entered the *Maṇḍapa* surrounded by his own people. He welcomed and adored the sage and enquired of him what should be done (by him).

Nārada said:

26. Those noble-souled lords have come with Indra at their head. So also the great sages surrounded by the Gaṇas. Mahādeva has come for the marriage celebration riding on his Bull.

27-30. (The first two hemistiches in verse 29 should have preceded verse 26.)[1]

Then after hearing his words the excellent Mountain Himavān adored him duly and spoke to Nārada the following great words very praiseworthy and sweet:

"Go to Śaṅkara along with these Mountains, viz. Maināka, Sahya and Meru, O highly intelligent one. Be quick and bring here Śiva whose feet are worshipped by both Suras and Asuras and who is accompanied by Devas and the excellent sages."

1. The wrongly ordered hemistiches:) On hearing the words of Mountain Himavān, the sage thought that it should be so and spoke these words to the King of Mountains.

31. Thinking that it should be so, that noble-souled one, the most excellent among sages, went quickly along with those leading Mountains. Hastening, he came to Śaṁbhu immediately.

32-34. Then Mahādeva was seen surrounded by Devas. Brahmā, Viṣṇu, Rudra, all the Suras and those who were close followers of Rudra asked Nārada: "Let this be spoken to us since we ask. (Otherwise) it is not spoken. Does each of these Mountains, Sahya, Maināka and Meru, want to give his daughter to Śaṁbhu? What is going on now?"

35-40. After keeping Brahmā in front of him (?), then Nārada, the excellent sage of great splendour, meaningfully spoke to Viṣṇu. Resorting to a lonely place, Nārada spoke these words to Surendra: "A great abode has been built up by Tvaṣṭṛ. All of us are fascinated by it. Has what had been done by you to that noble soul formerly, entirely been forgotten by you, O Lord of Śacī? Therefore, he is desirous of defeating you even while living in the abode of the noble-souled Mountain.

Oh, (I) have been deluded by that shining replica, that image of great likeness. Similarly Viṣṇu too has been made by him holding conch, discus, iron club etc. Brahmā too has been made by him. A bull of the nature of *Māyā* has been made by him and also the serpent Aśvatara. Similarly understand, O lord of the immortal ones, that many other things too have been carved by him."

41-43. On hearing his words, Devendra spoke these words to Viṣṇu: "I shall see it and return quickly. Wait here. Let me find it, under what pretext has he done this. He is dejected and distressed on account of (the death) of his son."

On hearing his words, Janārdana, the lord of Devas, spoke these words laughingly to Śakra who had become frightened:

44-48. "Formerly you had fallen into a swoon, O Indra, (in a clash) with Nivātakavacas. There the *Vidyā* (Magic Spell) *Amṛtā* was brought by me for rendering service (to you). It was due to the power of that great *Vidyā* that you could make this Himavān and other excellent Mountains devoid of wings. It was at my instance that all of them were made wingless, O Vāsava. Thanks to the power of the *Mahāvidyā*, Tvaṣṭṛ entered the *Maṇḍapa* now and did this by means of his *Māyā*. Stupid fellows desire to win success. There is not even an iota to be afraid of."

Thus Viṣṇu consoled those Devas who were arguing thus. They then said to Nārada:

49. "Does or does not the Lord of Mountains give his daughter? Let this be ascertained quickly. What has been done by him today? Speak everything, O Nārada, obeisance to you."

50. On hearing it, Śaṁbhu said these words laughingly: "If Mountain Himālaya gives his daughter to me, what have I to do with *Māyā*? O Viṣṇu, tell me exactly.

51. This is opined by learned men conversant with Logic (*Nyāya*) that the fruit must be achieved by some means or other. Hence all of you with Indra at your head seek only the object of desire. Go ahead quickly."

52. At that time even Śiva, the immanent soul of the universe, was deluded by god of Love having only five arrows. The lord of Bhūtas (goblins) has been (afflicted) by a greater Bhūta (i.e. god of Love). What will be the condition of others?

53. Śaṁbhu is highly splendid. In spite of that he has been won over by the bodiless lord of Love, just like an ordinary man of no culture.

54. Indeed Madana is very powerful. By him this entire universe including Devas and sages has been conquered by means of his mature prowess.

55. Indeed Anaṅga (god of Love) is the powerful king of all living beings and particularly of Devas. His order is strong.

56-57. With the womanly form of Pārvatī, Madana is invincible in all the three worlds. On seeing that lady, all the clever sages, Devas, human beings, Gandharvas, Piśācas, Serpents and Rākṣasas—do not dare to transgress the order of the noble-souled Madana.

58. O Brāhmaṇas, Madana cannot be pierced (*vettum*='to understand' also) by the power of penance or charitable gifts except through humility.

59-61. Hence the great anger of Anaṅga is excessively powerful. On seeing Īśvara thus deluded by Madana, Mādhava who was conversant with the proper use of words, said these words: "O lord, do not worry. What has been said by Nārada (is true). Everything wonderful that has been created in the *Maṇḍapa* by Tvaṣṭṛ was actuated by lord Madana."

Then Śaṅkara said to Madhusūdana:

62-63. "Indeed this *Maṇḍapa* has been made by Tvaṣṭṛ as one covered by *Avidyā* (Ignorance). But we will say, O Viṣṇu, that the *Maṇḍapa* (is made by him) alone. O highly fortunate one, marriage too has *Avidyā* as the root cause. Hence let us all go now for marriage celebration."

64-65. Keeping Nārada at the head, all the Devas including Vāsava and accompanied by Himavān went to the mansion of very wonderful features and variegated in form made by Viśvakarman. Therefore, that sacrificial chamber was excellent and very holy. It was honoured by many persons. That intelligent one (i.e. Viśvakarman) made that sacrificial chamber one that captivated the mind and was endowed with various wonderful features.

66. On entering, all the leading Suras and the sages were seen by Himavān who stood up in honour of them.

67. Similarly for their sake pleasing mansions were made by him. Gandharvas, Yakṣas, Pramathas, Siddhas, Devas, serpents and groups of celestial damsels could live in them happily. He made parks and gardens here and there for their sake.

68. On their behalf very valuable bathrooms with shower jets and enclosed spaces for toilet were made by him. They shone wonderfully. Those had been made by that noble-souled (Viśvakarman).

69. Amply spacious abodes for the purpose of the residence of all the Devas and the sages of sanctified souls were made by him.

70. Thus Viśvakarman expanded many abodes suitably and befittingly for those who stayed there.

71-73. Wherever these Bhairavas and others sat, Viśvakarman made abodes for them in those very same places. For Bhairavas, Kṣetrapālas, others who resided in the fields (sacred spots), the residents of cremation grounds, those who stayed on *Nyagrodha* trees (banyan trees), those staying on *Aśvattha* (the holy fig) trees, those who moved about in the sky, wherever they were seated, very beautiful great mansions were built by Viśvakarman. They were extremely suitable to those spirits.

74. Suras, along with Indra, Yakṣas, Piśācas, Rākṣasas, the groups of Gandharvas, Vidyādharas and celestial damsels were accommodated along with Gaṇas there alone by Himavān himself.

CHAPTER TWENTYFIVE

The Marriage Rituals

Lomaśa said:

1. All of them well-received and welcomed by Himādri sat (stayed) there along with their retinues and vehicles. Those Devas were highly delighted.

2. There itself (a mansion) of great dimensions was built by Viśvakarman for the residence of the Self-born Lord (i.e. Brahmā). It was endowed with excessive refulgence.

3. Similarly another abode that shone well, was very charming and of variegated features (and equipments) was made by Tvaṣṭṛ. It was reserved for Viṣṇu.

He himself built a very beautiful *Caṇḍīgṛha* (a common parlour?)

4. Similarly he built a huge white mansion of great lustre, well-adored by the excellent Devas. It was made resplendent with the great lustre of Kailāsalakṣmī (the presiding deity of fortune of Kailāsa).

5. It was there that Śaṁbhu was accommodated by Himādri making it well-furnished through his ample resources.

6-7. In the meantime, Menā came there along with groups of friends and attendants and surrounded by sages in order to perform the *Nīrājana* rite (ceremonious waving of lights) to Śaṁbhu. The entire space of the three worlds was filled with the sound of musical instruments. *Nīrājana* rite was performed for that ascetic (i.e. Śiva).

8. The great chaste lady Menā looked at the bridegroom and knew (his special characteristics). Recollecting what had been said by Girijā, Menā was struck with wonder.

9. "I see that the handsome features of Parameṣṭhin Maheśa are far more (beautiful) than what had been formerly said by Pārvatī in my presence. Now the handsomeness of Maheśa which cannot be described, has been seen by me."

10-13. Struck with wonder thus, Menā (went back) surrounded by the wives of Brāhmaṇas.

There Pārvatī was seated, being attended upon by friends and (married Brāhmaṇa ladies). The lady of excellent complexion appeared splendid with the pair of cloths that had not yet been washed (i.e. fresh from the loom). Her bodice was very excellent and divine (as) it was rendered splendid by various kinds of gems and jewels. It was liked by the goddess. It shone with the greatest glory. The daughter of the Mountain wore a necklace embellished with divine gems and jewels as well as very valuable bangles of pure gold. Seated there, Pārvatī was meditating upon Parameśvara.

14. In the meantime, Garga[1] spoke these words: "O clever ones, bring Śambhu quickly to our mansion first at this (auspicious) time for the celebration of the marriage."

15. On hearing the words of the noble-souled Garga, all the Mountains stood up along with their wives.

16-19. All of them were endowed with very great prosperity and affluence. They were well-adorned and had auspicious things in their hands. Their wives too were well-bedecked in ornaments. Those ladies with lovely glossy eyes were holding many presents and gifts (in their hands). To the accompaniment of the sounds of musical instruments as well as of the chantings of Vedic *Mantras* they came with their wives to the place where Lord Maheśvara was sitting surrounded by Pramathas and attended upon by Caṇḍī.

Śaṅkara, the benefactor of all the worlds, was surrounded and accompanied by the great sages and groups of Devas.

20. On hearing the loud sound of the musical instruments, all the servants of Śaṅkara suddenly got up along with Devas and sages.

21. Similarly, Gaṇas accompanied by groups of Yoginīs, the lord of Gaṇas of the same uniform splendour and all the Gaṇanāyakas (i.e. leaders of the groups of goblins) followed keeping Śiva at the head.

22. The group of Yoginīs was very fierce with their shouts resembling the sound of *Bherī* drums. They had kept at their

1. Garga—An ancient sage, a royal astrologer in King Pṛthu's court (Mbh, *Śānti*, 59.111.) A famous work on Astrology, *Garga-Saṁhitā*, is attributed to him and the present text, the authenticity of which is doubtful, is still believed to be his work. There is another Garga, the family priest of Yādavas. He was sent by Vasudeva to perform the thread ceremony of his sons at Gokula (BhP X.81ff). The Garga in SkP may be a different person of the same Gotra.

head the terrible Caṇḍī who was adorned with great prosperity and magnificence.

23. She wore serpent Karkoṭaka round the neck. She made a necklace of it. She wore scorpions and venomous reptiles like a *Padaka* (an ornament of the neck).

24. She wore as the ornaments of her ears, hands and feet of the heroes killed in battle. She wore the heads of others as ornaments upon her chest.

25. The hide of a tiger she wore (like a cloth). She was accompanied by the circle of Yoginīs. She was surrounded by Kṣetrapālas and Bhairavas.

26. Similarly she was surrounded by ghosts and goblins and Kapaṭas (spirits in disguise). There were the exceedingly terrible groups, Vīrabhadra and others, who had been commanded before by Śiva to destroy the *Yajña* of Dakṣa.

27. So also were Kālī, Bhairavī, the frightful Māyā, Tripurā and the auspicious Jayā, the cause of happiness and welfare.

28. These and many others of very fierce type were desirous of going, keeping Sadāśiva at their head, surrounded by Bhūtas and Pretas.

29-32. On seeing all these, Janārdana, the devotee of Śiva (said):

Viṣṇu said:

Honour the great sages, the immortal ones as well as Anasūyā and Arundhatī and keep them at the head (of the procession). O Lord, keep Caṇḍī to whom the Guardians of the Quarters bow down, very near you.

On hearing the words uttered by Viṣṇu, Sadāśiva, the Lord of the universe, laughingly said thus:[1] "O Caṇḍī, be pleased to stay here itself till the marriage is completely celebrated. O splendid lady, you know my feelings and emotions in the matter of what should be done and what should not be done."

33-36. On hearing these words of Śambhu of unmeasured splendour, Caṇḍī who had become much infuriated with Viṣṇu

1. Caṇḍī's behaviour being unsuitable to this occasion creates laughter among the readers, but caused embarrassment to the parties in the marriage ceremony.

spoke. Similarly all the other Pramathas said to Viṣṇu in great anger:

"Whenever Śiva appears, we too are present there, O Lord. Why were we prevented by you on this occasion of great festivity and happiness?"

On hearing those words, Keśava spoke these words directed towards Caṇḍī, Pramathas and others of the same type: "You have not been referred to by me. It does not behove you to be angry."

37. On being told thus by him, all the Gaṇas of whom Caṇḍī was the chief one resorted to an isolated place with burning sensations in their hearts at the statement of Viṣṇu.

38. By that time all the ministers of the Lord of Mountains came to Maheśa hurriedly in great flurry with their wives.

39. The sounds of five types of musical instruments and the loud sound of the chanting of the Vedic *Mantras* (were heard). They were accompanied by ladies who were singing (melodiously).

40. They came thus to the place where Śaṁbhu (was seated) surrounded by everyone. They came with pots (of water). Sadāśiva was bathed. He was adorned with all ornaments by women who were singing auspicious songs.

41. The sages, Devas, Gandharvas and others, the excellent Mountains and the women who were well-adored (adorned?) went in front of Śaṁbhu.

With a great umbrella held over his head (Śiva) shone very well.

42-44. He was fanned with chowries. He had a crown with which he shone excessively. Brahmā, Viṣṇu, Candra and the Guardians of the Quarters went ahead endowed with great refulgence. They too shone well. Conchs, *Bherīs*, *Paṭahas*, *Ānakas* and *Gomukhas* (varieties of drums) were sounded. Musicians too accompanied the party. There was great auspiciousness (everywhere). The *Vāditras* (musical instruments) were repeatedly played in that great festival.

45-46. The blessed Arundhatī, Anasūyā, Sāvitrī and Lakṣmī (were present there) surrounded by the Mātṛs (Mother deities). Accompanied by them all, the sole kinsman of the universe shone with great refulgence. He was surrounded by the Moon, the Sun, the Fire-god and the Wind-god along with the excellent Guardians of the Quarters and great sages.

47. He was fanned directly by Pavana (Wind-god); the umbrella was held aloft by Śaśī (the Moon-god); the Sun stood in front as lamp-bearer. Viṣṇu accompanied by Śrī remained at the side.

48. Devas accompanied by the sages showered him with flowers scattering them all round. Śaṁbhu went towards the great mansion, the ground of which had been paved with gold and which appeared splendid with great prosperity.

Worshipped by human beings, Devas and Dānavas with great service and attendance, Śaṁbhu entered that mansion.

49. Śaṁbhu who arrived there thus entered the *Yajñamaṇḍapa* (i.e. the hall erected for the purpose of the holy rite). Parameśvara was eulogized by Devas by means of songs of praise.

50-51. The excellent Mountain made Maheśa get down from the elephant. He was made to sit on a raised seat and the great rite of *Nīrājana* was performed by Menā along with her friends and the priest. Everything such as the offering of *Madhuparka*[1] etc. was performed there itself.

52. Urged by Brahmā, the priest, the holy Lord performed various preliminary rites connected with the splendid and auspicious ceremony fit for the occasion.

53-55. The slender-bodied Pārvatī was seated on an altar inside the *Maṇḍapa*. She was adorned with all ornaments. Hara was directly brought there by Viṣṇu and Brahmā. Persons beginning with Vācaspati began to look into the *Lagna* (auspicious hour). Sage Garga was seated in the *Ghaṭikālaya* (i.e. the room where the water device called *Ghaṭikā Pātra* to know the exact time is kept). When the stipulated hour was reached *Praṇava* (was uttered).

56. Proclaiming "*OM PUṆYA*" (auspicious) etc., Garga made the bride join her palms in reverence. Thereafter, Pārvatī took a handful of *Akṣata* (rice grain) and showered it on Śiva.

57-59a. Rudra was worshipped by her with curds, *Akṣata*, *Kuśa* grass etc. Pārvatī of beautiful face was filled with great joy

1. A respectful offering made to a guest or a bridegroom after his arrival at the door of the father of the bride. It generally consists of honey, ghee, curds, milk.

on looking at Śaṁbhu for whose sake a great penance, very difficult for others to perform, had been performed by the great goddess.

The life-giver of all living beings in the universe had been attained on account of that penance.

59b-60. Thereafter, the Bull-bannered great Lord was told by Nārada and other sages beginning with Garga and Sanaka: "O Three-eyed one, worship Pārvatī reciprocally." Then that slender-bodied lady was worshipped with *Arghya, Akṣata* and other things.

61. Being worshipped by each other Pārvatī and Parameśvara, constituting the universe, shone then very much.

62-63. They were covered with the glory of the three worlds. They looked at each other (lovingly). The divine couple, the great goddess and the god, were then (honoured) by means of *Nīrājana* rite by Lakṣmī and Sāvitrī particularly as well as by Arundhatī. Similarly Anasūyā looked affectionately at Śaṁbhu and Pārvatī of great renown and performed *Nīrājana* rite with pleasure and love displayed in her eyes.

64. Similarly all the Brāhmaṇa ladies performed the *Nīrājana* rite again and again. All of them laughed joyously on looking at the chaste lady and Śaṁbhu.

Lomaśa said:

65. In the meantime, urged by the preceptor Garga, Himālaya accompanied by Menā began the rite of offering the virgin.[1]

66. Menā, the better-half of Himādri, the highly fortunate lady adorned with all the ornaments took up the golden pot.

67-69. Then Viśvanātha, the bestower of boons, was told by Himādri: "After due consultation with Brahmā, Viṣṇu and the noble-souled preceptor Garga, I am today performing the rite of offering the virgin to the Trident-bearing Lord of Devas, O Brāhmaṇas. May the procedural *Mantras* suitable for this occasion be recited."

1. This is *Kanyādāna* (giving the bride to the bridegroom). In this ceremony the father of the girl says that the bridegroom should not prove false to the bride in *Dharma, Artha* and *Kāma* (the three *Puruṣārthas* in life) and the bridegroom pledges, he won't do so (*nāticarāmi*). This is done even now (vide *Pāraskara Gr. S.* I.3). See also *infra* ch. 26.3.

Agreeing that it should be so, the excellent Brāhmaṇas who were aware of the (proper) time (of the ceremony) said:

70. "O dear one, let your *Gotra* and lineage be mentioned.[1] O highly fortunate one, say." On hearing these words, the pleasant-faced one turned his face away; one who should not be bewailed attained a pitiable state.

71-75. Lord Maheśa who had a pitiable face when he had no reply to offer, was seen in such a state by the excellent Suras, sages and groups of Gandharvas, Yakṣas, ascetics and Siddhas. Then Nārada did something funny.

Nārada, the son of Brahmā, took out his Vīṇā. Then the intelligent one was prevented: "O holy Lord, do not play your lute." On being requested thus by the Mountain, Nārada spoke these words: "Bhava was directly asked by you to mention his *Gotra*. O Mountain, his *Gotra* and family is *Nāda*' (Pure Sound) alone. Śaṁbhu is well established in him. Hence, Śaṁbhu is identical with *Nāda*. Hence, O scorcher of enemies, this Vīṇā is played now by me.

76. O Parvata (Mountain), Devas beginning with Brahmā do not know his *Gotra* and family; what then to say of others?

77-78. You are confounded. You do not know anything about what should be said or should not be said. All worldly objects are external to Maheśa. O Mountain, whatever is originated, whatever has a birth, becomes dead. There is no doubt about it. This Virūpākṣa (one with uneven eyes) is devoid of form and features. (Hence) he is called *Akulīna* (having no family).

79. O excellent Mountain, your son-in-law is undoubtedly one without a *Gotra*. No criticism or comment should be made in this matter by you who are very learned.

80. All people do not know Hara. Why should I talk much on this, O Lord? Even these sages are confounded, O glorious one, because they are ignorant of him.

81-82. Brahmā does not know him (and his) head, the head of Parameṣṭhin (the great Lord).

Viṣṇu went to the nether worlds (and the foot of the Lord)

1. A humorous situation. Śiva, the creator and destroyer of the universe, is *Gotra-less* but is asked about his *Gotra* and lineage. The Lord is *Nāda* himself as is later shown by Nārada and explained that he is without a *Gotra* (vv 71-74).

was not seen. The whole range of the three worlds has been pervaded by that unfathomable *Liṅga.* Understand this. What purpose is served by this?

83. That (*Liṅga*) has certainly been propitiated by this daughter of yours, O Himālaya. How is it that you do not know exactly, O great Mountain.

84-85. This universe is created by these two. It is sustained by these two."

On hearing these words of the noble-souled Nārada, all of them, the chief of whom was Himādri and at whose head was Indra, became surprised in their minds and they said: "Well-done! Well-done!"

On realizing the majesty of Īśvara all those clever ones (sages) became overwhelmed by surprise. They spoke to one another:

The sages said:

86-87. It was at his bidding that this wide world was born. This is greater than the greatest, being of the form of self-consciousness. Everything becomes the object of the imagination of Parameśvara who is independent. This noble-souled one has the three worlds for his own form.

CHAPTER TWENTYSIX

The Marriage Celebration of Śiva and Pārvatī: Auspicious Festivities

Lomaśa said:

1. Then those excellent Mountains beginning with Meru became bewildered. They all addressed Himavān, the great Mountain, simultaneously.

The Mountains said:

2. O Mountain, let the offering of the daughter in marriage be performed today. It is your good fortune that the glorious Śaṁbhu has been obtained by you (as the son-in-law). No

hesitation should be entertained within your heart. So let her be given to Īśvara (Lord Śiva).

3-4. On hearing the words of his friends and on being urged by god Brahmā, Himālaya made this good resolve. He made the offer with the *Mantra* "O Parameśvara, I am giving this daughter to you as your wife. Accept her."[1]

To this great Rudra, to Śaṁbhu, the Lord of the Devas, to Maheśa his daughter was given by the noble-souled Lord of Mountains.

5-6. The lotus-eyed couple were brought out from the altar. Pārvatī and Parameśvara were made to sit outside the *Vedī* (altar) by the preceptor, the noble-souled Kaśyapa. Then for the sake of *Havana* (offering into the sacred fire) the (sacred) fire was invoked, O Brāhmaṇas.[2]

7-10. Brahmā was seated on the seat of Brahmā (the priest presiding over a sacrificial ceremony) near Śiva, while the rite of oblation to the fire was going on. The sages who were experts (in their field), who were conversant with various schools of philosophy, conversed with one another. Some of them who were engaged in Vedic discussion, expatiated on what has been accepted (in the Vedas). "It is like this." "It is not like this." "It is like this and not otherwise." "It should be done." "It should not be done." "It should be (partially) done and (partially) not be done." As they said like this the medley of their voices was heard in the place near Śiva (in the presence of Śiva). Sticking to their own opinions, they were speaking to one another. All of them were devoid of the knowledge of Reality. Their intelligence (and knowledge) was limited to the Vedas only.

1. This is formal *Kanyādāna.*

2. This is *Agnisthāpana* and *Homa* or *Havana*. Sacred fire is 'established' and ghee is oblated into it with *mantras*. The difference of opinion among the Brāhmaṇas referred to in vv 7-10 is due to the great divergence about the number of *āhutis* (oblations) and the *mantras* to be recited, in different *Gṛhya-sūtras*. See *Gṛhyasūtras of Āśvalāyana* (I.7.3 and I.4.3-7), *Āpastaṁba* (IV.1 : prescribes 16 *āhuti's* and 16 *mantras*), *Mānava* (I.8).

As the marriage rite is not completely described (including important rites such as *Saptapadī, Lājāhoma*) it is difficult to ascertain the *Gṛhya-sūtra* followed by the author. Positive mention of *Nāndīmukha* tentatively points to *Baudhāyana Gr. S.*

11. On hearing the words of those (Vedic scholars) who were desirous of defeating one another, Nārada laughed and spoke these words in the presence of Śiva:

12-14. "You are all great disputants taking delight in Vedic discussion. But, O Brāhmaṇas, keep quiet, meditating on Sadāśiva in your hearts. He is the Ātman, the Supreme Soul, greater than the greatest. Obeisance to that Lord who is the immanent soul of all, by whom this universe is created, through whom everything functions and in whom the whole universe becomes merged. That Lord is present now in the abode of the Lord of Mountains, O Brāhmaṇas. It was from his mouth that all of you clever people were born."[1]

15. Those excellent Brāhmaṇas were spoken thus by Nārada. Those excellent Brāhmaṇas were enlightened by means of words of advice.

16. As the *Yajña* was going on, Brahmā, the grandfather of the worlds, saw the feet and the beautiful moon-like nails of the goddess.

17. On seeing them the Lotus-born Lord was immediately agitated (sexually). Being overwhelmed by the god of Love, his semen was discharged on the ground.

18. As the semen virile trickled down, the grandfather (Brahmā) became ashamed. That thing worthy of being concealed and very difficult to be overcome, he pressed down by means of his feet.

19. Many thousands of sages, the Vālakhilyas, were born therefrom. All of them approached him crying out, "O father, O father."

20-21. Those Vālakhilyas were then told by Nārada who got very angry (with them): "O ye Baṭus, all of you go to the mountain Gandhamādana. You must not stay here. You are not wanted (here)."

On being ordered thus by Nārada, all the Vālakhilyas hastened to that mountain.

22-23. Then Brahmā was consoled by Nārada through auspicious words. By that time, the rite of oblations to fire (*Havana*) by noble-souled Maheśa was concluded and the Brāhmaṇas enga-

1. Cf *Brāhmaṇo'sya mukham āsīt*—RV, X.90,12.

ged themselves in *Śāntipāṭha*.[1] The cardnial points, i.e. the whole of the world became pervaded by the great *Brahmaghoṣa* ('loud sound of chanting the Vedas')

24. Then the *Nīrājana* rite was performed to the Lord by the wives of Devas. Similarly, he was adored and worshipped by the wives of the sages.

25. The auspicious and charming young ladies too, of the Lord of the Mountains, performed the rite of *Nīrājana*. Those who were experts and conversant with good music (delighted everyone) with songs. Similarly the great sages (propitiated the Lord) by means of eulogies.

26. Himālaya, the noble-minded great Mountain, gave them very valuable gems and jewels. He was delighted and he wished to please others.

27. The Lord who was stationed on the altar along with his wife and the groups of Suras and Siddhas, shone then. The sole (i.e. the most) handsome one (the Lord) in the universe was accompanied by all his Gaṇas and Pārṣadas. He was delighted in his mind.

28. In the meantime, the sages, Gandharvas, Yakṣas and many others with Brahmā and Viṣṇu at their head came there.

29. The noble-souled great Lord of Mountains endowed with the greatest refulgence, honoured and worshipped all of them and gave them good gems and jewels, clothes, ornaments, betel leaves and scented water.

30. Then all the leading Suras duly honoured Śiva and took their food. All of them gathered together and rejoiced.

31-32. They sat in rows and took food with *Liṅgins* and *Śṛṅgins* (types of Gaṇas). Some of the Gaṇas sat separately. Nārada and others pleased the Lord with witty remarks and jocular comments of different sorts. The group of Caṇḍī with many female attendants took their food. All of them had their (respective) vessels.

33-34. Vetālas and Kṣetrapālas shared their food equally. So also Śākinīs, Ḍākinīs, Yakṣiṇīs, the Mothers and others.

---

1. Recitation of passages from Vedas and Upaniṣads as part of the valedictory ceremony.

There were sixtyfour Yoginīs and Yogins too. There were others too: ten crores of Gaṇas and a core of noble souls.

35. So also, all the sages and others beginning with learned Devas. Other Yogins have already been mentioned by me.

36-38. Yoginīs have also been mentioned. I shall mention their food to you. Some of them brought the pure (raw) meat of rhinoceros and ate it along with the bone. Some who were hungry ate their entrails. Some of them brought huge and heavy heads of buffaloes. Some of them danced. Other Pramathas began to cry and shriek. Some of them in the form of Rudra remained quiet. Others remained staring at still others.

39. Bhairava who was standing in the middle of the circle of Yoginīs began to dance. Others, Bhūtas and Vetālas blurted out "Don't, Don't".

40. On seeing their festivities like this, the slayer of Madhu spoke these words laughingly to Śaṅkara, the benefactor of the worlds:

41-42. "Prevent these Gaṇas, these inebriated fellows now. What should be done on this occasion should be done with wisdom, O Mahādeva. So prevent them."

On hearing it, Lord Rudra said to Vīrabhadra:

Rudra said:

43-47. Prevent those mad and heedless ones and particularly the intoxicated ones.

Vīrabhadra was told thus by Śaṁbhu, the great god (*Parameṣṭhin*). On being ordered by the intelligent Vīrabhadra and prevented by him, the reckless Pramathas kept quiet. In the middle of Yoginīs, Bhūtas, Pramathas, Guhyakas, Śākinīs, Yātudhānas, Kūṣmāṇḍas, Kopikarpaṭas (?) and others, Bhūtas, Vetālas, Kṣetrapālas and Bhairavas—all these intoxicated Pramathas and others became calm.

Thus the marriage celebration was very elaborate. It was performed by Himādri with great auspiciousness and splendour.

48. Four days passed. With full mind, with great sincerity, the worship of the Trident-bearing Lord of Devas was performed by Himādri.

49-52. After worshipping and adoring Mahādeva with robes,

jewels and ornaments as well as with big and small gems, he became engaged in worshipping Viṣṇu. Himavān worshipped and honoured Viṣṇu along with Lakṣmī with splendid robes and ornaments. So also he honoured Brahmā. He honoured Lord Indra along with his preceptor (Bṛhaspati) and Indrāṇī. He honoured the Guardians of the Quarters severally.

Caṇḍī too was honoured along with Bhūtas, Pramathas and Guhyakas with robes and jewels and different kinds of gems and jewels. All others too who had come there were worshipped and honoured.

53. Thus all the Devas, Sages, Yakṣas, Gandharvas, Vidyādharas, Siddhas, Cāraṇas, human beings and groups of celestial damsels were duly honoured.

CHAPTER TWENTYSEVEN

The Birth of Kumāra Kārttikeya

Lomaśa said:

1-2. Similarly all the Mountains were exquisitely worshipped by Viṣṇu, viz. the Mountain Sahya, Vindhya, Maināka, Gandhamādana, Mālyavān, Malaya, Mahendra, Mandara and Meru.[1] These were very scrupulously honoured and respected by Viṣṇu.

3-5. Śvetagiri was made white (?),[2] Nīlādri (Blue mountain) also was made so (blue). Udayādri, Śṛṅga, the great Astācala, Mānasādri, mountain Kailāsa, the most excellent one among

1. Most of these are still known by their old names like Sahya (the Western Ghats), Vindhya etc. But those which are not in the present map of India but were a part of Purāṇic India are known by the following current names:

Gandhamādana—The northern ridge of the great Hindukush arch with its northern extension—the Khwaja Mohammad range.

Mālyavān—Sarikol range to the east of Pamir (Meru).

Meru—The Pamirs.

2. Probably *Śvetaḥ kṛtaḥ* is a misreading for *Śvetakūṭaḥ*, the name of a mountain.

Mountains, and the mountain Lokāloka—all these[1] were honoured by Parameṣṭhin (god Brahmā). Thus all those excellent Mountains were honoured by him. Similarly all the residents of those mountains were also honoured by him.

6. Along with Brahmā, everything relevant and befitting (the occasion) was done by Viṣṇu. On the next day, the procession *Varayātrā*[2] was taken out.

7. A majority of Gaṇas and all the groups of Suras went to the mountain Gandhamādana along with Himādri and kinsmen.

8-11. All the Pramathas, the Gaṇas of Caṇḍī and many others who had come to Himālaya for the marriage celebration of Śiva, were duly honoured by Śiva, O Brāhmaṇas. On seeing the couple they attained great delight. Śaṁbhu accompanied by Pārvatī and Pārvatī along with Śaṁbhu were in fact like a flower and its fragrance or like the word and its connotation. They are *Prakṛti* and *Puruṣa* united into one form. That couple of great lustre shone very well while riding on an elephant.

12-18. Brahmā was then seated in an aerial chariot. Viṣṇu was on his Garuḍa. Indra rode on Airāvata. Kubera sat in his Puṣpaka chariot. Varuṇa rode on his shark (crocodile); Yama on his buffalo; Nairṛta rode on a ghost. The great Fire-god was seated on a goat. Pavana (Wind-god) rode on a deer and Īśa on a bull. Thus the Guardians of the Quarters (came to the procession) of the supreme god (Śiva) along with the Planets. Similarly Pramathas and others came there along with their armies.

The Mountains like Himādri the great Mountain, Ṛṣabha, Gandhamādana, Sahya, Nīlagiri, Mandara, Malayācala, Kailāsa of great splendour and Maināka of great lustre, these and other Mountains became engaged in honouring Śiva. All of them were glorious, highly refulgent and charming. All of them came there along with their wives and sons. All those Mountains beginning with Meru were powerful and handsome. In the

1. Mountains not found in the present map of India:
Śṛṅga (*gin*)—Kara Tau—Kirgiz—Ketman Chain.
Śveta—Nura—Tau—Turkistan—Atbashi Chain.
Udayācala, Astācala, Lokāloka are unidentifiable mythical names.

2. *Varāt* in Marathi and *Varaghoḍā* in Gujarati.

context of *Varayātrā* ('procession of the bridegroom'), they devoted themselves to the worship of Śiva.

19-22. The Mountains beginning with Meru were seated (in their proper places) by Nandin there. The celebration of *Varayātrā* was duly carried out by Himādri as mentioned (before). They returned along with all kinsmen.

Himavān of great renown stationed in his own abode shone very well, due to the great splendour arising from the contact with Śiva. The great Mountain became famous and well-renowned in the three worlds, because Śaṅkara was delighted with him, due to the offering of the daughter.

Blessed indeed are those noble-souled ones at the tip of whose tongues the two-syllabled name (*Śi-va*) is always present. They shall accomplish their purpose and be contented.

Those people who utter the two-syllabled name '*Śi-va*' in their hearts are undoubtedly Rudras in the form of human beings.

23. Lord Śiva is pleased with the slighest offering or gift, even with a leaf.[1] Mahādeva is always pleased even with the (gift of) water.

24. Indeed Sadāśiva becomes pleased with (the gift of) a leaf, a flower or water. Hence Śiva should be regularly adored by all. He is the donor of good luck unto men here.

25. The unborn great lord is one great luminous refulgence. He is greater than the greatest. He is the great Ātman. He has no inter-space, is devoid of aberrations, has no lord (above him), is devoid of all hindrances, free from doubts and devoid of desire.

26. He is unsullied, is of eternal form. Obstacle-less as he is, he has perpetual bliss. He is the eternally liberated one. The Lord of Devas of this nature was adored by those Devas and others. Bhava (Śiva) worthy of being worshipped by the whole universe was eulogized and meditated upon. He was worshipped and contemplated upon. This omniscient lord is the perpetual bestower of everything.

27. Himavān was already very famous on account of all of his good qualities. He was noble-souled and the most excellent one among the Mountains. (After the marriage) he became one worthy of being saluted by the Lord of the universe.

1. Cf. BG, IX.26.

28. Going back to his own abode along with Menā, the Lord of Mountains of virtuous soul, bade farewell to all the Mountains.

29. After they had gone, Himavān, the most excellent one among and the king of Mountains, (lived happily) with his sons, grandsons and great-grandsons by the favour of Mahādeva.

30. Then at Gandhamādana, the great god (Śiva) who had resumed his own form, decided in his mind to indulge in sexual dalliance with Girijā in an isolated place.[1]

31-33. Indeed their mutual sexual contact took place through their great penance. Now that their sexual intercourse was begun, that alone became their penance.

It was a mysteriously wonderful phenomenon not liked (by Devas), because it could be compared to *Pralaya*[2] (ultimate anni-

---

1. The artistic presentation of the love-sport of Śiva and Pārvatī in *Kumārasaṁbhava* VIII stands in sharp contrast with the Purāṇic narration thereof.

2. Mbh, *Śalya*, 44.6-13 records the following stages of Skanda's birth: (1) Falling of Śiva's semen in the fire, (2) Fire-god's pregnancy, (3) Fire-god transfers the foetus to Gaṅgā by *Niyoga*, (4) Gaṅgā aborts it in *Śara*-grass on the mountain, (5) The foetus continues to grow in the grass, (6) Six sonless Kṛttikās claim him as their son, (7) Skanda develops six mouths to suck the milk of the six mothers.

This original outline of the story shows the following developments in the SkP, which are not mentioned in the Mbh, *Śalya*:

(1) The sexual intercourse between Śiva and Pārvatī created *Pralaya*—destruction of the world of mobile and immobile beings (vv 31-33).

(2) Gods depute Agni (the Fire-god) to disrupt the intercourse. Agni secretly enters Śiva's harem and loudly demands alms. Infuriated at this interruption, Śaṅkara rushes to kill Agni. Pārvatī intervenes but gives Śiva's semen in the joined palms of Agni and makes him drink it and curses him to be omnivorous (vv 24-43).

(3) Agni became pregnant and all Devas being recipients of food through the medium of Agni (in sacrifices) received Śiva's semen. All gods became pregnant thereby and had unbearable pain (vv 44-46).

(4) Deputation of Devas with Viṣṇu to request relief from the torturing pain of pregnancy. Śiva relents and asks all Devas except Agni (the main culprit) to vomit the semen. The vomited semen became a mountain of gold (vv 47-64).

(5) Agni requests for relief. Śiva advises him to transmit it to women. Next morning at dawn, wives of seven sages performed bath in the river and feeling cold went to warm themselves near the fire though prohibited by Vasiṣṭha's wife Arundhatī. Agni transfers Śiva's semen to them (vv 65-74).

hilation). As that great sexual dalliance went on, Devas beginning with Brahmā were not very happy in the matter of deciding what should be done and what should not be done. On account of the semen virile (of Śiva), the entire universe consisting of mobile and immobile beings perished.

34. Brahmā and Viṣṇu, the bestower of spiritual (welfare), remembered Agni mentally. On being remembered, Agni hastened towards them.

35. On being deputed by them, Agni saw the beautiful palace of Śiva. In front of him, he saw Nandin of great lustre stationed at the entrance.

36. Agni whose colour resembled saffron became minute (in size) and entered the inner apartment of Śaṁbhu that consisted of many wonderful features.

37. After reaching the front-yard beautified with many mansions and paved with gems and jewels, the Fire-god sat there and said:

38-39. "O mother, from the harem give alms unto me who have only (my) hands as begging bowl." On hearing those words (of Agni) who had only the hands as begging bowl, the girl began to give him alms. Thereupon Śiva desisted from sexual dalliance and got up. He became very furious.

40. Raising his trident, Rudra assumed the terrible form of Bhairava. Śiva was prevented by Girijā from killing him (Agni). The girl (Pārvatī) gave alms to Agni *Jātavedas*[1] ('one who knows all created beings').

---

(6) Their husbands, finding them pregnant from somebody else, drive them out of their houses. Being homeless on the earth, they become Kṛttikās (Pleids) in the sky. But out of shame, they aborted on top of Himālaya Śiva's semen whence it flowed down into Gaṅgā and was surrounded by bamboos. It ultimately developed into a child of six faces on the bank of Gaṅgā (vv 75-80).

The present text of the Mbh is presumed to belong to the 4th cent. A.D. and the SkP to the 10th cent. Such has been the development of this legend during 600 years or so.

1. *Jātavedas*—(1) That from which is formed (got) *Vedas* (wealth).

(2) Mbh, *Sabhā* 31.42 states: That for which Vedas were created:

vedāstvam artham jātā vai
jātavedas tato hyasi|

(3) The third derivation is as suggested in the translation.

41. After taking the alms (the semen of Śiva) in the (palms of his) hand, it was eaten up[1] by Agni in her very presence. Girijā became furious and cursed him.

42. "O mendicant, on account of my curse you will quickly become *Sarvabhakṣa* ('omnivorous'—one who eats everything). You will meet with distress and pain in every respect on account of this *Retas* (semen virile) immediately."

43-44. On being told thus, Agni, the bearer of *Havyas* (offerings in the sacred fire), swallowed the *Retas* of Īśa and came to the place where all the Devas beginning with Brahmā were staying. After arrival he told them everything about the swallowing of *Retas* (semen of Śiva) and other incidents. All the groups of Devas beginning with Indra became pregnant.

45-46. Just as *Havis* (ghee offerings) reaches every god through Agni (so also the semen reached them). By means of the semen issuing out of the mouth of Agni, all the leading Suras became pregnant. They were extremely afflicted with anxiety; they sought refuge in Viṣṇu, the Lord and Master of Devas.

Devas said:

47. You are the saviour of all Devas. You are the lord of the worlds. Hence protection should be accorded, O Lord, kind and compassionate towards those who seek refuge.

48. Afflicted with this semen virile, all of us are about to die. All of us, the heaven-dwellers, are already frightened of Asuras.

49-50. (Afraid of Asuras) we sought refuge in Śaṅkara. We got his marriage celebrated (and thought thus): 'When a son is born to Rudra, all of us will be happy and free from fear in heaven.'

A (new) danger has beset us even as we were steadying ourselves with that thought. How is it possible to remain alive with this (Śiva's) semen.

51. The three aims (in the life) of ordinary persons are well prepared (with the help of fate). But without (favourable) fate, without the support of the Lord, it becomes adverse in character, not otherwise.

1. *bhikṣita* is most probably a misprint for *bhakṣita*.

52. Hence, considering that as the strength (and support) for all embodied beings in the matter of deciding what should be done and what should not be done, all of us think so.

53-55. On hearing that lamentation of Devas, the great Lord, the slayer of the enemies of Devas, spoke these words laughingly: "In view of the gravity of the situation (of the work), let Maheśa the great Lord, be eulogized."

Saying "So be it", all the Devas went to Hara with Viṣṇu as their leader. Brahmā and others and all the sages eulogized Hara:

56-58. "Om, obeisance unto Lord Bharga (Refulgence), to the blue-throated, to the beautiful, to the three-eyed lord, to the lord of three Vedas, to the supporter of the three worlds.

We bow to the Lord of three[1] notes (*Svara*), three *Mātrās*, three Vedas and three forms. Hail to the Trident-bearing Lord (bestowing) the three aims in life, to the *Tridhāma* (having three abodes) and to the *Tripāda* (having three positions). Save us, save us, O Mahādeva, from this semen virile, O lord of the universe."

59. When he was (thus) eulogized by Brahmā, the Bull-bannered Lord appeared there itself for the sake of the accomplishment of the objective of Suras.

60. At that time, the Lord, the sole kinsman of the universe, was seen by the noble-souled excellent Devas. He was worshipped exquisitely well. He was eulogized with various words of expressive nature and approved by the Vedas.

61. Even as the Devas continued eulogizing, Parameśvara said: "Do not be frightened, all of you, now afflicted with this semen virile.

62. Now itself, O Suras, you all should vomit it."

Thinking that it should be so, all those groups of Devas beginning with Indra, O Brāhmaṇas, vomited that semen virile of Śaṅkara.

1. The triads recorded in vv 57-58 are as follows:
(1) The three *Svaras* (accents) are *Udātta*, *Anudātta* and *Svarita*.
(2) *Mātrās* are units of time or foot in Metrics. They are *Hrasva* (short), *Dīrgha* (long) and *Pluta* (lengthened or prolated).
(3) Three Vedas—Ṛk, Sāman and Yajus.
(4) Three forms—Brahmā, Viṣṇu and Śiva.
(5) Three aims of Life—*Dharma*, *Artha* and *Kāma*.
(6) *Tridhāman*—Shining in the three worlds.

63. Abruptly that miraculous semen virile became as lustrous as heated gold and as huge as a mountain.

64. All those groups of Devas beginning with Indra became happy. Excepting Agni all of them became exceedingly delighted.

65. Śaṅkara the benefactor of all the worlds, was addressed (thus) by Agni: "O Mahādeva, O most excellent one among Devas, what should be done by me now?

66. Tell me that now, O Lord, whereby I shall always be happy so that I can continue to carry *Havya* (the oblations in sacrifices) unto Devas."

67-68. Then Śiva said directly even as the Devas were listening: "Let the semen be discharged in some womb." Thereupon Agni laughingly said to Lord Śaṅkara: Your semen is unbearable. How can this semen which blazes like poison, be borne by ordinary persons?"

69. Then Lord Maheśvara said to Agni: "Let the semen be discharged every month in the body of those who are warmed up in the menstruation period.

70. Saying "So be it" and accepting his words, the Fire-god of great lustre, who was shining with great splendour and whose power and influence is very great, sat there in *Brāhmamuhūrta*[1] (before dawn).

71-73. The wives of the sages got up very early in the morning. Those chaste ladies who habitually took early morning baths were afflicted with chillness. They saw the blazing fire and wanted to warm themselves. They were prevented from doing so by Arundhatī. Although they too were prevented from doing so, the Kṛttikās warmed themselves. While they warmed themselves thus, minute particles of the semen virile (of Śiva) entered the pores in their skin at the roots of the hair quickly.

74-76. Agni then got rid of the semen virile and became reposed and tranquil. Then the wives of the sages went to their respective abodes. They were cursed by the sages. They became the constellations Kṛttikās moving about in the sky. At that time all of them became distressed due to their deviation from chastity.

---

1. *Brāhmamuhūrta*: the last half-watch of the night: *paścimārdha-prahara* (*Mitākṣarā*).

They discharged the semen virile on the top of the mountain Himavān.

77-80. Abruptly that semen virile, having the lustre of heated gold, (floated) in Gaṅgā. It was quickly encircled by *Kīcakas* (hollow bamboos).

On seeing the infant with six faces, all the Devas became joyous. They were ultimately told by Garga: "Let it (the child) be (conveniently) taken away. This son of Śaṁbhu, thanks to the grace of Śaṁbhu, shall become eternal and *Sarva* (identical with all)." Kārttikeya of great strength was born on the banks of Gaṅgā. (Kārttikeya,) the son of Gaṅgā sat up after a day and a night had passed. Śākha and Viśākha were exceedingly powerful (?). This Ṣaṇmukha was very powerful.

81. When Ṣaṇmukha ('six-faced' god Skanda) was born of Gaṅgā as the son of Śaṅkara, Girijā immediately experienced that milk was oozing out from her nipples.

82. Looking at Śiva, she said: "O Śaṁbhu, there is great exudation of milk (from my breasts, why is it so?). O Mahādeva, let it be looked into." Though omniscient, Mahādeva spoke to her like an ignorant one.

83. Nārada came there and told them about the birth of the child: "A beautiful son is born to Śiva and Śivā."

84. On hearing those words, O Brāhmaṇas, all the Pramathas became most delighted in their minds. Gandharvas became eager to sing.

85. In view of the birth of a son to the noble-souled Śaṅkara the mountain (Kailāsa) became dazzlingly brilliant and shone with many flags, banners, festoons and sprouts as well as with aerial chariots.

86-87. Then all the groups of Suras, Sages, Siddhas, Cāraṇas, Demons, Gandharvas, Yakṣas, all attended upon by groups of celestial damsels—all these gathered together immediately and along with Śaṅkara they proceeded ahead to see Gāṅgeya (Skanda, 'Gaṅgā's son') stationed on the sand-bank (of Gaṅgā).

88. Then the Lord mounted on his bull along with Girijā and was accompanied by other Suras beginning with Indra.

89-90. Then conchs, *Bherīs* (drums) and many other musical instruments were played. At the very same time, the Gaṇas beginning with Vīrabhadra followed the lord of all. They were excited with sportive spirit and they played different kinds of musical instruments. They played stringed musical instruments of different kinds.

91. Some were engaged in dances. Others were musicians. Those who eulogized and those who were being eulogized sang songs of praise.

92. Those Suras, Siddhas, Yakṣas, Gandharvas, Vidyādharas and Serpents and such others were delighted in their minds in the company of Śiva. They went ahead in order to see the son of Śaṅkara, the bestower of boons.

93. When they looked at Gāṅgeya resembling Śaṅkara, they saw that the three worlds were pervaded by great splendour.

94-96. The infant (boy) enveloped in refulgence was of the lustre of heated gold. His bright face was endowed with glorious magnificence. His beautiful face with a fine nose and eyes twinkling with a smile, was pleasant. He was beautiful in every limb. On seeing the exceedingly miraculous Gāṅgeya of renowned Ātman, the infant (boy) with solar radiance, Pramathas and all the Gaṇas beginning with Vīrabhadra, saluted him.

97-99. They flocked round him on the left and the right and waited upon him. Similarly, Brahmā, Indra surrounded by Suras, sages, Yakṣas and Gandharvas surrounded the boy. They prostrated on the ground like a log of wood. Some bent down their necks (in reverence). Others bowed down their heads honouring him as the immutable lord. In that great festival, different kinds of musical instruments were played. The sages recited the *Śānti* verses on that festival.

100-101. In the meantime Śaṅkara, the Lord of Girijā, reached the place. He quickly dismounted from his bull along with Pārvatī, O sages of holy rites.

Accompanied by Bhavānī and filled with great pleasure, the lord, the sole kinsman of the universe, saw his son. With great affection, the lord of all, having the (bodies of) serpents (as ornaments) became delighted. He was surrounded by Pramathas.

102. With great excitement, Pārvatī embraced Guha. Flooded with great love, she made him suck her breasts that exuded milk.

103. Then the infant-lord was given great ovation and the

Nīrājana (waving of lights) rite was performed by Devas who rejoiced in the company of their wives. The whole of the firmament was pervaded by great shouts of victory.

104. All of them served the infant-lord—the sages with the loud chants of the Vedic passages, the musicians with songs and those who played musical instruments with the same.

105. Giriśa (i.e. Śiva) took on his lap that infant-lord dazzling with great brilliance. The spouse of Bhavānī shone as the most excellent one among those blessed with sons. He was endowed with glory.

106-107. The couple were delighted together. On being sprinkled (with sacred waters) by the sages and being surrounded by excellent Suras, Kumāra (the infant-lord) played in the lap of Śaṅkara. With both hands he caught hold of and pressed Vāsuki that was round the neck (of Śiva).

108-110. After pressing his face, he counted his hands, not in the correct order, saying one, three, ten and eight. Lord Śaṁbhu told Girijā about this laughingly.

Due to the gentle smile (of the infant), Lord Maheśa in the company of Girijā attained the greatest joy. On account of the affection, his speech faltered. The sole lord of the worlds, the sole kinsman of the universe did not say anything.

CHAPTER TWENTYEIGHT

Preparations of Devas and Daityas for War

Lomaśa said:

1. After placing Kumāra in his lap, Rudra, the valorous Bharga, the lord of the universe, said to Devas including Indra:

2. "What is to be done by my son, O Devas? Let it be stated."

Then all of them together said to Lord Paśupati:

3. "A threat has come from Tāraka to all the worlds, O

Lord. You are the saviour. You are the master of the worlds. Hence let protection be accorded.

4. Today itself, O Lord, Tāraka shall be killed by Kumāra Kārttikeya. Hence we shall go today itself in our endeavour to kill Tāraka."

5-9. Thinking that it should be so, Suras started at once keeping Kārttikeya, the son of Śaṅkara, at the head. All of them, with Brahmā and Viṣṇu as leaders, had soon gathered there.

On hearing about the preparation of Devas, Tāraka, the mighty one, marched against Suras to fight them with a great army. The great army of Tāraka that had come (there) was seen by Devas.

Then an ethereal voice said consoling them: "All of you have started after keeping the son of Śaṅkara at the head. You will become victorious after defeating Daityas in the battle."

10. On hearing the ethereal voice, all the Devas became enthusiastic. Keeping the infant-lord (Kumāra) at the head, they got rid of all their fears.

11. When all the Suras who were desirous of fighting had arrived, the invincible daughter of Mṛtyu came there to woo Kumāra.

12. Formerly she had been urged by Brahmā to resort to great penance (to enable herself to attain) Kumāra by means of that great penance. That beautiful lady named Senā,[1] the daughter of Mṛtyu, came there.

13. On seeing her, all of them said to Lord Paśupati: "A very beautiful lady has come for this Kumāra."

14. At the instance of Brahmā she was wooed by Kumāra. Then Kumāra, the son of Śaṅkara, became *Senāpati* ('Lord of Senā', also 'commander-in-chief of the army').

15. Then conchs and drums (such as) *Bherī*, *Paṭaha*, *Ānaka*, *Gomukha* and *Dundubhi* as well as *Mṛdaṅgas* of loud sound were sounded.

16. The entire firmament was filled with that loud sound.

---

1. Mbh does not know 'Senā' as the daughter of Mṛtyu—both of male and female Mṛtyu. BhP. V mentions one 'Sena' but he is a prince—a male. Skanda is called *Senā-pati* which means 'commander of the army' (of Devas).

At that time, Gaurī, Gaṅgā and Mothers and Kṛttikās told one another, "This is my son. This is my son."

17-18. Thus all of them—Mothers and others—who were engaged in arguments were forbidden by Nārada: "Do not commit any foolishness. He is born of Pārvatī and Śaṅkara for the sake of accomplishing the task of Devas."

Then all the Kṛttikās along with the Mothers became silent.

19-21. Then all the wives of the sages, the Kṛttikās, were told by Guha: "All of you resort to the constellations and stay there forever."[1] So the groups of mothers also were established in the firmament by the lord. Accepting the daughter of Mṛtyu hurriedly, Kārttikeya, the infant-lord, the son of Śaṅkara, said to Indra: "Go back to heaven along with Suras."

22-23. Kumāra was told by Indra: "Indeed all of us have been harassed by Tāraka. We have been driven out of heaven and we have dispersed to all the ten directions. Now what are you asking of us who have been ousted from our positions, O magnanimous one?"

On being told thus by the *Vajra*-bearing Lord (Indra), the son of Śaṅkara laughed and said to Indra: "Do not be afraid." Thus he granted him freedom from fear.

24. Even as the noble-souled son of Śaṅkara was saying thus, Rudra went back to Kailāsa along with Pārvatī and Pramathas.

25. The great Daitya, surrounded by the armies of Daityas came (there). Great war drums were played. They were as terrifically loud as (the sounds at the time of) the great Deluge.

26-28. There were intensely harsh sounds of martial musical instruments. Wonderful drums such as *Diṇḍimas* and *Gomukhas* were sounded. There were many trumpets and large and harsh-sounding military drums like *Kāhalas* and *Kharaśṛṅgas*.

Different kinds of musical instruments were played when Daityas gathered there. The heroes shouted and roared along with Tāraka. Nārada spoke these words to Tāraka, a thorn unto Devas:

---

1. The credit of transforming the wives of six sages—the 'mothers'—into the constellation Kṛttikā (Pleiades) is given to Skanda.

Nārada said:

29. O excellent one among Asuras, effort has already been made by Devas for slaying you. There is no doubt about it. What is said by me cannot be otherwise.

30. This son of Śarva has been intended for you. After knowing this, O mighty one, try (to save yourself) with great concentration.

31-35. On hearing the words of Nārada, the intelligent Tāraka laughingly spoke these words:

"Go to Purandara, O great sage, and report my words immediately and truthfully: 'You wish to fight with me, keeping (the infant) Kumāra at the head; you are resorting to a foolish step if you wish to do so. It cannot be otherwise. Depending upon a man named Mucukunda, you stayed in Amarāvatī on the strength of his glory and not otherwise. You are now standing before me relying on the power of Kumāra. I will kill you, O dull-witted one, along with the Guardians of the Quarters.' Tell him this, O celestial sage. Do not tell Devendra anything else."

36. Thinking that it should be so, the holy sage Nārada went to Suras whose leader was Śakra. The intelligent (sage) repeated to them all that was uttered by the leader of Asuras along with derisive laughter.

Nārada said:

37. O Devas, let my words be heard. They should not be misunderstood. What has been said by Tāraka along with his followers may be heard.

Tāraka said:

38-39. I will kill you, O stupid one; my speech cannot be otherwise. You who had been honoured by the Guardians of the Quarters, have resorted to Mucukunda. I would rather not fight with you, a coward who has resorted to a man despite (your) being a Deva.

40. On hearing his words all the Devas including Vāsava said to Nārada, the excellent sage, referring to Kumāra:

41-43. "Indeed, O celestial sage, you know the relative

strength and weakness of Kumāra. How is it that his (Tāraka's) words were uttered before me as if you had become ignorant?"

Nārada laughed and spoke these words in his presence: "I too laughed satirically and spoke (befitting) words to Tāraka. O immortal Suras, understand ye all that Kumāra will be victorious. What I say will (surely) take place. There is no doubt about it."

44. On hearing the words of Nārada, all the Devas became joyous. They jointly rose up desirous of fighting with Tāraka.

45. Placing Kumāra on an elephant Devendra proceeded ahead accompanied by the big army of Suras and surrounded by the Guardians of Quarters.

46. Then *Dundubhis* were sounded. Many *Bherīs* and musical instruments were played. Lutes, flutes and *Mṛdaṅgas* were played. There were the vocal songs of Gandharvas.

47. After giving the elephant to Mahendra, Kumāra rode in an (aerial) chariot. It was studded with many gems and jewels. It was equipped with many wonderful features. It was extremely spacious and equipped with various marvels.

48. Getting into the aerial chariot that son of Śaṅkara of great fame shone well. He was accompanied by all the Gaṇas. He was endowed with great glory and radiance. The great lord was fanned with chowries of great lustre.

49. The umbrella (offered by) Varuṇa was held above the head of Kumāra by Candra (Moon). It had great refulgence on account of jewels. It was fitted with many precious gems and stones. It was made highly splendid by means of the rays of the Moon.

50. Then all the Devas assembled together with Indra at their head. They were accompanied by their respective armies. All those mighty ones were desirous of fighting.

51-53. Yama came with his followers. The Wind-god came with Maruts; Varuṇa with *Pāthas* (waters) (or *Yādas*—aquatic animals); Kubera with Guhyakas; Īśvara with Pramathas; Nairṛta with *Vyādhis* (ailments). Thus all the eight Guardians of the Quarters joined together desirous of fighting. In order to kill Tāraka they had as their leader Senāpati, the son of Śaṅkara, the most excellent one among the knowers of the Ātman worthy of being saluted by the entire universe.

Thus desirous of fighting, they descended to the earth. They stood within the doab in the middle of Gaṅgā and Yamunā.

54. (Some of) the dependents of Tāraka came from Pātāla, with all types of subsidiary armies. They moved about (here and there) desirous of killing Suras in battle.

55-56. Tāraka who shone in an aerial chariot came (there). (The Daitya) of great splendour had an umbrella held over his head. Being fanned with chowries, the king of Daityas shone well.

57. Thus Devas and Daityas stood in the region between Gaṅgā and Yamunā.[1] They had separate arrays of soldiers. They were accompanied by great armies.

58-60. They kept the elephants on one side, different kinds of horses (on another side). Chariots of various kinds set with many gems and precious stones stood (on another side). There were many foot-soldiers who were splendidly equipped with javelins, tridents, axes, swords, mallets, iron clubs, steel-tipped arrows, nooses and maces. The two armies of Suras and Daityas shone (while they faced) one another. They were desirous of killing one another. They were being eulogized by their kinsmen.

CHAPTER TWENTYNINE

The Battle Between Suras and Tāraka

Lomaśa said:

1. The two armies, that of Suras and that of Daityas, had all the four divisions of an army. They had many wonderful (weapons and equipments). They roared at each other like clouds at the advent of the rainy season. They shone well.

2. In the meantime, Devas and Asuras began to dance and jump with one another. All of them of great strength fought one another.

3. The fight between Daityas and Devas was very tumultuous and exciting. Within a moment the whole (battlefield)

1. The battle between Tāraka and Kumāra and their armies took place in Antarvedī or the *Doab* between Gaṅgā and Yamunā. But the exact location is not recorded.

became marked (coloured) with mutilated trunks and severed heads.

4. Hundreds and thousands fell on the ground. The arms of some were cut off by terrible blows of swords.

5-6. Indeed Mucukunda was very powerful. He was (famous) in the three worlds (as a man) of unmeasured courage and valour. Tāraka was then hit in the chest with all might with a sword by the intelligent Mucukunda. Enduring that blow, Tāraka laughingly spoke these words:

7. "O dull-witted fellow, what is it that has been achieved by you through your strength? I do not wish to fight with you. It is shameful to fight with a human being."

8-9. On hearing the words of Tāraka, Mucukunda spoke: "O chief Daitya, you have been (well-nigh) killed on being struck by me. You do not deserve to be otherwise. Experiencing the blow of my sword, you will never stand in front of me. I am going to kill you. See my valour, O king of Daityas; be steady."

10-11. After saying thus, when the heroic Mucukunda of great strength struck with his sword, he was hit with a javelin. The son of Māndhātā fell down in the battlefield. Though fallen, the slayer of inimical warriors got up instantaneously.

12. Getting ready to kill Tāraka, the lord of Daityas then, the exceedingly powerful son of Māndhātṛ, the sole conqueror of the world, seized a bow and took a *Brahmāstra* (i.e. the miraculous missile with Brahmā as its presiding deity).

13. That warrior of great force and speed who became very furious and whose eyes were full-blown, got ready to fight with Tāraka. At that time Nārada, the son of Brahmā, spoke thus to Mucukunda, the human warrior:

14. "Tāraka cannot be killed by a human being. Hence do not discharge this great missile."

15. On hearing the words of Nārada, the celestial sage, Mucukunda asked: "Who will then be his slayer?"

16-17. Then Nārada of divine vision and great splendour said: "Kumāra will kill him. This Kumāra is the son of Śiva. Hence all of you should stand (ready). Fight jointly. Restrain yourself, O Mucukunda of great intellect. Stand ready."

18. On hearing these fascinating and auspicious words uttered by that (sage) of great refulgence, all the Suras became com-

pletely calm and quiet along with that most excellent one among human beings.

19. Then *Dundubhis* were sounded. Conchs were blown. Different musical instruments were played by both Suras and Asuras.

20-21. Asuras who had prepared (for a fight) with Devas roared. Vīrabhadra who was born of the anger of Śiva, became exceedingly furious. Accompanied by many Gaṇas, he approached Tāraka of great strength, after making Mucukunda and Suras stand behind him.

22-23. Then all the Pramathas kept Kumāra at the head and fought in the battle. There the Gaṇas beginning with Vīrabhadra killed the enemies with tridents, swords, daggers, nooses, axes and iron clubs. In that mutual clash of Suras and Asuras, all of them struck and killed one another.

24. Struck hard by Vīrabhadra with his trident, Tāraka fell down there at once. He was in a swoon for a short while.

25. Within a *Muhūrta* (=24 minutes) Tāraka, the great Daitya, regained consciousness and got up. He struck (back) Vīrabhadra with great force.

26. Vīrabhadra, the powerful follower of Śiva, whose splendour was great, attacked Tāraka who had a javelin, with a terrible trident.

27. Fighting thus, they struck at each other. A tumultuous duel took place between those two noble souls.

28-30. Then Suras became mere spectators in that war. The three worlds were filled with the loud sounds of *Bherīs*, *Mṛdaṅgas*, *Paṭahas*, *Ānakas*, *Gomukhas* and *Ḍamarus*. By means of that loud sound, those two combatants of great strength shone splendidly. They were exceedingly excited and shattered completely on account of blows. Enraged furiously with each other, they resembled Budha (Mercury) and Aṅgāraka (Mars).

31-32. Nārada then revealed to Vīrabhadra the details about his (Tāraka's) death. Vīrabhadra then did not like those words that Nārada said about the death of Tāraka. Just as Rudra so also Vīrabhadra was exceedingly powerful.

33. Fighting thus they struck at each other. They vied with each other in roaring like two lions.

34. While those two were thus fighting on the ground, Vīra-

bhadra was prevented by means of various words by Nārada, the noble-souled (sage), the most excellent one among those who had perfect knowledge.

35. On hearing those words coming out of Nārada's mouth, Vīrabhadra who had become very furious replied to Nārada:

36-38. "I will kill Tāraka today. See my valour. Those heroes who make the master come down to the battle-ground are sinners and extremely unrighteous. Those who go to the battlefield but begin to ponder over (what they should do) should be known as cowards. They should never be talked to. O celestial sage, you do not know the reaction of (true) warriors. Those who keep the god of Death behind them, those who are devoid of any pain or distress in the battlefield, and those whose bodies are cut and pierced by weapons and missiles are undoubtedly praiseworthy."

39-40. After saying thus, Vīrabhadra of great power, spoke to Devas: "May Devas with Indra as their leader listen to my words. I will undoubtedly make the earth rid of Tāraka today."

41. He then took a trident and fought with Tāraka along with many (followers) who rode on bulls and held excellent tridents.

42. Those Gaṇas had matted hair; they had bull for their emblem. They struck with force. They kept Vīrabhadra at their head. They were as valorous as Vīrabhadra.

43. All of them wielded tridents. All of them had serpents as ornaments for their limbs. All of them were adorned with twisted and matted locks of hair. They had the crescent moon as their crest jewel.

44-45. They were blue-throated. They had ten arms, five faces and three eyes. They had the royal insignia of umbrellas and chowries. All of them had fiercely powerful arms. With Vīrabhadra at their head (the Gaṇas), with the valorous exploit of Hara, fought with Daityas who were the dependents of Tāraka for their subsistence.

46. Those Asuras were defeated again and again by the Gaṇas. They were forced to turn their faces (to retreat). Then an exceedingly frightful battle ensued between them and the excellent Daityas.

47. Though Daityas were experts in the use of great missiles,

the Gaṇas could not brook them. The Gaṇas became victorious. Defeated by the Gaṇas and therefore distressed very much, they (Asuras) intimated their discomfiture to Tāraka.

48. Tāraka who was desirous of fighting, was noble-souled and the most excellent one among Daityas, entered the army after keeping the bow well-bent, in the same way as a fish enters the ocean.

49. Indeed Vīrabhadra of great power fought (with Daityas) in the company of the Gaṇas.

The excellent Daitya of great strength, who became very furious, pounded and shattered all the Suras, the chief of whom was Indra, and the Gaṇas, Yakṣas, Piśācas and Guhyakas.

50. Then a tumultuous, exciting battle ensued between Devas and Dānavas, wherein Devas, Dānavas and Yakṣas took part collectively.

51. Roaring bulls killed the horses along with the horsemen. They struck at the chariots and killed the charioteers. They killed the elephants along with the elephant drivers.

52. All the Asuras were shattered and pierced (by the Gaṇas) who were driving in the chariots or riding on the bulls.

53-54. Many were completely destroyed. Some who were struck, fell down on the ground. Some entered Rasātala. Many fled (from the battlefield). Some of them sought refuge with the followers and servants of Rudras. Thus seeing his army destroyed and scattered, Tāraka, the protector of Asuras, became infuriated and he went ahead in order to kill the groups of Devas.

55. Tāraka, the king of Daityas, assumed ten thousand arms. He suddenly mounted a lion and killed them (i.e. the Gaṇas) in battle.

56. By the lion that had been equipped with an armour, some bulls were torn asunder. Similarly many Gaṇas were killed by Tāraka himself.

57. This was done by the noble-souled Tāraka then. The great Tāraka could not be tackled by all the Devas.

58-59. That Daitya of great and powerful arms became the destroyer of all the three worlds. The Daitya followers of Tāraka became superior in strength and invincible. They rode on great vehicles. They were terrific and fully equipped with armour. They were terrible strikers. The Gaṇas were swallowed by those Daityas and the bulls were killed by the lions.

60. Thus those Gaṇas were being killed in the battlefield. Viṣṇu laughed and said to Kumāra, the favourite (son) of Śiva:

Viṣṇu said:

61. Excepting you, O son of Kṛttikās, there is no one else who can kill this sinner. Hence, O mighty one, my suggestions should be carried out by you.

62. O Son of Śiva, you are born for slaying Tāraka. Hence slaying of Tāraka should be performed by you.

63. On hearing it, the great lord, the son of Pārvatī became angry. He laughingly said these proper words to Viṣṇu:

64-65. "The wonderful ways of fighting of the noble-souled (warriors) are being observed carefully by me. O Viṣṇu, I am not well-versed in deliberating upon what should be done and what should not be done. I do not at all know who are those who belong to us and who are our enemies. I do not know even why they are fighting and killing each other."

66. On hearing the words of Kumāra, Nārada spoke these words:

Nārada said:

67. You are Kumāra, O mighty-armed one, born of a part of Śaṅkara. You are the master and saviour of all the worlds. You are the ultimate goal of Devas.

68. O heroic one, a very severe penance was performed by Tāraka formerly, whereby Devas have been defeated and heaven conquered.

69. He attained invincibility by means of severe penance. Indra and the Guardians of the Quarters have been defeated by him.

70-71. All the three worlds have been conquered by this vicious-souled one himself. Hence Tāraka, the sinful person, should be killed by you. The welfare of everyone should be caused by you, the lord.

On hearing the words of Nārada, Kumāra, the great lord, descended from his aerial chariot and began to walk on foot.

72-74. The son of Śiva in the form of an infant-boy, began to run about on foot. He took up in his hand a javelin of great potentiality, endowed with much refulgence like a great comet.

On seeing (the Infant-Lord) who was advancing towards him, who was very fierce, whose form was unmanifest and who was the most excellent one among mighty persons, the Daitya spoke:

"This Kumāra (the Infant-Leader) belonging to the excellent Suras is the destroyer of the enemies (of the excellent Suras). I shall be the sole warrior fighting with him. I shall kill all heroic Gaṇas, the great Īśvaras and the Guardians of the Quarters immediately."

75. After saying this that ever mighty one proceeded towards Kumāra in order to fight. That Tāraka seized a javelin of exceedingly wonderful nature and spoke these words:

Tāraka said:

76. How and why is an infant placed in front of me by you all? O ye Devas, you are all shameless ones whose king happens to be Purandara.

77-80. Whatever has been done by him is all known (to me). Sleeping ones were bound and tortured; beings within the womb have been aborted and caused to fall down. Bahurūpa, the Asura, was killed by the son of Kaśyapa. Namuci, a great hero, was killed. Vṛtra was killed too.

This Devendra, the slayer of Bala, is desirous of killing Kumāra. This Kumāra, O Devas, shall undoubtedly be killed by me to-day.

Formerly, O Vīrabhadra, many Brāhmaṇas have been killed by you in the course of Dakṣa's *Yajña*. I shall show you today the fruit of that action, O highly intelligent one, in the course of the battle, O you expert in battle."

81-82. After saying thus that noble-souled lord of Daityas, the sole and excellent hero, took up his *Śakti* of great and wonderful qualities. That Tāraka is the most excellent one among those conversant with fighting.

Thus the son of Diti was attacked by the greatest Puruṣa (Lord). He was surrounded by leading Asuras. That powerful Tāraka who usually came out victorious in battles resolved to fight and kill (the Lord).

CHAPTER THIRTY

Tāraka Is Slain

Lomaśa said:

1. As the demon Tāraka came there leaping and bouncing, boasting and swaggering, Indra, the most excellent among the intelligent ones, hit him with great force with his *Vajra* (thunderbolt).

2. Due to that blow of *Vajra*, Tāraka was made alarmed and afflicted. Although he fell down, he got up and struck his (Indra's) elephant with his javelin.

3. He made Purandara who was on his elephant, fall down on the ground. When Purandara fell down, there was a great cry of distress.

4-5. Hear what was done by Tāraka there itself, O Lord. He stamped his foot on Indra who had fallen and snatched the *Vajra* from his hand. Looking at Indra who had been struck, he struck him with *Vajra* with great force.

6. Vīrabhadra raised his trident. That infuriated lord of great strength wanted to protect Purandara. With his trident of great lustre, he struck Tāraka, the Daitya.

7. On being struck by the trident, Tāraka fell on the ground. Although he fell down, Tāraka of great splendour rose up again (to his feet).

8. With his great javelin, he struck Vīrabhadra on his chest. Vīrabhadra fell down due to the blow from his javelin.

9. Devas along with the Gaṇas, Gandharvas, Serpents and Rākṣasas lamented again and again with a great cry of distress.

10. The exceedingly powerful Vīrabhadra, the slayer of enemies, suddenly got up. He lifted up his trident whose lustre was

like that of lightning. It (i.e. the trident) shone continuously and brilliantly with its radiance. It illuminated the canopy of the cardinal points with its refulgence and had the splendour of the discs of the Sun and the Moon, the fire and the galaxy of stars.

11-13. When (the lord) of great strength was about to kill him with his trident, he was prevented by Kumāra (saying), "O highly intelligent one, do not kill him."

Kārttikeya of great strength and lustre roared. Then he was greeted by "*Jaya*" ('Be victorious') by the living beings stationed in the sky. The hero then attempted to kill Tāraka with his great javelin.

14. The fight between Tāraka and Kumāra there became unbearable. It was extremely terrible and it caused fear (in the minds) of all living beings.

15. With *Śaktis* (javelins) in their hands, they fought each other. As they took the risk (and fought furiously) the hands of both of them became pierced by the *Śaktis*.

16-17. Like two lions of great strength, they dodged each other. They (resisted and) struck each other's *Śakti* (with a clang). The two great warriors continued the excellent fight following the tactics known as *Vaitālikī Gati* ('the movement of a conjurer?'), the *Khecarī Gati* ('the movement of a sky-walker') and the *Pārvata Mata* ('opinion of Parvata, mountain or a Gandharva of that name').

18-20. Taking their respective advantageous position, those two warriors of great strength and valour, who were experts in fighting, struck each other with the edges of their *Śaktis* in the course of the battle. They hit, cut and pierced, the head, the neck, the arms, the knees, the hips, the chest and the back. Thus the warriors of great strength desired to kill each other and continued to fight.

All the Devas, Gandharvas and Guhyakas became mere spectators.

21-22. They said to one another: "Who will win in this fight?" At that time an ethereal voice said consoling them: "O Suras, indeed this Kumāra will kill Tāraka today. O Suras, do not be anxious. All of you stay happily in heaven."

23-24. On hearing that voice uttered in the sky at that time, Kumāraka who was surrounded by Pramathas became desirous of killing Tāraka, the lord of Daityas of fierce form. Kumāra of great strength and superior power struck Tāraka, the excellent Asura, between the nipples with his *Śakti.*

25. Without minding that blow, Tāraka, the leading Daitya, who became furious, struck Kumāra also with his *Śakti.*

26. On account of that blow from the *Śakti*, the son of Śaṅkara became unconscious. Within a short while he regained consciousness and was eulogized by the great sages.

27. Just as a haughty and excited lion becomes desirous of striking (elephants), so also the valorous Kumāra struck Tāraka, the Daitya.

28. Thus Kumāra and Tāraka fought with each other. They were excessively agitated and they were engaged in a duel with *Śaktis.*

29-30. With a desire to defeat each other, they exerted themselves to a very great extent. While they engaged themselves in fighting each other with great force, they had wonderful (facial) expressions. They struck each other with the keen edges and sharp points of their *Śaktis*, wielding them dexterously. All Gandharvas, Devas and Kinnaras remained (as mere) onlookers.

31. They became exceedingly surprised. They did not say anything. (Even) the wind did not blow. The Sun became devoid of lustre.

32-35. The following Mountains came there to meet Kumāra: Himālaya, Meru, Śvetakūṭa, Dardura, Malaya, Mahāśaila, Maināka, Vindhya Mountain, the great Mountain Lokāloka, Mānasottara Mountain, Kailāsa, Mandara, Mālya(vān), Gandhamādana, Udayādri, Mahendra, the great Mountain Astagiri—these and many other Mountains of great lustre came there to meet Kumāra. They were prompted by sincere love.

36. On seeing that the Mountains were frightened, the son of Girijā and Śaṅkara spoke to them enlightening them:

Kumāra said:

37. O highly fortunate ones, do not be afflicted and distressed. O Mountains, do not be worried. Even as all of you remain watching, I will kill the greatest sinner.

38. After thus consoling those Mountains accompanied by

the groups of Devas and mentally bowing down to Śaṁbhu, the intelligent Infant-Lord, fond of Hari, bowed down to his mother.

39. Thereafter Kārttikeya cut off the head of his enemy by means of his *Śakti*. That head of Tāraka fell down on the ground immediately. Thus Kārttikeya, the great lord, gained victory.

40-41. The groups of Devas, sages, Guhyakas, birds, Kinnaras, Cāraṇas, serpents and the groups of celestial damsels saw him with great delight. They eulogized Kumāra. Vidyādharīs danced and the musicians sang.

42-44. On seeing him victorious thus, all of them became filled with joy. Girijā came there with great delight and placed her son in her lap. Embracing him closely, she became very glad. Placing Kumāra endowed with the splendour of the sun in her lap, the slender-bodied Pārvatī of charming eyes fondled him. Śaṁbhu along with Pārvatī was honoured by the sages.

45. Seated in a noble seat, the chaste lady of measured speech, shone splendidly on being eulogized by the ascetics, Siddhas, Cāraṇas and serpents.

46. The *Nīrājana* rite was performed by Devas then to Pārvatī accompanied by Śaṁbhu and Kumāra. The chaste lady shone splendidly.

47. Himālaya came then surrounded by his sons as well as other Mountains beginning with Meru, by whom he was eulogized much.

48. Then all the groups of Devas beginning with Indra along with the sages, made a great shower of flowers on Kumāra of unmeasured splendour. Keeping him in front and waving the lights ceremoniously for him, they shone well.

49. With the sound of songs and musical instruments as well as repeated chantings of different kinds of Vedic *Mantras*, he was well eulogized by those who were experts among the knowers of the Vedas.

50. This narrative named *Kumāravijaya* is very wonderful. It dispels all sins. It is divine. It yields all desired things unto men.

51. Those who glorify this exalted story of the greatness of Kumāra and his valorous exploits, become pure souls equipped with unmeasured good luck. They will assume infinite forms

without old age or death. This story yields pleasure to men. Whatever is desired in the mind will be achieved.

52. He who recites or listens to the story of the noble-souled Kumāra named *Tāraka(-vadha)* is released from all sins.

CHAPTER THIRTYONE

The Greatness of Śivaliṅga[1]

Śaunaka said:

1. After killing Tāraka in the battle, O Brāhmaṇas, what great deed was done by the noble-souled Kumāra? It behoves you to describe everything.

2-3. Kumāra indeed is another Śaṁbhu (i.e. Lord Śiva) by whom everything is pervaded. Śaṁbhu bestows the greatest position on being propitiated by penance (but) Kumāra always yields immediate benefit unto men on being visited (i.e. through his vision).

Indeed those who have committed great sins, those who are not religious at all, even the Cāṇḍālas (who cook dog's meat), become rid of their sins by seeing (Lord Kārttikeya). There is no doubt about this.

4. On hearing the words of Śaunaka, the exceedingly intelligent disciple of Vyāsa recounted the story of the noble-minded Kumāra.

Lomaśa said:

5. In the battle Kumāra killed Tāraka who could not be vanquished or killed by Devas, O excellent Brāhmaṇas. He gained victory.

6. The greatness of Kumāra is narrated in all sacred texts, in the Vedas, the good Āgamas and the Purāṇas.

1. Though the chapter is named so, it describes the meritoriousness of the vision of Kumāra.

7. So also in the Upaniṣads and the two systems of Mīmāṁsā. Kumāra of such a nature, O Brāhmaṇas, cannot be (adequately) described.

8-9. By mere sight, he sanctifies the entire universe.

The king of Manes (i.e. Yama) heard about the saviour of this world. Keeping Brahmā, Viṣṇu and Vāsava at the head, he hurriedly came to Śaṅkara, the benefactor of all the worlds. The Lord of the Southern Quarter eulogized (Śaṅkara) with great self-restraint and mental purity:

10-11. "Obeisance to Lord Bharga (the refulgent god), obeisance to the lord of Devas, to Mṛtyuñjaya ('conqueror of Death'), to Rudra, to Īśāna ('controller of the world'), to Kapardin ('one with matted hair'). Obeisance to the blue-throated (Nīlakaṇṭha), Śarva ('the destroyer of all'), to the lord having a form with sky as a limb. Obeisance to Kāla, the lord of Kāla; obeisance to the lord in the form of Kāla."

12. On being eulogized by Yama, the lord Īśvara said: "Why have you come? Speak everything to us."

Yama said:

13. May my words be heard, O Lord of Devas, a great expert in the use of words. Only with a great penance, O Śaṅkara, you are (propitiated and) satisfied.

14. Brahmā, the grandfather of the worlds, becomes gratified by great holy rites. There is no doubt about it that he is the lord (i.e. and bestower) of boons always.

15. So also Lord Viṣṇu who can be comprehended only through the Vedas and who is the eternal Lord, is delighted by many *Yajñas*, fasts and other holy rites.

16. He grants *Kevalabhāva* ('salvation') whereby one is liberated. All men (conform to) my opinion. My words cannot be otherwise.

17. When he is pleased, he grants all worldly pleasures and the riches of heaven etc. On being bowed down and not otherwise, the Sun-god grants health.

18. O Śambhu, the great god Gaṇeśa, if we offer *Arghya*, *Pādya* etc. and sandal paste and repeat the *Mantras* duly, makes our task free from obstacles.

19. So also all the other Guardians of the Quarters bestow

benefits in accordance with their capacity. O Śaṅkara, they are pleased with *Yajñas*, study of the Vedas, charitable gifts etc.

20. This has caused a very great surprise to all the living beings here that the gateway to heaven has been opened wide.

21. By the vision of Kumāra, O Mahādeva, even all the sinners have become heaven-dwellers. There is no doubt about it.

22-27. What should be done by me in the matter of deciding what should be done and what should not be done? (Hitherto) only those persons of meritorious deeds, such as those who are habituated to speak the truth, the quiescent ones, liberal donors, free and independent ones, those who have conquered their sense organs, non-covetous ones, those who are devoid of lust and base attachments, the performers of *Yajñas*, those who abide by righteous deeds and those who have mastered the Vedas and the Vedāṅgas, attained heaven.

O Śaṁbhu, the goal attained by these meritorious persons, is now attained by base men and Cāṇḍālas by the mere vision of Kumāra of wonderfully miraculous activities. O Lord of Devas, by seeing the son of Śiva in the month of Kārttika on the day of Kṛttikā constellation, people attain the good goal along with crores of the members of their family, avoiding my region. By seeing Kumāra, even Cāṇḍālas attain good position immediately. What shall I do?

28. On hearing the words of Yama, Śaṅkara, spoke these words:

Śaṅkara said:

29. There are good emotions in the minds of the people of meritorious deeds whose sins have come to an end, O Dharma.

30. There is a great desire in them to go to a good holy spot or to visit good people. This desire is caused by previous *Karmas*.

31. It is only at the end of many births and rebirths that a feeling of devotion to me is generated in the minds of living beings. O Yama, it is the result of many repeated experiences in the course of many births with all feelings.

32. Hence all those in whom good feelings of devotion arise are meritorious ones. What has been the outcome of the repeated experiences of various births need not cause surprise.

33. Women, children, Sūdras, those who cook dog's flesh (Cāṇḍālas) and base-born fellows who are born among sinners or stay with them become pure persons, O Dharma, due to the impressions of the previous births.

34-36. They attain white mind (i.e. purity of mind) and through it they derive knowledge in all matters. Due to the previous actions and the working of fate, all become Suras and the Guardians of Quarters beginning with Indra. Those groups of *Bhūtas* (beings or goblins), these sages and these deities are born in that manner. Even in the case of Kumāra, you need not have any surprise. In connection with the seeing of Kumāra, O Dharmarāja, know from me the following things.

37. Words accompanied by action yield fruits to everyone. Pilgrimage to all the holy spots, *Yajñas,* and different kinds of charitable gifts—all these should be performed for the sake of the purity of mind. There is no doubt about it.

38. The Ātman is purified through the mind; (one must purify and redeem) the Ātman through the Ātman. I am the (immanent) Soul established in all living beings.

39. I am stationed in the Ātman of all mobile and immobile beings perpetually. I am in yogic communion with them mentally, without anything in between. I am speaking the truth unto you.

40. I am beyond all *Dvandvas* (i.e. mutually opposed pairs such as pleasure, pain etc.). I am devoid of doubtful alternatives. I am abiding directly in myself. I am eternal. I am in yogic communion perpetually. I am devoid of desire. I am immutable. I am excluded from the controversies of the different *Kalpas.* I am infinite but can be comprehended by enlightenment.

41. All living beings are seen pursuing worldly existence because they have forgotten their Ātman which is single and characterized by enlightenment.

42. I, Brahmā and Viṣṇu, we three are the causes of *Guṇas.* We are the causes of creation, sustenance and annihilation. It cannot be otherwise.

43-46. We are all caused by the *Karma* enveloped by *Ahaṁkāra* ('Egotism'). You people, all the Devas, human beings, the birds etc., the beasts etc. and many others have separate existence because you all possess these *Guṇas*. You are scattered in the ocean of worldly existence. You are fallen in a mirage and you are fascinated and subdued by *Māyā*.[1] We, all the Devas, profess to be learned, scholarly and wise. We are all rogues engaged in false arguments. We blame and defame each other.

47. *Traiguṇas* (i.e. those who come under the control of the three *Guṇas*) are immersed in the ocean of worldly existence. They are not aware of the reality. They are persons with deep attachment to worldly pleasures. They possess lust, anger, fear, hatred, pride and rivalry.

48-49. Not conversant with reality, they blame and defame one another. They are extroverts and do not see within themselves. Hence one should understand all these as unreal, being differentiated by *Guṇas*. They should see the sole ultimate reality in that object which is beyond the *Guṇas*.

50. Hear that it is the greatest abode, wherein difference transforms itself into identity, attachment into absence of attachment and anger into freedom from anger.

51. Sound does not illuminate it because it is *Kṛtaka* (a 'product', that which is caused) like a *Ghaṭa* (pot). Indeed, O Dharma, sound is evolved (created) because it is directed towards *Pravṛtti* (action).

52. The place wherein natural opposite pairs (*dvandvas*) such as *Pravṛtti* and *Nivṛtti* (i.e. manifestation and disappearance or activity and inactivity) merge, is considered eternal.

53. It has nothing intervening in between. It is devoid of *Guṇas*. It is *Jñapti* (i.e. pure knowledge) alone. It is unsullied. It is free from aberrations. It is devoid of desires. It is pure existence. It is to be understood only through knowledge. It is self-established, self-luminous, refulgent and comprehensible through enlightenment.

54. Those who are endowed with perfect knowledge speak of this as *Jñāna* ('knowledge'). They observe it in the form of their

1. The *Māyāvāda* of Śaṅkara seems to be well-established at the time of this Purāṇa showing the latter's post-Śaṅkara date. The philosophical exposition in vv 46-63 and later in vv 68-77 contains an exposition of Śaṅkara's Advaita doctrine.

own self in everyone. After understanding it as something beyond all and comprehensible only through perfect knowledge, they establish themselves in their own self and impartially.

55. They go beyond the worldly existence which has no beginning, which is caused by *Māyā* and which cannot be deliberated on because of *Māyā*. O king of the dead ones, after abandoning *Māyā* they attain the state of freedom from doubts. They are rid of the sense of *my-ness* and are devoid of attachment.

56. The worldly existence has (unreal) fictitiousness or fancy (*Kalpanā*) as its root. Indeed *Kalpanā* (fictitiousness) is comparable to untruth. Those by whom *Kalpanā* is eschewed attain the ultimate goal.

57. The notion of silver (presumed) in an oyster shell, the notion of a rope in a serpent,[1] the notion of water in a mirage—all these are definitely unreal, not otherwise.

58. *Siddhi* ('spiritual attainment') is the ability to act as one desires. The unreal thing is dependence. One who is bound is called *Paratantra* ('dependent on another'). One who is liberated has the sense of freedom.

59-62. Whence can be bondage to those who, having realized that soul is one, have eschewed the sense of *myness* and have no external restraints? The bondage (is fictitious and non-existent) like the sky-flower, or the horn of a rabbit. So the worldly existence is unreal. Of what avail is much talk? Of what avail is fruitless blabbing?

Those who are desirous of attaining the greatest region avoid *Mamatā* (feeling of my-ness or possession). They are the wise ones, the learned ones. They are devoid of attachment and have conquered their sense organs.

Those who have cast off *mamatā*, those who have eschewed covetousness and anger, attain the greatest region, (as) they are devoid of love and anger.

63. As long as lust and greed, attachment and hatred persist, they do not attain spiritual beatitude. They will know only the words (of the scriptures).

1. A wrong statement about *Adhyāsavāda*. It should be 'the notion of a serpent in a rope'.

Yama said:

64. Word comes out of sound; but knowledge is devoid of word (sound). How then was it said by you, O lord, that word is non-eternal?

65. The greatest Brahman is *Akṣara* ('Imperishable'). Word is of the nature of *Akṣara* ('syllable'). Hence it is heard that 'word' is mentioned by you as *Nirīkṣaka*[1](?) ('that which observes').

66. Whatever has to be explained can be explained only through words. How can it be explained without words? Let all these be recounted, O Śaṁbhu, in the matter of deciding what should be done and what should not be done.

Śaṅkara explained:

67. Listen attentively to these truthful words (of great meaning). By hearing this nothing that should be known remains (unknown).

68. All the sages expound knowledge. They are devoid of sins. They repeatedly practise knowledge. Those who are conversant with knowledge know what is knowledge.

69-70. It is only after knowing the three (things), viz. (i) knowledge, (ii) object of knowledge and that (iii) which is comprehended and attained, that it can be described how and by whom it should be known and what is it that was intended to be spoken. I shall explain these things succinctly. Understand it from me. The only and single one (i.e. Brahman) appears to be many in the light of difference.

71. Just as the ground viewed from a *Bhramarikā* ('merry-go-round') appears to be whirling, O Yama, so also the Ātman appears to be many, due to the idea of difference.

72-73. Hence after critically examining it, it should be known through *Śravaṇa* ('listening attentively'); it should be meditated upon through close application of the process of *Manana* ('deliberation') in particular.

After comprehending the Ātman, one can easily be released from bondage. This entire universe consisting of mobile and immobile beings is a network of magical delusion.

1. Probably *Nirakṣara* 'perishable' instead of '*Nirīkṣaka*.'

74. This great extensive worldly existence is full of *Māyā* characterized by *Mamatā* ('sense of my-ness'). After driving out *Mamatā* one is liberated from bondage easily.

75. Who am I? Who are you? Whence are the others? All these are based on the great *Māyā.* Just like the fleshy protuberance from the neck of a goat, the entire world is worthless and aimless.

76. (All) this is fruitless and devoid of permanent appearance. It is a showy mass of smoke without any essence. Hence with all effort, remember the Ātman, O Yama.

Lomaśa said:

77. Directed thus by Śaṁbhu, the king of the dead ones became enlightened himself and realized the Ātman.

78. He became famous as the dispenser absorbed in dispensing the fruits of the *Karmas* of all men and living beings.

Sages enquired:

79. It may be described what highly wonderful feat was accomplished by the noble-souled Kumāra after killing Tāraka in the battle.

Sūta replied:

80. When the Daitya Tāraka was killed, Mountains, the chief of whom was Himavān, approached there and eulogized Kārttikeya with sweet words.

The Mountains prayed:

81. Obeisance to the lord of auspicious form. We salute you, the cause of auspiciousness unto the universe. Hail to you, O kinsman of the universe; obeisance to you, the sanctifier of the universe.

82. We bow down to you by whom, merely through your sight, Cāṇḍālas have been made excellent ones. We seek refuge in you, the sole kinsman of the universe.

83. Hail to you, O son of Pārvatī. Obeisance to you, O son of Śaṅkara. Obeisance to you, O son of Kṛttikās. Obeisance to you who are born of the Fire-god.

84. Obeisance to you, O lord worthy of being worshipped very well by the excellent Devas. Obeisance to you, O lord, the most excellent one among the possessors of perfect knowledge. Obeisance to you, O most excellent one among Devas. Be pleased, O lord worthy of being sought refuge in and competent to destroy all agonies, O Lord.

85. On being praised thus by Mountains, Kārttikeya, the son of Umā, was pleased in his mind and became eager to grant them a boon.

Kārttikeya said:

86. O excellent Mountains, listen to my words now. You will be served (resorted to) by both *Karmins* (i.e. those who are devoted to holy rites) and *Jñānins* (i.e. those who are devoted to the path of knowledge).

87. Stones served with great effort are found only in you. At my instance, let them purify the universe. There is no doubt about it.

88. All mountain regions will become holy spots and not otherwise. They will become divine temples of Śiva and other holy shrines.

89. There is no doubt that at my instance they will become splendid and great pilgrim-spots of various forms.

90. This excellent Mountain Himavān who is my maternal grandfather and is highly fortunate, will be the bestower of fruits on ascetics.

91-94. Meru, this lord of Mountains, will be the support (of all). The excellent Mountain Lokāloka and the Mountain of the Rising Sun, of great fame, will become the lord himself in the form of a *Liṅga* and not otherwise. The following Mountains will be the destroyers of sins: Śrīśaila, Mahendra, Sahyācala, Mālyavān, Malaya, Vindhya, Gandhamādana, Śvetakūṭa, Trikūṭa and Mountain Dardura.[1] These and many other Mountains are the embodiments of *Liṅga*. At my instance these will become the destroyers of sins.

1. Nīlgiri hills—De 53.

95. Thus the son of Śaṅkara granted boons to those Mountains. Then Nandin spoke (to the lord) honoured by all the Āgamas:

Nandin said:

96. O Lord, the Mountains have been made embodiments of *Liṅga* by you. How should the shrines of Śiva be worshipped by all the Devas?

Kumāra said:

97. *Liṅga* should be known as the shrine of Śiva, the trident-bearing lord of Devas. (It should be worshipped) by all human beings and Devas beginning with Brahmā, diligently without any lethargy.

98-101. *Liṅgas* made of sapphire, pearls, coral, lapis lazuli, lunar stone, *Gomeda*, ruby, emeralds, gold, silver, copper, brass and zinc, *Liṅgas* made of precious stones and metal have been described to you. Only the pure ones should be worshipped. They are the bestowers of all desired objects. Among all these (that made in) Kāśmīra is the most excellent one. It gives all pleasures of this world and the next one to the devotee who worships.

Nandī said:

102. How is it that you have told that *Bāṇa-liṅga*[1] is the most excellent and worthy of being worshipped? Explain everything, O Lord of holy rites.

Kumāra said:

103. The stones that are seen in the waters in the middle of the river Revā, shall be in the form of *Liṅga*, by the favour of Śiva and not otherwise.

104-106. Their roots should be made smooth and placed over the *Piṇḍikā* ('pedestal'). They should be scrupulously worshipped by one who has the initiation called *Śivadīkṣā*.

One shall worship Śiva joined to the *Piṇḍī* in accordance with the injunctions of the scriptures.

1. *Liṅga*-type stones formed in Narmadā are called *Bāṇa-liṅgas*. See vv 103-105 below.

The Lord of the universe should bestow boons on the worshipper, not otherwise.

The five-lettered *Mantra* should always be in the mouth (of the worshipper); the mind should be directed towards the contemplation on Śiva; he must have impartiality towards all living beings. He should be dumb in giving expression to slander. He should be an impotent fellow in regard to other men's wives.

CHAPTER THIRTYTWO

The Burning of Kāla[1]

Lomaśa said:

1. Thus all the rites pertaining to the worship of Śiva (*Śiva-dharmāḥ*) were narrated by him, O Brāhmaṇas. It was out of grace that the Pāśupata doctrines were explained in details in particular.

2. Doctrines enshrined in various Āgamas were declared truthfully in accordance with the principles. The different sects of *Kāpālikas* were described succinctly as well as in details.

3. Various kinds of holy rites were recounted to Nandin then.

The sages said:

4. The highly auspicious story of Kumāra which has nothing to surpass it, has been completely heard by us, O highly fortunate one. We shall enquire of something more.

5. The narrative of the leonine king Śveta is wonderfully mysterious. By means of his boundless devotion, Śiva-Rudra has been gratified by him.

---

1. This chapter illustrates Śiva's kindness and alertness in protecting his devotees. Kāla, the supreme destroyer of the world, was burnt down by Śiva in order to protect his devotee, King Śveta, and he was resuscitated at the request of the victim-King.

6. Those who worship Lord Mahāśaṁbhu devoutly, are great devotees of noble souls. They are experts both in the path of spiritual knowledge (*Jñāna*) and of religious rites (*Karman*).

7. Hence all of us enquire of you about the story of Śaṅkara as you and none else know everything through the favour of Vyāsa.

8. On hearing the words of those sages, Lomaśa said:

Lomaśa said:

9. Let that wonderful anecdote be listened to, O highly fortunate ones. Even as that king was enjoying all sorts of royal pleasures, the mind of that noble-souled Śveta was directed towards virtue and piety.

10. He protected the subjects righteously and ruled the earth. He was heroic and truthful in speech. He was well-versed in the Vedas. He was a constant and faithful devotee of Śiva.

11. That king administered the kingdom in accordance with his capacity. With devotion, he always worshipped Śaṁbhu, the great lord, the Supreme Being, greater than the greatest, the quiescent one, the ancient lord in the form of the Supreme Spirit.

12-14. His whole life was spent in worshipping the Supreme Lord. Let the story of this highly fortunate (king) be listened to. My words cover Śiva's story and are full of wonders. Neither mental agonies nor physical ailments harassed the king. No natural calamity afflicted him. The people were free from all the *Ītis*[1] (i.e. abnormal calamitous phenomena such as excessive rain, drought etc.) and were devoid of afflicting distresses.

15. In the realm of that king medicinal herbs grew naturally without being cultivated. Ascetics and Brāhmaṇas and common people adhered to the discipline of the four castes and stages of life.

16. No one had, at any time, the misery due to the death of a son. No one was insulted. There were no deadly (diseases). No one ever suffered from poverty.

17. Thus a great deal of time passed even as that noble-

---

1. *Īti*: Plague or any calamity of the season such as drought, excessive rainfall, swarms of locusts, foreign invasions etc.—MW, 17.2.

souled king successfully engaged himself in the worship of Śiva, O Brāhmaṇas.

18-19. Once, Yama sent his messengers to that king who was worshipping Śaṅkara, the bestower of the greatest aim in life (i.e. salvation). At the instance of Citragupta, the messengers were deputed and instructed, "Let Śveta be brought." Thinking that it should be so, the messengers came to the temple of Śiva.

20. Desirous of taking the king away, the messengers of Yama who had nooses in their hands and were very frightful, came there and looked for the king hurriedly.

21-23. Then the messengers could not carry out the command of Dharma. After knowing this, Yama himself came there. He suddenly lifted up his baton and was desirous of taking the king away. The deity of great arms saw the king engaged in the meditation of Śiva. He was endowed with great devotion to Śiva. He was quiescent and possessed of pure spiritual knowledge. On seeing the king, Yama became highly excited.

24-26. Immediately the king of dead ones became excessively agitated and remained (motionless) as though he was painted in a picture.

The deity who in the form of Kāla, caused perpetual destruction of the subjects, came very furiously to that king at that very same instant. (He was armed) with a sword of very sharp edge and a big shield.

He (Yama) overwhelmed by fear was standing at the entrance. Kāla spoke to Yama, the son of the Sun:

27-28. "Why was this great king not taken away by you, O Dharmarāja? O Yama, (though) you are assisted by your messengers, you appear to me to be frightened. Do not delay, O deity of good holy rites. At my instance do everything quickly)."

On being told thus by Kāla, Dharma spoke these words befitting the occasion:

29. "I shall do according to your command. There is no doubt about this. This devotee of Śiva cannot be tackled by us.

30. Due to fear from the Trident-bearing Lord, we stand (motionless) as though painted in a picture."

On hearing Yama's words, Kāla became infuriated. Hurriedly he took up the sword intending to kill the king.

31-36. As he furiously entered the temple of Śiva, resembling twentyfour Suns, he was seen by Śiva, the Pināka-bearing Lord (who thought): 'This (deity) is desirous of killing my devotee, the excellent king Śveta. He is absorbed in his own soul by way of meditation. His mind has become purified by the bright light of pure knowledge. Without any differentiation he meditates upon his Ātman in the form of the innermost Ātman. He is self-luminous. He is greater than the greatest standing in front of him. The king is thinking about the foot of Śiva who is of the nature of the Supreme Being, the cause of salvation and complete identity in form.' Kāla was rushing at him and was seen by Sadāśiva, the slayer of Kāla. The rogue was approaching him undeterred arrogantly. When he was seen midway between himself and Nandikeśvara by Śiva, the lord of the universe, the affectionate kinsman of devotees, he was stared at with the third eye by the great Lord who wanted to protect his devotee. He became reduced to ash in an instant.

37. He burned Kāla who had many colours, who had opened his month very wide, whose form was extremely terrible and frightening, whose sole food was the universe and who was very fierce. He was burned by a series of flames.

38-40. The groups of Devas who had gathered together along with Yakṣas, Gandharvas, Piśācas, Guhyakas, Siddhas, groups of celestial damsels, all the sky-walkers, serpents, birds and the Guardians of Quarters, saw Kāla enveloped in flames and stationed in front of Īśvara.

The king then regained consciousness and looked again and again at Kāla who had come to kill him and who was then being burnt by fire. Without being excited, he prayed to Rudra who resembled the fire of Kāla:

The king said:

41. Obeisance to Rudra the quiescent one, who is the moonlight unto himself, is the creator of himself, who is perpetual and subtle. I bow to the lord of the luminaries.

42. You alone are indeed the saviour, O Lord of the universe. You are the father, mother, friend and comrade. You alone are the kinsman and relative. You are Īśvara, the lord of people and of all the worlds.

43. What has been done by you, O Śaṁbhu? Who is this who has been burned in front of me? I do not know what has taken place here; what great thing has been carried out and by whom.

44. On hearing this expression of the pain of that (king) who was praying thus, Śaṅkara spoke these words enlightening that king:

Rudra said:

45. This Kāla was burnt by me in front of you for your sake. He was seen being burnt and overwhelmed by a great mass of flames.

46. On being told thus by Śaṁbhu that excellent king became humble before Śiva and spoke these words to him:

47. "What misdeed has been committed by this (Kāla), O Śaṁbhu? Tell me exactly. O Bhava, what for has he been reduced to this plight, ending with his death?"

48. On being requested by him the Supreme Lord said: "O great king, he is one who swallows all living beings.

49. O lord, it was for the purpose of swallowing you that this cruel one had come near me now. Hence, O lord, O great king, he was burnt by me.

50-51. Desiring the welfare of many persons, I have killed him particularly.

Those who are sinners, those who engage themselves in unrighteous activities, those who cause the annihilation of the worlds and those who propagate heretic doctrines—all these are to be killed by me."

On hearing the words of Rudra, Śveta spoke thus:

52-53. "It is on account of Kāla that the whole world always performs meritorious deeds: Some abide by righteous activities; some are endowed with great devotion; some are engaged in *Upāsanas* ('devotional rites'); others become *Jñānins* ('possessors of knowledge'); some practise spiritual pursuits; and some are liberated.

54. Indeed Kāla is the annihilator of all mobile and immobile beings. Similarly, he is the matchless protector too (of all).

He is the creator as well of the vital air of all living beings. Hence revive him back to life.

55-56. If you are intent on creation, resuscitate Kāla quickly. If you are inclined to annihilate all living beings, then (revive him) and give this work, O Śaṁbhu, to the noble-souled Kāla. Without Kāla nothing will take place, O Śaṅkara."

57. On being requested thus by that valorous king, Śaṁbhu carried out his suggestion. He did what his devotee desired (him) to do.

58. Śaṁbhu, the great Pināka-bearing Lord, resuscitated him and made his form as it had been before. He was then fixed by him in his place, in the middle of the messengers of Yama.

59. Approaching (the Lord) with shyness, he eulogized the Bull-bannered Lord. After bowing down to the fire stationed in front, this Kāla spoke these words in great dismay:

Kāla said:

60. O slayer of Kāla, O lord of Tripura, O destroyer of the three Puras. Indeed Madana was made *Anaṅga* (bodiless) by you, O lord of the universe.

61-62. A very wonderful feat was perfromed by you in destroying the sacrifice (*Yajña*) of Dakṣa. Kālakūṭa, the poison, unbearable to everyone, the great poison that caused destruction of all, was swallowed by you, O Śaṁbhu, as it was unbearable to all. The whole range of the three worlds was pervaded in the form of *Liṅga* by the great lord.

63. It is called *Liṅga* by all the Suras and Asuras because it absorbs the world within it. Devas with Brahmā and Viṣṇu at their head do not know its limits and extremities.

64. They do not know the greatness of the *Liṅga* as well as the great lord of Devas.

Hail to you, the Supreme Lord. Obeisance to you, O cause of the auspiciousness of the universe. I bow to you, the blue-throateded one; I salute that lord with matted hair.

65. Repeated obeisance to you, the cause of causes. Salutations to you, the auspicious soul of all auspicious things. Obeisance to the lord in the form of knowledge of all the learned ones conversant with knowledge. You are the primordial God. You are the ancient *Puruṣa*.

66. You are everything, O sole kinsman of the universe. You can be comprehended only through the Vedāntas; you are of exalted magnanimity; you are worthy of being glorified by all magnanimous persons. You alone are honoured by the whole universe, O lord of the universe.

67. You protect; you annihilate all the three worlds, O great lord. You are the creator. You and none else, are the lord of all living beings.

68. Thus the lord of the universe was eulogized by Kāla. Kāla then said to king Śveta enlightening him as it were:

Kāla said:

69. In the whole of the mortal world, there is no one greater than you by whom the lord who is invincible in all the three worlds, has been conquered.

70. This universe of the mobile and immobile beings has been killed by me. I am the conqueror of all the Devas. I cannot be transgressed by anyone.

71. I have now become your follower, O great king. Grant me protection from fear of the trident-bearing Parameṣṭhin, the lord of the Devas.

72. On being addressed thus by Kāla, Śveta laughingly spoke in a voice as majestic as the sound of clouds:

The King said:

73. There is no doubt about this that you are the greatest form of Śiva. You are Kāla in the form of sustenance and annihilation of all living beings.

74. Hence you are the most adorable of all. You are the controller of all. It is on account of their fear of you that all those who perform rites seek refuge in Parameśvara with various emotional feelings, desirous of dedicating themselves.

Sūta said:

75-76. Kāla who was thus saved by the excessively righteous king regained consciousness by the grace of Śiva alone. The lord was eulogized by Yama in the company of Mṛtyu and messengers of Yama.

After bowing down and praising Śiva and the king Śveta, (Kāla) went to his abode, O Brāhmaṇas. He considered himself as born once again.

77. In the company of his wife Māyā, he frequently recollected the great story of Śiva and became surprised more and more.

78-79. He said to all the messengers himself: "O messengers, let my words be heard quickly; what I suggest in my speech should be carried out scrupulously. It should not be otherwise."

Kāla instructed[1]:

80-83. The following persons should never be brought to my region: Those who apply *Tripuṇḍra* (upon their forehead); those who have matted hair; those who wear *Rudrākṣa*; those who are called by the names of Śiva; those who assume the guise of the men of Śaiva cult either for the sake of livelihood or out of fear; even men who have committed sins or practised evil conduct if they are wearing Śaiva garments. All these should never be brought to my region by you. They should be scrupulously avoided even if they are always sinful. What then about others, O messengers—others who worship Sadāśiva, Śaṁbhu, with great devotion? They are undoubtedly Rudras themselves.

84. He who wears even a single *Rudrākṣa* on his head and the *Tripuṇḍra* mark in the middle of the forehead, the good persons who repeat the five-syllabled *Mantra*—these are to be honoured by you all and never otherwise.

85. The nation, the country or the village where no wise devotee of Śiva is seen—is it different from a cremation ground? They (may) call that nation (*rāṣṭra*) *deśa*—a small place. I speak the truth unto you.

86. The persons in that village where there exist no persons who practise devotional rites of Śiva, should be chastised well.

87. Thus Yama commanded his servants. Thinking that it should be so, they remained quiet on being much surprised.

---

1. These instructions are intended to show the great efficacy of Śaivism.

88. Such is Sadāśiva, the sole lord of the worlds, the sire of the worlds. He is one and only one. He is the bestower and the chastiser, possessor of his supreme powers (*Bhāva*[1]), emotional feelings. He is eternal, the sole kinsman of the universe.

89-90. After burning Kāla, lord Mahādeva granted freedom from fear to Śveta, the king of kings, the most excellent one among the rulers of the earth.

Having attained freedom from fear, the lofty-minded king Śveta resolved (to strive for salvation) and by means of supreme devotion became liberated.

91. On being honoured by Devas, sages and Serpents, this Śveta, the most excellent one among kings, attained *Sāyujya* (identity) with Śiva.

92. Thus *Siddhi* (liberation) is within the palm (i.e. within the reach) of those persons who are devoted to Maheśa, the Sire of the universe. I am speaking the truth unto you.

93. Even a Cāṇḍāla can become an excellent man by the favour of Śaṅkara. Hence Śaṅkara should be worshipped with all efforts.

94-95. It is only after the end of many births that devotion to Śiva is born in *Jñānins* with great intellect. Śaṅkara should be worshipped in every birth. Of what avail is too much talk on my part? Sadāśiva should be worshipped.

96. In this context they cite this ancient mythological legend in regard to the wonderful holy rite performed by a Kirāta (forester) by whom the whole universe consisting of mobile and immobile beings was redeemed.

---

1. MW p. 754.

CHAPTER THIRTYTHREE

The Greatness of Śivarātri Vrata[1]

The sages said:

1. What was the name of that Kirāta? What holy rite was performed by him? O great Brāhmaṇa, narrate it. We are very eager.

2. We wish to hear everything. Let it be described exactly. Excepting you, there is no one else, O foremost one among eloquent people. Hence recount everything, O lord of Brāhmaṇas, to us who wish to hear.

3. On being told thus by the noble-souled Śaunaka, (Lomaśa) narrated every thing done by the Puṣkasa[2] (? Forester).

Lomaśa said:

4. Once there was an excessively terrible vicious man named Caṇḍa.[3] He used to associate with cruel people. He was roguish and of bad conduct. He used to terrorize all living beings.

5-6. With a net that evil-minded one used to capture and kill fish incessantly. That wicked fellow killed different kinds of deer, beasts of prey and porcupine as well as rhinoceros by means of arrows. Sometimes he furiously killed birds. The sinner killed Brāhmaṇas in particular. The forester of great sins was wicked himself and was a favourite of all wicked people. The wife of that Puṣkasa was also very terrible, like him.

7-8. Even as he amused himself thus, many years passed by. He continued to be engaged in those sinful activities and much time passed.

---

1. *Śivarātri* falls on the fourteenth day of the dark half of Māgha. It is sacred to Śiva. Observance of fast on that complete *Tithi*, worship of Śiva and keeping vigil that night in performing devotional service etc. to Śiva are the main features of the *Vrata*.

2. *Puṣkasa* is a hyper-Sanskritisation of Prakrit *Pukkasa*—name of a forest tribe.

3. The story of a vicious Cāṇḍāla called Caṇḍa illustrates how service to Śiva performed without knowing it and observance of fast on that day forced by unforeseen circumstances leads even a sinner to inclusion in the Gaṇas of Śiva.

9. Once that sinful fellow sat on a Bilva tree at night with the bow in his hand. He wanted to kill a wild boar and he kept awake even without winking. He had stored some water in his quiver, lest he should be distressed due to hunger and thirst.

10. It was the fourteenth day in the dark fortnight of the month of Māgha (January-February). He was looking in front for the animal and unintentionally he (plucked and) made many Bilva (*Aegle Marmelos*) leaves fall down.

11-15. Sometimes in anger he plucked a number of Bilva leaves and dropped them down. Wafted (by the wind) they fell upon a *Liṅga* that was at the root of the Śrīvṛkṣa (Bilva tree). Sometimes that wicked fellow gargled and that water fell on the *Śivaliṅga*. The leaves of the Bilva tree also fell. In such a manner, by sheer good luck and happy coincidence the action of that forester became a worship of Śiva.

With mouthfuls of water the great rite of bathing was performed; with the numerous leaves of the *Aegle Marmelos* the great rite of worshipping too was carried out in ignorance, O Brāhmaṇas, by that evil-minded Puṣkasa. On the fourteenth day in the black fortnight of the month of Māgha when the crescent moon was about to rise (at dawn), that Puṣkasa of evil conduct got down from the tree. Coming near the water-pond he began to catch (and kill) fish.

16. The wife of that Puṣkasa was known by the name Ghanodarī. She was vicious and she used to steal other people's wealth. She was engaged in committing sins.

17. In the evening she started from her house and stood outside the city gates. Desirous of meeting her husband on his arrival, she was watching the road to the forest.

18-22. When even after a long time her husband did not return, the huntress began to think:

'All the other hunters and fowlers have returned in the evening today. The four cardinal points and the intermediate quarters have been covered with mass of darkness. Two *Yāmas* ($2\times3=6$ hours) have gone by in the night. Has the forester come yet? Was he torn to pieces by a lion because he had coveted the mane? Was he tortured and afflicted by the poison of serpents because he was about to remove the gems and jewels from the hoods of serpents? Did he meet death on being hit and struck by the tips of the curved teeth of boars? Did he fall down on the ground from the top of a tree which he climbed up because he coveted honey? Where shall I enquire? Whom shall I ask? To whom shall I go?'

After lamenting thus in various ways, she returned to the house.

23. Throughout that day, nothing was eaten by her. Even water was not taken in. The fowler's wife spent the whole of the night thinking about her husband.

24. At dawn when everything was free from impurities (i.e. darkness), the Puṣkasī went to the forest in a hurry, taking with her food for him to eat.

25. Wandering in the forest, she saw a big river. On seeing her own husband seated on its bank, she became delighted.

26. She placed the food on the bank and began to cross the river. On seeing (her), he brought the fish caught in his net.

27. By that time, Caṇḍa was told by her: "Come quickly. Take your food. I have observed fast throughout the day and food has been brought for your sake.

28. What has been done by you today? What was done yesterday, O dull-witted one? Was not anything taken in by you, O stupid fellow? You sinner, did you refrain from taking food?"

29-30. That couple of pure holy rites took their bath in the river. When he went (to the other bank) for taking his food a dog came that way. All the food was eaten by it. The fierce woman became infuriated and proceeded to kill the dog.

31. "Our food has been eaten by this sinful wretch. What will you eat, O dull-witted one? You will have to remain hungry now."

32-35. On being (reproachfully) told thus by her, Caṇḍa who had become a favourite (devotee) of Śiva,[1] spoke to her: "I have been gratified by the food that has been eaten by the dog. Of what avail is this perishable body bereft of long life? This ill-fated body of momentary existence is being worshipped in the world. Those who are overwhelmed by emotional attachments and go on nourishing their body, are foolish ones. They

1. The transformation of a wicked Cāṇḍāla into a pious devotee of Śiva is due to the observance of *Śivarātri Vrata* even without knowing it.

should be known as sinners, excluded from both the worlds. Hence abandon false pride and unrestrained anger. Be composed by means of discrimination (between good and evil). Be steady by means of the intellect based on reality (i.e. through knowledge of reality)."

36. That fierce woman was extremely enlightened by the Puṣkasa then. That Puṣkasa had carried out the rite of keeping awake on the *Caturdaśī* night.

37. In view of the connection with *Śivarātri,* he attained that perfect knowledge which is undoubtedly produced at the time of *Śivarātri.*

38. Two *Yāmas* (i.e. six hours) passed and *Amāvāsyā* started. Many Gaṇas deputed by Śiva came there.

39. Many aerial chariots also came there near him. Those aerial chariots and the Gaṇas were seen by him.

40. The Puṣkasa spoke to them with great devotion: "From where have you come? All of you wear *Rudrākṣa* beads.

41. Some of you are riding in aerial chariots. Some have mounted bulls. All of you resemble the crystal. All of you have the crescent moon as coronet.

42. All of you have matted hair. Hides are your garments. (Bodies of) serpents have been worn as ornaments. You are equipped with all glorious features. Your heroism is like that of Rudra. Explain specifically and exactly what is proper unto you."

43. On being asked by Puṣkasa, then, all the lotus-eyed *Pārṣadas* (attendants) of Rudra, the lord of Devas, said very humbly:

Gaṇas said:

44. O Caṇḍa, we have been sent by the great god Śiva. Come on. Hurry up. Get into the vehicle along with your wife.

45. The worship of the *Liṅga* of Śiva has been performed by you at night. As a result of that good rite you have attained Siva's presence.

46. Told thus by Vīrabhadra, the Puṣkasa too laughingly said the following words relevant to the occasion, in accordance with his own intellect.

The Puṣkasa said:

47. What (good) has been done today by me who have been a sinner, a violent tormentor, an evil-minded Puṣkasa interested in hunting?

48. I have been perpetually committing sins. How can I go to heaven? How was the worship of *Liṅga* performed? Let it be explained.

49. My curiosity has been roused much. I am asking you for the exact state (of affairs). Explain, O deity of great fortune, everything in due order.

50. As the Puṣkasa put these questions properly, (Vīrabhadra) described the Śaiva rites entirely with great joy.

Vīrabhadra said:

51. Mahādeva, the lord of Devas, Īśvara, the lord of refulgent ones, Maheśa, the consort of Umā, is delighted today, O Caṇḍa.

52. In the month of Māgha, the worship of *Liṅga* was performed by you incidentally. It is the cause of the delight of Śiva. Undoubtedly you have become sanctified today. The worship was incidentally performed on the *Śivarātri* night.

53. O Caṇḍa, the leaves of the Bilva tree were plucked by you who were on the lookout for a wild boar. At the same time, they fell on the head of the *Liṅga*. Hence you have become full of merits, O holy lord.

54. Similarly the great rite of keeping awake was performed by you on the tree. The Lord of the universe is delighted at that keeping awake.

55. Under the pretext of watching (the arrival) of a wild boar, you had no sleep on the *Śivarātri* night. Nor did your wife sleep.

56. The noble-souled lord, the most excellent one among Devas, is delighted on account of that fast and keeping the vigil. In order to please you, the lord of great magnanimity, the bestower of boons, granted you all festivities.

57-60. On being told thus by the intelligent Vīrabhadra, the Puṣkasa got into the excellent aerial chariot even as the Gaṇas,

Devas and all living beings were watching. *Dundubhi*-drums were sounded. *Bherīs* and many musical instruments were played. The instruments like lutes, flutes and *Mṛdaṅgas* went ahead of him. The lords of Gandharvas sang; groups of celestial damsels danced. All the groups of Vidyādharas, Siddhas and Cāraṇas eulogized. The Puṣkasa was being fanned with chowries. He was honoured with various kinds of umbrellas. He was brought to Gandhamādana with great festivities and celebrations.

61. This Caṇḍa attained the presence of Śiva on account of that holy rite. By fasting on the *Śivarātri* night, he attained the greatest region.

62-63. Even a Puṣkasa and that too by means of an incidental (holy rite) attained Sadāśiva. What then in the case of those who have great faith in attaining Śiva, the great Ātman?

There is no doubt about this that those who offer flowers etc., fruits, scents, betel leaves and rich foodstuffs in this world to god Śiva are Rudras themselves.

64. Everything was incidentally performed by Caṇḍa, a Puṣkasa, who was of insignificant intellect. Still his action was fruitful.

The sages enquired:

65. What is the benefit? What is its purpose? By whom was it performed formerly? Wherefrom did this *Vrata* originate? By whom was it laid down, O holy lord, formerly?

Lomaśa said:

66. When the entire universe was created by Brahmā Parameṣṭhin, the wheel of Time[1] also was evolved formerly along with the zodiacs.

67. There are twelve zodiacs and the main constellations are twentyseven in number, for the sake of achieving the objectives.

68. The Wheel of Time is very fierce with these zodiacs and constellations. Accompanied by this *Kālacakra* ('Wheel of Time'), *Kāla* sportively creates this universe.

69. *Kāla* creates, protects and destroys everything from

1. VV 66-67 explain the concept of Time and its sub-units.

Brahmā down to a blade of grass, O Brāhmaṇas. Everything is connected with *Kāla*.

70. Indeed *Kāla* is very powerful. It is the only one (of its kind). (There is) nothing else than *Kāla*. Hence all these (visible worlds) are of the nature of *Kāla*. There is no doubt about it.

71. The leader of all the leaders of the world is *Kāla* at the outset because of *Kālana* (calculation?). The worlds are born therefrom. The creation comes next.

72. From the creation, *Lava* (i.e. the smallest unit of time) is born. From *Lava*, *Kṣaṇa* (moment) is born; from *Kṣaṇa*, *Nimiṣa* (i.e. winking time) is born. This occurs continuously in all living beings.

73. Sixty *Nimiṣas* make one *Pala*.[1] Fifteen days and nights make one *Pakṣa* (fortnight).

74. Two *Pakṣas* make one *Māsa* (month); twelve *Māsas* make one *Vatsara* (year). Knowledge should be acquired from experts by a person desirous of knowing *Kāla*.

75. From *Pratipad* (first day of the lunar fortnight) if we calculate up to the full-moon day, the fortnight becomes complete (*Pūrṇa*). Hence full-moon day is called *Pūrṇimā*.

76. The day on which the moon is complete is called *Pūrṇa* (*Pūrṇimā*). It is a favourite day of Devas. The day on which the moon vanishes is called *Amā* by learned men.

77. It is a great favourite of Pitṛs beginning with Agniṣvāttas. All these thirty days have certain auspicious times. Listen to some special features of them, O excellent Brāhmaṇas.

78-79. Among the *Yogas*[2] (particular division of time; there

---

1. Probably some lines are missing after this in the text, as there is a gap between *Pala* and *Pakṣa* (a fortnight).

2. *Yoga*—Astronomically, *Yoga* corresponds to 13 degrees and 20 minutes—being the sum of the Longitudes of the Sun and the Moon. That is, it is the time during which the Sun and the Moon together cover 13 degrees and 20 minutes of space. But there is no direct astronomical phenomena corresponding to it. *Yogas* are 27 in number making together 360 degrees.

The following are the *Yogas*:

Name		*Deity*
1. Viṣkambha	—	Yama
2. Prīti	—	Viṣṇu

are 27 such *Yogas*) *Vyatīpāta*[1]; among stars *Śravaṇa*; among *Tithis* (Lunar days) *Amāvāsyā* (new-moon day) and *Pūrṇimā* (full-moon day) and *Saṅkrāntis* (i.e. when the sun passes from one zodiac to another)—these should be known as sacred ones for the rites of charitable gifts. *Aṣṭamī* (i.e. the 8th day in a fortnight) is a favourite[2] of Śambhu and *caturthikā* (the 4th day) of Gaṇeśa.

80. The fifth day (is a favourite) of the king of Serpents; the

---

3. Āyuṣmat	—	Candra
4. Saubhāgya	—	Brahmā
5. Śobhana	—	Bṛhaspati
6. Atigaṇḍa	—	Candra
7. Sukarman	—	Indra
8. Dhṛti	—	Āpaḥ
9. Śūla	—	Sarpa
10. Gaṇḍa	—	Agni
11. Vṛddhi	—	Sūrya
12. Dhruva	—	Pṛthvī
13. Vyāghāta	—	Pavana
14. Harṣaṇa	—	Rudra
15. Vajra	—	Varuṇa
16. Siddhi	—	Gaṇeśa
17. Vyatīpāta	—	Śiva
18. Varīyas	—	Kubera
19. Parigha	—	Viśvakarman
20. Śiva	—	Mitra
21. Siddha	—	Kārttikeya
22. Sādhya	—	Sāvitrī
23. Śubha	—	Kamalā
24. Śukla	—	Gaurī
25. Brahman	—	Aśvinau
26. Aindra	—	Pitṛs
27. Vaidhṛti	—	Aditi

1. *Vyatīpāta*—It is a *Yoga* when the Moon and the Sun are on the opposite sides of either solstice and their minutes of declination are the same.

viparītāyanagatau candrārkau krānti-liptikāḥ|
samastadā vyatīpāto bhagaṇārdhe tayoryutau||
Sūryasiddhānta XI.2.

There are generally 13 *Vyatīpātas* in a year. *Śrāddha* is recommended on this *Yoga*.

VV 78 and 79a enumerate auspicious occasions for religious gifts.

2. VV 79a-82 state what *Tithi* (Lunar day) is specially favourite with what deity.

sixth day that of Kumāra (Skanda). It should be known that the seventh day (is a favourite) of the Sun and the ninth day is a favourite of Caṇḍikā.

81. It should be known that the tenth day is (a favourite) of Brahmā; the eleventh day that of Rudra; the twelfth day is a favourite of Viṣṇu; and the thirteenth day that of Antaka (i.e. god of death).

82-83. The fourteenth day is a favourite of Śaṁbhu. There is no doubt about it. The *Caturdaśī* of the dark half which extends to the mid-night is a *Tithi* (Lunar day) on which one should observe fast. It is very excellent and is conducive to the attainment of *Sāyujya* (identity) with Śiva. The *Tithi* of *Śivarātri* is well-known as the destroyer of all sins.

In this context they cite this ancient legend.[1]

84. There was a certain Brāhmaṇa widow of fickle mind. She loved a certain Cāṇḍāla. She became his beloved through sheer lust.

85. A son was born to her and the Cāṇḍāla of evil mind. His name and soul were both vicious and he was unbearable. He was excluded from all holy rites.

86-87. Urged by sinful nature, he began sinful actions always. He was a gambler, an addict to liquor, a thief and a defiler of the bed of his elders. He was a vicious hunter, a veritable Cāṇḍāla through his action also. Always engaged in evil actions and being vicious though he was, once he happened to go to the temple of Śiva on the *Śivarātri* night. He stayed there in the presence of Śiva.

88-89. By chance he heard the scriptural texts of the cult of Śiva from close quarters. Now and then, he happened to visit Śiva in the form of *Liṅga* that was self-born. Though he was a wicked fellow he attained a meritorious birth due to the holy rite of staying in the presence of Śiva and keeping awake on the *Śivarātri* night.

---

1. This, being a Śaiva Purāṇa, re-emphasizes the importance of *Śivarātri* by relating legends etc. Vicitravīrya in this legend (vv 84-98) is not the Mbh King who was the son of Śantanu (Mbh, *Ādi*. 95.49-50; 101.3). The Vicitravīrya in this legend is the son of Citrāṅgada (v 90).

90. He enjoyed pleasures in the meritorious worlds and spent there many many years. (Ultimately) he became the son of Citrāṅgada with all the characteristics of a great king.

91. He was known by the name Vicitravīrya. He was very handsome and was fond of beautiful women. After attaining the vast kingdom, he became a very great supporter of all.

92. Practising devotional services unto Śiva, he became engaged in holy rites of the Śiva-cult. He was desirous of performing the worship of Śiva in accordance with the scriptural texts of the Śaiva cult. He scrupulously performed the rite of keeping a vigil at night, in the presence of Śiva.

93. Singing the songs of praise of the deeds of Śiva, he used to shed tears of joy frequently from his eyes. He used to experience a thrill of rapture.

94. The whole life passed away thus, when he devoted his attention to the meditation of Śiva. Indeed, Śiva is easy of access to brutes as well as the wise and the learned.

95. In order to serve and for the sake of obtaining happiness, the only (deity) is Sadāśiva.

By observing fast on the *Śivarātri* he obtained excellent knowledge.

96. Everything is acquired, including equality with all living beings, through knowledge. After realizing Sadāśiva alone, the immanent Soul of all, identical with all, he attained liberation.

Without Śiva there is no object here or elsewhere.

97. Thus one obtains the rare knowledge of the Lord, unconnected with the terrestrial worlds.

After obtaining the (spiritual) knowledge, the king became a beloved (devotee) of Śiva.

98. He attained the liberation of the form of *Sāyujya* by observing fast on *Śivarātri* night. What had been obtained by him formerly has been told by me.

99. Being bereaved of the daughter of Dakṣa (the furious lord Śiva) struck his extensive mass of matted hair (on the ground). At that time, the deity well-known as Vīrabhadra, the destroyer of Dakṣa's *Yajña*, was born from the forehead of Śiva, the supreme Ātman.

100. Many have been redeemed formerly through the holy

rite of *Śivarātri.* They achieved *Siddhi* formerly, O Brāhmaṇas. The souls beginning with Bharata,[1] achieved *Siddhi.*

101-102. Māndhātā, Dhundhumāri, Hariścandra and other kings achieved *Siddhi* through this holy rite alone.

Thereafter, Giriśa engaged himself in sports in the company of Girijā, on the top of the king of mountains. The Supreme Lord (*Pareśa*) in the company of Bhavānī played the game of dice earnestly.

CHAPTER THIRTYFOUR

Śiva Loses to Pārvatī in a Game of Dice[2]

Lomaśa said:

1. The lord of the universe, the lord of Devas, ruled the kingdom while dwelling on Kailāsa accompanied by many Gaṇas and in the company of the great (deity) Vīrabhadra.

2. Rudra was accompanied by the Sages and Devas beginning with Indra. Brahmā was engaged in eulogizing him. Viṣṇu remained there like a servant.

---

1. As a propagandist of Śaivism, famous ancient persons are claimed as devotees of Śiva. The *Who's Who* of the kings mentioned in vv 100-102 is as follows:

(1) Bharata—son of Duṣyanta and Śakuntalā (Mbh, *Ādi*, 2.95-96) or the son of the 1st Jain Tīrthaṅkara Ṛṣabha.

(2) Māndhātā—Son of Yuvanāśva of Ikṣvāku race (Mbh, *Vana*, Ch. 126).

(3) Dhundhumāri—Original name, Kuvalāśva, son of Bṛhadaśva of the Solar race (Mbh, *Droṇa*, 94.42). He killed demon Dhundhu and got the epithet Dhundhumāra (-māri) (Mbh, *Vana*, 204.32).

(4) Hariścandra—Son of Triśaṅku of Ikṣvāku race, famous for truthfulness and charity (Mbh, *Sabhā*, 12.10-18).

2. The author of SkP is a fine storyteller with a sense of humour. In this chapter and the next he describes how Śiva lost everything to Pārvatī in gambling and left his wife and palace in a huff. Pārvatī enticed him to return by assuming the guise of a young Śabarī girl.

3. Along with the groups of Devas, Indra devoted himself to the duties of serving him. Candra (the Moon-god) became the bearer of the umbrella and Vāyu (the Wind-god) that of chowries.

4. Jātavedas (the Fire-god) was his permanent cook; Gandharvas were the musicians, bards and panegyrists of the Pināka-bearing god Śiva.

5-6. Many Vidyādharas and the groups of celestial damsels danced in front of him. Thus Lord Śiva ruled the kingdom without any suspicion or fear on the mountain Kailāsa.[1] He was accompanied by his valorous sons, Gaṇeśa and Skanda, as well as Girijā. He moved about here and there (supervising everything).

7. The wicked mighty Daitya named Andhaka, a great enemy of Devas, was pierced by him with his trident and placed in the sky for a long time.

8. He killed the Asura in the form of an elephant and removed his hide which was (later) made by him his divine robe. The burning of the three Puras (the demon Tripura) was carried out by him. With Viṣṇu as the deity incharge of the protection of *Bhūtas* (living beings), the lord who was handsome in all his limbs, shone well.

9. (Once) desirous of seeing him, the holy lord Nārada of divine vision went to the excellent mountain Kailāsa which was white like the moon.

10. On seeing that highly powerful mountain served by the great *Sudhā* (Gaṅgā?), the mountain that had very great wonderful features and was white like camphor, Nārada was struck with wonder. He entered the Gandhamādana mountain.[2]

11. The mountain Gandhamādana was endowed with many wonderful features. It was rendered very splendid by means of blazing sun-stones. It possessed great splendour and it was filled with singing Vidyādharī maidens.

---

1. v.l. The 4th pāda of the verse:
mahatā vikrameṇa ca 'with great valour'.

2. The Purāṇa identifies Gandhamādana and Kailāsa mountains. It indicates a later period for this Purāṇa, as the author was not aware of the different locations of the two mountains.

12. There were many *Kalpa* (i.e. wish-yielding)-trees round which creepers had entwined themselves. Excellent *Kāmadhenus* (were seen) in the thick shades (of those trees).

13. There were many bees greedily hankering after the fragrance of the *Pārijāta* grove. There were many swans of sweet voice (*Kalahaṁsas*) sporting about in the lakes.

14. Peacocks made there loud sounds of *Kekā* joyously. All the birds chirping with the *Pañcama* note were very gay and delighted (as if inebriated).

15. Elephants of bright lustre rejoiced in the company of she-elephants. Similarly lions roared in the company of tigers.

16. Bulls, the chief among whom was Nandin, bellowed continuously. There were many divine trees and parks of sandal trees.

17. There were trees such as *Nāga*, *Punnāga*, *Bakula* and *Campaka*. There were wild rose-apple trees as well as golden *Ketakas*.

18-19. There were *Kalhāras* (i.e. white esculent water-lilies), *Karavīras*, *Kumudas* (lilies) of many types. There were *Mandāras*, *Badarīs* (jujube), *Kramukas* and *Pāṭalas* (trumpet trees) and, many other trees along with the creepers winding round them. There were many parks (seen as) twice as many (i.e. double) on that mountain.

20. The wonderful flood of Gaṅgā suddenly coming out of the sky fell on the top of that mountain. It appeared very splendid.

21. A well (plenty) of waters whereby the universe becomes sanctified, was also seen double by the noble-souled Nārada.

22. Everything was seen double then on being looked at by that noble-souled great Nārada, O Brāhmaṇas.

23. Observing everything thus, the holy lord and sage Nārada hurriedly went ahead desirous of meeting Śiva.

24. When he stood at the entrance, he saw a very surprising thing. Two gate-keepers were seen there. (Actually) they had been made artificially by Viśvakarman.

25-26. Nārada was deluded by them. He asked them then: "I wish to enter. I am desirous of meeting Śiva. Hence permission should be granted to see Śiva."

On seeing them as if they had not heard (his words), Nārada became surprised.

27. With his vision born of knowledge he saw (the truth) and became silent. After realizing that they were artificial, the lofty-minded sage entered.

28. Similarly others, of the same form as those (two) were seen by that noble-souled (sage). Sage Nārada, the holy lord, was joyously bowed to by them.

29. He saw these and many other wonderful things (there). Then he clearly saw lord Tryaṁbaka accompanied by Girijā.

30. The chaste lady, the daughter of the King of Mountains, was occupying half of the seat of the noble-souled Śaṅkara. The whole of the three worlds is pervaded by her.

31. The slender-bodied young woman Gaurī had sparkling bright eyes of great beauty. It was on account of her that Śaṁbhu, the great lord, was rendered worthy of being accepted.

32. The lord (who was really) without any emotional aberrations (*vikāras*) was made weak and imperfect through *vikāras*[1] (by her).

That goddess was seen by him as though joined to half of the body of Siva.[2]

33. Similarly Śaṁbhu, the lord of the three worlds, was seen by Nārada, as being served by Suras and Asuras. The lord had the lustre of pure gold.

34-35. His lotus-like feet were served by Śaṅkha, the excellent serpent. He was served by the following serpents: Dhṛtarāṣṭra, Takṣaka in particular, the great serpent Padma and Śeṣa in particular. He was continuously served by other excellent serpents. Vāsuki had become a necklace of great lustre and was retained in the neck.

36. Kaṁbala and Aśvatara were his perpetual ear-rings. Other excellent serpents were ensconced at the root of his matted hair.

37-44. He was covered by serpents of many colours and types, e.g. Takṣaka, Kulika, Śaṅkha, Dhṛtarāṣṭra of great lustre,

1. '*vikāra*' may be taken as 'a change' of form or nature.

2. This is the *Ardhanārīśvara* concept. In Trika-Śaivism of Kashmir, Śiva and Śakti form one body as it were.

Padma, Daṁbha, Sudaṁbha, Karāla, Bhīṣaṇa—these and many other serpents formed parts of Hara who was the most worthy of being worshipped in the three worlds.

Some excellent serpents shone with a single hood. Some had two hoods, some three hoods of great lustre. Similarly others had four, five, six, seven, eight, nine, ten, eleven, twelve, eighteen, nineteen hoods. Some serpents had forty hoods. Others fifty, sixty, seventy, eighty, ninety, hundred, thousand, ten thousand, hundred thousand, one hundred million, a hundred billion hoods.

Those serpents with endless number of hoods are the serpents adorning Śiva as ornaments. All these were seen then by the noble-souled Nārada.

45. All those serpents were endowed with learning and they possessed precious stones and jewels. They had unmeasured lustre. They were highly refulgent as the ornaments of the neck.

46. His (i.e. Lord Śiva's) excessively beautiful matted hair was marked (adorned) by the crescent moon. He shone well with his third eye in his forehead.

47-48. Mahādeva had five faces. He had ten arms and his neck was dark in colour like emerald. His broad chest was very beautiful. His hips were big. The highly great pair of feet of Rudra were extremely splendid.

49. The matchless lotus-like foot of Śaṁbhu was seen (by the sage). It was resplendent and beautiful. With its reddish tinge of the (cloud at) dusk, it was highly auspicious. It dispelled distresses. It radiated masses of splendour. It was greater than the greatest. It was the seat and support of the graceful play of beauty. It was the cause of the increase of the happiness of all. The foot (i.e. the pair of feet) of Śaṁbhu was very holy.

50. After seeing the lord greater than the greatest (he saw the goddess). The greatest goddess Satī endowed with beauty and charm was splendid and fascinating. She shone with the greatest prosperity of the auspicious state of wifehood and blessedness.

51-52. After seeing the couple who were pure and refulgent throughout the three worlds, were really non-different but had (apparent) difference, were really devoid of *Guṇas* but had (apparent) *Guṇas*, who were really devoid of shape and size but had apparent shape and size, were free from ailments and the bestowers of happiness, Nārada, the beloved (devotee) of the Lord, saluted them joyously. He repeatedly (prostrated) and got up. Then he eulogized the lord and the goddess of the universe.

Nārada said:

53. O excellent ones among Devas, I bow down to you both who are greater than the greatest through your *Kalā* (skill and ingenuity). The couple who shine and who constitute the seed of the universe consisting of the mobile and immobile beings, are seen by me.

54. You two are the parents of all the worlds. Only today have you been realized by me truly. There is no doubt about this that it is due to your favour.

55. They were thus eulogized by the noble-souled Nārada. Along with Pārvatī, Lord Śaṁbhu was delighted and gratified.

Mahādeva said:

56. Are you happy, O Brāhmaṇa? What shall I do for you?

On hearing those words of Śaṁbhu, Nārada spoke these words:

57. "I had the pleasure of seeing you today. O Lord, I am gratified thereby. (I have acquired) everything through this vision. I have no doubt about this.

58-59. I came here to the excellent mountain Kailāsa just for some sports. O Lord, you are always stationed in the hearts of men. Yet, it is necessary for all living beings to see you."

Girijā said:

60. What play should there be with you? Mention it to me quickly.

On hearing her words, he spoke laughingly:

61. "The game of dice of various types is seen here, O Mahādevī. Two can have the game of dice. There is great happiness in playing the game of dice."

62. Satī who had been annoyed with the sage spoke to him

as he stopped after saying this much: "How do you know the renowned game of dice, the gambling game of learned men?

63. You are the son of Brahmā. You are a sage. You make learned men conform to discipline through various well-known words. You always wander through all the three worlds. There is no other person of lofty mind (like you)."

64. On being told thus by the goddess, Nārada of divine vision, laughingly spoke these words to Girijā in the presence of Śiva:

Nārada said:

65. I do not know gambling, nor do I resort to it. I am an ascetic and a servant of Śiva. Why do you ask me (thus), O Princess (most) sacred among the greatest of the leading Yogins?

66. On hearing those words, Satī (chaste lady) Girijā laughingly spoke to him: "You know everything, O Baṭu. See, I shall play the game of dice today with Maheśa in front of you."

67. After saying thus, the daughter of the Lord of Mountains, the most beautiful lady in the world, took up the dice cubes. Even as the great sage stood witness, she stayed there and played the game with Bhava.

68. The couple earnestly engaged in the game were observed by the sage Nārada. With his mind (pleasantly) influenced by surprise, the learned sage went on observing (the game) and he was extremely gratified.

69. The chaste goddess engrossed in the game of dice was surrounded by her friends and attendants. She clashed with Śiva and played the game of dice fraudulently.

70. Opposed by great fraud he put the stake and Bhavānī was defeated by Śiva when he appeared to smile at it.

71-72. Together with Śiva, Nārada laughed at her satirically. Seeing that she had lost the game and hearing the satirical laughter as well as the derogatory remarks of Nārada, Pārvatī became extremely furious. She hastened to reply to him (suitably) after catching hold of his neck and attempting to turn him out.

73. The two crest jewels (of Girijā) charmingly sparkled.

Beautiful in that anger, her splendid face was seen by Hara again and again (with great pleasure). They then played the game of dice.

74-75. Śaṅkara, the benefactor of the worlds, was told by Girijā: "I have lost the game. The wager has been already given. It is not otherwise. What are you going to stake now? Let it be mentioned."

Then the Three-eyed Lord spoke to Pārvatī:

76. "For your sake, O Bhavānī, this great ornament is being offered as wager: (my famous crest-jewel) the crescent moon, the great necklace as well as the pair of ear-rings.

77. O slender-bodied lady, let me be defeated by you and these ornaments be taken by you easily."

Then the game of dice with Śaṅkara was resumed.

78. Thus both of them, great experts in the art of gambling, went on playing. Then Śaṅkara who had (staked) many ornaments was defeated by Bhavānī.

79. The extremely beautiful Gaurī laughed and said to Śaṅkara: "O Śaṅkara, give me now itself the wager that you have lost."

80. Then Maheśa laughingly spoke these words of truth: "I have not been truly defeated by you, O slender-bodied one. Let it be pondered over.

81. I am invincible unto all living beings in every respect. Hence, O chaste lady, these words should never be spoken. Gamble as much as you please. I will win once again. See."

82-83. Then Aṁbikā said to Maheśa, her husband: "You have been defeated now by me. There is no wonder in this." After saying thus the lady of excellent face held Śaṁbhu by the hand and said: "O Śaṅkara, you have been defeated. There is no doubt. But you do not know."

Thus Girijā laughed gracefully and looked at him fascinatingly. He was attacked with words of merriment: "O Lord, the most auspicious of all auspicious things, O enemy of Smara, give me what has been lost (by you) and what had been promised (by you)."

Śiva said:

84. I am invincible to you, O lady of wide eyes. There is no

doubt about this. Let what had been said arrogantly be pondered over truly.

85. On hearing his words she laughed and said: "O Lord, Mahādeva is invincible indeed to everyone.

86. But by me alone you have been defeated in the game of dice. You do not know anything in regard to what should be done and what should not be done as well as what was intended to be said."

87. Thus the couple were engaged in argument. Nārada, the excellent sage, laughingly spoke these words:

Nārada said:

88. O lady with large eyes extending up to the ears, listen to a statement conducive to the auspiciousness of the universe. Was this (Lord), the most excellent one among the great fortunate people, defeated by you? Why do you utter lies?

89. Mahādeva, the greatest sire of Devas, is indeed unconquered. He is called *Arūpa* ('formless'), *Surūpa* ('of beautiful form') and *Rūpātīta* ('one who is beyond all forms').

90. He is one and one alone. He is the Supreme. He is the splendour (of the luminous things). Śaṅkara is the lord of the three worlds. He is the immanent soul of the universe. He is the benefactor of the worlds.

91. O goddess, how is he defeated by you? He cannot be defeated (by anyone) in all the three worlds. O lady of excellent face, you do not know Śiva because of your womanly nature and feelings.

92. On being addressed thus by Nārada, Pārvatī became excessively angry. Incited by jealousy, the chaste lady spoke these words of censure:

Pārvatī said:

93. Nothing should be spoken out of fickleness, O son of Brahmā. Obeisance to you. I am afraid of you, O celestial sage. Welfare unto you. Be quiet.

94-96. Why is Śiva alone spoken highly of by you, O celestial sage, too many (times)? It was by my grace that Śiva was born, Śiva who is cited as Īśvara. There is no doubt about this that he has become well-established through me.

On hearing many such (taunts and censures) Nārada kept quiet. On seeing that (such a situation) had arisen, Bhṛṅgī spoke these words:

Bhṛṅgī said:

97. You must not talk too much, O beautiful lady. My master is invincible and devoid of aberrations, O lady of good waistline.

98. You possess only womanly temperament, O lady of excellent face. You do not know the Lord who is greater than the greatest. Formerly, O Bhavānī, you had come to Ugra, the great lord, after keeping Kāma in front of you.

99. Has this ever been remembered by you? (Do you recollect) what has been performed by the Pināka-bearing Lord formerly? O beautiful lady, tell us (if it is so). Indeed Kāma was made *Anaṅga* (bodiless) by him. The park belonging to that Mountain, your father, had been burned.

100. It was after that, that Śiva, the Supreme Soul, the lord, greater than the greatest, was propitiated by you.

101. On being told thus by Bhṛṅgī, she became excessively angry. Even as Maheśa was listening, the infuriated lady spoke these words to Bhṛṅgī:

Pārvatī said:

102. O Bhṛṅgī, it is out of partiality that these words are spoken to me. You are a favourite of Śiva, O stupid one. Hence you have this attitude of difference.

103. I am of the nature of Śiva, O foolish one. Śiva is permanently stationed in me. How then could you use words showing difference between Śiva and Śivā?

104. Those words that bestow auspiciousness, uttered by Pārvatī were heard by Bhṛṅgī then. The infuriated Bhṛṅgī spoke to Pārvatī in the presence of Śiva:

105. "In the course of the *Yajña* of your father Dakṣa, the censure of Śiva was heard by you. Due to the hearing of what is displeasing and disquieting, the body was abandoned by you at the very same instant.

106. O lady of slender body, what is done by you now, out of excitement? Don't you know a person who censures Śiva.

107. How were you born of the most excellent one among the Mountains, O lady of excellent complexion? How were you subjected to great distress, O lady of good waistline, on account of a severe penance.

108. Now you do not have devotion combined with love for Śiva. You are a beloved of Śiva, O lady of slender limbs. Hence I am speaking thus to you.

109. There is nothing greater than Śiva in all the three worlds. You must have devotion combined with love for Śiva, O lady of excellent complexion.

110. You are a devotee, O great goddess, O most excellent one among highly fortunate ones. Let him be served scrupulously as he has been attained by you by means of penance. Śiva is the most excellent one.

111. He is the lord of all. You must not do otherwise. It behoves you not to do otherwise."

On hearing Bhṛṅgī's words Girijā spoke to him:

Girijā said:

112. O Bhṛṅgī, be quiet and steady. Otherwise go away. You do not know what should be said and what should not be said. Why do you babble like a ghost?

113. By which man or woman was Śiva brought here by means of penance? Who am I? Who is this as understood by you? You speak to me with the attitude of difference.

114-115. Who are you? By whom have you been united? Wherefore do you talk too much? I will curse you. What will Śiva do now?

On being spoken to reproachfully by Bhṛṅgī, the chaste lady then cursed: "O stupid Bhṛṅgī, O favourite one of Śaṅkara, be devoid of flesh."

116-117. After saying thus, Pārvatī, the goddess, beloved of Śaṅkara, became furious. She held Śaṅkara by the hand. The lady of slender limbs took away the serpent Vāsuki from his neck.

118. Similarly she removed many other ornaments also. The

infuriated lady hurriedly took away the ornaments of Śaṁbhu. His crescent moon and his excellent elephant hide were removed.

119. The serpents Kaṁbala and Aśvatara that had been worn by Maheśa as ornaments were removed by the great goddess laughingly with tricky words.

120. Even his loincloth was taken away laughingly with the utterance of tricky words.

At that time the Gaṇas and the friends (of Pārvatī) felt embarrassed and ashamed.

121-122. (The friends and others) turned their faces away. Bhṛṅgī of great penance, Caṇḍa, Muṇḍa, Mahāloman, Mahodara and many other Gaṇas became miserable. On seeing them in that plight, Maheśa became ashamed.

123-126. Śaṅkara who became angry spoke these words to Pārvatī:

Rudra said:

All the sages are laughing satirically. Similarly Brahmā, Viṣṇu and these Devas, Indra and others—all of them are laughing (at me). O splendid lady, what has been done by you? You are born of a (good) family, O slender-limbed one. Why do you behave like this? If you know for certain, O lady with excellent eyebrows, that I have been defeated by you, do like this. Give me the loincloth alone. Give me the loincloth only. It does not behove you to do otherwise.

127. On being told thus by Śaṁbhu, the Yogin, Pārvatī, the chaste lady of charming face, laughed and spoke these words:

128. "What have you to do with a loincloth? You are a sage of sanctified soul. (Some time back) you wandered through Dāruvana with the cardinal points alone for your garment (i.e. you were naked).

129. Under the pretext of begging for alms, the wives of the sages were enchanted. While you were going, you were greatly adored by them.

130. Your loincloth fell down (penis?) there. Nothing else was uttered by the sages. Hence what you have lost in the gambling game, should be abandoned by you."

131. On hearing it, Rudra the great lord became angry with Pārvatī. He stared at her angrily with his third eye.

132. On seeing Śaṅkara furious, all the groups of Devas as well as the Gaṇakumārakas (i.e. sons of the Gaṇas or son-like Gaṇas?) became overcome by great fear.

133-135. All of them said to one another slowly with suspicion and fear: "Rudra is angry now with Girijā. Just as Madana was burnt so also she (will be burnt). The words cannot be otherwise." Those Gaṇas and all the celestial sages who were discussing thus were looked at by the goddess with the glowing gesture of married blessedness. The chaste lady spoke laughingly to the *Satpuruṣa* (the Supreme Being, the Principle of Existence):

136-138. "Of what avail is your stare with your greatest eye? I am not Kāla nor Kāma nor the sacrifice of Dakṣa. I am not Tripura, O Śaṁbhu, nor Andhaka, O bull-emblemed Lord. What will come out of your staring thus? In vain have you been a Virūpākṣa (i.e. of uneven three eyes) before me."

Parameśvarī spoke these and many other similar words. On hearing those words, the lord became inclined to go away:

139-141. 'A forest alone is the excellent (resort) today. A lonely forest is really the best resort now. One who is alone, who has kept his mind and soul under control and who has eschewed all possessions is really happy. He is a learned man. He is wise. He is the knower of the greatest truth. He, by whom lust and attachment have been eschewed, becomes liberated and happy.'

After thinking thus, Śrī Śaṅkara of great compassionate nature abandoned Girijā and went away to the wonderful forest region. Separated from his beloved wife, he went to the Siddhāṭavī ('forest of the Siddhas'), full of Paramahaṁsas ('great Yogins of high spiritual power').

142. On seeing Śaṅkara come out, all the inhabitants of Kailāsa, all the Gaṇas beginning with Vīrabhadra came out and followed him.

143-144. Taking up the umbrella, Bhṛṅgī went behind him. The chowries used for fanning resembled Gaṅgā and Yamunā. Taking them up, the intelligent Nandī went behind him. The bull went ahead and shone along with the aerial chariot.

145-146. With all these splendid things, Mahādeva shone with refulgence. The goddess Pārvatī went to the harem with dejected mind. Surrounded by many friends, attendants and others, Girijā mentally thought about Parameśvara.

147-149. Leaving off the Gaṇas then, Śaṁbhu went very far off. Mahādeva left behind Gaṇeśa, Kumāra, Vīrabhadra and others, Bhṛṅgī, Nandin, Caṇḍa, Somanandin and other inhabitants of Kailāsa. Mahādeva of great penance went alone and single. He went far into the forest. (Ultimately) Śiva reached Siddhavaṭa.

150-153. A divine seat was made by the Earth for him. It was made wonderful by means of saffron, jewels, Siddharatnas ('precious gems') and lapis lazuli. It was polished and brightened by whitewash. Maheśa, the lord of Yoga sat there.

He sat in the lotus posture. Maheśa, the most excellent one among the knowers of Yoga, kept his eyes shut and meditated on the pure Ātman by means of Ātman.

Mahādeva, the moon-crested lord, shone during the meditation.

The noble-souled Śeṣa was his Yogapaṭṭa (upper cloth). Vāsuki, the great king of serpents, was tied round the waist.

The Ātman was eulogized by him. The Ātman was considered the immanent soul of everything. He who was to be known through Vedāntas cannot behave like worldly men. He was single and infinite without any limit or boundary. He cannot be guessed or known by Logic. He is of the form of self-enlightenment. The sole lord of the worlds remained thus visualizing the (Supreme Spirit) greater than the greatest.

CHAPTER THIRTYFIVE[1]

Pārvatī as Śabarī Brings Back Śiva: *Śiva's Coronation*

Lomaśa said:

1. When Mahādeva went to the forest, Girijā became dejected on account of separation. The lady of slender limbs did not get any pleasure in the mansions or apartments.

2. The splendid lady of slender body brooded over Śiva with all feelings. Understanding that Śivā was worried and anxious (about Śiva), her friend Vijayā said:

Vijayā said:

3. O splendid lady, it was by means of a great penance that you attained Śiva. In vain was a false game of dice played with Śaṅkara, the ascetic.

4. There are many defects in playing at dice. O sinless lady, have they not been heard by you? Seek the forgiveness of Śiva, O slender lady of great cleverness, immediately.

5-6. O gentle lady of excellent face, go, go along with us (to the forest). Before Śaṁbhu has not gone far off, go to Śaṅkara and seek his pardon. If you do not seek the forgiveness of Śiva, later on you will certainly have to regret it. You will become miserable.

7. On hearing the words uttered by Vijayā, (the goddess) of great equanimity and courageousness, laughingly spoke these words to her friend Vijayā—wondrous words of truthful nature:

8-11. "Formerly he had been surrounded by great prosperity but he was defeated by me. He is shameless[2] (or above the sense of shame). I have nothing to do immediately. Without me, he will continue to be ugly and hideous (or formless). Lord

---

1. This concluding chapter of the *Kedāra-khaṇḍa*, tells us how Pārvatī in the guise of a Śabara girl enticed Śiva back and the apologizing Śiva amicably lived together with her afterwards.

2. VV 8-11. A clever use of *pun*. Every epithet of Śiva which is apparently derogatory is really complimentary, e.g. *virūpa*: (i) of ugly form; (ii) formless or transcending form.

Maheśa had been rendered as one with forms and say not otherwise. Neither communion nor separation can exist between us, with him and with me. Maheśa who is without form and shape has been made one with form and shape by me. This entire universe consisting of the mobile and immobile beings along with the excellent Devas, has been created by me for the sake of his sport. O Vijayā, see my sport along with the causes of origin and existence."

12. After saying thus, the goddess Girijā, the (cause) of all auspiciousness, became desirous of going to Maheśvara after assuming the form of a female Śabara huntress.

13. (She assumed the form of a) dark-complexioned slender lady. Her teeth were like the buds of *Śikhara* (a variety of jasmine). Her lips resembled the round *Bimba* (a variety of red plum) fruit. She possessed a fine neck. She had to bend down slightly on account of the weight of the heavy breasts. Her smooth glossy tresses had grown abundantly. She was very slender and thin in her waist. The buttocks were large. Gaurī's thighs were like the golden plantain stem. She was *Pallīyuktā* (? accompanied by her friends who looked like the members of the hut or family). She had very fine bangles. She adorned herself with the plumes and feathers of a peacock.

14. She held in her hand a bow that resembled a lotus-stalk. There was a quiver on her back. It had been made of *Ketaka* leaves. (From a distance) she saw Giriśa. The lady of beautiful face thus went along, served and accompanied by many friends and attendants.

15. Through the loud humming sound of the bees, she made the three worlds reverberate. Girijā (appeared) to revive *Manmatha* again and again.

16. The royal swans became at that instant filled with love and desire. Bees and peacocks—all of them were lovelorn and so had heart-burn.

17. She went to the place where Maheśvara was seated engaged in trance and meditation. He was seen by the goddess extremely fascinated by the sound of bees.

18-19. Mahādeva woke up from his trance. On seeing the Śabarī, Maheśa immediately became afflicted with love. He went near Girijā and was about to seize her by the hand, when the chaste lady suddenly vanished from his presence.

20. Immediately after seeing it, the lord had his wrong notion dispelled. Śaṁbhu wandered around but did not see the dark-eyed lady.

21-22. He experienced pangs of separation. He became love-lorn. Śaṁbhu who was the enemy of Madana, whose form was perpetual knowledge and who was devoid of delusion, became deluded. He saw Girijā once again. He spoke to the huntress the following weighty words, very relevant to the occasion:

Śiva said:

23. Listen to my words, O lady of slender limbs. After hearing them, it behoves you to do accordingly. Who are you? To whom do you belong, O slender-limbed lady? Let this be told exactly, O lady of beautiful waist and of great fortune.

Śivā said:

24. I am searching for my husband who is omniscient, who bestows all objects, who is independent and devoid of aberrations and who is the most excellent lord of all the worlds.

25-28. On being told thus, the bull-emblemed lord replied to Girijā thus: "O gentle lady, I am the most suitable husband for you and none else. O beautiful lady, O beautiful lady of excellent face, let this be truthfully pondered over."

On hearing the words of Rudra, she spoke smilingly: "O noble one of great fortune, you may say that the husband sought after by me is you yourself and not otherwise. But welfare unto you, I shall tell you something. You are devoid of *Guṇas*. You are the scorcher of enemies. The beautiful lady by whom you had been wooed before by means of great penance, has been abandoned by you in the forest in a trice.

29. It is very difficult for all living beings ever to propitiate you. Hence what has been said before me by you, should not be said again."

30-31. On hearing the words of Śabarī, the Bull-emblemed Lord replied: "Do not say so, O lady of large eyes. That poor ascetic woman has not been abandoned. If she is abandoned by me, O lady of slender body, can anything be spoken? After knowing me wretched and pitiable, O lady of large eyes, O lady of good waistline, you must carry out my suggestion."

32. On being earnestly requested thus in various ways by the Trident-bearing Lord, Girijā laughingly spoke these words of ridicule and reproof:

33-34. "O lord of Yogins, you are an ascetic. You are free from attachment. You are unsullied. You are one revelling in the Ātman. You are beyond *Dvandvas* (i.e. mutually opposed pairs such as pleasure-pain) and you are the lord by whom Madana was slain. You are Virūpākṣa himself and you have been seen by me. It is impossible for me to attain you. You cannot be conquered by anyone. Hence what has been suggested to me before, should not be said by you again."

35. On hearing her words, the slayer of Madana said: "Be my wife. It does not behove you to do anything otherwise."

36-37. After saying this, the lord who was afflicted with love seized the huntress by the hand. She said smilingly to him in a respectful manner:

"Let me go, let me go. This is not proper, O lord, to do, especially by an ascetic. Do not use force. Request my father. Do not attack me otherwise."

Mahādeva said:

38. O lady of splendid face, where is your father living? Tell your father quickly. I shall see him after presenting my prostrations.

39. On hearing these words uttered by him, the Bull-bannered Lord was brought to her father by that slender lady of dark eyes.

40-41. He was the excellent Mountain Himavān stationed on the peak of Kailāsa. He had great lustre. He was surrounded by many serpents. He was standing at the entrance and was pointed out to Śaṅkara by the goddess: "O lord, this is my father. Without shyness request him (for my hand). He will give me (to you). O ascetic, do not delay."

42. Thinking that it should be so, he suddenly bowed down

to Himālaya and spoke these words: "O most excellent one among the lords of Mountains, O highly intelligent one, give your magnificent daughter (to me), the extremely distressed one."

43. On hearing these pitiable words, Himālaya got up. Holding Maheśa (by the hand), the Lord of Mountains himself spoke:

44-46. "What do you say, O lord? This is improper for you now. You are the donor (reputed) in all the three worlds. Universe consisting of mobile and immobile beings has been created by you." Thus the great Mountain Himālaya engaged himself in eulogy. Then there came Nārada, the excellent sage.

He laughingly spoke these words: "O Trident-bearing Lord, obeisance to you. O Śaṁbhu, listen to my words, the great words full of the essence of reality.

47. Association with young women only adds to affliction and distress. You are the master, the lord of the worlds, the great lord, greater than the greatest. Ponder over everything, O lord of Devas. It behoves you to speak truthfully."

48. On being enlightened thus by the noble-souled Nārada, Śaṁbhu, the great lord, became enlightened and laughed.

Śiva said:

49-53. O Nārada, truth has been spoken by you in this matter. It is not otherwise in any respect. Downfall for men is surely caused by association with young women. There is no doubt about it. Your words cannot be otherwise. I have been fascinated by this lady and brought to Gandhamādana.

This is a mysteriously wonderful activity caused by a ghost-like creature. Hence I am not staying near this Mountain. I am going now itself once again to another forest.

After saying thus, he went along the path that is hard to be attained even by Yogins, that is unfathomable and that has no support. On understanding this, Nārada spoke these words to Girijā, the Lord of Mountains and to the *Pārṣadas* immediately:

54. "This is Maheśa, the lord of the universe, the destroyer of Tripura, the lord of great reputation. He should be saluted, eulo-

gized and entreated for pardon truthfully [*or paramārthataḥ*: for the sake of the greatest aim in life]."

55-56. On hearing these words uttered by Nārada, all the Mountains of great lustre (went to the Lord) keeping Girijā at their head. All of them fell (at the feet of) Śaṅkara, the benefactor of all the worlds, like a long rod. All Pramathas, Guhyakas and others bowed down and eulogized him (i.e. Śiva).

57. On being eulogized, the Lord came to Gandhamādana. The lord of all was ceremoniously crowned by Aṅgiras along with noble-souled ones.

58. At that time *Dundubhi*-drums were sounded and many musical instruments were played. All the Suras beginning with Indra threw showers of flowers.

59. The Lord of Yogins worthy of being saluted by the entire universe, was entreated and surrounded by many groups of Suras beginning with Brahmā. He was accompanied by Girijā. On being entreated by them, he condescended to sit on a divine seat where he shone with great magnificence and all kinds of auspicious things.

60. The acts of the noble-souled Maheśa, O Brāhmaṇas, of this sort are destructive of the sins of those who listen to them. They (i.e. the acts) are innumerable.

61. All those stories of Rudra heard (by us) are great. What more shall I tell you?

The sages said:

62. Thus the act of Śaṅkara has been described by you. By this story itself we are undoubtedly satisfied.

Sūta said:

63-64. Everything has been heard by me by the grace of Vyāsa. The wonderful form of Śaṅkara is vast and contains within it the wonderful features of the Vedas. It is of the nature of perfect knowledge and it has been described (to you). Those who are endowed with great faith and listen to as well as narrate with love and devotion the wonderful story of the greatness of Śiva, this story which is dear to Śiva and which is called *Śiva-śāstra*, attain the great goal.

:: END OF KEDĀRAKHAṆḌA ::

INDEX

CORRECTIONS

Page	*Line*	*Misprint*	*Correction*
1	Fn. 3 line 2	*Svarrgārohaṇika*	*Svargārohaṇika*
22	21-22	There should be one line space between these lines	
76	17	Śiva	Śivā
119	23	chaiming	claiming
123	4	born	borne
186	19	Śailāda	Śilāda
191	last	pro ud	proud
201	22	Śiva	Śivā
213	16	Śīva's	Śiva's

Whispers in the Village

By the same author

THE NEW RECTOR
TALK OF THE VILLAGE
VILLAGE MATTERS
THE VILLAGE SHOW
VILLAGE SECRETS
SCANDAL IN THE VILLAGE
VILLAGE GOSSIP
TROUBLE IN THE VILLAGE
VILLAGE DILEMMA
INTRIGUE IN THE VILLAGE

A COUNTRY AFFAIR
COUNTRY WIVES
COUNTRY LOVERS
COUNTRY PASSIONS